T0192180

Communications
in Computer and Information Science   1702

Rationale

The CCIS series is devoted to the publication of proceedings of computer science conferences. Its aim is to efficiently disseminate original research results in informatics in printed and electronic form. While the focus is on publication of peer-reviewed full papers presenting mature work, inclusion of reviewed short papers reporting on work in progress is welcome, too. Besides globally relevant meetings with internationally representative program committees guaranteeing a strict peer-reviewing and paper selection process, conferences run by societies or of high regional or national relevance are also considered for publication.

Topics

The topical scope of CCIS spans the entire spectrum of informatics ranging from foundational topics in the theory of computing to information and communications science and technology and a broad variety of interdisciplinary application fields.

Information for Volume Editors and Authors

Publication in CCIS is free of charge. No royalties are paid, however, we offer registered conference participants temporary free access to the online version of the conference proceedings on SpringerLink (http://link.springer.com) by means of an http referrer from the conference website and/or a number of complimentary printed copies, as specified in the official acceptance email of the event.

CCIS proceedings can be published in time for distribution at conferences or as post-proceedings, and delivered in the form of printed books and/or electronically as USBs and/or e-content licenses for accessing proceedings at SpringerLink. Furthermore, CCIS proceedings are included in the CCIS electronic book series hosted in the SpringerLink digital library at http://link.springer.com/bookseries/7899. Conferences publishing in CCIS are allowed to use Online Conference Service (OCS) for managing the whole proceedings lifecycle (from submission and reviewing to preparing for publication) free of charge.

Publication process

The language of publication is exclusively English. Authors publishing in CCIS have to sign the Springer CCIS copyright transfer form, however, they are free to use their material published in CCIS for substantially changed, more elaborate subsequent publications elsewhere. For the preparation of the camera-ready papers/files, authors have to strictly adhere to the Springer CCIS Authors' Instructions and are strongly encouraged to use the CCIS LaTeX style files or templates.

Abstracting/Indexing

CCIS is abstracted/indexed in DBLP, Google Scholar, EI-Compendex, Mathematical Reviews, SCImago, Scopus. CCIS volumes are also submitted for the inclusion in ISI Proceedings.

How to start

To start the evaluation of your proposal for inclusion in the CCIS series, please send an e-mail to ccis@springer.com.

Rodrigo Pereira dos Santos ·
Marcelo da Silva Hounsell
Editors

Grand Research Challenges in Games and Entertainment Computing in Brazil - GranDGamesBR 2020–2030

First Forum, GranDGamesBR 2020
Recife, Brazil, November 7–10, 2020
and Second Forum, GranDGamesBR 2021
Gramado, Brazil, October 18–21, 2021
Revised Selected Papers

Springer

Editors
Rodrigo Pereira dos Santos 🅾
UNIRIO
Rio de Janeiro, Brazil

Marcelo da Silva Hounsell 🅾
UDESC
Joinville, Brazil

ISSN 1865-0929   ISSN 1865-0937 (electronic)
Communications in Computer and Information Science
ISBN 978-3-031-27638-5   ISBN 978-3-031-27639-2 (eBook)
https://doi.org/10.1007/978-3-031-27639-2

This Springer imprint is published by the registered company Springer Nature Switzerland AG
The registered company address is: Gewerbestrasse 11, 6330 Cham, Switzerland

Preface

The Brazilian Computer Society (SBC) published the "Grand Challenges in Computer Science Research in Brazil 2006–2016" based on a series of seminars. The effects of such strategic action have inspired different Computer Science communities towards the identification of specific research challenges. In this context, the establishment of a common view on the theoretical and practical challenges in the field of Games and Entertainment Computing is required as a strategy for driving efforts regarding the existing problems faced by researchers and practitioners.

This volume contains 12 chapters as the extended versions of the selected papers published from two editions (2020 and 2021) of the Forum on Grand Research Challenges in Games and Entertainment Computing in Brazil (2020–2030). The event was co-located with the Brazilian Symposium on Games and Digital Entertainment (SBGames), promoted by the SBC Special Committee of Games and Digital Entertainment (CEJOGOS). With this book, entitled "**Grand Research Challenges in Games and Entertainment Computing in Brazil - GranDGamesBR 2020–2030**", SBGames celebrates 20 editions of a successful symposium for researchers and practitioners who are interested in opportunities and challenges related to games and entertainment computing.

This initiative was prioritized with the aim of identifying research opportunities for this decade in the field of Games and Entertainment Computing. GranDGamesBR Forum focused on advancing research questions that will be important to science and the country and world for 2020–2030, including challenges to both academia and industry as well as multidisciplinary actions regarding (but not limited to) the main tracks of SBGames: Computing; Education; Culture; Arts and Design; Industry; Healthcare; and Others. In 2020 (2021), we received 12 (12) submissions, from which 4 (8) were accepted and invited to submit chapters to this volume.

The topics included in this volume cover the following fields connected to games and entertainment computing: game design, educational games, games evaluation, game-based learning, player experience, human-computer interaction, the games industry, business models, game software ecosystems, ethics, serious games, cyberdemocracy, emotional design, computer graphics, cognitive simulation, immersive entertainment, virtual/augmented/extended reality, gamification, and the creative process.

All the accepted chapters were peer reviewed by three to five qualified reviewers chosen from our scientific committee based on their qualifications and experience.

The book editors wish to thank the dedicated scientific committee members and the authors for their contributions to this rich material, as well as CEJOGOS members for their valuable support since this initiative was proposed in SBGames 2019 in its 18th edition in Rio de Janeiro, Brazil. We also thank Springer for their trust and for publishing the GranDGamesBR chapters.

January 2023   Rodrigo Pereira dos Santos
                                                          Marcelo da Silva Hounsell

Organization

Organizing Committee

Rodrigo Pereira dos Santos	UNIRIO, Brazil
Marcelo da Silva Hounsell	UDESC, Brazil

Scientific Committee

Alan Carvalho	Fatec São Caetano do Sul/Impacta Faculty, Brazil
Aline Job	University of Caxias do Sul, Brazil
Ana Carla Amaro	University of Aveiro, Portugal
Ana Paula Bacelo	PUCRS, Brazil
André Rodrigues da Cruz	CEFET-MG, Brazil
André Tavares da Silva	UDESC, Brazil
Bernardo Aguiar	Unisinos, Brazil
Cláudia Werner	COPPE/UFRJ, Brazil
Davi Viana	UFMA, Brazil
Débora Barbosa	Feevale University, Brazil
Edirlei Lima	European University of Lisbon - IADE, Portugal
Eduardo Albuquerque	UFG, Brazil
Ellen Barbosa	ICMC/USP, Brazil
Flávia Santoro	UERJ, Brazil
Heitor Costa	UFLA, Brazil
Helton Biscaro	USP, Brazil
Isabel Nunes	UFRN, Brazil
Ivaldir de Farias Júnior	UPE, Brazil
João Bernardes Júnior	USP, Brazil
Joaquim Cavalcante-Neto	UFC, Brazil
Johnny Marques	ITA, Brazil
José Gilvan Maia	UFC, Brazil
José Maria David	UFJF, Brazil
Lúcia Lemos	PUC-SP, Brazil
Luciano Medeiros	UNINTER, Brazil
Luis Paulo Mercado	UFAL, Brazil
Marcos Arrais	PUC Minas, Brazil
Marcos Borges	Unicamp, Brazil
Nelson Zagalo	University of Aveiro, Portugal

Contents

Challenges in Evaluating Players'
Interaction with Digital Games

Ticianne Darin$^{(\boxtimes)}$ ⓘ, Nayana Carneiroⓘ, David Mirandaⓘ, and Bianca Coelho

Federal University of Ceara, Fortaleza, CE, Brazil
ticianne@virtual.ufc.br, {nayanatcl,biancasmd}@alu.ufc.br

Abstract. Evaluating the quality of the player's interaction with a digital game considering human factors is not a trivial task. In addition to considering technical issues, it is necessary to explore the player's perspective carefully, focusing on their satisfaction, motivation, and expectations regarding the game. Thus, human factors evaluation in games raises new challenges for academia and industry, such as defining the factors to be explored, the appropriate choice of methods to be applied, the use, translation, and validation of attitude scales, and the availability of resources, among others. The pursuit of the maturation and systematization of studies and practices related to evaluating the player's interaction and experience is an international challenge, which has moved the efforts of research and practice communities but is still commonly neglected in the Brazilian context. Thus, it is necessary to encourage the development of national studies and initiatives in this area to develop better-grounded practices suited to our cultural context and the needs of the Brazilian market.

Keywords: Digital games · Human factors · Interface and interaction evaluation

1 Introduction

Technological advances in recent years have allowed the creation and development of increasingly varied, robust, and engaging games that cross different devices – such as computers, consoles, mobile, and wearable devices – and present themselves with a multitude of genres and dynamics. Amidst such variety, all games share the fact that they are designed with the goal of providing engaging and meaningful experiences for their players, which is the heart of digital games [83].

Thus, digital games are intricate interactive computer systems that usually focus on recreational interaction (not necessarily functional, as in productivity systems) and are generally designed to generate positive emotions, satisfaction, and player engagement. Because of their diverse characteristics, several factors regarding the players and their surroundings may affect the experience lived by the player while playing – or the *player experience* (PX). PX can be understood

R. P. d. Santos and M. d. S. Hounsell (Eds.): GranDGamesBR 2020/2021, CCIS 1702, pp. 1–24, 2023.
https://doi.org/10.1007/978-3-031-27639-2_1

as the construct that describes the qualities of interactions between a player and a game, typically investigated during and after one's interaction with digital games [60,81]. Thus, this term deals with the individual perception of the player-game interaction process [34] (how the player perceives and responds to their interaction with a game), and it also highlights the subjective and psychological nature of this construct.

Therefore, a deep understanding of the interaction between players, games, and everything surrounding them is essential to creating games that achieve their goals. The search for this understanding necessarily involves the study of **human factors**, more specifically, **human characteristics** – which include psychological, physiological, and anatomical aspects, group factors, individual differences, psychophysiological state variables, and factors related to the task being performed [73] – in this case, the "task" of playing. Delving deeper into the analysis of these human characteristics during the game evaluation allows not only to improve game design but also to design games that offer more attractive, engaging, and satisfying experiences, besides identifying unwanted aspects or low acceptance by players [30]. It means that, in addition to the conceptualization and development of the game, it is crucial to reason about the evaluation process.

An evaluation process that considers the human factors adequately results in: (i) games with higher technical quality by evaluating the adequacy of interfaces, devices, modalities of interaction, and feedback according to the player's context, as well as their physical and cognitive limitations and abilities; and (ii) games that offer a more engaging and immersive experience, considering how the mechanics, narrative, and other game elements affect the goals of the experience designed for the game, as well as the player's behavior and social, cultural, and cognitive aspects.

However, *how* to do this is admittedly a challenge, despite the advances made in the last two decades [30]. Unlike common misconceptions, a deep understanding of player-game interaction cannot be obtained with shallow and frivolous procedures. For example, to evaluate player satisfaction after a playtest, it is not enough to question players about how much they liked or disliked the game. Satisfaction – as the various constructs that describe the quality of player interaction – is a multidimensional construct and involves immersion, fun, aesthetics, and motivation, to name a few [66]. One of the main challenges for the international gaming research community has been the lack of a set of methods and tools that allow measuring entertainment experiences in a sensitive, reliable and valid way, properly considering human factors [8,16,30,48]. This situation is even more incipient in the Brazilian community, where a renewal of our understanding and *modus operandi* is imperative.

1.1   International Scenario *vs.* Brazilian Scenario

In the international community, digital games research increasingly addresses human factors in games, which is demonstrated by the integration of Human-Computer Interaction (HCI) principles in the gaming area. Different sub-areas with thought-provoking research questions emerged, including player-centered design, human-centered game design, Games User Research (GUR), and Player-Computer Interaction. The topic of digital game evaluation has been presented at the ACM CHI Conference on Human Factors in Computing Systems (the leading international conference for the field of HCI[1]) consistently over the years. For instance, a search in the conference proceedings for articles that jointly present the term game in the title and the term game evaluation in the abstract results in 621 articles, of which 295 were published between 2016 and 2021[2].

In fact, such interest culminated in the creation of the ACM SIGCHI Annual Symposium on Computer-Human Interaction in Play (CHI Play) in 2014, an international and interdisciplinary conference series for researchers and professionals across all areas of play, games, and HCI. As stated by its organizers, "CHI Play grew out of the increasing work around games and play emerging from CHI over the last several years"[3]. Other evidence that this topic has aroused increasing interest from the international community can be identified in the proceedings of different conferences, such as the International Conference on the Foundations of Digital Games (FDG), the Symposium on Computational Intelligence and Games (CIG), the International Games Innovation Conference (IGIC), and the Games Entertainment Media Conference (GEM).

In Brazil, the Brazilian Symposium on Games and Digital Entertainment (SBGames) – the most significant academic event in Latin America in the area of games – is correlated to the Brazilian Symposium on Human Factors in Computational Systems (IHCBr). Only in recent years, the IHCBr community has started to explore human facets and characteristics in evaluating games and applications for digital entertainment from different perspectives. This fact can be exemplified by the creation of the Workshop on Interaction and User Research in Game Development (WIPlay) at the IHCBr 2019 and by the works and discussions on evaluating human factors in digital games. Likewise, recent research by the SBGames community has addressed GUR concepts and the adaptation of HCI design and evaluation methods for games in specific contexts, which demonstrates the Brazilian community's perception of the need to consider human factors properly in games evaluation.

However, a current challenge for these communities is developing a systematic effort to promote transversal reflection on the different dimensions of human factors in developing and evaluating games and thinking of a research agenda in this area for the Brazilian community. Often, digital games are evaluated with a simplified approach around isolated human factors, which can lead researchers to make incorrect assumptions and obtain misleading results. Another consequence is the planning and conducting of player research based on the game developer's personal experience and limited knowledge of the correct application of player research methods and instruments, which compromises the quality of the results, especially when considering the characteristics and objectives of games in different domains.

---

[1] https://sigchi.org/conferences/conference-history/chi/.
[2] Search updated in April 2022.
[3] https://sigchi.org/conferences/conference-history/chiplay/.

Therefore, evaluating human factors in the player interaction with digital games can be considered a Grand Challenge for the next ten years of research in Computer Science in Brazil [25], and we need to stimulate the maturity of this area in technical-scientific terms. Following the thought of Jeroen Bourgonjon [13], we highlight that digital games deserve scholarly attention, not only as a mere product or medium for research but also as a social practice and a place for meaning-making and learning.

Gaming is intrinsic to human nature. The earliest stage of culture is in the form of play, and that culture proceeds in shape and the mood of play, as Huizinga said in his seminal work *Homo Ludens* [38]. However, culture is constantly transforming. In our digital and hyper-connected world dealing with the challenges of a brand new generation born playing digital games in all genres, sizes, and shapes, we must address social-cultural challenges from multiple perspectives when creating games. In this chapter, we contribute by offering a perspective founded on GUR and HCI. These areas tackle universal and transversal issues that affect how players interact – and perceive their interaction – with digital games in the most diverse contexts. We do not, however, presume to encapsulate in this chapter all the possible challenges related to the inherent human complexity. Instead, we encourage the Brazilian research community to discuss further and ampliate the challenges we propose wearing the lenses of their specialties, including – but not limited to – Cognitive and Social Sciences and Design.

2   Main Challenges

There is a need to promote reflections and systematically develop the critical view of the Brazilian community about the dimensions and human characteristics applied in the design and evaluation of digital games, providing coherent instrumentation for this context. To stimulate the development of research tackling this issue, in this chapter, we point out some of the main challenges in evaluating digital games considering human factors (summarized in Fig. 1), namely: **(C1)** Strength of the body of knowledge about PX; **(C2)** Promoting the proper assessment of human factors affecting the PX; **(C3)** Avoid and combat abusive and unethical practices and reveal the different parameters that guide human motivation itself; and **(C4)** Foster evaluation in the industry context, based on practices developed in academia. In the following subsections, we discuss each challenge, highlighting underlying needs upon which our community can act to deal with the presented issues.

2.1   C1: Strength of the Body of Knowledge About PX

There are different views in the literature regarding what is meant by the term *player experience* (PX), which dimensions make up this construct and, consequently, which human characteristics should be considered and how to measure them – a question already discussed by several authors, for example, [74,81].

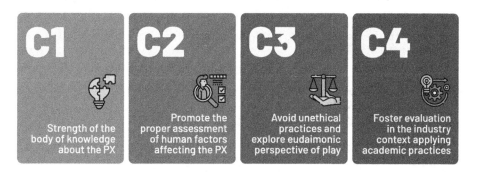

Fig. 1. Main challenges in evaluating digital games considering human factors

The lack of consensus or clarity on this subject is reflected in published research and market practices. For instance, it is common to find studies that use the term PX or variants – e.g., gaming/game experience, gameplay experience, user experience (UX), or just experience – without considering conceptual differences or stating which theoretical views and concepts they embrace as fundamentals, as already identified by other works [16,81].

Such negligence can generate confusion and inconsistencies in practices of interaction and experience evaluation since works that propose to explore supposedly the same constructs evaluate entirely different ones and apply methods that are sometimes contradictory. This situation makes it difficult to systematize and mature technical procedures, contributing to the construction of diffuse and poorly grounded knowledge. The miscellanea of understanding regarding what the terms mean creates divergence about which constructs should be evaluated and how they should be approached, resulting in the misuse of instruments and concepts [12,16]. In Brazil, this scenario is further aggravated by the inappropriate use of instruments in a foreign language (usually in English) translated into Portuguese without concern for the validity of the constructs that make up the psychometric scales or even modified to measure other constructs allegedly. This means that conclusions drawn in these cases are, at the very least, debatable [25,57].

In a general analysis, this panorama reveals two key underlying needs that our community should explore to overcome this situation (Fig. 2): (i) the need to investigate the PX qualities; and (ii) The need to translate and validate psychometric instruments to evaluate PX qualities. We discuss them in detail in the remainder of this section.

The Need for a Shared and Solid Comprehension of the PX Definition. A central aspect in the study of games has been the search for understanding and an attempt to measure the "experience lived by the player while playing" [81]. However, as we mentioned above, there is no consensus in the

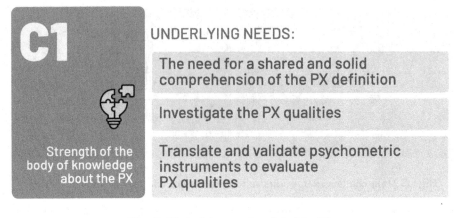

Fig. 2. Underlying needs related to C1

literature on nomenclature, taxonomy, or definition to refer to this experience [74,81]. This lack of consensus has roots in the fact that the overall user experience understanding changes according to the socio-cultural context and between professional positions, making a global consensus unattainable [22].

In the case of game design, different terms are often used interchangeably without enough reasoning about their definitions and what they represent for the studies [81]. Although this conceptual and terminological issue has been somewhat discussed, the views are still widely divided in the literature [74].

Some authors consider PX the UX in games [60]. Others disagree, as is the case of Lazzaro (2008), who states that UX is the experience of using a system and deals with how easy and suitable the system is for the task the user expects to perform in it (with a focus on productivity), while PX is the experience of playing a digital game, focused on how well a game supports and delivers the kind of fun the player wants [51]. This perspective is also concerned with possible impediments to the player's fun and enjoyment. Furthermore, Wiemeyer and his colleagues (2016) state that, strictly speaking, PX is a more appropriate term than game experience and its variants (or even UX) since it is the person of the player who lives this specific experience and not the game (focus on the player) [81]. Besides, this term is already widely used in the digital games literature [61].

Discussions about these terms indicate that, although it is common to confuse gameplay with player experience, the terms include aspects that are quite different [7]. However, understanding the differences between definitions and how practitioners and researchers employ them is necessary because how they understand the experience in games can explain differences and choices in game design and evaluation [22].

The Need to Investigate the PX Qualities. There is also a lack of clarity on which constructs compose the Player Experience, or what constructs one should consider when aiming to evaluate it. Since the idea of PX can be extensive, subjective, and specific to the context of digital games, such experiences are often formally explored through constructs such as flow, affect, presence, engagement, motivation [43], among others.

The literature is filled with different views on this dilemma, but many researchers and practitioners do not seem to give the proper attention to this matter. Once we cannot evaluate or measure what we cannot understand, this blurred comprehension tends to produce inconsistencies in our practices, as already identified in some domains of games studies [12,16]. Therefore, the PX and the qualities of the player-game interaction must be further investigated, and it is necessary to invest efforts to identify notions and properties that allow analyzing and measuring this type of experience in a more "palpable" and systematic way [74]. Besides, there is much space for empirical research investigating PX qualities and their influences on game design. Considering our context, we can observe a lack of experimental studies on this topic [2,5], which could help path the way to move forward theory and impulse the development of new evaluation technologies and methodologies to serve both academia and the game industry.

The Need to Translate and Validate Psychometric Instruments to Evaluate PX Qualities. Instead of relying solely on game analytics or modifying existing attitude scales in an *ad hoc* way, which affects their validation, the Brazilian community must invest efforts in translating and culturally adapting valid instruments to our context, considering the particularities and needs of our users.

A recent literature mapping on instruments to evaluate PX showed that among the 58 cataloged instruments, only eight were developed in a language other than English (Portuguese and Dutch) [12]. The authors identify it as an obstacle to understanding PX components and dimensions since language is a cultural expression, and it is essential to assimilate the felt experience.

The study by Miranda, Li & Darin (2021) highlights that most valid self-report questionnaires are developed and validated in the English language and cannot be used by non-native speakers [57]. Even when used by people fluent in English, cultural differences between native and non-native English speakers jeopardize the validity of standardized questionnaires. This language issue is exemplified in studies demonstrating that using English in a product in non-native English-speaking countries affects text comprehension, irrespective of whether the respondents' (self-)reported English proficiency is high or low [35]. This means that the use of questionnaires in different languages can compromise the validity of the research, regardless of the participants' proficiency level.

Several studies have translated and adapted psychometric questionnaires for different languages and areas over the years. For PX in Brazilian Portuguese, however, there are yet few initiatives – we can cite as examples: the MEEGA+ KIDS [79], a customized translation of the MEEGA+ instrument meant to evaluate educational games with children in K-12; the UES-BR [57], a contextual adaptation and translation of the User Engagement Scale (UES); and, more recently, the PX-BR [5], a summarized instrument focused on immersion/presence, fun, and gameplay and based on international instruments already validated. However, these initiatives should be more systematic instead of isolated, contributing to player interaction research by enabling the Brazilian community to rely on tools already established for native English speakers. We highlight that, as psychometric scales explore reasons and attitudes, they should be combined with investigating observable phenomena, such as actions, expressions, and behaviors, to explore human factors in the gaming context better.

2.2 C2: Promote the Proper Assessment of Human Factors Affecting the PX

Digital games are artifacts that unfold their full potential in interacting with human players, allowing them to craft their experience individually [61]. Thus, a diversity of factors must be considered to understand how a person's characteristics and internal state affect their experience with a game – those can be called PX factors. The study of PX factors aggregates knowledge from many disciplines (e.g., neurophysiology, psychology, and sociology) [81]. Although there is no consensus on what exact factors constitute PX [60], there is a shared comprehension that PX is a multidimensional and multilayered construct [67]. Consequently, several psychophysiological models have been developed to explain the complex PX's structure and the diverse components that influence this experience – the reader can find more on this topic in [2,81].

While there is a need for a holistic evaluation of the human factors in this context, it is common to focus on evaluating engagement metrics in the game industry. Large world-renowned technology companies openly promote the role of engagement in raising businesses profit: Facebook, for example, presented the results of a survey that highlighted the power of engagement to maintain the use of games and, consequently, increase revenue [31]; Google has associated engagement with the players' "inclination to spend" in apps of this genre [36]; Activision Blizzard also highlighted that engagement means gains for the game [11]. User engagement is, in fact, an essential element for the player-game interaction and is desirable in all human activity mediated by machines [49]. Engaging with a digital artifact means being captivated by it and, consequently, feeling motivated to use it [52]. However, it is also necessary to consider how other human factors and characteristics are affected by this construct, trying to stimulate the well-being of users of digital games and gamified applications in different domains.

Speaking of motivation, that is another example of a valuable concept for HCI and games. Human motivation has been extensively studied over the last two centuries in the most different areas of knowledge (e.g., education, marketing, social sciences, and semiotics). From the perspective of neuroscience, motivation is defined as the precursor of all behavior performed by an individual [80]. Thus, to understand human motivation, it is necessary to understand a complex and multifaceted structure that involves cognitive, emotional, and biological mechanisms and takes into account the goals, purposes, and meaning of each individual [70].

However, jointly evaluating these and other factors that motivate and explain the interaction of people with games is not a trivial task [30]. Game Analytics tools are often used in games evaluation based on events that allow tracking metrics, such as user retention and acquisition, monetization, player progression, and engagement. Indeed, the use of dashboards and data mining techniques facilitates understanding what players do in a game and where development efforts can focus. However, these tools only provide starting points for investigating human factors. They are not enough to generate an understanding of how the player is affected by the pragmatic and hedonic aspects of the game's interaction and interface in the long term – and therefore, they are not the best way to approach the problem.

As mentioned before, for a long time, the gaming research community has been trying to overcome the scarcity of a set of adequate methods and tools that allow measuring entertainment experiences in a sensitive, reliable and valid way [9,30], in addition to addressing different PX constructs, which include both physical and psychological factors [16]. In this context, this challenge brings some underlying issues that require attention from our community (indicated in Fig. 3), so we can take advantage of the advances produced by the international community and contribute to overcoming this gap. These needs involve considering: (i) multiple human factors using quali-quantitative approaches, (ii) the game focus, and (iii) how the PX changes over time.

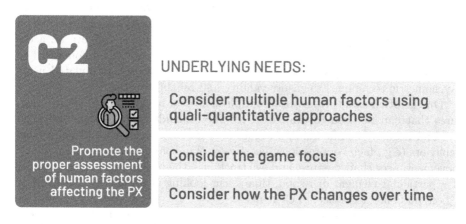

Fig. 3. Underlying needs related to C2

The Need to Consider Multiple Human Factors Using Quali-Quantitative Approaches. Human Factors can be defined as a scientific discipline concerned with understanding interactions among humans and other elements of a system [6]. The focus of this discipline is on the application of knowledge about human abilities, limitations, behavior patterns, and other characteristics to the design of systems that require interaction between people and system components, such as hardware, software, tasks, environments, and work structures [73] – including games.

The search for understanding the characteristics of the player-game interaction, the generated experience, and its impact requires the study of human factors, more specifically, of human characteristics, which include psychological, physiological and anatomical aspects, group factors, individual differences, and psychophysiological state variables [73].

Several characteristics such as the players' profiles and motivations [18], and their physical and cognitive characteristics [27] can impact how a group of persons engages with a game. Hence, they should be considered during the game design in formative evaluations. i.e., before or during implementation to improve the design and performance of the game for its target players and purposes.

In this perspective, evaluation efforts focus on the experience lived by the players while interacting with the physical and digital interface of a game in different stages of development. It should be performed during the design process and after the game is ready. To accurately evaluate the players' experience, it is necessary to adopt appropriate techniques and tools for the different stages of maturity of the game under development, the players' characteristics, and game goals. For that matter, combining quantitative and qualitative methods and objective and subjective measures is essential.

Objective measures, such as eye-tracking and heart rate measurements, and subjective ones, such as interviews and self-report questionnaires, have been widely used to evaluate Player Experience. Self-report questionnaires, for example, are subjective measures that allow collecting emotional information from a person. An evaluation that uses this type of instrument can achieve an accurate and less intrusive measurement, being easier to apply when compared to objective methods [3,32]. This type of instrument should be formulated using psychometric techniques to ensure validity and reliability [75].

On the other hand, behavioral and physiological metrics are objective measures that can be used to evaluate PX. They include verbal behaviors (positive and negative comments and suggestions for improvement) and non-verbal behaviors (e.g., facial expressions, heart rate, skin conductance, pressure mouse movement, user chair posture, and eye tracking – the proportion of users looking at a particular element or region, time spent looking at a particular element or region, and time to notice an element).

Behavioral measures can offer greater sensitivity and reliability than self-report measures, as affective responses tend to be difficult to explain verbally or cause participants to act by their perception of the evaluators' goals. While self-report measures provide the user's perception of their behavior, behavioral measures allow the verification of actual behavior through psychophysiological measures. Emotions are related to various psychophysiological measures, and the measures are associated with various emotions and constructs of the PX. However, further exploration is still needed to identify which emotions are best captured and by which psychophysiological measures [54].

Although a wide variety of methods can be used and combined in this type of evaluation, the gaming research community still faces a scarcity of adequate methods and tools that allow measuring the PX in a sensitive, reliable and valid way [48]. Reflections of this are seen in the sometimes confusing way researchers and practitioners have been evaluating the player-game interaction – as pointed out in works such as [16]). It seems that the apparent confusion regarding terms and definitions in the literature may have influenced the practice of this type of evaluation.

An example is that *ad hoc* questionnaires are commonly used to evaluate PX – which is an intrinsically subjective construct. Questionnaires are a valuable method, but if poorly done, they can result in questionable data [50]. Besides, they are often used because they are the easiest method, not because they are the most appropriate [16, 26, 50]. Perceptions like these emphasize that it is necessary to carefully analyze the evaluation methods' suitability to the defined objectives and highlight the need to build a robust and versatile set of methods appropriate to this domain.

Thus, one of the available alternatives is to opt for a less extensive but deeper investigation or combine methods that produce complementary insights. For example, Carneiro, Viana & Darin (2021) explore qualitative methods to evaluate PX in location-based games and propose the VALERIE guide, which aims to help prepare and conduct semi-structured interviews to investigate players' perceptions about the experience lived with a game [19]. The authors encourage combining interviews with other methods, defending the use of a mixed approach to evaluate the player-game interaction and, mainly, the PX. This type of approach is already widely recognized in the literature of games studies and other research areas [23, 30].

Therefore, to obtain a deeper understanding of human characteristics in game evaluation, it is necessary to triangulate the data collected through quantitative and qualitative evaluation approaches, which use both self-reported and objective measures. Approaches that rely on applying multiple complementary methods can offer a more in-depth view of the phenomenon studied, allowing us to understand how player characteristics affect and are affected by the gameplay and the PX [30].

The Need to Consider the Game Focus. The evaluation of PX should be driven by the player's goals while engaged with that experience. Digital games offer some of the most intense, rich, and immersive experiences of all interactive products, serving not only serious purposes as a means of education but also as tools for entertainment, persuasion, and self-expression. They also foster different cultural practices formed around them (e.g., streaming, modding, and game journalism). Understanding the goals and context should help evaluators decide what constructs are relevant to their context.

The pleasure of playing games for entertainment is often associated with feelings of being in control, competence, and improved mood after the game due to the satisfaction of psychological needs [55]. Researchers have investigated, for example, if a less challenging game can be more enjoyable for offering ample opportunities to satisfy competence needs, or if players have more pleasure when they reach a rare moment of triumph in a game, and how both situations differ concerning player motives [14]. The conceptualization of gaming pleasure has potential theoretical implications for PX research, namely that gaming pleasure should be understood as the valence of the player's experience. In contrast, the intensity of the PX can best be represented by the players' immersion, involvement, or engagement, that is, the extent to which players' attention is maintained by the game's challenges and the game's environment [14]. The more immersive a game is, the more intense the player's experience will be, eventually culminating in cognitive absorption and time distortion, directly related to the engagement construct.

Focusing on the pleasure of the experience, one of the most common types of games for entertainment today is *casual games*, widely used by the most diverse profiles of people. In short, casual games can be understood as fun, fast-access and easy-to-learn games that require little time to play and no previous experience or specific skills [46].

While casual gaming is, in some ways, quick access to fun, immersive, and engaging experiences, it is not a style of play that appeals to all individuals. This is due to the myriad of personal factors that interfere with the preference of human beings when playing a particular game [62].

Other games aim beyond entertainment and induce players to learn content or skill that enhances their mental models, possibly, while having fun – these games are called "serious games" [56]. Serious games are often used for training, advertising, simulation, and education, and are designed for different computing devices or video game consoles [76]. These games allow people to experience unfeasible situations in the real world for a variety of reasons, such as safety, cost, time, and human limitations.

Consequently, they help improve our performance in various tasks and skills. Serious games are premised on using entertainment to teach and/or improve the skills of their users. They can be used in education, security, and health and allow dramatic representations of a subject or problem being studied. It also allows players to assume realistic roles, face problems, formulate strategies, make decisions, and have quick feedback on the consequences of their actions [56]. Serious games and their mechanics are thus used in different contexts. Lately, they have been applied in the most diverse domains, including digital government and therapeutic applications. In such cases, the PX will not – and should not – be evaluated as in entertainment games.

The Need to Consider How the PX Changes over Time. As discussed, it is necessary to invest in quantitative and qualitative evaluation techniques capable of generating relevant results to identify game quality problems. For the most, both approaches are employed in assessments that occur during the interaction or after a single interaction [24]. However, there are concerns about biased results of evaluations that consider only a single episode of use of a system caused by the so-called "novelty effect" [42].

In HCI, the novelty effect is considered one of the biggest challenges that need to be overcome to determine the practical potential of an application [44]. There is no consensus on when the "novelty effect" ends. However, it is known that one of the most effective ways to mitigate it is to carry out long-term assessments - or "longitudinal evaluations" [42]. It is known that longitudinal evaluations can reveal the real impact that interaction had on users [69], as not necessarily the good or bad sensations experienced at the time of interaction will have a positive or negative impact on their perception [40].

Historically, longitudinal evaluations in HCI have been avoided, as they are considered expensive and tiring for both users and researchers [53]. Another preponderant factor was the belief that long studies were unnecessary since the technology industry evolves very fast, making technologies quickly obsolete to be evaluated at length [50]. However, in a short time since the initial contact with the system, the changes identified in the user experience with systems from different domains became evident, causing evaluations aimed at understanding changes in experience over time to be stimulated [41]. Long-term evaluation methods can make researchers understand the evolution of the user's affections towards the product, which makes it possible to map the necessary stages for a product to be integrated into the daily lives of users [10]. In parallel, evaluations identified that users tend to abandon interactive digital systems produced by the industry very quickly – some studies report two weeks, for example [33] –, which also stimulated concerns about the changes that occur in their experience over time [21].

In this context, UX specialists introduced the HCI community to the concept of "accumulated UX", that is, the experience formed through a series of episodes of use and periods of non-use, which can last months, or more [69]. Although other approaches can be used as alternatives for assessing accumulated UX – such as cross-sectional and retrospective studies [40,59] –, longitudinal assessments, in which there is a continuous collection of user data, constitute the most complete and least biased approach [47] and can equally be applied to games research. The difficulties related to conducting this type of evaluation have been overcome by the diffusion of software that facilitates continuous evaluation techniques [78], using commercially available APIs and SDKs to collect devices data over long periods [37], and by the Internet of Things technologies, such as wearable devices, which facilitate the collection of psychophysiological data in several sessions [82].

However, it is still necessary to identify how to support lengthy PX evaluations that keep people motivated to participate in research and facilitate the organization of data by researchers [39,68]. Above all, it is still necessary to orchestrate the extensive literature on PX methods and instruments to conduct longitudinal evaluations suitable for different domains (e.g., web applications, games, and ubiquitous systems) since each domain may require specific methods [17].

2.3 C3: Avoid and Combat Abusive and Unethical Practices and Reveal the Different Parameters that Guide Human Motivation Itself

Focusing too much on a single interaction feature – such as engagement – tends to have negative consequences for the player. If, on the one hand, there is an industry profiting more and more from people's engagement in games, on the other hand, there are people who develop unhealthy conditions due to addiction. According to the World Health Organization (WHO), gambling addiction is a reality for many people worldwide. WHO defines gaming disorder as "a pattern of gaming behavior ("digital-gaming" or "video-gaming") characterized by impaired control over gaming, increasing priority given to gaming over other activities to the extent that gaming takes precedence over other interests and daily activities, and continuation or escalation of gaming despite the occurrence of negative consequences" [64].

In a highly competitive scenario, the game industry has been betting on developing standards quite unethical, which bears some degree of risk for players, sometimes using dark patterns to lead the player to addiction. One of the causes of the increase in people in a state of addiction is the fact that developers have sought, over the last few decades, to produce increasingly engaging digital artifacts (in order to stimulate use) while not giving the same importance to the well-being of users [65], giving rise to the so-called "engagement-addiction dilemma". This dilemma is characterized by the high tension between the exploitation of game elements for an exacerbated increase in engagement and the triggering of obsession on the players' part [20].

When studied through one of the traditional perspectives, the eudaimonic perspective, well-being is shown as a "way of living" [28]. This means that well-being, from the eudaimonic perspective, is not exactly a static state but a condition that surrounds the flow of life. Thinking of a habit as games, which occur throughout life, suggests understanding this phenomenon as something that goes beyond a given moment.

Thus, a game experience is said to be meaningful (meaningful play) when eudaimonic needs are satisfied. This means that experiences that allow the player to understand human nature or even allow the understanding of the truths of life can be considered significant [63].

Understanding well-being and meaningful experiences help understand one's psychological motivations and needs. Research that orbits this field of study is essential to understanding how to trigger positive potentials and, consequently, allow us to unravel the nuances of human nature itself and favor its development [29]. It is common knowledge that games are one of the most popular entertainment activities globally [15]. Understanding the game experience through the eudaimonic perspective allows us to understand the experience as a whole in the long term. So, this knowledge can be applied in a design context to provide more valuable game experiences from the user's perspective.

Few works have been approaching unethical practices in game design. Some examples of initiatives in this regard in the Brazilian community are the discussion about what should be considered ethical and unethical in a game, under the perspective of Aristotle, Augustine, and Kant [1], and the proposal of the Radiant Patterns [58] to offer game designers an alternative to lead the players to a state of well-being, satisfying one or more basic psychological needs (autonomy, competence, relatedness). There is much room for Brazilian researchers to contribute with ethical discussions and practices in game design and motivate future work towards developing policies to protect players.

2.4 C4: Foster Evaluation in the Industry Context, Based on Practices Developed in Academia

The context of game development is intrinsically linked to the industry. In the SBGames Industry track, for example, no works in the last three years discuss the evaluation of human factors in human interaction with digital games. Some works have proposed and reported their design processes, in which evaluation is one of the steps. Still, they present a perspective that can make it difficult to understand and adapt to human factors: "*after* the game is ready to be evaluated", when, often, there is no more design time to consider human factors in greater depth. Consequently, alpha, beta, and gold tests are applied, using quick methods to obtain players' opinions without evaluating the human factors themselves.

This scenario may be a consequence of the fact that the gaming market in Brazil is still not very mature and has experienced relatively recent growth [72]. Many developers still seem to have not cultivated a holistic understanding of the need to assess human factors, as they consider that the most critical thing in a game is gameplay, narrative, soundtrack, and graphics – no human factors included [4]. At the international level, however, large game development companies invest in research of their users' cognitive, psychophysiological, individual, and group factors to provide the best gaming experience [45].

The Self-Determination Theory (SDT) is a promising bridge between academia and industry. SDT is an empirical psychological theory of human motivation and personality that seeks to understand how biological, social, and cultural factors affect inherent human capacities for psychological growth, engagement, and well-being [71]. It suggests that the processes of motivation, internalization, and well-being are potentiated by the satisfaction of three basic psychological needs – autonomy, competence, and relatedness.

Due to its practical characteristic in identifying conditions that facilitate or impair motivation and satisfaction, SDT has been used in several areas, such as education, health, and technology [71]. In HCI, SDT has been relevant in game studies mainly because it allows a greater understanding of what constitutes an engaging experience, considered one of the intersections of areas [77]. The main applications of the theory in HCI and game research have been investigating the motivational appeal of games, the PX, the construction of game design, and evaluating and testing in the industry [77].

Evaluating the player's interaction with a digital game, properly considering human factors, is not a trivial task since, besides considering technical issues, it is necessary to explore the player's perspective carefully, focusing on their relationship with the game, satisfaction, motivation, and fulfillment of their expectations. PX evaluation instruments as validated tools (ranging from self-reported scales to software) have been designed to systematically collect qualitative data, measure quantitative data related to experience constructs from various participants, and produce results based on psychometric properties. Nonetheless, this type of evaluation raises many challenges for academia and industry, such as the definition of factors to be explored, the appropriate choice of methods to be applied, the use, translation, and validation of attitude scales, and the availability of resources, among others. The search for maturity and systematization of studies and practices related to evaluating player interaction and experience is an international challenge, which has driven efforts by research and practice communities; therefore, to deal with such a challenge, we need to foster communication between academia and the gaming industry.

3 Practical Initiatives and Success Evaluation

Internationally, the evaluation of human characteristics has been widely studied, with emphasis on GUR, a field of research and practice that has been consolidated by combining efforts of academics and practitioners to deepen the understanding of player-game interaction and PX. GUR has been promoted in publications, projects, and events such as CHI and CHI Play. Such initiatives can serve as a reference and aspiration in advancing the presented challenges. Thus, the Brazilian community as a group can lead some actions to collaborate with the general promotion of this grand challenge:

- To widely disseminate the work on the challenges produced by the Brazilian gaming community to encourage the scientific community in general to develop research in the area;
- Promote contests, awards, or multidisciplinary competitions that propose the analysis, creation, and application of human factors assessments in different gaming contexts;
- Encourage the creation of teaching materials and teaching practices on the subject to support teachers in the area;
- Encourage the creation of interdisciplinary and inter-institutional research groups on the topic;
- Insert disciplines that address Evaluation of Interaction and Research with Users in undergraduate and graduate courses in Digital Game Design and correlated courses;
- Seek partnerships between university and industry for cooperation in projects that allow the exchange of experiences and mutual improvement.

Regarding the SBgames, our main academic event on games, the proposed challenges tackle subjects regarding all of its tracks and directly connect to the Computing track. However, this subject is not directly mentioned among the topics of interest listed in its calls, and it is necessary to punctuate it to increase its visibility. It is also possible to indicate it in the Art & Design and Industry tracks, emphasizing other perspectives, such as individual, cultural, and social factors in game development, and case studies of the evaluation of these factors in the industry, including gaps between academic research and the applied practice. As mentioned before, other national events have also little explored the area, as is the case of the IHCBr, which only recently promoted a workshop on interaction and research with users in digital games, with works related to this grand challenge.

Assessing the success of research that meets the discussed challenges is not easy because a gradual culture change is necessary due to the nature of the problem. Quantitative metrics may not be enough; on the other hand, qualitative metrics are difficult to track. So, to estimate the progress on the proposed challenge, we must develop diverse evaluation mechanisms that allow us to embrace the particularities of the Brazilian scenario and identify advances made by research labs, companies, or other groups in their activities related to Game Design and Research. As an initial list of possibilities, we suggest the community survey periodically:

- The number of publications by Brazilian authors in conferences, journals, magazines, and books that cite and discuss human factors or report the evaluation of human characteristics in digital games;
- The number of publications by Brazilian authors in conferences, journals, magazines, and books proposing methods aligned with the challenge or reporting the conduction of studies to this end;
- Instruments, methods, and tools developed for the evaluation of physical, psychological, or social factors in specific contexts or audiences;
- Research projects approved by the Ethics Committees of universities involving the evaluation of different human factors in games;
- The number of standardized psychometric instruments translated and validated into Brazilian Portuguese;
- Decrease in the number of published articles in which the evaluation concludes the inappropriate use of psychometric instruments and methods;
- The number of software records developed for the evaluation of human factors in the interaction with games;
- Teaching materials on the topic created and disseminated to the research and practice community;
- The number of workshops, keynotes, masterclasses, courses, and forums held at events promoted by academia or industry on human factors evaluation in games and correlated topics.

4   Research Agenda

In this sense, the Brazilian community would benefit from a research agenda that contemplates the grand challenge's different aspects, as discussed in this chapter. In Table 1, we gather recommendations to tackle the presented issues

Table 1. Summary of recommendations for a research agenda

Recommendation	Related main challenge
Efforts to evolve, translate, culturally adapt **and validate** attitude scales and other instruments already presented in the game literature	C2
Development and validation of self-reported verbal and non-verbal scales **based on psychometric models**	C1, C2
Development and validation of computational tools for behavioral and psychophysiological measures in a **less intrusive way** during gameplay	C2, C4
Discussion of **ethical issues** involved in games evaluation and development of proper strategies and evaluation tools to tackle them	C2, C3
Development of tools and processes **appropriate to the reality of small game companies** that provide efficient ways to consider human factors during the game development process	C2, C4
Conducting and publishing **case studies to foster a formative evaluation culture in the industry** during the game development process, instead of evaluating only at the end of the process	C1, C4
Adaptation and evaluation of qualitative and quantitative **data collection techniques for specific domains and audiences,** considering the impact of games on cultural and social contexts	C1, C2
Identify, apply, propose and systematize good practices and guidelines **to evaluate games with specific audiences,** such as children, the elderly, and people with disabilities	C1, C2, C3
Identification of relevant human factors **for evaluating games in specific domains and with specific goals** (e.g., cognitive impact of games for skills development)	C1, C2
Systematic discussion of **terms, concepts, methodologies,** and their implications and appropriate applications throughout game research and development community	C1
Foster the **intercommunication of results and interchange of practices** between academia and the gaming industry	C4
Increase the opportunities and diversify the participation modalities for the **national and international Game Industry involvement in SBGames** for interaction on practices, strategies, and their bases	C4
Identification of ambiguities and promotion of consistent discussions of the theories involved in game development	C1
Deepen theoretical discussions on philosophical concepts related to the multiple game elements and their implications in the cognitive and psychological aspects of player-game interaction	C3
Conduct experimental studies to analyze physical, psychological, and social factors and promote transparency and replication in research by making available the artifacts used or produced in the experiments	C1, C2

that can be gradually translated into actions by individuals and their research groups or by the Brazilian gaming community as a whole.

Regarding Challenge 4, the gaming research community has the possibility of impacting the gaming industry in Brazil through the development of tools and processes appropriate to the reality of small companies, considering the size and complexity of their projects, restrictions, and team resources, but that provide adequate inputs for considering human factors in games evaluation. Following the example of the international GUR community, we can also conduct case studies to foster a culture in the industry that evaluation should not only occur at the end of the project.

5 Conclusion

Since digital games are intricate interactive computer systems designed to generate positive emotions, satisfaction, and player engagement, methods and techniques are needed that can be incorporated into the industry and allow a holistic assessment of the human factors involved in this interaction.

However, how to jointly evaluate the human factors that motivate and explain the interaction with games is a research challenge recognized by the international community of HCI and GUR. Given the complexity of this scenario, there is a need to create and adapt methods and techniques for evaluation and data collection that allow evaluating the player's interaction with these games considering human factors and the specific characteristics of the domain.

This chapter seeks to stimulate the community to investigate the conceptual and practical relationship between the player experience constructs and the evaluation of human factors in digital games and gamified applications.

The gaps in the evaluation of human factors in the interaction with digital games in the Brazilian scenario reveal challenges to be explored in the coming years by the research and practice communities, aiming at the maturity of the area and a better insertion of Brazil in the international gaming scenario. In addition to promoting this grand challenge, we can carry out actions such as proposing workshops at relevant events related to digital games; encouraging research aimed at developing and validating methods and techniques for this type of evaluation; formally translating validated instruments into Brazilian Portuguese; negotiating the acquisition of equipment – to name a few. With the advancement of efforts and discussions, the community should evolve the suggested metrics to obtain qualitative data and verify the effects on academia and industry practices. Thus, this proposal constitutes a first step towards renewing reflections and practices in the area.

References

1. Joselli, M.: A ética e os games:"morais, imorais ou amorais?". Um estudo sobre a ética em games segundo Aristóteles, Santo Agostinho e Kant. Proceedings of XIII Brazilian Symposium on Games and Digital Enterteinment (SBGAMES'14), 448–456 (2014)
2. Abeele, V.V., Spiel, K., Nacke, L., Johnson, D., Gerling, K.: Development and validation of the player experience inventory: a scale to measure player experiences at the level of functional and psychosocial consequences. Int. J. Hum. Comput. Stud. **135**, 102370 (2020)
3. Adams, A., Cox, A.L.: Questionnaires, In-Depth Interviews and Focus Groups. Cambridge University Press, Cambridge (2008)
4. Amelio, C.: A indústria e o mercado de jogos digitais no brasil: evolução, características, obstáculos e análise comparativa. Trabalho de Conclusão de Curso. Universidade Federal de Minas Gerais (2018)
5. Aranha, R.V., Nunes, F.L.: Player experience with Brazilian accent: development and validation of PX-BR, a summarized instrument in Portuguese. In: XVIII Brazilian Symposium on Information Systems, pp. 1–8 (2022)
6. IE Association: Definition and domains of human factors and ergonomics (2020). https://iea.cc/what-is-ergonomics/. Accessed 17 Apr 2022
7. Barbosa, S.D.J., da Silva, B., Silveira, M.S., Gasparini, I., Darin, T., Barbosa, G.D.J.: Interação humano-computador e experiência do usuario. Auto publicação (2021)
8. Bernhaupt, R.: Game User Experience Evaluation. Springer, Heidelberg (2015)
9. Bernhaupt, R., Mueller, F.F.: Game user experience evaluation. In: Proceedings of the 2016 CHI Conference Extended Abstracts on Human Factors in Computing Systems, pp. 940–943 (2016)
10. Biduski, D., Bellei, E.A., Rodriguez, J.P.M., Zaina, L.A.M., De Marchi, A.C.B.: Assessing long-term user experience on a mobile health application through an in-app embedded conversation-based questionnaire. Comput. Hum. Behav. **104**, 106169 (2020)
11. Blizzard, A.: Social connection in a virtual world (2021). https://www.activisionblizzard.com/newsroom/2021/10/social-connection-in-a-virtual-world. Accessed 20 Dec 2021
12. Borges, J.B., Juy, C.L., de Andrade Matos, I.S., Silveira, P.V.A., Darin, T.D.G.R.: Player experience evaluation: a brief panorama of instruments and research opportunities. J. Interact. Syst. **11**(1), 74–91 (2020)
13. Bourgonjon, J.: The meaning and relevance of video game literacy. CLCWeb: Comp. Lit. Cult. **16**(5), 8 (2014)
14. Brockmyer, J.H., Fox, C.M., Curtiss, K.A., McBroom, E., Burkhart, K.M., Pidruzny, J.N.: The development of the game engagement questionnaire: a measure of engagement in video game-playing. J. Exp. Soc. Psychol. **45**(4), 624–634 (2009)
15. Brühlmann, F., Schmid, G.M.: How to measure the game experience? Analysis of the factor structure of two questionnaires. In: Proceedings of the 33rd Annual ACM Conference Extended Abstracts on Human Factors in Computing Systems, pp. 1181–1186 (2015)
16. Carneiro, N., Darin, T., Viana, W.: What are we talking about when we talk about location-based games evaluation? A systematic mapping study. In: Proceedings of the 18th Brazilian Symposium on Human Factors in Computing Systems, pp. 1–13 (2019)

17. Carneiro, N., Melo, B., Cavalcante, L., Castro, R., Andrade, R.M., Darin, T.: Mobili: development and use of a usability checklist for mobile games and applications. In: 19th Brazilian Symposium on Software Quality, pp. 1–9 (2020)
18. Carneiro, N., Miranda, D., Pereira, G., Mendonça, G., Darin, T.: A systematic mapping on player's profiles: motivations, behavior, and personality characteristics. J. Interact. Syst. **13**(1), 257–273 (2022). https://doi.org/10.5753/jis.2022. 2572. https://sol.sbc.org.br/journals/index.php/jis/article/view/2572
19. Carneiro, N., Viana, W., Darin, T.: VALERIE: a guide to qualitative evaluation of player experience in location-based games using interviews. In: Proceedings of the XX Brazilian Symposium on Human Factors in Computing Systems, pp. 1–7 (2021)
20. Charlton, J.P., Danforth, I.D.: Validating the distinction between computer addiction and engagement: online game playing and personality. Behav. Inf. Technol. **29**(6), 601–613 (2010)
21. Cho, M., Lee, S., Lee, K.P.: Once a kind friend is now a thing: understanding how conversational agents at home are forgotten. In: Proceedings of the 2019 on Designing Interactive Systems Conference, pp. 1557–1569 (2019)
22. Coelho, B., Andrade, R.M.C., Darin, T.: Not the same everywhere: comparing the scope and definition of user experience between the Brazilian and international communities. Int. J. Hum.-Comput. Interact. **38**(7), 595–613 (2022). https://doi. org/10.1080/10447318.2021.1960727
23. Creswell, J.W., Creswell, J.D.: Research Design: Qualitative, Quantitative, and Mixed Methods Approaches. Sage Publications (2018)
24. Darin, T., Andrade, R., Sánchez, J.: Principles for evaluating usability in multimodal games for people who are blind. In: Antona, M., Stephanidis, C. (eds.) HCII 2019. LNCS, vol. 11573, pp. 209–223. Springer, Cham (2019). https://doi.org/10. 1007/978-3-030-23563-5_18
25. Darin, T., Carneiro, N.: Avaliacao de fatores humanos na interacao com jogos digitais. In: 2020 19th Brazilian Symposium on Computer Games and Digital Entertainment (SBGames). SBC-Proceedings of SBGames, pp. 2179–2259 (2020)
26. Darin, T., Coelho, B., Borges, B.: Which instrument should I use? Supporting decision-making about the evaluation of user experience. In: Marcus, A., Wang, W. (eds.) HCII 2019. LNCS, vol. 11586, pp. 49–67. Springer, Cham (2019). https:// doi.org/10.1007/978-3-030-23535-2_4
27. Darin, T., Andrade, R., Sánchez, J.: Usability evaluation of multimodal interactive virtual environments for learners who are blind: An empirical investigation. Int. J. Hum Comput Stud. **158**, 102732 (2022)
28. Deci, E.L., Ryan, R.M.: Hedonia, eudaimonia, and well-being: an introduction. J. Happiness Stud. **9**(1), 1–11 (2008)
29. Deci, E.L., Ryan, R.M.: Self-determination theory (2012)
30. Drachen, A., Mirza-Babaei, P., Nacke, L.E.: Games User Research. Oxford University Press, Oxford (2018)
31. Facebook IQ, M: Strategic considerations for mobile gaming engagement campaigns (2019). https://www.facebook.com/business/news/insights/strategic-considerations-for-mobile-gaming-engagement-campaigns. Accessed 20 Dec 2021
32. Fuentes, C., Herskovic, V., Rodríguez, I., Gerea, C., Marques, M., Rossel, P.O.: A systematic literature review about technologies for self-reporting emotional information. J. Ambient. Intell. Humaniz. Comput. **8**(4), 593–606 (2017)
33. Garg, R.: An analysis of (non-)use practices and decisions of internet of things. In: Lamas, D., Loizides, F., Nacke, L., Petrie, H., Winckler, M., Zaphiris, P. (eds.)

INTERACT 2019. LNCS, vol. 11749, pp. 3–24. Springer, Cham (2019). https://doi.org/10.1007/978-3-030-29390-1_1

34. Gerling, K.M., Klauser, M., Niesenhaus, J.: Measuring the impact of game controllers on player experience in FPS games. In: Proceedings of the 15th International Academic MindTrek Conference: Envisioning Future Media Environments, pp. 83–86 (2011)

35. Gerritsen, M., et al.: English in product advertisements in non-English-speaking countries in Western Europe: product image and comprehension of the text. J. Glob. Mark. **23**(4), 349–365 (2010)

36. Google: Change the game: Driving inclusivity and belonging in gaming (2019). https://static.googleusercontent.com/media/play.google.com/pt-BR//about/changethegame/assets/static/pdf/white-paper-2019.pdf. Accessed 20 Dec 2021

37. Harrison, D., Marshall, P., Berthouze, N., Bird, J.: Tracking physical activity: problems related to running longitudinal studies with commercial devices. In: Proceedings of the 2014 ACM International Joint Conference on Pervasive and Ubiquitous Computing: Adjunct Publication, pp. 699–702 (2014)

38. Huizinga, J.: Homo Ludens. Reprint (1944)

39. Irizar-Arrieta, A., Casado-Mansilla, D., Garaizar, P., López-de Ipiña, D., Retegi, A.: User perspectives in the design of interactive everyday objects for sustainable behaviour. Int. J. Hum. Comput. Stud. **137**, 102393 (2020)

40. Karapanos, E., Martens, J.B., Hassenzahl, M.: Reconstructing experiences with iScale. Int. J. Hum. Comput. Stud. **70**(11), 849–865 (2012)

41. Karapanos, E., Zimmerman, J., Forlizzi, J., Martens, J.B.: User experience over time: an initial framework. In: Proceedings of the SIGCHI Conference on Human Factors in Computing Systems, pp. 729–738 (2009)

42. Kjærup, M., Skov, M.B., Nielsen, P.A., Kjeldskov, J., Gerken, J., Reiterer, H.: Longitudinal studies in HCI research: a review of CHI publications from 1982–2019. In: Karapanos, E., Gerken, J., Kjeldskov, J., Skov, M.B. (eds.) Advances in Longitudinal HCI Research. HIS, pp. 11–39. Springer, Cham (2021). https://doi.org/10.1007/978-3-030-67322-2_2

43. Klarkowski, M.W.: The psychophysiological evaluation of the player experience. Ph.D. thesis, Queensland University of Technology (2017)

44. Koch, M., von Luck, K., Schwarzer, J., Draheim, S.: The novelty effect in large display deployments-experiences and lessons-learned for evaluating prototypes. In: Proceedings of 16th European Conference on Computer-Supported Cooperative Work-Exploratory Papers. European Society for Socially Embedded Technologies (EUSSET) (2018)

45. Kou, Y., Li, Y., Gui, X., Suzuki-Gill, E.: Playing with streakiness in online games: how players perceive and react to winning and losing streaks in league of legends. In: Proceedings of the 2018 CHI Conference on Human Factors in Computing Systems, pp. 1–14 (2018)

46. Kuittinen, J., Kultima, A., Niemelä, J., Paavilainen, J.: Casual games discussion. In: Proceedings of the 2007 Conference on Future Play, pp. 105–112 (2007)

47. Kujala, S., Miron-Shatz, T., Jokinen, J.J.: The cross-sequential approach: a short-term method for studying long-term user experience. J. Usab. Stud. **14**(2) (2019)

48. Lankes, M., Bernhaupt, R., Tscheligi, M.: Evaluating user experience factors using experiments: expressive artificial faces embedded in contexts. In: Bernhaupt, R. (ed.) Game User Experience Evaluation. HIS, pp. 113–131. Springer, Cham (2015). https://doi.org/10.1007/978-3-319-15985-0_6

49. Laurel, B.: Computers as Theatre. Addison-Wesley, Boston (2013)
50. Lazar, J., Feng, J.H., Hochheiser, H.: Research Methods in Human-Computer Interaction. Morgan Kaufmann, Burlington (2017)
51. Lazzaro, N.: Why we play: affect and the fun of games. Hum.-Comput. Interact. Designing Diverse Users Domains **155**, 679–700 (2009)
52. Lehmann, J., Lalmas, M., Yom-Tov, E., Dupret, G.: Models of user engagement. In: Masthoff, J., Mobasher, B., Desmarais, M.C., Nkambou, R. (eds.) UMAP 2012. LNCS, vol. 7379, pp. 164–175. Springer, Heidelberg (2012). https://doi.org/10.1007/978-3-642-31454-4_14
53. MacKenzie, I.S.: Human-computer interaction: an empirical research perspective (2012)
54. Maia, C.L.B., Furtado, E.S.: A study about psychophysiological measures in user experience monitoring and evaluation. In: Proceedings of the 15th Brazilian Symposium on Human Factors in Computing Systems, pp. 1–9 (2016)
55. Mekler, E.D., Bopp, J.A., Tuch, A.N., Opwis, K.: A systematic review of quantitative studies on the enjoyment of digital entertainment games. In: Proceedings of the SIGCHI Conference on Human Factors in Computing Systems, pp. 927–936 (2014)
56. Michael, D.R., Chen, S.L.: Serious Games: Games That Educate, Train, and Inform. Muska & Lipman/Premier-Trade (2005)
57. Miranda, D., Li, C., Darin, T.: UES-BR: translation and cross-cultural adaptation of the user engagement scale for Brazilian Portuguese. Proc. ACM Hum.-Comput. Interact. **5**(CHI PLAY), 1–22 (2021)
58. Miranda, D.M., Pontes, R.M., de Gois Ribeiro Darin, T.: It's dark but just a game: towards an ethical and healthy game design practice. In: Proceedings of the 21st Brazilian Symposium on Human Factors in Computing Systems, IHC 2022. Association for Computing Machinery, New York (2022). https://doi.org/10.1145/3554364.3559144
59. Montero, H., Krawczyk, P., Topolewski, M., Pallot, M., Huotari, J., Lehtosaari, H.: Repeated cross-sectional study of a mobile app user-experience. In: 2020 IEEE International Conference on Engineering, Technology and Innovation (ICE/ITMC), pp. 1–8. IEEE (2020)
60. Nacke, L., Drachen, A.: Towards a framework of player experience research. In: Proceedings of the Second International Workshop on Evaluating Player Experience in Games at FDG, vol. 11 (2011)
61. Nacke, L., et al.: Playability and player experience research. In: Proceedings of DIGRA 2009: Breaking New Ground: Innovation in Games, Play, Practice and Theory. DiGRA (2009)
62. Nacke, L.E., Bateman, C., Mandryk, R.L.: BrainHex: a neurobiological gamer typology survey. Entertainment Comput. **5**(1), 55–62 (2014)
63. Oliver, M.B., Raney, A.A.: Entertainment as pleasurable and meaningful: identifying hedonic and eudaimonic motivations for entertainment consumption. J. Commun. **61**(5), 984–1004 (2011)
64. World Health Organization: Addictive behaviours: Gaming disorder (2020). https://www.who.int/news-room/questions-and-answers/item/addictive-behaviours-gaming-disorder. Accessed 20 Dec 2021
65. Peters, D., Calvo, R.A., Ryan, R.M.: Designing for motivation, engagement and wellbeing in digital experience. Front. Psychol. **9**, 797 (2018)
66. Phan, M.H., Keebler, J.R., Chaparro, B.S.: The development and validation of the game user experience satisfaction scale (guess). Hum. Factors **58**(8), 1217–1247 (2016)

67. Poels, K., de Kort, Y.A., IJsselsteijn, W.A.: D3.3: game experience questionnaire: development of a self-report measure to assess the psychological impact of digital games (2007)
68. Regani, S.D., Xu, Q., Wang, B., Wu, M., Liu, K.R.: Driver authentication for smart car using wireless sensing. IEEE Internet Things J. **7**(3), 2235–2246 (2019)
69. Roto, V., Law, E.C., Vermeeren, A.P., Hoonhout, J.: User experience white paper: bringing clarity to the concept of user experience (2011)
70. Ryan, R.M.: The Oxford Handbook of Human Motivation. OUP, USA (2012)
71. Ryan, R.M., Deci, E.L.: Self-determination Theory: Basic Psychological Needs in Motivation, Development, and Wellness. Guilford Publications (2017)
72. Sakuda, L.O., Fortim, I.: Ii censo da indústria brasileira de jogos digitais. Ministério da Cultura, Brasília (2018)
73. Salvendy, G.: Handbook of Human Factors and Ergonomics. Wiley, Hoboken (2012)
74. Sánchez, J.L.G., Vela, F.L.G., Simarro, F.M., Padilla-Zea, N.: Playability: analysing user experience in video games. Behav. Inf. Technol. **31**(10), 1033–1054 (2012)
75. Sauro, J., Lewis, J.R.: Quantifying the User Experience: Practical Statistics for User Research. Morgan Kaufmann (2016)
76. Susi, T., Johannesson, M., Backlund, P.: Serious games: an overview (2007)
77. Tyack, A., Mekler, E.D.: Self-determination theory in HCI games research: current uses and open questions. In: Proceedings of the 2020 CHI Conference on Human Factors in Computing Systems, pp. 1–22 (2020)
78. Van Laerhoven, K., et al.: Experiences from a wearable-mobile acquisition system for ambulatory assessment of diet and activity. In: Proceedings of the 4th International Workshop on Sensor-Based Activity Recognition and Interaction, pp. 1–8 (2017)
79. von Wangenheim, C.G., Petri, G., Borgatto, A.F.: MEEGA+ KIDS: a model for the evaluation of games for computing education in secondary school. RENOTE **18**(1) (2020)
80. Wasserman, T., Wasserman, L.: Motivation, Effort, and the Neural Network Model. Springer, Heidelberg (2020)
81. Wiemeyer, J., Nacke, L., Moser, C., et al.: Player experience. In: Dörner, R., Göbel, S., Effelsberg, W., Wiemeyer, J. (eds.) Serious Games, pp. 243–271. Springer, Cham (2016). https://doi.org/10.1007/978-3-319-40612-1_9
82. Yang, S., et al.: IoT structured long-term wearable social sensing for mental well-being. IEEE Internet Things J. **6**(2), 3652–3662 (2018)
83. Yang, W., Rifqi, M., Marsala, C., Pinna, A.: Towards better understanding of player's game experience. In: Proceedings of the 2018 ACM on International Conference on Multimedia Retrieval, pp. 442–449 (2018)

The Pursuit of Fun in Digital Games: From the Sandpit to the Console and Beyond

Diego Fellipe Tondorf$^{(\boxtimes)}$ (iD) and Marcelo da Silva Hounsell (iD)

Department of Computer Science, Graduate Program in Applied Computing, Santa Catarina
State University (UDESC), Joinville, Santa Catarina, Brazil
`diegodft@hotmail.com`, `marcelo.hounsell@udesc.br`

Abstract. Fun has long been considered inherent in the act of playing. Some
authors argue that it is an element always present in games, and others that it is
not, that there are several types of fun and several factors that change the perception of fun, but fun has always been associated with positive effects on players.
As a subjective concept, and dependent on context and player experience, understanding fun in games is a challenge for developers. With the development of the
industry and the research on digital games, it became necessary to create new artifacts for the design and validation of fun. Understanding fun is also essential for
serious games, which have been criticized for not being fun. Thus, better understanding fun and how to achieve it is a big challenge where crucial outcomes could
benefit application areas such as education, health, and others. But the roadmap
for such an area of research has not been established. This chapter presents fun
as a grand challenge in games and digital entertainment and proposes a path for
future research.

Keywords: Digital games · Game design · Fun

1 Introduction

Playing a game and going to a playground are inherent concepts in the construction of
individuality and society [1]. As children, we spent time playing alone or with others,
and we unconsciously trained our bodies and minds. In the old days, before video games
became popular, going to the playground, playing at the sandpit, getting together with
friends, and spending the day without worries were what motivated children who were
always having fun.

Game nowadays is mostly in the digital environment such as consoles, computers,
or mobile phones, and so is fun, as shown in a survey where 44% of respondents were
young people [2]. But in the playground, there were elements already known to bring
fun (equipment, sand, space, hiding, other children, freedom, scream and imagination),
but what is fun in the digital environment? What elements of digital space promote fun?

Fun is inherent in the act of play [3–6]. Is that real? Is it always true? The fact is that
when you play you are looking for fun, and it can come in many different forms and
factors. But, when we play, will we always have fun? Will it always be satisfying?

R. P. d. Santos and M. d. S. Hounsell (Eds.): GranDGamesBR 2020/2021, CCIS 1702, pp. 25–46, 2023.
https://doi.org/10.1007/978-3-031-27639-2_2

Digital games are spaces where the player can, through pre-defined rules (mechanics), interact with the digital space (dynamics) to acquire experiences (aesthetics). This perspective comes from the MDA framework [7] which pragmatically presents how the path to the game experience works, and this experience is the result of the rules imposed on the player through the interactions made by him.

With a rapidly growing industry [8] the search for innovative and successful products is constant, and these elements relate directly to creativity [9] and the fun [10] that the game brings to the player.

Fun is a precursor to a greater player acceptance, better player experience, higher sales, higher profits, greater satisfaction, more vitality for the industry, more jobs, etc. Some of the advantages that games present are [11]: increase in player motivation, which generates interest and curiosity; reach player's emotional, engaging, and elevating interest and effort in the game; provide immediate feedback and adaptability, thus decreasing stress and providing balanced cognitive, emotional or physical challenges. Fun is therefore an inherently multidisciplinary area of research.

Fun can even be found in watching someone else streaming a video gameplay. Even by only watching the play, this can improve the viewer's mood. Some other values gained from watching streamings are [12]: escapism; audiovisual pleasure; leisure; immersion; novelty; excitement; sense of belonging; relationships; cohesion; interactions; respect; self-fulfillment; security; self-respect; specialization.

Fun is considered a part of the game [3] or, at least, it is expected from a game [13]. But what is fun? How is it experienced? How can it be guaranteed or improved in a game? Beyond these, because of the multi-facets of fun, there are a plethora of questions.

Some research related to fun have already been made in the area of games.

- According to Prensky [3], digital games, lead to fun and pleasure. This fun is part of a learning process, promoting and motivating engagement based on the experience of the game. Thus, fun can, and should, be used to improve outcomes in educational games.
- The time spent feeling joy, a deep pleasure that we have experienced for a long time and marks our lives, is described by Cziksentmihalyi [14] as "Optimal Experience", better known as Flow. Although not directly related to fun, flow is related to sensations we have when playing, because they are pleasant and make us lose track of time.
- Albuquerque [10] groups fun together with pleasure and satisfaction and considers fun as the player's intrinsic motivation also. For the author, fun is something complex and varied, there is confusion about understanding the topic, and understanding this phenomenon is an arduous task.
- The compilation in the area of human-computer interaction (HCI) made by Blythe et al. [5] presented several points and observations about usability and experiences which were divided into theories and concepts; methods and techniques; and case studies. According to the authors, there are differences between pleasure and fun, with fun being related to distraction while pleasure is related to absorption [5, p. 95].
- Lazzaro [15] presents a view where fun comes from the emotions felt by the player, which are divided into 4 groups: (a) Hard fun, related to the emotions generated from meaningful challenges, strategies, and puzzles; (b) Easy fun, which holds the attention by presenting light elements (no effort required from the player), game

ambiguity, incompleteness and details; (c) Altered states, which generate emotions through perception, thoughts, behaviors and other people, and; (d) People factor, creates opportunities through players' competition, cooperation, performance, and display.

- For Wang, Shen, and Ritterfeld [13] games are expected to be fun, however, the fun may depend on the player and the context. In their research, they divide fun into 27 factors, grouping them into 5 categories: technological capability; game design; aesthetic presentation; entertainment game experience, and; narrativity. These 27 factors were coded by 4 experienced gamers, who used inductive and deductive approaches from 60 game reviews by other gamers published on game review websites.

- Noticing the academia's emerging interest in games, Koster [4] created a book from his knowledge of the games industry. For him, fun depends on context, is defined by the feedback the brain gives when absorbing patterns for learning purposes, and consists mainly of practicing and learning.

Understanding how fun is experienced in games; working with these concepts and being able to ensure minimal fun in games to engage the player and improve outcomes; elucidating the problems that diminish or take away fun; creating new forms of fun and new fun media; seeking new players and recovering old ones; among others; are game-related issues of such a "funny" industry. So, one of the great challenges in the field of digital games (both from a practical and scientific point of view) is to understand how to promote fun in digital games, and what are the consequences of achieving fun. Therefore, this chapter will present the pursuit of fun aiming at its constructs and outcomes as well as its meaning.

2 Going Deeper

This section details some aspects that have been associated with fun.

2.1 Funology

The book called Funology [5] presents various research concerning fun and usability. It compiles multiple viewpoints aligning them with the area of HCI. Several terms are commonly used interchanged to fun: enjoyment, pleasure, and attraction. But they do not refer to the same experience, nor they are deducible to a simple definition. Throughout history, the word "fun" has had several meanings associated to it, such as [5]: diversion, amusement, jocularity, to fool, to cheat or hoax, low cant word, and humor.

Fun depends on context, as well as amusement and pleasure. Fun is never guaranteed, various activities (like playing for example) can be fun at certain times just as they can be boring depending on the context. To enjoy some activity requires a context, a previous experience, and an expectation (or even the lack of it), from enjoyment, which can come from fun and pleasure.

There are also differences between fun and pleasure. Although they are related to similar things each has a different meaning and purpose. Fun does not mean the absence of pain, just as joy does not mean the absence of seriousness [5], games can generate fun and pleasure, and one does not necessarily need the other to be generated, but both are related. While fun is related to distraction, pleasure is related to absorption, by having fun we are distracted from the world, or we can say that we are in "flow" as presented by Csikszentmihalyi [14], while with pleasure we enjoy something more deeply. This doesn't mean that we can't have fun without pleasure or have pleasure without having fun.

2.2 Keys to the Emotion

To Lazzaro et al. [15] fun is an emotion that drives the player's experience. From 12 player experience models, 4 keys to the emotion of fun from games without stories were created. Each key is a reason that make people play a game. Both for the player and for the game, each key to have fun is valued differently. These 4 keys are:

Hard Fun
Hard Fun comes from meaningful emotions, being related to challenges, strategies, and puzzles. Players who prefer this type of fun seek to overcome obstacles. The emotions usually felt are frustration and triumph. When playing a game for Hard Fun players seek to see how good they are; to finish the game; to have multiple objectives; to value strategy over luck.

Easy Fun
Unlike Hard Fun, Easy Fun comes from elements such as ambiguity, incompleteness, and detail. To achieve Easy Fun players look for the experience, the focus is more on keeping the player's attention than on having some win condition. Players who enjoy this kind of fun look for new worlds; exhilaration and adventure; understanding and being part of the game. Immersion activates the player's sense of curiosity, thus holding their attention to detail.

Altered States
The Altered States key is related to context, to how the player felt during and/or after the game. Some players use the game as a "therapy", in which case the game serves as a mean for the player to alter their current state, and it depends on not only how the game explores the provided but also how the player seeks that experience. Gamers typically experience exhilaration or relief in addition to playing to clear their minds, feel better or evade boredom.

The People Factor
Another type of key to fun comes from the People Factor, where these emotions come from elements such as competition, cooperation, performance, and spectacle. This key is based on multiplayer mode. Players who enjoy this kind of fun prefer games that they can play with friends, either by cooperating with them or competing against them; in these games, it is the people who move and give meaning to the game, not only its mechanics. Players who use this key look for the game as a form of social interaction.

2.3 Fun Factors

Wang, Shen, and Ritterfeld [13] presented factors that lead to fun in a game, these factors range from direct elements such as a visual presentation to more complex and subjective elements such as presence. For them, games are expected to be entertaining, however, what fun is may vary according to individual players and their contexts. Furthermore, what makes games fun may not have the same effect in serious games. These fun factors, classified by experts, come from reviews of players about games and are related to various elements of game design. Some can be changed directly by the developer as visual presentation or control, for example, and; some are complex and need more elements involved such as overall game design and gameplay experience.

In the overall classification scheme, the most frequent fun factors presented in players' reviews were Overall Game Design and Visual Presentation. Also, the most frequently presented fun factor in both negative and positive reviews is Overall Game Design, which shows that this fun factor is the most relevant and perceived by the player. When they talk about Overall Game Design, Overall Technological Capacity, Overall Aesthetic Presentation, and Overall Entertainment Game Play Experience they are talking about elements that are in addition to several factors. So these 4 factors are a set that is considered as a generalist form of a review commentary, it is also a way of looking at the game by separating it into factor groupings. Factors such as usability, control, challenge, and visual presentation are expected to make the game playable and serve as prerequisites for enjoying the game.

2.4 Game Feel

There is no standard definition for Game Feel, many designers describe it in different ways, relating it to intuitive controls, physical interactions with virtual objects, player feelings, and aesthetic appeal. There are 3 main blocks of Game Feel [16], being real-time control, related to interactivity; simulated space, related to physical interactions with the virtual world; and polishing, related to any effect that enhances interaction without changing the base simulation. Pichlmair and Johansen [17] performed a survey, where they evaluated several related works and presented a list of sets of elements, each set with several game design elements, that are related to game feel, these sets being: action and movement; event signification; time manipulation; persistence; scene framing, and; summary. Although not based on fun, many game feel components are related to game design components, and thus related to the fun that game feel components generate.

2.5 Be Aware of Fun

Despite being associated to many positive outcomes fun can lead to negative outcomes, such as excessive game time, for example. Some game constructs and elements can be used to attract the player's attention and keep him in the game for a longer period of time than is healthy. Excessive use of digital games can lead to loss of control and various psychological and physical consequences. For instance, in a sample of 1945 players, 156 (8%) reported problems such as social anxiety, high caffeine consumption or excessive playing time [18].

Besides possibly harming the player by excessive gaming time, for susceptible people who have had no strong moral upbring, gaming can triggers negative behaviors, such as violence, racism, terror, and homophobia, for example. These elements in a certain context and for a certain player can have negative returns. Thus, game content should be well explained by developers besides taking care of the chosen age group. These problems are more related to the psychological part of the game constructs and is out of the scope of this chapter (which has been dealt with elsewhere [18]).

3 Where Do I Find Fun?

Several authors [4, 5, 7, 11, 13, 15, 19, 20] have commented on fun, what is fun, types of fun, and even factors of fun in games, but where fun can be found? What are the related elements and sets of elements that can lead to fun? This is truly an important question where the best answer is perhaps, "it depends".

3.1 Context

Fun depends on at least 3 main factors related to the context, regarding the current, past and future state of the player:

- People, place, and mood: A game can be fun with friends and extremely boring alone, funny if you are happy or sad if you are in a bad mood, challenging or frustrating according to the will to overcome the goal. Several variables can change the level or type of fun obtained, which are related to the current state of the player and the world around him.
- Previous experience: The player's previous experience should impact the enjoyment of the game, positively or negatively. A stressful day can leave the player stressed and end up taking it out on his teammates in the game taking the fun out of both. Or on the contrary, he can use this stress to focus on the game and forget about the problems, resulting in decreased stress and increased fun. When playing a game that is very similar to what one played in childhood, it activates euphoria and nostalgia, and maybe this is the reason for that person's enjoyment of that game.
- Expectation: The current context and previous experience are determining factors in the experience of fun, but the expectation is also relevant since the player plays because he expects something from the game. This expectation leads to fun once the player gets what he is looking for, or generates frustration if he or she doesn't get it, or sometimes, even fun due to the breach of expectation. When winning against a difficult boss the player thinks that the game is over, only to be surprised to discover that the boss has a second life; when entering the main map and marveling at the beauty of the game, the way he was expecting; when unwittingly entering a secret place, or seeing a hint of a secret place and finding it on purpose; are examples of expectations and that can alter the level of fun.

3.2   Game Components

Previous, current, and future experiences alone do not make games fun, it only influences the fun being generated. Articulating game components is what generates fun. Components include mechanics, dynamics, technology, aesthetics, and narrative [6, 7]. These are the components in a general way, that offers many possibilities, and each of these possibilities can alters the player's perception of fun.

The mechanics of a game are the rules of its world. They should be easy to understand so that the player has no problems with the gameplay, they should be well structured to not unbalance the game in any way, and designed for interaction since it is through the mechanics that the player interacts with the game.

Dynamics are how the sets of mechanics interact with each other: kicking a ball makes no sense without a goal; running makes no sense if it is in a straight line and without challenges, and; there is no way to play a fighting game without opponents. There are several examples of sets of mechanics that lead to game dynamics, for instance [21]. The dynamics must make sense and lead the player to the intended experience.

In the case of technology, there is the software and the hardware, that have been growing and evolving a lot recently. As for software, we have current mechanics, more realistic elements, optimized games and more platforms, chats, games with massive number of players, and even retroportability where you can play old games on your current machine. As for hardware, we see technological advances to new and more precise controls, different or realistic controls for simulations, the consoles themselves with more processing power, virtual reality glasses, and mobile devices.

The aesthetics of the game is not only related to the visible part, the whole part that brings experience to the player, whether by any of the other elements mentioned above or the sum of them, is part of the aesthetics. Audio and visual elements, mechanics, dynamics, technology, and narrative, all of them (and also the lack of one or another) corroborate the aesthetics of the game. The game can be extremely violent and visceral, or maybe cute and light, fast and frenetic, or maybe calm and slow, with a complex and emotionally heavy story, or just an animal in the middle of the street making a mess. These are examples of types of games, not that one is more fun than the other, but to show that there are several types of game aesthetics, and each player will strive for one or the other.

Last but not least, another of the main elements of the game is the narrative [6]. The narrative is the story of the game, as well as the elements that make up the story, such as the characters, worlds, places, and possible outcomes in a game. When talking about the narrative we need to understand why that world exists, and what builds it. If it weren't for the narrative of a princess in danger in the clutches of a turtle hand, the plumber would just be a guy eating mushrooms and jumping on turtles around the world; or defending the base from alien attack would just be someone shooting in the air; or before that, without being a game related to ping pong it would just be a ball walking on a screen. The story of the game, is not only the playable narrative but also the whole mythology of that world, is extremely important to give the player the mood and the flavor of the game.

3.3 Game Experience

The experience is mainly related to the aesthetics of the game because it is the sum of all the game elements (aesthetics included) [7] and the experience can be changed according to the context. In this way, with the elements of games, depending on the context, we have the experience, which is the result of playing the game. It is, like the context: previous, because the player expects a certain experience from the game; current because it is when playing that the player acquires the experience; future, because the player, when having the experience with the game, will have a different or at least updated vision from when he opened the game to play it.

Experience can come in many forms, a game can make the player feel extremely strong; or on the contrary, show him that there are stronger enemies and he needs to improve to defeat them; be quick and reflexive; be strategic and thoughtful; encourage cooperation to win a goal; competition to show skill; surprise you with something new and need quick response, or inform you of everything that can happen in the game. Even frustration can generate fun [22]: some very difficult games a high level of frustration, but for players who enjoy it and if the game design is made in a way that reaches the limit of this frustration without taking away the player's will, players can relate this frustration to fun.

Games can vary their dynamics along the way: a fighting game can have some stages with puzzles; a game that focuses on player's skills suddenly can rely on luck. Game modes can become a completely new game: a shooter game can have the story mode, where a single player wants to understand the game and its world in an adventure; in the multiplayer mode, players are encouraged to compete by killing other players, and; in the survival mode, the player together with companions need to play in order to survive. Other games allow different dynamics so the player can develop different playing styles: a player can sneak through the challenge, or get the attention of all the enemies; a player can build a gigantic house just to blow up her in the end of the day. All these variations might be fun.

3.4 The Serious-Fun Paradox

Serious games have intentional and specific goals besides entertainment, but can they be fun? According to Blythe and Hassenzahl [5] "Fun cannot be serious and if it is, then it ceases, in this sense, to be fun.". However, a serious environment can be enjoyable, depending on the design chosen to distract or absorb the information. Nevertheless, the word "serious" in "serious games" has nothing to do to the game presentation – an usual misconception – but to the fact that those intentional and specific goals are a "serious" matter, particularly to the serious game design. Therefore, there is actually no paradox in claiming a serious game as fun, although some serious games do prioritize functions against fun sometimes.

As some authors argue, it is expected that a game would bring fun [13], games lead to fun [3] and fun cannot be serious [5]. But there are serious games, games designed for more than just entertainment and fun. Serious games should be fun [23], and also this fun can increase the results of the serious objective expected by the developers [24]. For a serious game, fun should aim to increase the results, it can't be a reason for the player to get distracted and lose focus. A game that uses body movements as mechanics can be colorful and vibrant to induce players to exercise; a game to convey a message or advertisement can use realism and focus to capture and hold the player's attention; simulators rely on being as realistic as possible and this can be fun too.

The prejudice that a serious game is not fun is a problem because fun depends on the context. If the player already enters the game expecting something tedious it will already change his experience. On the other hand, if the game is seen as a fun and an exciting way to solve a serious problem, the player will have a different and more positive experience.

Therefore, being fun is a must for serious games, as long as fun would make using the game more enjoyable and for a longer period of engagement, both outcomes potentialize benefits that can come embedded in using a serious game.

3.5 Fun!

So, in summary, it can be said that:

- Fun is an abstract concept, with different definitions and is difficult to explain.
- There are types of fun and types of players.
- There is a plethora of factors that alter the level of fun.
- Fun depends on context, past experiences, and expected experiences.
- Fun comes from the game elements, synthesized in a way that creates an experience.
- The experience in turn can be delivered in a variety of ways, with fun being one of the emotions felt during the process.

4 Research Directions

Once we have gathered a basic understanding of what is fun and had a glimpse of where it comes from, it must be said that there is no consensus and therefore it is still prone to further research.

Nevertheless, we need to go forward and understand how to imprint such a remarkable feature into a (serious) game and afterward, what are the consequences (hopefully beneficial) of achieving such an experience.

To cover these nuances and complex issues it is a good idea to have a plan to explore them that will be presented following research directions:

Table 1 presents a vision of medium and long-term goals for the development of this grand challenge in the area of digital games. It was divided into 4 dimensions depicted in Fig. 1: the conceptual, relative to the deep understanding of what fun is and what constitutes it; the projectual, relative to how these concepts are used from a practical point of view, in the design of new games; the scientific, relative to the guarantees of achieving fun and; the outcome, relative to what can be obtained due to the achievement of fun in the game.

Table 1. Fun game research directions.

Directions	5 years (medium-term)	10 years (long term)
Conceptual	Investigate the epistemological aspects to understand the fundamentals of fun	Create conceptual models to organize and group the factors related to fun
	Explore the underlying psychological aspects, thus obtaining what causes fun	Create theories of fun promotion, increasing results, and ensuring fun in games
Scientific	Investigate or create instruments for the evaluation of fun	Establish ethical aspects of fun, relating them to human factors
	Analyze methods of experimentation related to fun	Define a scientific paradigm for investigating and using fun in digital games
Projectual	Investigate the association of constructs to game design components: mechanics, aesthetics, dynamics, market, audiences/niches, narratives, technologies, etc.	Create game design methodologies using the constructs and concepts previously studied to foster fun
Outcome	Investigate what are the consequences and outcomes	Create casual models, organizing and grouping fun-related outcomes

Figure 1 shows that when taking fun as a central feature, it (still) raises questions about its concept and meaning; its scientific paradigm, and its practical design framework. All of these are handled towards desirable outcomes. All these directions are detailed in the following sections.

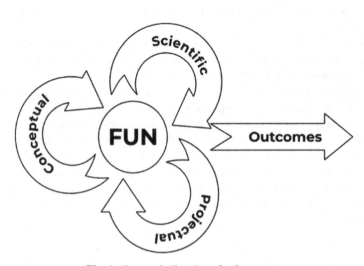

Fig. 1. Research directions for fun games

4.1 The Conceptual Direction

What is fun? In Portuguese, the word "diversão" comes from the Latin "diversĭo" and means to be the act or effect of amusement, pastime, recreation, the change or detour of attention, or a distraction [25]. The word fun has its origins in the Middle English 'fool' and pleasure from the Gaelic language and is also defined as a source of pleasure, being a function of the brain feeling good by releasing endorphin [4]. The word fun has been associated (erroneously) with concepts such as engagement, enjoyment, and play, among others. A simpler way to differentiate fun from enjoyment is to acknowledge that the latter is more commonly used as a reflexive verb – "I enjoyed that game" - while the former is frequently used as an adjective – "that is a really fun game". In this sense, it is possible to conceive that enjoyment could be an outcome of that game feature (fun).

So, one of the first and fundamental questions to explore is the real understanding of what is fun. Some questions that need to be answered include:

- Does fun equate to other experiences and feelings?
- Are there types of fun?
- According to the player's own experiences, will these types of fun impact the fun obtained from playing?
- Are there other feelings that compose to yield fun, such as happiness or moodiness, for example?
- Are these other feelings results or causes of fun?
- What are the feelings that take away the fun?
- How to decrease the chance of activating these feelings, or turn them into feelings that bring fun?
- A player on a sad day would find a game funnier (and act as some sort of remedy) or, on the contrary, he will be prevented from such feeling?

Regarding fun-related factors, which ones increase the most, and which ones decrease the most fun? Some authors have already studied these factors, raising those that can be related to fun [26], dividing them into types of fun [15], or also being considered the flow of the game [14]. These points help to align and better understand fun, but studies that prove the effectiveness of each factor and present results are needed. In addition, studies that demonstrate more factors or go deeper into them help to understand the motives of the players.

What are the intervening factors? Fun is related to the player's experience, so it is understood that it will vary according to a set of factors specific to the player. Elements such as age, sex or gender, cultural background, cognitive and physical conditions, health, context, emotions, type of player, and even global issues such as a pandemic, can alter the experience and perception of fun. There are current issues but past experience, context, and (future) expectation alter the player's perception of fun, but can this be proven? Are there patterns that can be studied to guarantee that any person with a specific characteristic has the predisposition to have fun in a certain game?

Also, the same player's perception of fun may vary over time, so in addition to factors promoting or impairing fun, factors of maintenance or change need to be explored. Thus, understanding fun requires a greater understanding of the individual and its whole state.

4.2 The Scientific Direction

From a scientific perspective, interventions involving the constructs of fun should be worked out to identify their influence and their magnitude. It is a must to find a suitable research paradigm. But, several questions arise, such as:

- Is it possible to isolate the constructs or they should be always considered altogether? By isolating each construct it would be possible to understand the problem in detail, but a construct is a part of the game, and the game is a set of several elements. As a consequence of studying, the construct may vary when relating it to the whole. On the other hand, by considering the whole game as the fun driver we can see if the game is fun or not, but understanding why it is fun or which of the constructs contributes the most to making it fun becomes difficult since the evaluation is done organically.
- Add, remove or modify the construct? When adding an element to the game one must be careful that this element makes sense in the design. Adding an element just because it is fun in another game can bring a big impact on the fun, but can this impact be good or bad? When removing an element (because it is considered a fun killer, for instance) there is the danger of breaking a series of mechanics and related dynamics. What are the risks in doing so and how will it impact the project? Online multiplayer games run usually with frequently changing mechanics, which creates engaging and balanced experiences, and to do this, they change their elements so that the largest group of players are interested in the game. A clear knowledge of which elements to change, how much to change, and what to change for are important issues when it comes to designing fun.

It remains to experiment and try different ways to understand these concepts, to create effective and assertive methods to obtain the results, thus getting quantitative and qualitative data about fun, concluding what is fun, or what generates fun. It is not an easy or practical task, for this, it requires several studies, and since fun is multifaceted, from several areas.

- An important step to understand how fun is achieved in games is to know how to measure it. Because it is subjective and dependent on the player, measuring it becomes somewhat difficult since each player will have different feedback from the game. Can it be measured directly or should we measure related aspects? What metrics can be used? Experience, usability, satisfaction, engagement, willingness to play again, presence, focus, and others are elements that are related to fun. However, it is necessary to understand which of these elements best reflects the player's fun, as well as the causes and consequences of fun. What is the best way to measure fun? Direct values such as yes or no [27], or numerical such as 1 or 5 [20, 28] to get a quick and practical result; descriptions will give better feedback on why, but depending on the player's ability to express themselves. Establishing a fun metric is key to building a scientific process where interventions can be better evaluated. Methods such as questionnaires get quick and practical feedback about fun but can be difficult to understand because they do not provide the feedback needed to conclude about fun. Descriptive questions can better explain what the player felt, but lack of experience or difficulty in expressing themselves in the results can confuse the analysis of the descriptions, using experts for this will result in more assertive and detailed data, but the general public is not experts and therefore the results may vary.

Another way to measure fun is by the physiological aspects of the player [29], such as heart rate, skin responses, brain waves, blood pressure, sweating, pupil dilation, and stress for example. Yet another way to measure fun is by body language, b observation can be analyzed the way the player behaves, and facial expressions (happy, sad, surprised, and so on) for example.

Game data can also be used as metrics, but they do not provide direct feedback from the player, because the values are taken directly from the game and not from the player. By analyzing the pattern of play and in which moments the player did not advance or advanced too quickly, one can have a parameter for analysis.

- What research design to use? A much-valued Randomized Controlled Trials (RCT) with a control group that is not exposed to a specific fun factor as opposed to an experimental group that is exposed seems impractical. Firstly, because some consider fun to be part of any gaming experience; secondly, because some would argue that each setup represents a different game once the dynamics would vary, therefore not comparable. Nevertheless, RCTs are much more reliable.

How to Measure Fun?
It is interesting to observe that although fun is regarded as an experience and therefore it is a multi-faceted phenomenon, there are some instruments that attempt to measure fun as a well-defined and isolated one. Yet, as an user perception. There is a clear advantage of doing so regarding simplicity and it might work well for a population that has difficulty in assessing the whole fun spectrum. This over-simplified solution hides away factors that might be contributing the most for such perception.

Methods
Evaluating a game is not an easy task, several variables change constantly. Also, there are many aspects to evaluate in a game, and among them, fun. Some methods that can be used for evaluation are [30]: interviews; questionnaires; focus groups; brainstorming; card sorting; field studies; contextual investigation; heuristic evaluation; cognitive journey; semiotic inspection; usability testing; communicability evaluation; paper prototyping; and, comparative evaluation method. Some of these methods are applied to (a) the players; (b) to professionals that would be using a game for a given purpose; (c) to the development team, and; (d) to more than one of the previous.

Fun is intrinsic and depends on the player, so one of the ways to measure fun is directly with them. Some ways to collect data from players are [30]:

- An interview aims to collect detailed and deep information from players, it allows them to collect information from players individually, thus understanding what their reasons for fun are. Besides, it is possible to deepen the questions, detailing their experience while playing the game. As for difficulties, the interview depends on trained personnel to execute it, besides demanding more time when there are many interviewees. Interviews seem more appropriate when research aims to explore openly what is happening and possibly when multiple aspects are in synergy.

- Questionnaires are quick ways to collect data, particularly quantitative ones. It allows you to collect information from many users almost simultaneously, and therefore facilitates and speeds up data gathering, as well as being relatively inexpensive and requiring little distribution effort. Creating a questionary requires care to avoid closed questions that induce answers and should be kept to a minimum and as objective as possible. Questionnaires seem to be more appropriate when a researcher has a clear target and a set of aspects that want to analyze.

- The focus group is a way to evaluate players' attitudes, opinions, and impressions. The focus group is a discussion that generates new ideas and provides a simultaneous collection of information from the players. Because it relies on a discussion between the players, the problem with a focus group is that it requires a lot of resources to recruit enough users for a good discussion.

- Brainstorming is another way of collecting discussions among the players; unlike the focus group, it aims to collect a prioritized list of the players' perceived needs and wants and is a systematic way of conducting the group. This form has the advantages of preparing, conducting, and analyzing data from the activity in a short period and with few resources, besides using little effort to conduct and analyze the data. Since it is a group activity, moderation demands effort and experience, and recruiting enough players can be resource-intensive.

- Card sorting is an activity that aims to identify how users group information or objects. It is a simple technique to conduct, it motivates the team to break down the product into components, it demands low effort to conduct and if done in a group it allows for to collection of data from several players at once. The problems with this activity are that it needs some effort to detail the information and definitions and that the effort for the analysis depends on the tool, the number of cards, and participants.

- The field study or contextual research seeks to understand the players in their environment and context, it allows to discover how the game is played, collect rich myths, and have ecological validity. As difficulties, it relies on a higher level of effort to prepare visits, and to conduct and analyze data.

Scales

Numerical scales such as Likert help to illustrate the numbers with graphs and comparisons; graphical scales such as the Fun Toolkit [20] help players (in this case children) who have difficulty in expressing; while a selection of words to describe the game as in ESFQ [31] limits the options but gives a more targeted feedback.

Besides asking players about fun straightway, it seems interesting to gather a variety of related data once players might misunderstand the actual meaning of fun (it looks simple but when you ask for it all blurs out).

Other metrics to be gathered and related to fun included: data related to the game session such as playing time or improvement in results and scores; psychological data such as game experience, willingness to play again, and level of satisfaction; and data related to the player's physiology such as heart rate, facial expressions, and brain waves.

Ethics

In any research involving individuals, ethical concerns must be included. To decrease the possibility of players being bothered by the game or the evaluation, some actions need to be taken:

- Research must be careful of players' social, mental, and physical problems; players must not be forced to perform the activities; warnings about the type of content in the game must be given; the purpose of the evaluation should be made clear; an informed consent must be given from individuals; the risks and benefits of the activity must be accounted for; foreseeable harm must be avoided; and, the social relevance of the research must be clear.
- The data obtained in the game sessions must be kept and cared for properly, respondents should be anonymous and not receive benefits as this may alter their answers, or they may answer in any way just to get the benefits.
- Some elements that may be sensitive to certain audiences include: flashing lights; social issues such as homophobia, racism, and prejudice in general; violence; gore; acid humor; and, nudity; among others. When implementing these elements in games, one should be careful if the target audience fits into this context, because, as deplorable as they may be in real life, depending on the context and the player, the game can still be fun.

4.3   The Projectual Direction

Some existing game design frameworks do mention fun as a result of their approach but they either consider fun the resulting experience or, do not point out specific steps towards fun.

Frameworks

Some of the game design frameworks are presented below:

The MDA framework [7] is a formal approach to understanding games that follows a tripartite structure. In it, fun is the result and experience delivered to the player from the aesthetics. The aesthetics are the result of the game system, and the dynamics, are the sets of mechanics that act in the game and with the player. The mechanics are the rules and components that control the game. In other words, when considering MDA the fun is the experience of the game, the result of its rules acting according to the dynamics created.

The Elemental Tetrad [6] is a widely used and discussed game development framework. It helps to visualize, divide and classify the elements present in the development of a game. It is divided into 4 elements of equal importance being more or less visible to the player: the mechanics, the game rules; the story, the sequence of events; the aesthetics, the appearance, either sound or visual; and the technology, related to the hardware and software used. It does not focus on fun but it is an important way to visualize the basics of game design.

On the Elemental Tetrad the higher the element is the more visible to the player it is. In contrast, the lower the element the less visible to the player the element is. Also, they are in a way that every element has connections to the other elements. On MDA Framework the higher the element is, the closer to the player it is. Different from the Elemental Tetrad, MDA follows a sequence, where the game mechanics (made by the designer) lead to the dynamics and consequently to the aesthetics of the game (experienced by the player). Both can be visualized in Fig. 2.

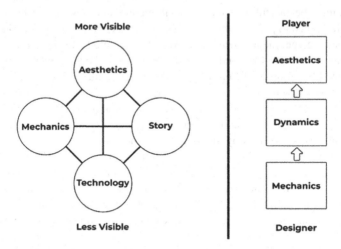

Fig. 2. Elemental Tetrad and MDA (adapted from [6] and [7])

There is a practical need for a framework and/or game design methodology that incorporates fun as one of its main goals. If such help can be developed, fun can evolve from a fluke to a discipline for a given project. It becomes a science per se, not an empirical subject. But them, some questions arise:

- How do articulate the constructs of fun among themselves?
- How fun factors should be fine-tuned to specific contexts?
- Who should be responsible for such a feature - a specialist or all team members?
- When fun factors should be reasoned about? When to apply checkpoints? Understanding how to use these constructs to optimize and improve results with the target audience is a big challenge.
- Which fun factor to consider? When studying fun, a specific construct or element can be separated and analyzed, such as technology, exploring the differences in hardware, as in desktop or mobile for example; aesthetics and narrative by including more visible elements to the player or mixing them with diegetic interfaces; mechanics and dynamics by giving more freedom to the player or improving the feedback of actions. Moreover, for fun, it matters not only how each element works individually, but also the articulation between them, complementing them. A good balance between the elements so that the player does not feel stuck or lost in the gameplay is important for fun.

Understanding which elements to use and when to use them, and which not to use, is important for a good result in a game design. Checklists for minimal fun or no fun-killers in the game design should be described and studied. Beware of excessive components, such as very difficult enemies, complex building systems, long scenes or messages for example, as these can be fun for some and boring for others, a balance, or varied ways of playing can be crucial for fun in the game.

Some constructs of fun, already suggested in the literature, such as mechanics [13], are a broad set of features that the player performs or experiences, which is composed of challenges, rewards, control schemes, player actions, and object manipulations [21] that can be used concurrently. This suggests a combination of possibilities that is impractical to explore. So, more research on combined and single factors, and more abstract methodologies should be done. Besides, tests in new mechanics and ways of playing can show new ways to find fun. An example is a Virtual Reality, a technology that has existed for decades but is becoming popular in the last few years.

Some mechanics and dynamics are well known and even though they are old they are still of great value to consider in a game. Some examples of elements in games that have made a big difference and success in certain games are Increasing difficulty as you defeat enemies; a suspended time in the air before you can make a second jump; secrets; surprises; good feedback; a good story; good graphics and audio; open o community modification; multiplayer; cross-play; adaptation to new ideas, lies, and betrayals. Of course, these mechanics alone are not enough to promote fun in a game, there is always a doubt about how to articulate the factors among them, and for this end, designers need to be careful, so that the game does not become boring.

The history of games shows that we have gone from a simple pixelated ball bouncing on a screen to a plethora of game genres: arcade; platform; fighting; racing; simulator; massively multiplayer online role-playing game; shooting; real-time strategy; multiplayer online battle arena; sandbox world; battle royale; mobile, and augmented and virtual reality. Besides the genre of the game, other elements have changed over time such as: the quality of graphics and audio; the hardware, and particularly the game mechanics. What could be the next mechanic or set of mechanics to succeed and change the industry?

One must see that understanding the constructs is not enough. It is necessary to understand how to insert them into game design methodologies, including these fun constructs within the project conception, saving time and speeding up results. In this way, by including "fun" mechanics and elements in the game design, the experts can confirm that it fits with the game design and definition.

Special attention should be paid to Serious Games, which are digital games intentionally created for a purpose beyond fun [32] because design decisions for this type of software can eventually become conflicting between fun and purpose [33, 34]. In this case, not only the fun must be considered, but also the goal, and the balance of the fun with the goal, so that the goal is not forgotten for the sake of the fun, and vice-versa.

Players Profile
It should be acknowledged that players are the central piece of fun experience and they vary a lot.

One way to characterize players regarding their expectations and behaviors towards a game is by screening them against a player's taxonomy. There are some existing taxonomies out there such as: Bartle's [35]; Yee's [36]; Brainhex [37], MBTI [38], and;

QPJ-BR [39], among others. They all classify players using different criteria such as interest, type of interaction, response to the experience, among others. They might shed light to the relationship of players and fun.

Regarding the player side, for instance, Bartle's [35] which is one of the very first taxonomy, might help to understand the types of players, and thus the types of components that these players find fun:

- The *Socializer* type will prefer to interact with players rather than the game world, and so mechanics like emotes, chats, dance, and group creator will help these players interact with other players.
- The *Killer* type will also prefer to interact with other players rather than the game world, but unlike Socializers they prefer to kill other players rather than socialize with them, so mechanics like duels, body looting, declaration of war, and player vs. player areas will draw the attention of these players.
- The *Achievers* have a more aggressive way of interacting with the game world, seeking to complete it. In this case, mechanics such as achievements and completion metrics can make the player continue to play.
- The *Explorers* are in the game for the journey, not to complete it but to be in the game, this type of player likes hidden achievements or places of difficult access with different rewards such as easter eggs or extra history of the game for example.

It is noteworthy that players do not fall into only one type, and even if they have a predominant one, this can and usually change constantly but, knowing the predominant type of player in your target audience is important for the game design project.

4.4 The Outcome Direction

When having fun, there are various (measurable?) responses of the body and mind. These responses can be considered as the results of fun. What are these responses? What happens to these responses will depend on the past and current experiences of the player, as well as the expectation of the future experience.

Fun has been found to have the potential to keep people performing physical activities [40] for example. This task requires discipline and effort. Significant results like this can (should) be drivers for better games, particularly for serious games that have been receiving criticism for not being fun [3, 32, 41].

Whether understood or not on how fun is achieved, some consequences or expectations have been attributed to it:

- Does fun lead to engagement?
- Does fun lead to better attention or lasting memory?
- Does fun lead to motivation?
- Does fun lead to learning?
- Are these outcomes, and possibly others, dependent on or enhanced-by fun?
- Does fun result in emotions like happiness for example, or are the emotions that result in the fun? Knowing which emotions are related to fun, and what the results of the player having experienced these emotions are important points to understand about enjoyment in games.

5 "Apples and Pears"

For a complex and multidisciplinary research challenge - such as fun - to mature, it is expected that more tacit knowledge could be generated and tested. Although futuristic and outreached, some measurements can be seen for this grand challenge.

The number of people from various background involved in the area is considered an important factor on maturing the understanding of fun - teachers, game designers, psychologists, (biomedical/electrical) engineers, computer scientists, physiotherapists, etc. - they all have some contributions to give as long as fun is related to a human interacting with its surroundings.

Also, the number or researchers involved, and the number of scientific papers published in the area might give a glimpse of the maturing progress.

Other palpable progress measurements (yet non revolutionary [42]) can be foreseen for this Grand Research Challenge:

- More exploratory research on features that might or might not influence the perception of fun.
- More descriptive research on correlations between individual or set of constructs and the perception of fun.
- More descriptive research on correlations between the perception of fun and possible outcomes.
- More clear and practical ways to measure fun and/or its constructs.
- Composition of guidelines for game design for fun to specific niches (being types of individuals, game genre, game themes, etc.).
- More validated reference models that better support the research on fun.
- More trustful frameworks that make it easy to reason and achieve fun games.
- More explicative research on methodology proposals embedded with theories related to fun (neurological, psychological, anthropological, sociological, etc.).

6 Final Considerations

Unlike "going to the sandpit", fun in digital games seems to be more complex and involves many different areas, from the psychological, with the subjective and descriptive aspects of fun, to the physiological, with the body's responses when having fun, to the technological, related to the consoles, input and output devices and methods used to obtain the design of games. But its importance goes beyond because achieving fun can lead to significant consequences.

From a game design point of view, fun reflects the overall game experience. Understanding how to apply it, and which elements are related to it, will help create new artifacts that are focused and deliver better results.

However, there is a long way to go once the foundations of the concept are still to be understood, it lacks a specific metric and an appropriate research paradigm and also, a fun-focused game design methodology or framework.

Figure 3 rescues Fig. 1 by summarizing the challenges presented in previous sections.

The evolution of the various dimensions of this challenge can be evaluated by the volume of productions in terms of papers, technical reports, and other instrumental and informational materials. In other words, this refers to the importance of academic work in performing scientific research. In this context, one of the first methodological approaches to be used could be (systematic) reviews to identify the state of the art of each dimension.

The "digital sandpit" shapes our society in a way yet to be understood but one of its main drivers, the fun in it, may be harnessed to achieve good and productive results. So let's have fun researching what is fun in digital games.

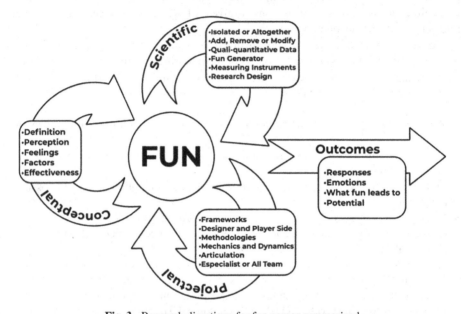

Fig. 3. Research directions for fun games summarized

Acknowledgments. The authors would like to thank the Coordenação de Aperfeiçoamento de Pessoal de Nível Superior - Brazil (CAPES-Brazil) - Funding Code 001 - for the master's scholarship, the Conselho Nacional de Desenvolvimento Científico e Tecnológico (CNPq-Brazil) for the DT2 productivity grants (process 313398/2019-4) and, the Fundação de Amparo à Pesquisa e Inovação do Estado de Santa Catarina (FAPESC-Brazil) for partial funding to the LARVA laboratory, T.O. No.: 2021TR851.

References

1. Huizinga, J.: Homo Ludens. Editora Perspectiva S.A., São Paulo (2000)
2. DATAFOLHA: Mercado de Games no Brasil. https://www.brasilgameshow.com.br/estudo-mercado-de-games/. Accepted 13 Aug 2021
3. Prensky, M.: Fun, play and games: what makes games engaging. Digital Game-Based Learn. **5**(1), 5–31 (2001)
4. Koster, R.: Theory of Fun for Game Design. O'Reilly Media Inc., Sebastopol (2013)

5. Blythe, M.A., Overbeeke, K., Monk, F.A., Wright, C.P.: Funology from Usability to Enjoyment. Kluwer Academic Publishers, New York (2004)
6. Schell, J.: A arte de Game Design. Elsevier Editora LTDA (2010)
7. Hunicke, R., LeBlanc, M., Zubek, R.: MDA: a formal approach to game design and game research. In: AAAI Work. - Tech. Rep. WS-04-04, pp. 1–5 (2004)
8. Sakuda, L.O., Fortim, I.: II Censo da Indústria Brasileira de Jogos Digitais. MINISTÉRIO DA CULTURA, São Paulo (2018)
9. Possamai, D.S., Hounsell, M.S., Gasparini, I.: A Criatividade no Design de Jogos Digitais : Um Mapeamento Sistemático da Literatura. Nuevas Ideas en Informática Educ., pp. 186–193 (2018)
10. Albuquerque, R.M.: Diversão Nos Videogames: Perfis De Usuários De Jogos Eletrônicos, p. 166 (2011)
11. Dörner, R., Göbel, S., Effelsberg, W., Wiemeyer, J. (eds.): Serious Games. Springer, Cham (2016). https://doi.org/10.1007/978-3-319-40612-1
12. Shen, Y.C.: What do people perceive in watching video game streaming? Eliciting spectators' value structures. Telematics Inform. **59**, 101557 (2021). https://doi.org/10.1016/j.tele.2020.101557
13. Wang, H., Shen, C., Ritterfeld, U.: Enjoyment of digital games: what makes them "seriously" fun? Serious Games Mech. Eff., pp. 25–47 (2009). https://doi.org/10.4324/9780203891650
14. Csikszentmihalyi, M.: Flow : the Psychology of Optimal Experience. Harper & Row, New York (1990)
15. Lazzaro, N.: Why We Play Games: Four Keys to More Emotion Without Story. Game Dev. Conf. 8 (2004)
16. Swink, S.: The Future of Game Feel. Morgan Kaufmann Publishers (2008)
17. Pichlmair, M., Johansen, M.: Designing Game Feel: A Survey. In: IEEE Transactions on Games, pp. 138–152 (2022). https://doi.org/10.1109/TG.2021.3072241
18. Porter, G., Starcevic, V., Berle, D., Fenech, P.: Recognizing problem video game use. In: Australian & New Zealand Journal of Psychiatry, pp. 120–128 (2010). https://doi.org/10.3109/00048670903279812
19. Marsh, T., Nickole, L.Z., Klopfer, E., Xuejin, C., Osterweil, S., Haas, J.: Fun and learning: the power of narrative. In: Proc. 6th Int. Conf. Found. Digit. Games FDG 2011, pp. 23–29 (2011). https://doi.org/10.1145/2159365.2159369
20. Read, J.C., MacFarlane, S.: Using the fun toolkit and other survey methods to gather opinions in Child Computer Interaction. In: Proceeding 2006 Conf. Interact. Des. Child. IDC 2006, pp. 81–88 (2006). https://doi.org/10.1145/1139073.1139096
21. Krause, K.K.G., Hounsell, M.D.S., Gasparini, I.: Um Modelo para Inter-relação entre Funções Executivas e Elementos de Jogos Digitais. Rev. Bras. Informática na Educ. **28**, 596–625 (2020). https://doi.org/10.5753/rbie.2020.28.0.596
22. Bothona, C., Nesteriuk, S.: Jogos Soulslike : como a diversificação de contexto pode ajudar a consolidar o gênero. In: SBGAMES, pp. 1–4 (2021)
23. Caserman, P., et al.: Quality criteria for serious games: serious part, game part, and balance. JMIR Serious Games. **8**, e19037 (2020). https://doi.org/10.2196/19037
24. Ketcheson, M., Ye, Z., Graham, T.C.N.: Designing for exertion: how heart-rate power-ups increase physical activity in exergames. In: CHI Play 2015 - Proc. 2015 Annu. Symp. Comput. Interact. Play, pp. 79–90 (2015). https://doi.org/10.1145/2793107.2793122
25. Editora Melhoramentos: Diversão. Michaelis On-line: https://michaelis.uol.com.br/moderno-portugues/busca/portugues-brasileiro/diversao
26. Li, R.Y., Wang, C.H.: Key factors and network model for location-based cultural mobile game design. Br. J. Educ. Technol. **51**, 2495–2512 (2020). https://doi.org/10.1111/bjet.12926
27. Jhones, E., Nascimento, F., Abreu, A.C.S., Lira, F.A.: Procedural Generation of Isometric Racetracks Using Chain Code for Racing Games (2021)

28. Petri, G., Von Wangenheim, C.G., Borgatto, A.F.: MEEGA+: um modelo para a avaliação de jogos educacionais para o ensino de computação. Rev. Bras. Informática na Educ. **27**, 52–81 (2019)
29. Mandryk, R.L., Atkins, M.S.: A fuzzy physiological approach for continuously modeling emotion during interaction with play technologies. Int. J. Hum. Comput. Stud. **65**, 329–347 (2007). https://doi.org/10.1016/j.ijhcs.2006.11.011
30. Barbosa, S.D.J., Silva, B.S., Silveira, M.S., Gasparini, I., Darin, T., Barbosa, G.D.J.: Interação Humano-Computador e Experiência do Usuário. Autopublicação, Rio de Janeiro (2021)
31. Moser, C., Fuchsberger, V., Tscheligi, M.: Rapid assessment of game experiences in public settings. In: ACM Int. Conf. Proceeding Ser., pp. 73–82 (2012). https://doi.org/10.1145/236 7616.2367625
32. Michael, D.R., Chen, S.L.: Serious Games: Games that Educate, Train, and Inform. Cengage Learning, Bostom, MA (2005)
33. Buchinger, D., Hounsell, S.: Design de Jogos Sérios Colaborativos-Competitivos : Lições Aprendidas, pp. 404–413 (2015)
34. Shen, C., Wang, H., Ritterfeld, U.: Serious games and seriously fun games: can they be one and the same? Serious Games Mech. Eff., pp. 48–61 (2009). https://doi.org/10.4324/978020 3891650
35. Bartle, R.A.: Designing Virtual Worlds. New Riders Publ., p. 741 (2004)
36. Yee, N.: Motivations for play in online games. CyberPsychology Behav. **9**, 772–775 (2006). https://doi.org/10.1089/cpb.2006.9.772
37. Nacke, L.E., Bateman, C., Mandryk, R.L.: BrainHex: a neurobiological gamer typology survey. Entertain. Comput. **5**, 55–62 (2014). https://doi.org/10.1016/j.entcom.2013.06.002
38. Myers, I.B.: The Myers-Briggs Type Indicator: Manual (1962). Consulting Psychologists Press, Palo Alto (1962). https://doi.org/10.1037/14404-000
39. Andrade, F., Marques, L., Bittencourt, I.I., Isotani, S.: QPJ-BR: Questionário para Identificação de Perfis de Jogadores para o Português-Brasileiro. Apresentado em novembro 7 (2016). https://doi.org/10.5753/cbie.sbie.2016.637
40. Rodrigues, F., et al.: A perceção de divertimento em jovens, adultos e idosos: um estudo comparativo. Cuad. Psicol. del Deport. **20**, 26–36 (2020)
41. Franzwa, C., Tang, Y., Johnson, A.: Serious game design: Motivating students through a balance of fun and learning. 2013 5th Int. Conf. Games Virtual Worlds Serious Appl. VS-GAMES 2013 (2013). https://doi.org/10.1109/VS-GAMES.2013.6624239
42. Kuhn, T.S.: A Estrutura das Revoluções Científicas (Tradução de Beatriz Vianna Boeira e Nelson Boeira). Editora Perspectivas S.A., São Paulo (2005)

Business Model for Indie Studios in Game Software Ecosystems

Bruno Xavier[1,2][(✉)] [iD], Davi Viana[3] [iD], and Rodrigo Santos[1] [iD]

[1] Federal University of the State of Rio de Janeiro, Rio de Janeiro, Brazil
blxavier@firjan.com.br, rps@uniriotec.br
[2] SENAI Innovation Institute for Virtual Production Systems,
Rio de Janeiro, Brazil
[3] Federal University of Maranhão, São Luís, Brazil
davi.viana@ufma.br

Abstract. The games industry is constantly growing. The emerging players are mostly software developers who join together with professionals from different fields to form independent (or indie) studios. This movement has resulted in an exponential amount of new products, and some big game companies have adopted a differentiated strategy to capture value in this scenario. This innovative strategy, explored with the concept of Software Ecosystems (SECO), led to the development of common technological platforms where players integrate their products. The competition between the players, the constant technological changes and evolution, and the need for agile and high-quality production due to the demands of the consumer market and the long-term financial sustainability bring challenges to the independent studios regarding their business planning. This chapter aims to present one of the grand research challenges on games and digital entertainment, more specifically related to business modeling for independent studios that work in Game SECO (GSECO). By presenting a unified agenda, we expect that the digital games industry and academia actors could join efforts to propose and validate solutions, leveraging the growth of the digital games' scenario.

Keywords: Digital games · Business models · Software ecosystems · Industry-academia integration

1 Introduction

The shortening of the distance between market players, caused by the advent of the Internet, resulted in new business opportunities and the emergence of software solutions to attend to these demands. As a consequence of a market

This work was conducted with the support of the Coordenação de Aperfeiçoamento de Pessoal de Nível Superior - Brazil (CAPES) - Funding Code 001. The authors also thank UNIRIO and FAPERJ (Proc. 211.583/2019) for partial support.

R. P. d. Santos and M. d. S. Hounsell (Eds.): GranDGamesBR 2020/2021, CCIS 1702, pp. 47–66, 2023.
https://doi.org/10.1007/978-3-031-27639-2_3

increasingly integrated with digital solutions, a different way to understand how business works appeared in the 1990s:s: business modeling. In parallel, after a few decades, with the actors and products network growth in the software industry, a differentiated strategy emerged. The development of a single software product switched to a collaborative approach, in which multiple solutions are integrated through a common technology platform [5]. This strategy is related to the concept of Software Ecosystems (SECO). The emergence of SECO has again changed how companies plan and execute their activities.

The games industry trajectory is an example of how changes in the software industry affect the business models of the players in the marketplace [8]. The trajectory of games based on digital technologies originated with the creation of the first computer game and the first videogame console in the 1950s [41]. The industry appropriated several technologies, and the emergence of SECO deepened the relationship with the software industry [60]. With the strategy brought by SECO, digital games have established themselves in the software landscape, having a significant presence on major distribution technology platforms such as GooglePlay and AppleStore [64].

The great demand for digital games has also enabled the emergence of platforms exclusively for this category, some focused on distribution (e.g., Xbox Live, Playstation Network, Steam, and Nintendo Store) and others focused on development (e.g., Unity and Unreal). The new players emerging in the Game SECO (GSECO) are mostly software developers who join together with professionals from different fields and form independent (or indie) studios. Independent studios are groups of actors who do not have a formal connection with the owners of the major distribution platforms and who also do not receive funding from main actors for the development of projects [52].

Some academic studies [34,35,53] and national market reports [18,52] report difficulties in managing and maintaining digital game businesses. In addition, some studies investigate digital game production in an international context. For example, Petrillo et al. [48] analyze problems in the development process of electronic games based on postmortem documents. Potanin [50] performed a cultural analysis of the business of videogame production and highlighted some characteristics of US publishers and markets in Australian game development in the years 2004–2009. Finally, Politowski et al. [49] report results of a survey on the software engineering processes and observed that iterative practices are increasingly present in digital game production processes, but some independent studios still use waterfall processes (about 30% of the analyzed projects).

The multidisciplinarity required for these businesses increases the complexity of independent studios' efficient and "lean" management. Such difficulties reinforce the challenge of business modeling performed by these actors immersed in GSECO. Based on this context, we present a unified agenda, which enables the collaborative participation and a joint effort of several fields involved in production and management, focusing on providing the growth of the actors' businesses and, consequently, of the national digital games scene.

2   Basic Concepts

Based on the motivation presented in Sect. 1, independent studios face challenges regarding their surveillance in an interconnected digital games industry. Such studios are part of GSECO, which is seen as a wider network of actors, including large companies, regulatory agencies etc., as well as platforms such as game engines and marketplaces supporting the contributions from the community of developers (i.e., new features, digital games etc.) to reach users' demands in the global context [8,14,19,22,39,53]. In the next sections, we explain concepts related to this grand challenge in this context: SECO, digital games, and business models.

2.1   Software Ecosystems

The term has several definitions in the literature [20,33]. The meaning of the word "ecosystem" itself comes from Biology and is used in different contexts to convey the evolving nature of processes, activities, and relationships [15,20]. By adding the word "software", a focus is given to the software components that form more complex software systems [20].

Briefly, a SECO is the interaction of artifacts and actors on a common technology platform, which results in a set of direct or indirect contributions and influences on a community of companies, developers and users [33]. A SECO can be divided into three dimensions, as illustrated in Fig. 1 [5]. The technical (or architectural) dimension addresses the common technology platform's life cycle, technical features, and architecture. The business (or transactional) dimension is related to knowledge flow, exploring issues about artifacts, resources, and information through the business view. Finally, the social dimension is related to the stakeholders, exploring how actors interacts within a network to achieve goals.

Fig. 1. SECO dimensions, adapted from [55].

An actor is any stakeholder (e.g., independent studio, end-user, developer, and others) and can play several roles in the ecosystem [27]. In turn, roles are categories that actors represent within a SECO [6,8,27,33]. Independent studios play the role of external actors, specifically as external developers, as they promote SECO and its products by proposing solutions with no formal ties with the technology platform owner. The owners of the SECO platforms (e.g., Google-Play, PlayStation Network, Steam, Unity, Unreal, among others) fit the role of keystone since they represent the dominant influential entity responsible for the sustainability of the ecosystem.

Sustainability in SECO can be understood as the ecosystem's ability to increase or maintain its user/developer community over time, ensuring survival from changes inherent to new technologies, products, competitors, users, and attacks/sabotages [15]. Sustainability is considered an essential aspect of the business dimension and a critical element for keystone [5,9,55] and is directly linked to the frequent collaboration of actors aiming at the promotion of the ecosystem [15]. As such, SECO must be concerned with maintaining/growing its user/developer community for extended periods, and the financial sustainability of the actors is a critical factor for SECO platforms.

2.2   Digital Games and Software Ecosystems

Games are an ancient element for humanity. There are records of games built-in dates around 3,000 years B.C. [17]. Another example is the world's oldest chess game, which dates back to around 700 B.C. [4]. New game modes and formats have emerged because of technological advances throughout human history. The era of digital games began with the release of the first computer game in 1952, and the first videogame console in 1958 and was consolidated with the creation of electronic entertainment in the 1980s [41]. Digital games can be understood as entertainment-oriented software [61], as some academic studies report this relationship between digital games and software industry [24,41,60].

With the growth of networks that arise from interactions between actors and software artifacts, SECO has emerged as a research topic [5,15,33,57]. Large companies in the software industry, such as Amazon, Apple, Google, Microsoft, and SAP, lead the development of SECO [54], which has contributed to the status of an important research topic. In the digital games domain, some companies, such as Valve Corporation, Epic Games, Unity Technologies, Blizzard Entertainment, Bethesda Games Studios, Facebook, Sony, and Nintendo, have also been exploring SECO concepts [8,19,22,56].

The new actors emerging in a GSECO are mostly software developers who group with other professionals and form independent studios. Independent studios are group of actors that do not have a formal connection with the owners of the large distribution platforms and also do not receive funding from main actors for the development of projects [52]. The growth of the digital games industry in recent years [18,52] and the challenges faced by studios [18,31,34,35,40,52] accentuate the need to explore the dynamics and relationships of these actors through the SECO perspective due the domination of SECO concepts in the games industry.

2.3   Business Models

Business modeling became a relevant subject after the advent of the Internet in the 1990s [58]. This term has several meanings in academic literature. Some references relate the term to a description, representation, architecture, conceptual tool, model, structural template, method, framework, or as a standard [67].

In order to organize the understanding of the studies in the area, Osterwalder et al. [46] created an evolutionary perspective of the studies on business modeling. As illustrated in Fig. 2, the first definitions appear with the works of Timmers [59] and Rappa [51]. Next, studies with definitions of components and descriptions that make up a more detailed definition of the term emerge in the field. As such, reference models and ontologies are created, making the logical and behavioral connection between the components. Finally, there are studies about conceptual tools and applications.

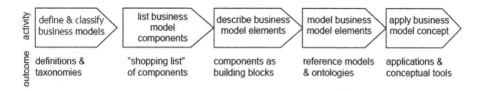

Fig. 2. Evolution of business model studies, adapted from [46].

Due to the theme evolution and the use for several purposes [67], some studies propose a categorization of the studies on business modeling. For this purpose, Pateli and Giaglis [47] propose a framework that classifies the works on business modeling into six subdomains:

- Definitions: definition of the objective, scope, and primary elements;
- Components: definition segregated into components;
- Taxonomies: categorization of business models;
- Conceptual Models: description of the relationships among components abstractly and rationally;
- Design Methods and Tools: methods, languages, standards, and software to automate model design;
- Change Methodologies: description of steps and actions to change models over time; and
- Evaluation Models: evaluation criteria or best practices when implementing a model;
- Adoption Factors: factors that affect model adoption.

An essential point for understanding the term "business modeling" is identifying the boundaries with other areas of knowledge. Some studies point out a relationship between business modeling and business strategy, but these are two distinct concepts [2,11,67]. Strategy refers to the choices by which the company competes in the market [11]. In other words, business modeling impacts and suffers impact by strategic business decisions.

There is also a relationship with business process modeling, which aims to specify actions and activities to execute the business. Thus, it is possible to understand that business modeling links strategy modeling and business process modeling, being an intermediate element [2,67], as illustrated in Fig. 3. Finally, in order to provide a standard definition, the excerpt from Osterwalder et al.'s work [46] is highlighted:

"[...] is nothing else than a description of the value a company offers to one or several segments of customers and the architecture of the firm and its network of partners for creating, marketing and delivering this value and relationship capital, in order to generate profitable and sustainable revenue streams." [46]

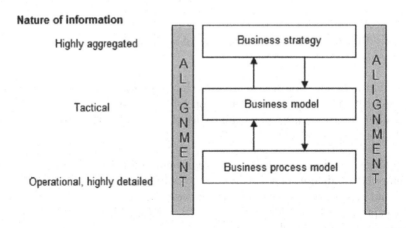

Fig. 3. Digital business layers, adapted from [2].

3   State-of-Art on Business Model for Digital Games

In order to understand how the digital games industry defines business models, we identified some prominent references in studies that dealt with the terms digital games and business model. Part of the studies investigates business models based on a simple perspective, explaining isolated aspects, such as reselling and monetization. This approach, allied with using the term "business model" to help in the argumentation or introduction, results in studies without the proper theoretical reference and, consequently, without a clear and well-grounded definition. We identified different works from a systematic mapping study on the definitions of the business modeling in the practice of digital games research and development, as well as how developers and companies play in the industry. The study protocol and results are detailed in [63]. We highlight that the studies were identified in the context of the digital games.

Among the studies that applied references to support the use of the term (Definitions subdomain), the definitions of Osterwalder et al. [46] and Timmers [59] stand out - for Osterwalder et al.'s definition, see Sect. 2.3. According to Timmer, a business model is an architecture for the product, service, and information flows, including a description of the several business actors and their roles, the potential benefits for the different business actors, and the sources of revenues [59]. More broadly, business modeling is associated with describing the logic of how a business creates value for its customers.

Some studies have also dealt with tools for business modeling. Among the tools, the Business Model Canvas, proposed in [45] and illustrated in Fig. 4, gained prominence due to the fact that it addresses almost all the subdomains of Pateli and Giaglis' framework [47]. Another study that stands out is the work of Afuah and Tucci [1], due to the framing in the subdomains.

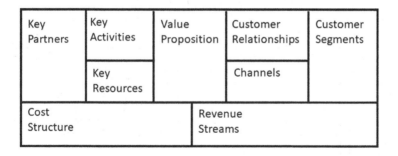

Fig. 4. Business Model Canvas, adapted from [45].

In the Components subdomain, the first structure is the Business Model Canvas [45]. In Osterwalder's works [16,42–46], there is an evolutionary sequence regarding the business modeling components. The framework, consisting of nine building blocks (Value Proposition, Customer Segments, Channels, Customer Relationships, Key Resources, Key Activities, Key Partners, Cost Structure, and Revenue Streams), aims to address innovation in business models by providing a shared language that can describe business models and methods for change and evolution. Similarly to the work of Osterwalder and Pigneur [45], the work of Lindgardt et al. [29] also focuses on innovation criteria in business modeling. The work addresses the concept of Business Model Innovation (BMI) and a survey approach was run to achieve an understanding of the components that make up the model, which is composed of two elements (Value Proposition and Operating Model) and six dimensions (Target Segment, Product or Service Offering, Revenue Model, Value Chain, Cost Model, and Organization).

In [36,37], a series of questions to identify key aspects of business modeling is explored. The six-component framework (Offering, Market, Internal Capability, Competitive Strategy, Economics, and Personal/Investor) was called as the MSA Framework, alluding to the authors' names (Morris, Schindehutte, and Allen). MSA Framework focuses on allowing its user to design, describe, categorize, critique, and analyze a business model for any company. In turn, in [21], the E^3-Value proposes an interdisciplinary approach with nine concepts (Actor, Value Object, Value Port, Value Offering, Value Interface, Value Exchange, Market Segment, Composite Actor, and Value Activity) to explore e-commerce. The study aims to explore requirements engineering based on concepts and terminology from business science, marketing, and axiology.

Regarding the Taxonomies subdomain, some authors have adopted a two-dimensional-based approach to generate the categories of their taxonomies on business modeling. The first citation goes to the work of Timmers [59], who created a classification based on two axes: Functional Integration (ranging from Single Function, Functional Integration, and Multiple Integrated Functions) and Degree of Innovation (ranging from Lower to Higher). The variation of these axes allowed the identification of 11 business model classifications, as illustrated in Fig. 5.

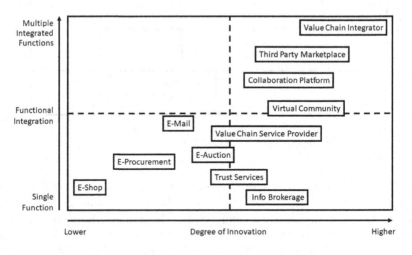

Fig. 5. Classification scheme, adapted from [59].

In [7], the authors created a scheme that simultaneously considers which actors in the economy (supplier, customer, or mediator/trader) initiate and maintain a business model and how (active or passive) they communicate with their business partners. With these axes, five classifications emerged, as illustrated in Fig. 6. Finally, as a more recent work identified in this context and still in a two-dimensional approach, Kortmann and Piller [26] created a categorization with the following axes: Value Creation and Collaboration, as illustrated in Fig. 7. On the horizontal axis (value creation), value creation can have one of three phases: Production, Consumption, or Circulation. There are three types of collaboration on the vertical axis: Firms, Alliances, or Platforms. These dimensions allow for nine different archetypes of business models.

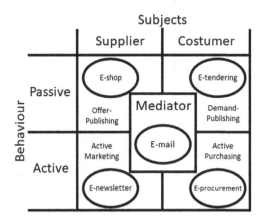

Fig. 6. Classification for business model, adapted from [7].

For the Conceptual Model subdomain, the highlights are from the works of Osterwalder and Pigneur [44], and Gordijn and Akkermans [21]. In [44], the relationship between the building blocks of Osterwalder's ontology is detailed. Figure 8 illustrates the elements of the ontology. In [21], Gordijn and Akkermans use a notation based on the UML (Unified Modeling Language) class diagram to represent the concepts of the E^3-Value ontology, as illustrated in Fig. 9. Finally, for this subdomain, it is important to highlight the work of Bouwman et al. [10], which defines the STOF Model elements.

In the Design Methods and Tools subdomain, the highlights were the same works as mentioned in the previous subdomain [21,42]. In [21], Gordijn and Akkermans created a language with graphical syntax to facilitate communication between business modeling stakeholders. Figure 10 illustrates an example of the graphical language with the appropriate caption for each of the nine components that make up the design tool. In [42], a formal language is elaborated, whose purpose is to describe and capture instances of the business model. The elements of its graphical representation were coded based on an XML (eXtensible Markup Language) structure, forming the Business Modeling Language (BM^{2}L). Figure 11 exemplifies the use of BM^{2}L with the Value Proposition component. The Business Model Canvas, presented in Fig. 4, later replaced BM^{2}L.

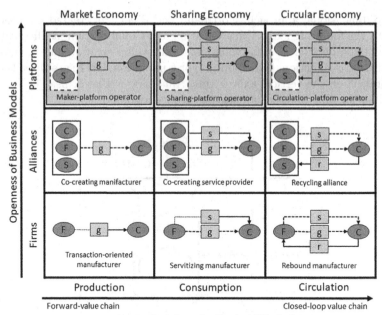

Fig. 7. Open business models in extended product life cycles, adapted from [26].

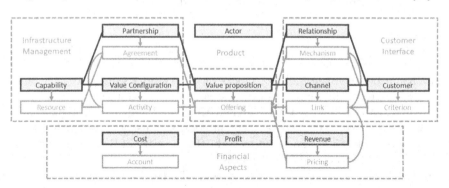

Fig. 8. Relationships between Business Model Ontology elements, adapted from [42].

In the Change Methodologies subdomain, the outstanding works describe some steps/stages for the elaboration and evolution of business models [12,13,28, 30]. In [12], for example, four different phases of change in a business model are suggested, as illustrated in Fig. 12. The first phase (box identified as "1") refers to materializing a business idea into a new venture. The second phase represents the extension of the business model, in which is possible to add activities to an existing model. The third phase is revising the business model, removing, modifying, or replacing parts of an existing model. Finally, the fourth phase is about closing or removing parts of the model.

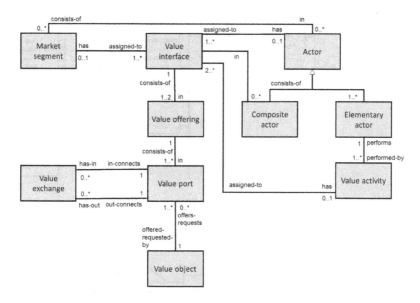

Fig. 9. Example of concepts relations of E³-value ontology, adapted from [21].

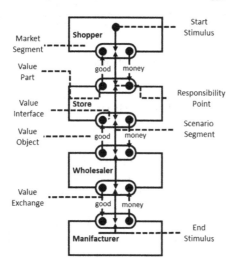

Fig. 10. An E³-Value model example, adapted from [21].

The Evaluation Models subdomain adds some metrics for evaluating models to the existing tools. Some works suggest metrics and steps for evaluation [1, 21,25,32], while Osterwalder and Pigneur's work [45] applies third-party tools and techniques integrated with the proposed business model. For the Adoption Factors subdomain, no works related to games were identified.

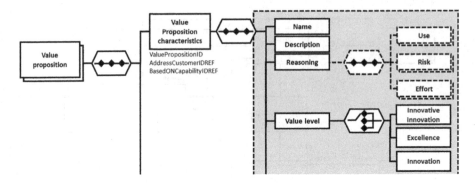

Fig. 11. BM^{2}L diagram/XML schema, adapted from [42].

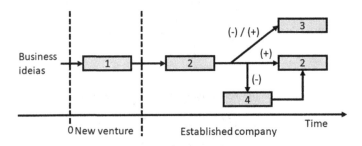

Fig. 12. Business model change, adapted from [12].

4   Business Modeling for Independent Studios in Game Software Ecosystems: Challenges and Opportunities

The business model challenges for independent studios in GSECO fall into two main approaches: (1) adoption of the SECO perspective and concepts by the digital games industry, and (2) development of the business model for the Brazilian context. The SECO perspective aims to bring digital game studios closer to the concepts and practices of the software industry, aiding in the understanding and appropriation of dynamics that underlie the industry. In turn, business modeling is the area of knowledge responsible for assisting in the "navigation" of actors in the SECO environment.

In the SECO literature, some studies highlight challenges that have synergy with digital games [3,15,23,57]. There are also national industry censuses [18,52] and academic studies related to digital games [8,53,64,66] that list specific problems and challenges of the industry in Brazil. Table 1 presents a consolidation of these challenges related to SECO dimensions for the next decade. These five grand challenges emerged from a clustering process made by the three researchers involved in the present work. The analysis was based on a systematic mapping study from the academic literature on business models for digital games [62,63] as well as from a survey research with researchers and practitioners in the Brazilian GSECO [66]. The selected studies on the models and the opinions on the benefits, pitfalls, and challenges served as the basis for organizing the challenges into five groups (or grand research challenges), as exposed in Table 1 and extended from [65]. Such analysis involved experts in SECO context and qualitative analysis. There is no priority or order of the proposed challenges, i.e., they can be investigated separately and in parallel.

Table 1. Business modeling challenges for independent studios in GSECO.

ID	Challenge	Dimension	Description
1	Interoperability and Solution Integration	Technical and Business	Investigate ways to address interoperability (syntactic, semantic, pragmatic, and technical) and integration between solutions and technologies for the digital games domain.
2	Software Engineering for Games	Technical and Social	Develop artifacts (e.g., templates, techniques, tools) that support game production and consumer relationships over the platform architecture and independent studios' products.
3	Ecosystem Modeling and Analysis	Business and Social	Identify the network of actors, their roles, and relationships along the digital game production chain to develop analysis strategies to benefit the Brazilian ecosystem.
4	Knowledge and Complexity Management	Technical, Social and Business	Stimulate strategies and the generation of tools to support sharing knowledge about projects, opportunities, technologies, and other subjects of interest to the sector.
5	Supply Network Sustainability	Business and Social	Adapt or create artifacts (e.g., models, frameworks, methods) under the sustainability dimensions (technical, social, environmental, economic, and individual) in the independent studios' business modeling.

4.1 Interoperability and Solution Integration

The challenge of **interoperability and solution integration** involves topics such as management, knowledge reuse, communication standards, extensibility, portability, cross-platform development, and backward compatibility to compose digital game solutions [53]. Security, reliability, modularity, and flexibility are important criteria when it comes to interoperability [38].

In the case of games, there is the possibility of integrations with several solutions of centralized platforms and external actors to delegate business activities or product functionalities, such as payments, location map, login, data persistence in the cloud, among others. However, these integrations bring challenges to extract value for the customer, and it is a topic to be further explored in both the technical and business dimensions.

4.2 Software Engineering for Games

In turn, the challenge of **software engineering for games** aims to cover pre-production, production, and post-production aspects, such as data collection and extraction, *feedback* from users, version management, solution certification, design patterns, automated testing, and development cycle models [3,18,52,53, 57]. One of the independent studios' problems is the initial relationship with consumers and their long-term loyalty. As such, the challenge arises due to the studio's uncertainty in maintaining themselves with the revenue coming from the games and low initial financial investment. The need for product success becomes fundamental, and this aspect highlights the need to convert the market potential into consumers. To mitigate this risk, it is necessary to have the consumer as the main target in the business modeling and create/evolve solutions to assist the production of digital games.

Another point of this challenge is integrating the games with the different game platforms/SECO solutions. The studio must investigate and adapt to contribute/participate in the platform's evolution over time. Maintaining and complying with quality and security criteria (e.g., General Data Protection Law) imposed by the platforms and communities is also an example of this adaptation. Modeling the architecture of the solutions also includes planning an entire process and possibly the studio's adaptation concerning technical and social issues. Finally, GSECO scenarios are constantly changing in the digital games industry. Furthermore, by involving professionals from different fields in the software development process, it increases the challenge of proposing a unified agenda and corroborates the importance of fostering further research.

4.3 Ecosystem Modeling and Analysis

The **ecosystem modeling and analysis** involves the identification of actors, roles, relationships, level of influence, tools for modeling, and the characterization of specific GSECO (e.g., games for education and health) [8,15,53,64]. Identifying the production chain is fundamental for strengthening the national scene and for the business modeling in independent studios. Such mapping will enable the maintenance of challenges, the integration between studios, and the elaboration of strategies with main actors (e.g., governments, investors, platform owners) that would be unreachable for independent studios.

We highlight the importance of the SECO perspective on business modeling for independent digital game studios. Digital games, which can also be understood as information systems [61], are immersed in a complex landscape with multiple disciplines and constantly changing technology [8,14,19,22,39,64]. In this context, the SECO perspective corresponds to a way to assist independent studios in understanding and planning for sustainability and longevity within the ecosystems they participate. Moreover, we highlight that several independent studios are currently playing on SECO platforms. As such, the understanding of such a socio-technical network is important for their survival over time, considering their scope/size and their immersion in a complex socio-technical network [8,14,19,22,39,53].

4.4   Knowledge and Complexity Management

The **knowledge and complexity management** aims to stimulate social inter-action in order to enable the dissemination of knowledge about methodologies, tools, professional courses, events, workshops, and infrastructure support for the exchange of production and management knowledge [15,52,53]. Social interaction for knowledge diffusion is an important aspect of the dissemination of new technologies, especially in the area of software [57].

For digital games, the knowledge required to design a product is complex and comes from several areas (e.g., management, accounting, marketing, software development, testing and quality, software engineering, among others). In the context of independent studios, the acquisition of some knowledge becomes more difficult due to the lack of access to certain technologies (e.g., virtual reality headsets, video cards, software licenses, among others) [52]. In this independent studios' context (multidisciplinary, complex, and with limited access), the focus is on building artifacts that support such topics, including infrastructure and channels for the relationship between the different actors. For example, they play as contributors to GSECO, providing courses, training, software components, arts and design artifacts for reuse, patterns, frameworks, applications etc.

4.5   Supply Network Sustainability

Finally, the **supply network sustainability** addresses aspects such as profit, competition, business capture, product portfolio, metrics and performance indi-cators, niche identification, taxes, fees, and access to financial resources. Sus-tainability is considered a basic aspect of the business dimension and a critical element for SECO keystones [5].

Lack of financial sustainability can result in the change/leaving of these actors, thus becoming a critical factor for the overall sustainability of the ecosys-tems and platforms. The lack of support in the relationship between developers and technology platform owners also contributes to this challenge prominence. These actors lack formal support from the companies, since they depend on them to reach their target audience and achieve the financial sustainability of their business. As such, these organizations must pay attention to the maintenance and growth of their ecosystem communities, with the sustainability of the actors being a crucial factor for SECO and a challenge highlighted in some studies [18,52,66].

5   Discussion and Future Directions

As a suggested evolutionary approach to the proposed grand research challenge, i.e., "Business Model for Indie Studios in Game Software Ecosystems", we sought to identify the benefits to be maintained and improved from market reports [18,52]. The main benefits of the current market are (1) networking and (2) knowledge sharing among actors. Thus, the first stages of the grand challenge to be addressed are **ecosystem modeling and analysis** and **knowledge and complexity management**. Besides being aligned with the current moment of the sector in Brazil, efforts on these challenges will allow the dissemination and, possibly, the adoption of SECO concepts, which will serve as a basis for the second stage of the grand challenge, i.e., the elaboration of business models for the national context.

In turn, based on the problems identified in academia and industry [8,53,64, 66], the following challenges guide further business modeling: starting with **interoperability and solution integration**, then copying with **software engineering for games**, and finally addressing **supply network sustainability**. These challenges require an appropriation of the business modeling subdomains. Table 2 present a vision for tracking and evolving each challenge over a 10-years period (2020–2030).

Table 2. Monitoring and evolution of the challenges throughout the decade.

ID	3 years	6 years	10 years
1	Investigate platform architectures and solutions for digital games.	Develop solutions for different levels of interoperability.	Develop reference architectures for specific digital games domains.
2	Specify methods, techniques, tools, strategies, and practices for developing software for digital games.	Evaluate experimentally the software engineering support produced in the context of different digital game domains.	Monitor software quality indicators for digital games with a focus on the maturity of the development process.
3	Identify and map actors, roles, and relationships in GSECO.	Develop tools to analyze software production networks for digital games.	Build repositories for sharing ecosystem data and experiences.
4	Define strategies for knowledge sharing and complexity analysis in the digital games industry.	Identify collaborative networks to engage different actors and disseminate knowledge from SECO and game production.	Apply systems thinking tools to support knowledge management focused on addressing complexity in production.
5	Identify elements of business modeling under the sustainability dimensions (technical, social, environmental, economic, and individual).	Develop sustainability-oriented business models for large production companies and independent studios.	Use the proposed models in different digital game domains to measure improvements in SECO sustainability indicators.

Business modeling is a concept present in digital-based companies, and the digital games industry needs to appropriate this concept and its tools. Business modeling and digital games are sometimes buzzwords in both academia and industry. We expect that this work helps in understanding the concept and tools used in further studies in digital games. New industry censuses and literature studies related to digital games are required to check the evolution of the grand research challenge in a controlled, evolving way. We also expect that this grand challenge can contribute to the growth of the Brazilian GSECO.

References

1. Afuah, A., Tucci, C.: Internet Business Models and Strategies: Text and Cases. McGraw-Hill Inc. (2002)
2. Al-Debei, M.M., Avison, D.: Developing a unified framework of the business model concept. Eur. J. Inf. Syst. **19**(3), 359–376 (2010)
3. Axelsson, J., Skoglund, M.: Quality assurance in software ecosystems: a systematic literature mapping and research agenda. J. Syst. Softw. **114**, 69–81 (2016)
4. Banaschak, P.: Early east Asian chess pieces: an overview. Issue August (1999)
5. Barbosa, O., Santos, R.P., Alves, C., Werner, C., Jansen, S.: A systematic mapping study on software ecosystems from a three-dimensional perspective. In: Software Ecosystems: Analyzing and Managing Business Networks in the Software Industry. Edward Elgar Publishing (2013)
6. Barnett, M.L.: The keystone advantage: what the new dynamics of business ecosystems mean for strategy, innovation, and sustainability (2006)
7. Bartelt, A., Lamersdorf, W.: A multi-criteria taxonomy of business models in electronic commerce. In: Fiege, L., Mühl, G., Wilhelm, U. (eds.) WELCOM 2001. LNCS, vol. 2232, pp. 193–205. Springer, Heidelberg (2001). https://doi.org/10.1007/3-540-45598-1_18
8. Berg, N.: Business model evolution in the game software ecosystem. Master's thesis, Universiteit Utrecht (2015)
9. Bosch, J.: From software product lines to software ecosystems. In: SPLC, vol. 9, pp. 111–119 (2009)
10. Bouwman, H., Faber, E., Haaker, T., Kijl, B., De Reuver, M.: Conceptualizing the STOF model. In: Bouwman, H., De Vos, H., Haaker, T. (eds.) Mobile Service Innovation and Business Models, pp. 31–70. Springer, Heidelberg (2008). https://doi.org/10.1007/978-3-540-79238-3_2
11. Casadesus-Masanell, R., Ricart, J.E.: From strategy to business models and onto tactics. Long Range Plan. **43**(2–3), 195–215 (2010)
12. Cavalcante, S.A., Kesting, P., Ulhøi, J.P.: Business model dynamics: the central role of individual agency. Acad. Manag. Proc. **2010**(1), 1–6 (2010)
13. Chesbrough, H.: Business model innovation: it's not just about technology anymore. Strategy Leadersh. **35**(6), 12–17 (2007)
14. De Prato, G., Lindmark, S., Simon, J.P.: The evolving European video game software ecosystem. In: Zackariasson, P., Wilson, T.L. (eds.) The Video Game Industry: Formation, Present State, and Future, chap. 8, pp. 221–243. Routledge (2012)
15. Dhungana, D., Groher, I., Schludermann, E., Biffl, S.: Software ecosystems vs. natural ecosystems: learning from the ingenious mind of nature. In: Proceedings of the Fourth European Conference on Software Architecture: Companion Volume, pp. 96–102. ACM (2010)
16. Dubosson-Torbay, M., Osterwalder, A., Pigneur, Y.: E-business model design, classification, and measurements. Thunderbird Int. Bus. Rev. **44**(1), 5–23 (2002)

17. Finkel, I.L.: On the rules for the royal game of UR. Ancient Board Games in Perspective, pp. 16–32 (2007)
18. Fleury, A., Sakuda, L.O., Cordeiro, J.H.D.: I censo da indústria brasileira de jogos digitais. NPGT-USP e BNDES, São Paulo e Rio de Janeiro (2014)
19. Fung, A.: Global Game Industries and Cultural Policy. Springer, Heidelberg (2017)
20. García-Holgado, A., García-Peñalvo, F.J.: Mapping the systematic literature studies about software ecosystems. In: Proceedings of the Sixth International Conference on Technological Ecosystems for Enhancing Multiculturality, pp. 910–918 (2018)
21. Gordijn, J., Akkermans, J.: Value-based requirements engineering: exploring innovative e-commerce ideas. Requirements Eng. 8(2), 114–134 (2003)
22. Inoue, Y., Tsujimoto, M.: New market development of platform ecosystems: a case study of the Nintendo Wii. Technol. Forecast. Soc. Chang. 136, 235–253 (2018)
23. Jansen, S., Brinkkemper, S., Souer, J., Luinenburg, L.: Shades of gray: opening up a software producing organization with the open software enterprise model. J. Syst. Softw. 85(7), 1495–1510 (2012)
24. Jantke, K.P., Gaudl, S.: Taxonomic contributions to digital games science. In: 2010 2nd International IEEE Consumer Electronics Society's Games Innovations Conference, pp. 1–8. IEEE (2010)
25. Johnson, M.W., Christensen, C.M., Kagermann, H.: Reinventing your business model. Harv. Bus. Rev. 86(12), 57–68 (2008)
26. Kortmann, S., Piller, F.: Open business models and closed-loop value chains: redefining the firm-consumer relationship. Calif. Manag. Rev. 58(3), 88–108 (2016)
27. Lima, T., Barbosa, G., Santos, R., Werner, C.: Uma abordagem socio-técnica para apoiar ecossistemas de software. iSys: Revista Brasileira de Sistemas de Informação 7(3), 19–37 (2014)
28. Linder, Cantrell: Changing Business Models: Surveying the Landscape. Accenture (2000)
29. Lindgardt, Z., Reeves, M., Stalk, G., Deimler, M.S.: Business Model Innovation. When the Game Gets Tough, Change the Game. The Boston Consulting Group, Boston (2009)
30. MacInnes, I.: Dynamic business model framework for emerging technologies. Int. J. Serv. Technol. Manag. 6(1), 3 (2005)
31. MacInnes, I., Hu, L.: Business models and operational issues in the Chinese online game industry. Telematics Inform. 24(2), 130–144 (2007)
32. Malone, T.W., et al.: Do some business models perform better than others? SSRN Electron. J. (2006)
33. Manikas, K.: Revisiting software ecosystems research: a longitudinal literature study. J. Syst. Softw. 117, 84–103 (2016)
34. Mäntymäki, M., Hyrynsalmi, S., Koskenvoima, A.: How do small and medium-sized game companies use analytics? An attention-based view of game analytics. Inf. Syst. Front. 22, 1–16 (2019)
35. Martins, G., Veiga, W., Campos, F., Ströele, V., David, J.M.N., Braga, R.: Building educational games from a feature model. In: Proceedings of the XIV Brazilian Symposium on Information Systems, pp. 1–7 (2018)
36. Morris, M., Schindehutte, M., Allen, J.: The entrepreneur's business model: toward a unified perspective. J. Bus. Res. 58(6), 726–735 (2005)
37. Morris, M., Schindehutte, M., Richardson, J., Allen, J.: Is the business model a useful strategic concept? Conceptual, theoretical, and empirical insights. J. Small Bus. Strateg. 17(1), 27–50 (2006)

38. Motta, R.C., De Oliveira, K.M., Travassos, G.H.: Rethinking interoperability in contemporary software systems. In: 2017 IEEE/ACM Joint 5th International Workshop on Software Engineering for Systems-of-Systems and 11th Workshop on Distributed Software Development, Software Ecosystems and Systems-of-Systems (JSOS), pp. 9–15. IEEE (2017)
39. Murphy-Hill, E.R., Zimmermann, T., Nagappan, N.: Cowboys, ankle sprains, and keepers of quality: how is video game development different from software development? In: 36th International Conference on Software Engineering, pp. 1–11 (2014)
40. Nahar, N., Huda, N., Tepandi, J.: Critical risk factors in business model and is innovations of a cloud-based gaming company: case evidence from Scandinavia. In: 2012 Proceedings of PICMET 2012: Technology Management for Emerging Technologies, pp. 3674–3680. IEEE (2012)
41. Neto, B., Fernandes, L., Werner, C., de Souza, J.M.: Reuse in digital game development. In: Proceedings of the 4th International Conference on Ubiquitous Information Technologies & Applications, pp. 1–6. IEEE (2009)
42. Osterwalder, A.: The business model ontology a proposition in a design science approach. Ph.D. thesis, Université de Lausanne, Faculté des hautes études commerciales (2004)
43. Osterwalder, A., Pigneur, Y.: An eBusiness model ontology for modeling eBusiness. In: BLED 2002 Proceedings, p. 2 (2002)
44. Osterwalder, A., Pigneur, Y.: An ontology for e-business models. Value Creation e-Business Models 1, 65–97 (2004)
45. Osterwalder, A., Pigneur, Y.: Business Model Generation: A Handbook for Visionaries, Game Changers, and Challengers. Wiley, Hoboken (2010)
46. Osterwalder, A., Pigneur, Y., Tucci, C.L.: Clarifying business models: origins, present, and future of the concept. Commun. Assoc. Inf. Syst. 16(1), 1 (2005)
47. Pateli, A.G., Giaglis, G.M.: A research framework for analysing eBusiness models. Eur. J. Inf. Syst. 13(4), 302–314 (2004)
48. Petrillo, F., Pimenta, M., Trindade, F., Dietrich, C.: What went wrong? A survey of problems in game development. Comput. Entertain. 7(1) (2009). https://doi.org/10.1145/1486508.1486521
49. Politowski, C., Fontoura, L., Petrillo, F., Guéhéneuc, Y.G.: Are the old days gone? A survey on actual software engineering processes in video game industry. In: Proceedings of the 5th International Workshop on Games and Software Engineering, GAS 2016, pp. 22–28. Association for Computing Machinery, New York (2016). https://doi.org/10.1145/2896958.2896960
50. Potanin, R.: Forces in play: the business and culture of videogame production. In: Proceedings of the 3rd International Conference on Fun and Games, Fun and Games 2010, pp. 135–143. Association for Computing Machinery, New York (2010). https://doi.org/10.1145/1823818.1823833
51. Rappa, M.: Managing the digital enterprise-business models on the web (2001)
52. Sakuda, L.O., Fortim, I.: II censo da indústria brasileira de jogos digitais. Ministério da Cultura, Brasília (2018)
53. Santos, R.: Ecossistemas de software no projeto e desenvolvimento de plataformas para jogos e entretenimento digital. In: Anais do XVI SBGames, pp. 1327–1337 (2017)
54. Santos, R., Barbosa, O., Alves, C., et al.: Software ecosystems: trends and impacts on software engineering. In: 2012 26th Brazilian Symposium on Software Engineering, pp. 206–210. IEEE (2012)

55. Santos, R., Werner, C.: ReuseECOS: an approach to support global software development through software ecosystems. In: 2012 IEEE Seventh International Conference on Global Software Engineering Workshops, pp. 60–65. IEEE (2012)
56. Santos, R., Werner, C.M.L.: A proposal for software ecosystems engineering. In: IWSECO@ ICSOB, pp. 40–51 (2011)
57. Serebrenik, A., Mens, T.: Challenges in software ecosystems research. In: Proceedings of the 2015 European Conference on Software Architecture Workshops, p. 40. ACM (2015)
58. Teece, D.J.: Business models, business strategy and innovation. Long Range Plan. **43**(2–3), 172–194 (2010)
59. Timmers, P.: Business models for electronic markets. Electron. Mark. **8**(2), 3–8 (1998)
60. Toftedahl, M., Engström, H.: A taxonomy of game engines and the tools that drive the industry. In: DIGRA - International Conference 2019: Game, Play and The Emerging Ludo-Mix (2019)
61. Wang, Z., Scheepers, H.: Understanding the intrinsic motivations of user acceptance of hedonic information systems: towards a unified research model. Commun. Assoc. Inf. Syst. **30**, 17 (2012). http://aisel.aisnet.org/cais/vol30/iss1/17
62. Xavier, B., Viana, D., Santos, R.: Business model for Brazilian indie game studios in game software ecosystems. In: XVII Brazilian Symposium on Information Systems, SBSI 2021. Association for Computing Machinery, New York (2021). https://doi.org/10.1145/3466933.3466956
63. Xavier, B.L.: Business model for independent studios in digital game software ecosystems. Master's thesis, UNIRIO (2020)
64. Xavier, B.L., Araujo, R.M., Santos, R.P.: Explorando o ecossistema de software de jogos digitais no município do rio de janeiro. In: Anais do XVII SBGames, pp. 1526–1533 (2018)
65. Xavier, B.L., Santos, R., Viana, D.: Modelagem de negócio para estúdios independentes nos ecossistemas de software de jogos digitais. In: Proceedings of SBGames 2020. XIX Simpósio Brasileiro de Jogos e Entretenimento Digital, pp. 1135–1138 (2020)
66. Xavier, B.L., Santos, R., Viana, D.: Software ecosystems and digital games: understanding the financial sustainability aspect. In: Proceedings of the 22nd International Conference on Enterprise Information Systems - Volume 2: ICEIS, pp. 450–457 (2020)
67. Zott, C., Amit, R., Massa, L.: The business model: recent developments and future research. J. Manag. **37**(4), 1019–1042 (2011)

Games as Mediating Platforms
in an Open and Digital World

Tadeu Moreira de Classe[1]([⊠])[iD] and Renata Mendes de Araujo[2,3,4][iD]

[1] Graduate Program on Informatics (PPGI),
Federal University of the State of Rio de Janeiro (UNIRIO),
Rio de Janeiro, Brazil
tadeu.classe@uniriotec.br
[2] Mackenzie Presbyterian University (UPM), São Paulo, Brazil
renata.araujo@mackenzie.br
[3] University of São Paulo (USP), São Paulo, Brazil
[4] Brazilian National School of Public Administration (ENAP), Brasília, DF, Brazil

Abstract. The complexity of social interactions has been pointed out as challenges in studies on social development, education, cultural diversity, behavior change, and innovation. The COVID-19 pandemics highlighted important issues of our modern society, especially regarding emotional and psychological issues: humans as artificial beings disconnected from the planet, anxious for socialization, mainly through virtual worlds. Stress, anxiety, hopelessness and depression are sources of concern, while pleasure - a fundamental aspect for human life - loses space. We argue that our society needs to recover the pleasure which relies on the learning aspects of life situations as well as to rebuild the way we interact for social or work purposes. In this chapter, we propose as a challenge for the games research community, to face the sophistication that encompasses how to conceptualize, model, design, evaluate, and play games which can turn our actions in the world more playful. We primarily approach games as enablers and agents for work relations, social change and innovation in organizations, with a special look to the Brazilian context.

Keywords: Cyberdemocracy · Serious games · Digital game design

1   Introduction

"Because games make us better and can change the world". With this thought in mind, McGonigal starts her book and invites us to think about how games can change the world we live in [54].

Digital games are a branch of the entertainment industry that annually moves billions of dollars, with Brazil holding the 13th position in this market [57]. The growth of this market in Brazil can be explained by the popularization of smartphones and tablets, and, according to the 2nd Census of the Brazilian

R. P. d. Santos and M. d. S. Hounsell (Eds.): GranDGamesBR 2020/2021, CCIS 1702, pp. 67–88, 2023.
https://doi.org/10.1007/978-3-031-27639-2_4

Digital Games Industry (2014–2018) [73], a growth of 182% of companies in the niche of digital game development in the country was identified. The importance of digital games is even pointed out in Brazilian government's strategies, such as in the Brazilian Strategy for Digital Transformation [14].

As tools for learning and virtualizing the world, the idea of translating complex interaction contexts into game environments is not a new deal. Games that support learning range from educational games used by children, to those that apply to organizational environments, military training games, advergames and newsgames, respectively for advertising or reporting on global issues [3].

However, digital games have been underused as tools for social and behavioral change. This reality begins to change with the emergence of non-governmental initiatives and organizations such as Games for Change[1] which aims to promote social development, education, cultural diversity and innovation through the use of digital games. Some of these games were produced by initiatives such as Half the Sky[2], focusing on awareness, fundraising and behavior change [30] and proposals that frequently appears in journals such as Simulation & Gaming[3]. Controversially, in several situations, games are also associated with harmful transgressions of social behavior [28].

Meanwhile, the world is increasingly connected as networks. We experience technological disruptions due to the convergence of collaboration, mobility, big data and artificial intelligence. We are also experiencing increasingly complex emerging challenges related to our own survival and the sustainability of life in the planet [58], recently highlighted with the occurrence of the COVID-19 pandemic. We have witnessed the phenomenon of social media expanding the communication channels between individuals, and ICTs being massively applied for opening businesses and public administration. The world is increasingly connected and open, bringing benefits and challenges to our society. A long list of aspects can be considered as implications of this opening: new forms of interaction, information sharing, privacy, security, values, reliability, diversity... the list is endless.

In parallel with technological disruption, we watch society getting sick. Stress, burnout, anguish, anxiety, depression, panic syndrome, among other situations of imbalance affect a large part of the world population, to the point of being included by the World Health Organization in the International Classification of Diseases (ICD) [59].

New teaching and learning methodologies, such as Transformative Learning [82], advises for the need to develop attitudes (so-called soft skills) for the development of important characteristics of personality, sociability and human action - ethics, resilience, commitment, collaboration, leadership, etc. The documentary *Tarja Branca* [66] brings a beautiful denunciation of how much humanity has become serious and, by separating the act of working (conquering) from the act of playing (pleasure), we have become sick, artificial and disconnected from the

---

[1] http://www.gamesforchange.org/.

[2] http://www.halftheskymovement.org/.

[3] https://journals.sagepub.com/home/sag.

planet. The documentary makes clear the urgency of playing, of reconciling the act of playing with the act of living, producing and acting in the world. But how to do it?

Life is a continuous learning process. According to Koster [46], the human being is a learning machine and, in order to learn, he/she needs to be stimulated since our birth. The act of playing is a simple way for a child to start with: they set goals, play and, while playing, they learn useful skills for their life [38]. However, at some point, given the complexity of everyday life and the economic, social and cultural pressures, we put challenges and games aside, get more and more serious and start "playing to survive" in the world.

We propose as a challenge for the game community, in particular for the Brazilian Scientific community, to design games which promote gamification and pleasure in our actions in the world, reconciling "play" and "work", using digital games as platforms for social interaction in distinct contexts of human activity, considering the open and increasingly digital world we live in. We describe this challenge from the point of view of a conceptual vision of cyberdemocracy and open world premises, approaching games as platforms for work and social change, as well as their potential to innovation. We start our endeavour by focusing on work and social relations inside organizations as well as their openness to the outside environment.

The chapter is organized as follows: Sect. 2 details the concepts that ground the proposed challenge; Sect. 3 discusses the challenge relevance; Sect. 4 details the challenge and its sub-challenges; Sect. 5 discusses ideas for monitoring advances towards the challenge goals; and, finally, Sect. 6 concludes this chapter.

2   Conceptual Background

2.1   Cyberdemocracy

The Information Systems Brazilian research community has settled down as one of this community's research challenge the case of how to cope with conceptualizing, building and providing information systems which promote broader and massive collaboration, knowledge management and participation [13]. Araujo [8] highlights the importance of regarding the new requirements brought by the open world to information systems specification, design, implementation and evaluation based on the epistemological view of cyberdemocracy, a conceptual view to approach these systems as digital ecosystems; a pragmatic view to describe and understand their dynamics by understanding their processes; and the desired implications or impacts on these systems' behavior and mindset through mutual accountability.

Cybernetics [84] is the interdisciplinary study of regulatory systems structure (physical as well as social systems) and is closely linked to control theory and general systems theory [12]. Complex systems affect their external environment and then adapt to it. In technical terms, they focus on control and communication functions: both external and internal phenomena from/to the system. This ability occurs naturally in living organisms and has been imitated in machinery and organizations [80]. Cybernetics is the science of control, the science of governance.

The concept of Democracy is usually understood as a government model where the power of making important political decisions comes directly from the citizens, or in its most usual form, through elected representatives [72]. Democracy refers to a set of cultural and historical processes and has a difficult definition, grounded on the notion of a political community where all people have the right to equally participate, debate and decide on political processes and, in the modern sense, in which certain rights are universalized from the principles of freedom of expression and human dignity. The concept, although closely linked to legislation and constitutionalism, is not limited to legal equality, and also depends on democratic access (i.e. the same for all) to spaces and social benefits. Democracy is a socially constructed concept, based on the creation and preservation of rights, where conflict is legitimate and necessary and sovereignty is popular, not belonging only to the ruler [15].

Based on these two concepts, Cyberdemocracy is understood as the assumption that in a digitally-enabled open world, information sharing and reconfiguration performed by individuals provide collaboration, plurality, empowerment and governance. The idea is that the more we produce, deliver and share information, more "intelligent" (in the sense of governance) and conscious the society can be. Cyberdemocracy can be seen as the intelligence that arises through the possibilities of public opinion and empowerment with the use of technology, leading to better levels of social and organizational systems governance. The relationship between communication (social power) and technique (power of action) is the basis for this new political dimension, providing each individual connected by technology a new relationship with space and time, a new dimension of collectively living [49]. Cyberdemocracy is a term that brings together the great aspects of contemporary society - connected, convergent, informed and collaborative - and the great challenges faced by organizations to follow it. Cyberdemocracy points to the challenges of these new ecosystems that involve citizens, institutions public policies, technology, information, practices, policies and processes [5].

2.2   Serious Games

In general, games focus on the player's entertainment. However, they can also be innovative tools for socialization, education, reflection, and training [55]. Games used for these purposes are known as "serious games". According to Abt [1], serious games design considers "serious" contexts (reason of the name), i.e., contexts committed to educating and training people instead of just entertainment.

Michel and Chen [55] reaffirmed the concept of serious games proposed by Abt, arguing that these games have the primary purpose of teaching players something beyond entertainment. It does not mean that these games should forget entertainment, but the real goal is in the message that the game will transmit to players and how that message will influence them in the real world

[67]. Therefore, the word "serious" does not imply a dull game, but it refers to the purpose and reason for creating the game [71].

In Petridis et al.'s studies [62], they concluded the existence of the potential to use serious games to improve the efficacy of formative programs, to increase organizational productivity, and to solve problems. To become more effective as a learning or training tool, serious games must not only fulfill learning or training requirements but, they should follow the domain competencies and give feedback to players in real-time [67].

There are different types of serious games categorized by their purposes and contexts [69]. Among the most known genres, Alves [2] highlighted: advergames; edutainment; game-based learning; newsgames; training and simulation; persuasive games; organizational dynamic; games for health; art games and militainment. Each of these genres represents distinct purposes, but all of them have the feature of communicating and/or teaching something, encouraging thoughts, opinions, attitudes, and persuading players. In this sense, movements like *Games for Change* argue in favor of these games as timely tools to social change in many contexts (educational, political, philosophical etc.) [4,31,39].

Independently of the context, when designers think of a game for reflection or teaching something, they are proposing new ways of learning, facing and overcoming challenges. Thus, as researchers in games and players, we envision the possibilities of games to change work and social relations in organizations, turning them more amusing, humorous and fun [31,39].

2.2.1   Serious Games Design

In the begining, game design was just a matter of coding games [9]. Designers had no formal and systematic support to game design. They just "codified" them. Through the years and more recently, the game industry has been worried about formalizing specific game design processes as well as optimizing their production [9]. However, those game design processes are put aside by game organizations due to its complexity [9]. What we know about game design processes are experiences and steps reported by game designers and researchers such as Salen and Zimmerman [74], Fullerton [34], Jesse Schell [76], and other authors.

Traditional approaches to support game design for entertainment follow steps such as conception, documentation, prototyping, production, programming, tests, and delivery [34,74]. However, these activities may change depending on the target audience, goal, marketing strategy, financial resources, and other organizational needs. It is still a great challenge to the games research and practice community on how to define effective approaches to support digital games engineering [53,60]. Literature describes different proposals for supporting serious game design. For instance, the DPE (design, play, and experience) framework [85] focuses on the relationship between how players overcome game challenges and the resultant effects that they learn and feel from playing the game. Siriaraya et al. [81] presented the PGD (persuasive game design) model for persuasive purposes, which composes a set of components, tools, and elements for the game design task. Classe et al. [25] developed the Play Your Process (PYP) method to support the design of business processes-based digital games, through systematic mapping of business process models into elements of game design.

Although we can find many serious game design proposals in literature, there is still ground for researching the theme, basically because of the diversity of application contexts and learning, understanding or changing behavior objectives [81]. The main challenge in any serious game design process is knowing and understanding the game application context and how to represent it as game elements. People involved in serious game design (artists, designers, programmers) must learn about the application domain to be described in the game. Therefore, to design a serious game, the development team must think about the expected learning goals and continuously care about them during the game design [42].

Another important issue is how to evaluate serious games. Designing these games is complex, and it is hard to say that they deliver the right message to players [10]. Many proposals consider serious games assessment and evaluation, such as [33] or MEEGA+ [61].

2.3   Business Process-Based Digital Games

Business process-based digital games are games with a purpose that present a business process in a playful, funny, and engaging manner, and that allow players to understand and learn how the process works, as well as to develop an awareness of the process objectives, practices, values, challenges, and limitations [18,22,63]. The *Play Your Process* method was developed to carry out the design of business process-based digital games and is fully described in [22]. It organizes the whole business process-based digital game development through game engineering concepts, guiding game designers from the game conceptualization to evaluation, starting from a business process model. The key activity in the method is the possibility of semi-automatically translating elements of a process model into game design elements, making the game design directly adherent to the process definition.

A business process-based digital game is, to some extent, an "adventure game" where players can effectively "play" the adventure of performing the organizational process. For example, consider the process model depicted in Fig. 1, which describes part of the process conducted in a Brazilian police department for finding missing persons, comprising case analysis, and its inclusion into the police department information system. To design this process as a game, the method guides the designer to map process elements into game elements: events ("Missing person reported", "Answer Closed", and "RO is sent") as start and winning condition of the game; actors ("Citizen" and "Police Station") as characters or scenarios in the game; activities (e.g., "Person Welcome" and "Case Analysis") as game tasks or phases; resources (e.g., "ROWEB" and "Documents") as tools or achievements in the game; and rules and decisions in the process into decisions in the game.

Following this process mapping activity suggested by the method, it is possible to build a game to allow the player to go through the process execution as defined in the model like an "adventure" game, and eventually, to learn about

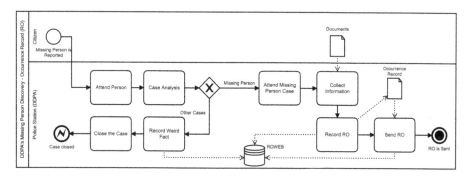

Fig. 1. Example of a business process model (Missing Person Discovery's BPMN Model).

the process designed in the game. The game designed using the method for the process depicted in Fig. 1 is described in [16].

Other activities besides process-game mapping are required to complete the game design: to understand the process context, aims, and expected organizational results (context analysis); to create the game concept where designers use their creativity to create an enjoyable game by defining its mechanics and aesthetics game project step; to work on prototyping and development, evaluation and publishing.

2.4 Values in Digital Games

Values are the moral and ethical principles that guide a person's life [36,70,77]. The idea that values can be incorporated into systems and technical devices (artifacts) has been the target of various approaches to studying technology, society, and humanity. In an ideal world, technology should promote not only instrumental values (efficiency, safety, reliability, and ease of use) but also social, moral and political values to which societies subscribe, hence, those who design systems have a responsibility to take these latter values into account [32].

Kheirandish et al. [44] discuss the role of values to design activities, highlighting the importance of having a list of values as a reference to supporting designers in identifying the relevant ones to be included in their target products. They developed the *HuValue* - a card-based design tool to help designers consider human values at different stages of the design process. Horn [37] argued that games are cultural artifacts that reflect designers' values and may reinforce or challenge players' values. These aspects give games the potential for social change and make us reconsider our relationship with the world. Darzentas and Urquhart [24] point out that game designers and players, as citizens, need systematic critical reflection on social, ethical, and political issues and games are a good starting point for framing and provoking critical discussion around values, being both cultural and educational tools.

Considering values in game design, the work of the American writer and game designer Mary Flanagan is noteworthy. Flanagan has dedicated her career to studying alternatives for game development that can add positive values - both for those who design the games but mainly for those who play them [32]. To address human issues in game design and promote the inclusion of values in design practice, she developed, together with Helen Nissembaum, a methodological framework, called Values at Play (VAP), or "Values at the Game", to promote the integration of values in the design process [32]. One of the essential features of VAP is the card game Grow-a-Game (GaG) [11], a brainstorming tool that helps designers incorporate values into their projects.

The use of cards as a way to identify relevant values for a game is also explored by Kheirandish and Rauterberg [45], in the *HuValue* tool; and by Raftopoulos [64], who presents a set of card-based tools to assist in the gamification design process for business, products, and services. Cards are used as a common tool for discussing values because many designers search for finding a balance between their values, those of users and other interested parties, and those of the surrounding culture. Therefore, it is essential to have a set of values to start with, and to decide which value must be designed in the game is only possible through an interpretative, collaborative, and brainstorming activity.

3   Relevance

When analyzing the research tracks of the Brazilian Symposium on Digital Games and Entertainment, (SBGames)[4], since its first edition in 2004, we will find tracks concerning games applied to complex contexts ("In2Games" and "GameArt" tracks). New tracks emerged in the following years: "Culture" in 2007; "Games For Change" in 2010 (closed in 2013); "Education" in 2018; and "Health" in 2019. This dynamics show how games in context have been considered as important to the research and practice in games.

As mentioned before, this challenge proposition is also aligned to the research challenges described by the Information Systems academic community in Brazil, particularly when examining the open world and cyberdemocracy principles - transparency, collaboration, sharing and empowerment [8]. In a world where transparency is a watchword, where diversity is considered a need and innovation and multidisciplinarity are key to solve complex global problems that anguish our society, this world must be open, connected, accessible, and its main actors (individuals) should be able to get organized without a previous predicted plan [78].

Business and organizations will keep themselves competitive if they learn how to manage their collaborators and internal processes in this new scenario, connected and open. In the meantime, the organizational internal environments need to cope with new forms of collaboration and interaction using technology, to guarantee the execution of work and business processes which comprise more

---

[4] Análise das trilhas nos sites dos anos anteriores - https://www.sbgames.org/.

simple, less bureaucratic tasks, performed with more autonomy and quality, highly connected to the external environment (clients) needs [68].

Our proposal is to reconcile these two visions to address the challenge of how to build innovative platforms for human interaction based on games, transforming everyday activities mediated by digital systems and tools into games, expanding connection, dialogue and pleasure.

4 Challenges

We propose to the scientific research community in games to join efforts to investigate how to expand everyday interactions within organizations and among organizations and society using games (Fig. 2). How to make individuals, society and institutions cooperate, look for essential communication aiming at the construction of an effective sharing process towards a common objective? How to manage permanently connected individuals which are both information providers and consumers, disconnecting them from old organizational interaction spaces (usually based on confrontation), to new spaces of community bond between them and with the organizations? How to strengthen the ties between organizations and people (workers, clients and citizens) as supporting actors in its governance, aiming at continuous improvement?

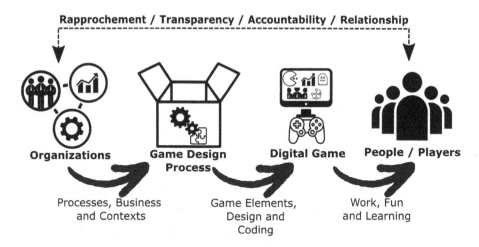

Fig. 2. Organization, games and people

The dynamics of the modern world have resulted in increasing the intricacy in the relationship among politics, economics and the media, making it challenging for people to keep up with daily events and react appropriately to changes in organizations and society. These complex contexts have brought barriers, for example between citizens and their representatives, where communication between them is minimal or distorted. Looking forward to shorten these distances, one step could be to try to make these complex contexts, political, economic, social, etc., minimally known and understood by individuals within the society [7].

We summarize the challenge as: **how to conceptualize and design games in order to expand mutual understanding between actors (society, clients, citizens, workers, organizations, regulators, etc.), particularly the understanding of complex organizational or social contexts, access to information, interaction and innovation, in a world increasingly connected and open.**

The design of these games must be based on the social, economic, cultural and educational contexts of the target players. Regarding individuals who have no technical skills, games must bring a simple language to allow easy dialogue with the players, make them understand the game, and associate it to the world they live. The potential use of these games need to be explored, analyzed and evaluated by society and institutions, which will bring to light relevant contexts as well as real organizational issues, and possible solutions including innovation and social entrepreneurship. We understand that this is a broad challenge, however, we direct our initial efforts to the Brazilian scenario.

This challenge comprises "sub-challenges", which were observed from insights and gaps in our research programs, as well as within SBGames (the Brazilian games research community), and in international forums. Each of these sub-challenges are discussed below.

4.1   Digital Games to Understand Organizational Processes

Games can be introduced in private or public organizational environments. In these contexts, games are usually associated to the possibility of promoting workers motivation, stimulating them to search for alternatives to improve the efficiency of organizational processes [48,52]. We argue that games can also be used to enable participants outside the organization (clients and citizens) to understand how the organization perform their processes in order to provide products and services, considering the inside context, obstacles, particularities and challenges [19,21].

This challenge can be summarized as: **how to carry out the *design* of digital games describing organizational contexts and processes, faithfully and efficiently, so that players (clients, citizens, workers) can understand the organizational functioning and to contribute to quality improvement?**

If we consider, for example, public organizations, digital games can be used to help citizens understand how the public organization performs in order to provide them a specific public service [26,63]. Simulation environments supported by digital games could be helpful for citizens and public administrators to experiment new possibilities and alternatives to public policies or service provision, allowing mutual understanding, quality improvement and innovation [83]. Games can be a "two-way street" where citizens can understand the organization and the organization workers can understand citizen needs and expectations.

Designing games in public contexts is a unique process when we take into the account that the game elements should simplify distinct and complex aspects such as social interactions, regulation, organizational rules and culture etc. It is also necessary to take into account cultural and social aspects of citizens, their values (ethical, moral, civic, legal, etc.), and bring them into the game design [25].

The Brazilian government and its institutions have performed significant legal and operational efforts to improve public service delivery. As a consequence, most public institutions nowadays provide basic information about their services online[5]. However, great part of these initiatives concerns possibilities with limited interaction with citizens (document download, filling forms, "talk to us" etc.). Owing most likely to process complexity, information available on the website is kept to a minimum, consisting of a brief service description and facilities to schedule an appointment. Brazilian citizens still have limited interface channels with the public bodies and to obtain information about services. Classe et al. [26] suggest the use of business process-based digital games (Sect. 2) in this context, as an alternative for explaining citizens how public services are provided. The idea is not to show just the service delivery aspects that the citizen already knows, but its internal details: rules, activities, actors, resources, bottlenecks, etc.

To illustrate this idea, let's consider one game designed for this purpose in the context of our research group: *The Missing Person Game*. The missing person discovery service is performed by the police department in Rio de Janeiro, Brazil. As reported by the police representatives at the Missing Person Police Department (DPPA), the service and its steps are usually unknown by the citizens, which leads to confusion and disappointment in service provision. The process modeled in Fig. 1 was used to design the game. The game narrative follows common cases the police department faces, like a missing boy who got lost in the subway while going to school. The game puts the player into the role of a police officer at the police department (Fig. 3A), and he/she must correctly perform the process tasks. At the same time, he/she attends to different citizens reporting missing persons. The game allows the player to experience the process used in the police department, considering the resources available to perform the process and facing the process challenges and difficulties. The cases that must be solved are based on real-life situations described by the police department staff, leading the player to contact with several social issues involved in the process (missing children, the elderly, mentally-ill persons, and criminals). The game is over when the player cannot solve the case in a specific timeframe or the character gives up the service. The player must collect information about the missing person. As in the real process, the officer must calm down the citizen while he/she tries to get enough information (e.g., ID, address, eye color, skin, birthmarks, and clothes) to find the person as fast as possible (Fig. 3B). The player must use the resources available for performing the tasks, such as information systems, and face frequent problems while using these resources (for instance, finding the password to access the system). Player success in the game comprises finding the missing person by performing the right task.

---

[5] https://acesso.gov.br/.

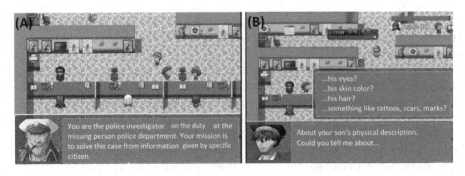

Fig. 3. A) Game introduction telling the player that he/she is the police officer and the aims in the game. B) Police officer investigation: requesting a physical description of the missing person.

Focusing private organizations, games can be used to add value to products and services, disclosing to customers relevant aspects of the production process. Additionally, they can be used as platforms to change work interactions within organizations, balancing work and pleasure. One possibility to find this balance is discussed in [52] and [79], proposing the use of business process-based digital games as tools for business process training. To cope with the design of games for this purpose, the authors propose the *PYP4 Training*, a variation of the game design method *PlayYourProcess* regarding training objectives [51].

To illustrate this idea, we describe the *Mediador Game* [79], designed in the context of The Judicial Centers for Conflict Resolution[6], agencies responsible for carrying out and managing judicial conciliation and mediation sessions. Although it is a public context, the conflict mediation process was a first attempt to design business process-based digital games form process training. The conflict mediation process comprises the selection of agents to hold mediation sessions, where parties can discuss and solve the existing conflict. The *Mediador Game* comprises the activities of scheduling a mediation session and the selection of mediators. This selection of mediators is important given that the success of mediation depends on their experience and knowledge.

The study highlighted the importance of addressing the training of the actors who assume the role of secretaries, since the turnover for providing this service is high. Particularly, it was observed the importance of training these actors in analyzing citizen's requests and selecting the mediator according to specific criteria. The process used for the development of the game is depicted in Fig. 4.

---

[6] http://www.tjrj.jus.br/web/guest/institucional/mediacao/cejusc.

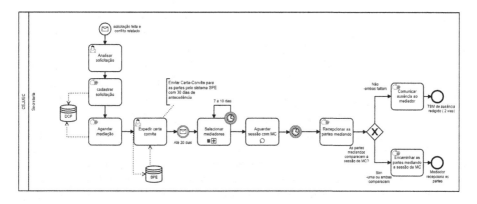

Fig. 4. Mediator selection process

The game puts the player in the role of the secretary who receives different conflict resolution requests and need to perform all the activities to select the appropriate mediators and to schedule a conflict resolution session with all the involved parties (Fig. 5).

Fig. 5. Mediator selection

The design of business process-based digital games for understanding organizations comprises a set of challenges: **Methodology:** Improvements on methodologies for building games to explain and understand organizational complexity are mostly welcome. Play Your Process is just one proposal, grounded on the assumption that organizations benefit form business process management approaches [27]. Another approach is the proposal of how to systematize business process-based interactive narratives, showing business process models as games in interactive fiction style [29]. **Evaluation:** Digital games evaluation is an important matter in the game research community. The evaluation of the kind of games we propose in this challenge is still an open research issue. The question is how to objectively evaluate if the organizational context is correctly represented in the game, if the players were able to learn and if their learning impacts the organization performance and changes social and work relations. **Supporting tools:** Designing the games proposed herein requires and brings many opportunities for the development of design supporting tools: game modeling, automatic translation of organizational models to game elements [17], narrative design tools [29], new game design documents and even specific game engines [43]. **Continuous change:** Organizations change continuously and fast, pressured by market competitiveness or innovation. Game design is a time consuming task what may hamper continuous delivery of new versions of the game whenever the organizational process change. It is important to think about approaches to keep the game design frequently updated upon organizational change. **Game design viability:** organizations can model a business process in several levels of complexity. Depending on the process model complexity, designing a game based on PYP can be an arduous task. Thus, it is essential to discuss the viability of this approach. To what extent it is valid, and to what it is not.

4.2   Digital Games, Open Data and Accountability

Information transparency is a determinant factor in building democratic environments. Its definition relates to information availability truthfully and straightforwardly and allows society to audit for governmental acts. Usually, information transparency relies on the relation between the information publicity of governmental actions and the society's role in supervising the public actors [75].

In Brazil, some laws aim to increase public transparency. The Information Access Law[7] allowed society to access public accounts, see the personal spending of public actors, follow the government's public works, and enable citizens to supervise governmental actions. Although this law aims to publicize governmental data, not even the information is simple. The governmental institutions deliver raw data (tables, texts, and others), and outside people (usually ordinary citizens) can not understand them [35].

In terms of game design, transparency information can be helpful to build games as informational tools that help society to people supervise the public spending. By playing these games, citizens could know that public money is applied, investigate irregularities, and complain to regulatory institutions. All of those actions performed inside a virtual world [65].

Therefore, we can summarize this **challenge: how can we use open and public data to design digital games that support information transparency and accountability?**

To illustrate the idea, let's imagine the scenario that a public institution publishes all data about maintenance in the city's streets (resurfacing, illumination, sewer treatment, and others). In this context, just data availability is insufficient for the society to supervise if the work is or was concluded because usually, they do not know the origin, the validity, or the meaning of the data.

---

[7] http://www.planalto.gov.br/ccivil_03/_ato2011-2014/2011/lei/l12527.htm.

In this sense, we can bring this context to digital games. Using open data on game elements, we can give transparency to the public information and provide social accountability in a gameful environment.

Recent research is looking into how to design games for transparency and fight against corruption. In its findings, the study found levels to develop games to support information transparency: **Reflection games:** the main objective of these games is to provide simple forms to present open data and enable people to understand, think, and reach their conclusions about the information. **Games for behavior changing:** these kinds of games focus on persuasive concepts to present public data and call the attention of citizens to harmful situations, trying to change the people's minds about how to do the right thing. **Whistleblower Games:** these games encompass the highest level of support for information transparency. At this level, we can provide methods that allow players to analyze public and real situations and complaints with regulatory bodies. This process helps social accountability, making society the supervisor of governmental actions.

Each level has different challenge complexity. The main challenge is to make the open and public data more comprehensive for people in the first one. In the second one, the challenge relies on changing people's behavior through the game information. And in the last one, the main challenge is to make people denounce situations such as corruption or lousy use of public resources to regulatory agencies. This last one still involves the challenge of raising awareness of the regulatory agencies to consider the game denounces as serious complaints and investigate them.

4.3   Values in Games for an Open World

If we desire the design of games for mediating social and work interactions within or outside organizations, values are a fundamental issue. Technology, as a human-made artifact and used by humans, has the potential of becoming imbued with human beliefs, values and attitudes. Technology can be interpreted and adopted by humans differently from how it has been designed as much as it has the potential to change human behavior [50].

The challenge here is **how to design values in digital games mediating social and work relations**. As discussed previously in this chapter, designing values comprise i) the existence of a set of relevant values to start with, ii) a multi perspective debate on what values are important to a specific design, and iii) a method to implement these values in the game. We motivate the Brazilian research community to work on these three aspects, regarding different domain, business and social contexts.

Take, for instance, the case of public organizations in Brazil. Jansen et al [20] developed a set of artifacts to cope with how to design values in business process-based serious games for Brazilian public services. They developed a card deck named VAPBr[8] (Fig. 6), containing specific values for public services based

---

[8] VAPBr: https://ciberdem.mack.com.br/wp-content/uploads/2020/03/VAPBr-Cart as-e-Regras-Ciberdem-1.pdf.

on Brazilian legal documents and national guidelines for public service delivery, searching for explicit or implicit values in Brazilian democratic culture and practice. The Brazilian Federal Constitution[9] (BFC), the country's main democracy letter and the Federal Government's Digital Governance Strategy[10] (DGS) were the main references for building VAPBr card deck. The same authors suggested the use of narratives as a way to introduce values in these games [40]. They propose the PYP-VBr[11], a method for discussing and selecting relevant games for public processes-based digital games using VAPBr and for implementing theses values using narratives, particularly those narrative styles attached to the Brazilian culture.

Fig. 6. VAPBr cards examples (in Portuguese)

What different sets of values should be proposed by the research community as tools for designing games in specific work and/or social contexts? What different alternatives for designing these values could be applied to build games as mediating platforms in these contexts?

4.4   The Paradox of Games

In spite of the fact that we do believe that games can change work and social relations and bring fun, pleasure, collaboration and learning to our lives, we would be very naive to assume that games have only a positive side. As discussed by different authors [47,50], technology brings no neutrality in its inception and will be interpreted by humans and probably differently used from what had been imagined for its purpose. Digital games are not different on this matter. There

---

[9] Brazilian Federal Constitution: http://www.planalto.gov.br.
[10] Federal Government's Digital Governance Strategy: https://www.gov.br/.
[11] PYP-VBr: https://ciberdem.mack.com.br/index.php/metodos/.

is a lot of debate on how games may be agents of violence and prejudice as well as blamed for damage to health, emotions and social life.

It is also worth to discuss how humans can change technology use according to their needs, desires and expectations. Take, for example, the population of China being submitted to a social credit system based on gamification concepts [41] and the human potential to "play" and trick with technology [56].

We strongly suggest our research community to adopt system thinking, sociotechnical approaches and multidisciplinarity as key to the future of game design research, amplifying the scope of our research to go beyond the technical side of game design [6, 23].

In this sense, we do not know yet to what extent games will be able to improve people and organizations' relationships. Approaches, metrics and methodologies for this purpose are still unknown. Therefore, we understand that assessing the impact of games in this context is part of the challenge for which we invite the research community to join with us.

5   Progress Assessment

The assessment of the challenges progress is possible through covering research initiatives, programs, projects and their outcomes in the research community. First of all, it is crucial to motivate and follow the sound adoption of theories and research methods to cope with the sociotechnical nature of the research in games as mediating platforms for work and social life. Another important aspect is to observe the results on development and evaluation of games in different organizational contexts. We could also monitor research indicators related to the use of games in complex contexts (ex. number of scientific publications in conferences and journals); results on technological diffusion (ex. intellectual property and technological artifacts); projects and initiatives related to games for complex contexts (ex. funding, number of projects, non-profit initiatives, academic courses, events etc.). Additionally, it is important to motivate innovation, consulting and technology transfer projects between universities and industry on the theme. Moreover, we understand that monitoring proposals from the game industry, governmental organizations, and society is necessary. New business opportunities involving complex contexts can arise from the "social entrepreneur" approaches, even games created by citizens or external clients.

6   Conclusion

This chapter presents challenges addressed to the scientific game community to reflect upon, understand, model, design, play and study the adoption of games to promote the gamification of our actions in a open, interactive, and digital world. Our motivation comes form the growth of game research in different fields, such as education, health, culture, industry, society, etc. We also experienced the arising and growth of a "game culture" from mobile devices, wearables, and e-sports.

When we treat the challenges proposed in this chapter, we will be attempting to use the potential of digital games as social interaction platforms, probably improving communication, organizational transparency, accountability, interchange of experience among people and innovations in distinct contexts. The design of these games can translate the bureaucratic contexts, which are sometimes incomprehensible, into a more playful language. It may have the potential to improve satisfaction while people better understand and interact the context they are in.

We invite the Brazilian research community to join us in this effort and to walk closer to MacGonigal's ideas: we could change the world through games once they bring us to the most powerful state of knowledge building, our act of play.

Acknowledgements. This work was partially supported by the Brazilian National Research Council (CNPq), under the grant number #313210/2019-5, and by the MackPesquisa support fund. Additionally, this work was supported by the State of Rio de Janeiro Research Support Foundation (FAPERJ) under the grant number E-26/010.002459/2019.

References

1. Abt, C.C.: Serious Games. University Press of America (1987)
2. Alves, E.S.: Jogos Sérios para Ensino de Engenharia de Software. Master's thesis, Faculdade de Engenharia da Universidade do Porto, Portugal (2018). https://repositorio-aberto.up.pt/bitstream/10216/68502/2/27255.pdf
3. Andrade, V.C.G., Araujo, R., de Classe, T.M.: Jogos digitais e serviços públicos: um levantamento. RelaTe-DIA **11**(1), 1–20 (2018)
4. Antle, A.N., Tanenbaum, T.J., Macaranas, A., Robinson, J.: Games for change: looking at models of persuasion through the lens of design. In: Nijholt, A. (ed.) Playful User Interfaces. GMSE, pp. 163–184. Springer, Singapore (2014). https://doi.org/10.1007/978-981-4560-96-2_8
5. Araujo, R.M.: Sistemas de informação para a ciberdemocracia. In: Humanidades Digitais e o Mundo Lusófono, pp. 249–266. Editora FGV (2021)
6. Araujo, R., Fornazin, M., Pimentel, M.: Uma análise sobre a produção de conhecimento científico nas pesquisas publicadas nos primeiros 10 anos da isys (2008–2017). iSys-Braz. J. Inf. Syst. **10**(4), 45–65 (2017)
7. Araujo, R., Taher, Y., Heuvel, W.J.V.D., Cappelli, C.: Evolving government-citizen ties in public service design and delivery. In: Electronic Government and Electronic Participation-Joint Proceedings of Ongoing Research of IFIP EGOV and IFIP ePart 2013 (2013)
8. de Araujo, R.M.: Information systems and the open world challenges. In: Boscarioli, C., Araujo, R.M., Maciel, R.S.P. (eds.) I GranDSI-BR - Grand Research Challenges in Information Systems in Brazil 2016–2026, chap. 4, pp. 42–51. Special Committee on Information Systems (CE-SI). Brazilian Computer Society (SBC), Porto Alegre (2017)
9. Bateman, C., Boon, R.: 21st Century Game Design (Game Development Series). Charles River Media, Inc. (2005)

10. Bellotti, F., Kapralos, B., Lee, K., Moreno-Ger, P., Berta, R.: Assessment in and of serious games: an overview. Adv. Hum.-Comput. Interact. **2013**, 1 (2013)
11. Belman, J., Nissenbaum, H., Flanagan, M., Diamond, J.: Grow-a-game: a tool for values conscious design and analysis of digital games. In: DiGRA Conference, vol. 6, pp. 1–15 (2011)
12. Bertalanffy, L.: Teoria Geral de Sistemas. Editora Vozes (2008)
13. Boscarioli, C., Araujo, R.M., Maciel, R.S.P.: I GranDSI-BR - grand research challenges in information systems in Brazil 2016–2026. Special Committee on Information Systems (CE-SI). Brazilian Computer Society (SBC), Porto Alegre (2017)
14. Brasil: Estratégia brasileira para a transformação digital. Technical report, Ministério da Ciência, Tecnologia, Inovações e Comunicações (2018). http://www.mctic.gov.br/mctic/export/sites/institucional/estrategiadigital.pdf. Accessed 3 Aug 2020
15. Chaui, M.: Cultura e Democracia. Secretaria de Cultura do Estado da Bahia (2012)
16. Classe, T., Araujo, R., Xexeo, G.: Desaparecidos rj-um jogo digital para o entendimento de processos de prestação de serviços públicos. In: XVI Simpósio Brasileiro de Jogos e Entretenimento Digital (SBGames 2017). Curitiba (2017)
17. Classe, T., Araujo, R.M., Xexéo, G.B.: Process model game design: uma ferramenta para apoio a sistematização de design de jogos digitais baseados em processos de negócio. English title: Process Model Game Design: A Tool to Support the Systematization of Digital Games Based on Business Process). In: XVII Simpósio Brasileiro de Jogos e Entretenimento Digital (SBGames 2018) (2018)
18. de Classe, T.M., Araujo, R., Xexéo, G.: Jogos digitais baseados em processos de negócio. Simpósio Brasileiro de Jogos e Entretenimento Digital. SBGAMES (2019)
19. de Classe, T.M., de Araujo, R.M., Xexéo, G.B.: Construção de jogos digitais sérios para processos de serviços públicos. Sociedade Brasileira de Computação (2018)
20. de Classe, T.M., Janssen, F., Araujo, R.: VAPBr: values in digital games for public service in Brazil. Int. J. Serious Games **8**(4), 25–48 (2021)
21. Classe, T.M., et al.: Jogos para os cidadãos. J. Eletrôn. Fac. Vianna Júnior **10**(1), 16 (2018)
22. Classe, T.M.D., De Araujo, R.M., Xexéo, G.B., Siqueira, S.: He play your process method for business process-based digital game design. Int. J. Serious Games **6**(1), 27–48 (2019)
23. Connolly, R.: Why computing belongs within the social sciences. Commun. ACM **63**(8), 54–59 (2020)
24. Darzentas, D.P., Urquhart, L.: Interdisciplinary reflections on games and human values. In: Proceedings of the 2015 Annual Symposium on Computer-Human Interaction in Play, pp. 805–810 (2015)
25. De Classe, T.M., De Araujo, R.M., Xexéo, G.B., Siqueira, S.: The play your process method for business process-based digital game design. Int. J. Serious Games **6**(1), 27–48 (2019)
26. De Classe, T.M., De Araujo, R.M., Xexéo, G.B., Siqueira, S.W.M.: Public processes are open for play. Digit. Gov.: Res. Pract. **2**(4) (2021). https://doi.org/10.1145/3474879
27. Dumas, M., La Rosa, M., Mendling, J., Reijers, H.A.: Business Process Management. Springer, Heidelberg (2013)
28. Escola, E.B.: Videogames violentos não criam assassinos. Brasil Escola (2020). https://brasilescola.uol.com.br/sociologia/videogames-violentos-nao-criam-assassinos.htm. Accessed 10 Aug 2020

29. Ferreira, M., Classe, T.: Design de narrativas para jogos digitais baseados em processos de negócio. In: Anais Estendidos do XVII Simpósio Brasileiro de Sistemas de Informação, pp. 73–77. SBC, Porto Alegre (2021). https://doi.org/10.5753/sbsi. 2021.15359, https://sol.sbc.org.br/index.php/sbsi_estendido/article/view/15359

30. Fisher, J.: Digital games for international development: a field theory perspective. Int. Commun. Gaz. **81**(6–8), 707–726 (2019)

31. Flanagan, M.: Making games for social change. AI Soc. **20**(4), 493–505 (2006)

32. Flanagan, M., Howe, D.C., Nissenbaum, H.: Embodying values in technology: theory and practice. In: Van den Hoven, J., Weckert, J. (eds.) Information Technology and Moral Philosophy, pp. 322–353. Cambridge University Press, Cambridge (2008). https://doi.org/10.1017/CBO9780511498725.017

33. Fu, F.L., Su, R.C., Yu, S.C.: EGameFlow: a scale to measure learners enjoyment of e-learning games. Comput. Educ. **52**(1), 101–112 (2009)

34. Fullerton, T.: Game Design Workshop: A Playcentric Approach to Creating Innovative Games. CRC Press, Boca Raton (2014)

35. Gomes, W., Amorim, P.K.D.F., Almada, M.P.: Novos desafios para a ideia de transparência pública. E-Compós **21**(2), 1–21 (2018)

36. Hessen, J.: Filosofia dos valores. Rev. Portuguesa Filosofia (1945)

37. Horn, M.S.: Beyond video games for social change. Interactions **21**(2), 66–68 (2014). https://doi.org/10.1145/2568372

38. Huizinga, J.: Homo ludens. Editora Perspectiva SA (2020)

39. Jacobs, R.S.: Serious games: play for change. In: The Video Game Debate 2, pp. 19–40. Routledge (2020)

40. Janssen, F., Pimentel, M., Araujo, R.: Valores em jogos baseados em processos de prestação de serviços públicos para cidadãos brasileiros. In: Simpósio Brasileiro de Jogos e Entretenimento Digital (SBGames). SBC (2019)

41. Jones, K.: The game of life: visualizing Chinas social credit system (2019). https://www.visualcapitalist.com/the-game-of-life-visualizing-chinas-social-credit-system/. Accessed 20 Apr 2022

42. Kelly, H., et al.: How to build serious games. Commun. ACM **50**(7), 44–49 (2007). https://doi.org/10.1145/1272516.1272538

43. Keshi, F.: Engine de construção de jogos baseados em processos de negócio. Trabalho de Conclusão de Curso (Graduação em Ciência da Computação) - Universidade Presbiteriana Mackenzie (2020)

44. Kheirandish, S., Funk, M., Wensveen, S., Verkerk, M., Rautterbergh, M.: A comprehensive value framework for design. Technol. Soc. **62**, 101302 (2020). https://doi.org/10.1016/j.techsoc.2020.1013022

45. Kheirandish, S., Rauterberg, M.: Human value based game design. In: 2018 2nd National and 1st International Digital Games Research Conference: Trends, Technologies, and Applications (DGRC), pp. 6–16. IEEE (2018). https://doi.org/10.1109/DGRC.2018.8712077

46. Koster, R.: Theory of Fun for Game Design. O'Reilly Media, Inc. (2013)

47. Lang, K.R., Jarvenpaa, S.: Managing the paradoxes of mobile technology. Inf. Syst. Manag. **22**(4), 7–23 (2005)

48. Leitão, T.M., Navarro, L.L.L., Cameira, R.F., Silva, E.R.: Serious games in business process management: a systematic literature review. Bus. Process Manag. J. **27**, 685–721 (2021)

49. Lemos, A., Lévy, P.: O futuro da internet: em direção a uma ciberdemocracia planetária. Paulus 13, São Paulo (2010)

50. Lévy, P.: tecnologias da inteligência, As. Editora 34 (1993)

51. Lopes, T.N., Araujo, R.: Jogos baseados em processos de negócio: aplicação no treinamento de processos de negócio. In: Anais Estendidos do XVII Simpósio Brasileiro de Sistemas de Informação, pp. 83–87. SBC (2021)
52. Lopes, T.N., Araujo, R.: Um mapeamento sistemático da literatura sobre aplicação de jogos digitais no treinamento de processos organizacionais. iSys-Braz. J. Inf. Syst. **14**(2), 96–125 (2021)
53. Mangeli, E., et al.: Games with purpose development methodology by ludology laboratory. In: Developments in Business Simulation and Experiential Learning: Proceedings of the Annual ABSEL conference, vol. 49 (2022)
54. McGonigal, J.: Reality is Broken: Why Games Make Us Better and How They Can Change the World. Penguin (2011)
55. Michael, D.R., Chen, S.L.: Serious Games: Games that Educate, Train, and Inform. Muska & Lipman/Premier-Trade (2005)
56. News: Berlin artist uses handcart full of smartphones to trick google maps' traffic algorithm into thinking there is traffic jam (2020). https://www.abc.net.au/news/2020-02-04/man-creates-fake-traffic-jam-on-google-maps-by-carting-99-phones/11929136. Accessed 20 Apr 2022
57. Newzoo, B.: Global games market report 2019. Amsterdam: gamesindustry.com (2019). https://newzoo.com/insights/trend-reports/. Accessed 3 Aug 2020
58. ONU: Conheça os novos 17 objetivos de desenvolvimento sustentável da onu. Nações Unidas Brasil (2020). https://nacoesunidas.org/conheca-os-novos-17-objetivos-de-desenvolvimento-sustentavel-da-onu/. Accessed 10 Aug 2020
59. Organization, W.H.: International classification of diseases (2019). https://www.who.int/standards/classifications/classification-of-diseases. Accessed 13 Apr 2020
60. Paschali, M.E., Bafatakis, N., Ampatzoglou, A., Chatzigeorgiou, A., Stamelos, I.: Tool-assisted game scenario representation through flow charts. In: ENASE, pp. 223–232 (2018)
61. Petri, G., von Wangenheim, C.G., Borgatto, A.F.: MEEGA+: an evolution of a model for the evaluation of educational games. INCoD/GQS **3**, 1–40 (2016)
62. Petridis, P., et al.: State of the art in business games. Int. J. Serious Games **2**(1), 55–69 (2015)
63. Pflanzl, N., Classe, T., Araujo, R., Vossen, G.: Designing serious games for citizen engagement in public service processes. In: Dumas, M., Fantinato, M. (eds.) BPM 2016. LNBIP, vol. 281, pp. 180–191. Springer, Cham (2017). https://doi.org/10.1007/978-3-319-58457-7_14
64. Raftopoulos, M.: Playful card-based tools for gamification design. In: Proceedings of the Annual Meeting of the Australian Special Interest Group for Computer Human Interaction, pp. 109–113 (2015). https://doi.org/10.1145/2838739.2838797
65. Rangel, J.A., Emer, M.C.F.P., Neto, A.G.S.S.: Jogo serio como facilitador de denúncias e detecção de fraudes em Órgãos públicos governamentais. Simpósio Brasileiro de Jogos e Entretenimento Digital (SBGames) (2017)
66. Rhoden, C.: Tarja branca-a revolução que faltava. documentary. Maria farinha filmes, São Paulo (2014). https://mff.com.br/films/tarja-branca/. Accessed 27 June 2022
67. Rocha, R.V.D., Araujo, R.B.D.: Metodologia de design de jogos sérios para treinamento: ciclo de vida de criação, desenvolvimento e produção. In: XII Simpósio Brasileiro de Jogos e Entretenimento Digital (SBGames 2013), pp. 1–10 (2013)
68. Rogers, D.: Digital Transformation. Practical Guide. Publishing Group Tochka, Moscow (2017)
69. Rogers, S.: Level Up! The Guide to Great Video Game Design. Wiley, Hoboken (2014)

70. Rokeach, M.: The Nature of Human Values. Free Press (1973)
71. Romero, M., Usart, M., Ott, M.: Can serious games contribute to developing and sustaining 21st century skills? Games Cult. **10**(2), 148–177 (2015)
72. Rosenfield, D.L.: O que é democracia. Brasiliense (2017)
73. Sakuda, L.O., Fortim, I.: 2° censo da indústria brasileira de jogos digitais. AbraGames. Ministério da Cultura, Brasília (2018)
74. Salen, K., Zimmerman, E.: Rules of Play: Game Design Fundamentals. MIT Press, Cambridge (2003)
75. Santos Leite, B.M., Nishijima, M., Sarti, F.M., Chaim, M.L.: An analysis of the SICLOM information system employing misuse case diagrams. Health Policy Technol. **10**(4), 100576 (2021)
76. Schell, J.: The Art of Game Design: A Book of Lenses. AK Peters/CRC Press (2019)
77. Schwartz, S.H., Bilsky, W.: Toward a universal psychological structure of human values. J. Pers. Soc. Psychol. **53**(3), 550 (1987). https://doi.org/10.1037/0022-3514.53.3.550
78. Shirky, C.: Here Comes Everybody: The Power of Organizing Without Organizations. Penguin (2008)
79. Silva, T.G., Lopes, T.N., Araujo, R.: Mediador game: um jogo baseado em processo de negócio para treinamento organizacional. In: Anais Estendidos do XVII Simpósio Brasileiro de Sistemas de Informação, pp. 29–32. SBC (2021)
80. Simon, H.: Les sciences de l'artificiel. Folio Essais (2004)
81. Siriaraya, P., Visch, V., Vermeeren, A., Bas, M.: A cookbook method for persuasive game design. Int. J. Serious Games **5**(1), 37–71 (2018)
82. Taylor, E.W.: Transformative learning theory. In: Transformative Learning Meets Bildung, pp. 17–29. Brill Sense (2017)
83. Thiel, S.K., Reisinger, M., Röderer, K., Fröhlich, P.: Playing (with) democracy: a review of gamified participation approaches. JeDEM-eJ. eDemocr. Open Govern. **8**(3), 32–60 (2016)
84. Wiener, N.: Cybernetics: Or Control and Communication in the Animal and the Machine. MIT Press, Cambridge (1948)
85. Winn, B.M.: The design, play, and experience framework. In: Handbook of Research on Effective Electronic Gaming in Education, pp. 1010–1024. IGI Global (2009)

Balancing Game Elements, Learning, and Emotions in Game Design

Gabriel C. Natucci[✉] and Marcos A. F. Borges

School of Technology, University of Campinas,
Pascoal Marmo St., 1888, Limeira, SP, Brazil
g091247@dac.unicamp.br, marcosborges@unicamp.br

Abstract. Games have been shown to be an effective method for various purposes, from pure entertainment to fostering learning outcomes through serious and game-based learning approaches. However, the design of games is not an easy feat, regardless of whether they are focused on emotional outcomes or learning. There are many components that must be considered during game design, such as pedagogical theories, game elements, player experience, as well as cognitive-affective and sociocultural foundations. The balance of such components is one of the greatest challenges designers, researchers and educators must face in the next few years, especially considering that some of these components and their interactions have been neglected in research until recently, such as the importance of emotions in learning and their temporal influence in moderating player experiences. In the context of serious games, where learning and/or non-entertainment goals are as important as the entertainment itself, addressing this challenge is even more difficult. This work outlines and discusses the complexities of this balancing challenge, suggesting research opportunities related to new design tools and methods that consider all aspects enumerated above.

Keywords: Game design · Emotional design · Player experience · Game-based learning · Serious games · Games user research · Human-computer interaction

1 Introduction

The use and development of games for educational purposes is getting increasing research attention in the last decade, with positive attitudes and high acceptance from both scholars and students regarding game-assisted learning [104]. Typically games and their elements in learning can take three distinct forms: i) using game elements and techniques in non-gaming environments, a practice known as gamification [21]; ii) the development of games whose purpose is other than just entertainment, known as Serious Games (SG) [19]; and iii) the redesign of a pedagogical activity through the use of serious or entertainment games, a practice known as Game-based learning (GBL) [71].

© The Author(s), under exclusive license to Springer Nature Switzerland AG 2023
R. P. d. Santos and M. d. S. Hounsell (Eds.): GranDGamesBR 2020/2021, CCIS 1702, pp. 89–112, 2023.
https://doi.org/10.1007/978-3-031-27639-2_5

Particularly, SGs and their use in GBL practices have been associated with several learning and cognitive benefits in the literature, like increasing knowledge acquisition and learner's engagement [10,89]. Even 21st-century skills such as problem-solving and creativity have been positively improved with SGs and GBL [40,76]. SGs and GBL also have been shown to be at least equal to traditional instructional approaches [44] or even more effective [89,102].

Regardless of their effectiveness in learning, SGs and GBL are still far from being fully understood. The exact causal relationship between specific game elements (e. g. mechanics, aesthetics) and their impact on player behavior and learning is yet to be determined. Current methods and tools in game design still lack a proper integration with pedagogical approaches [44,104]. In a systematic review of SGs and GBL, Wu et al. [103] shows that in over 658 studies, only 91 presented an underlying pedagogical theory (less than 13.68%). Similarly, in a systematic review conducted by Bakan and Bakan [6], 90 of a total of 190 studies presented a pedagogical theory explicitly. Furthermore, the majority of studies in game design struggle to provide generalizable results that can shed light on SGs/GBL and their impact on players, focusing on single games rather than general game elements [10].

This lack of generalization can be explained by the inherent complexity of studying and designing games. Even the concept and definition of what constitutes a game and its underlying elements is still a topic of debate. In this context, a game element can be broadly defined as a cornerstone component of a game, related to its mechanics (e. g. rules, progression, randomness), aesthetics (e. g. art style, sounds, user interface) and narrative (e. g. story, characters, quests) [77]. These elements can either interact, define or mediate several game foundations related to the player experience, such as affect (i. e. emotions), engagement, motivation, cognition, and social/cultural foundations [71]. Both game elements and foundations can interact with one another, increasing their complexity. For instance, engagement itself is a rather multifaceted element, comprised also of cognitive and affective foundations [36]. Affect in general has also been shown to have great influence in learning contexts where achievement matters [66], as well as influencing engagement, motivation and cognition [36,48,73].

Furthermore, the design of SGs and GBL requires the right balance between hedonic (i. e. game elements, affective foundations, motivation, engagement) and utilitarian (i. e. learning and pedagogy) aspects [30]. However, achieving this balance is also hard, making it even more difficult to understand the full impact of SGs and GBL and creating challenges for educators and industry game designers. According to a Delphi focus group study involving game design researchers, some of the greatest challenges educators face are transferring pedagogical theories into game elements as well as creating game challenges that are motivational and not explicitly didactic [17]. Similarly, Theodosiou and Karasavvidis [94] conducted a case study with 95 teachers acting as game designers in an undergraduate game design course, mapping their challenges and problems when developing SGs. One of the major findings was that pedagogical theories were not easily transferable into the game design practice, with teachers struggling to use basic game elements and combining them into useful experiences [94].

Considering the complexity of designing games in general, these problems are not unique to educators, scholars and GBL/SGs approaches. According to an extensive gray literature review in the game design industry conducted by Politowski et al. [75], developers still struggle with game design complexity, scope, vision as well as the fun (i. e. affective) aspects of games, even though game-design-related problems have been diminishing in recent years. While these problems are somewhat similar, there is still a disconnection between academic and industry game design practices [27,64] which further increases the complexity of fully understanding games in terms of their impact and overall generalizability of findings. According to Greenwood et al. [27], academics need to learn more about industry practices and vice-versa. Research should also be proposed in a collaborative and action-oriented/empirical basis, bringing together industry partners, opinions and limitations. This scenario leads to the understanding that not only a formal mapping between game elements and their foundations is lacking, but because of that educators and designers fail to create and propose effective game experiences in order to achieve their goals, whether it is an entertainment or educational one. Inspired by this scenario, this work will simply refer to game or General Game (GG) as an umbrella term for SGs, games utilized in GBL practices and commercial/entertainment games, keeping in mind that all these game classes present affective and learning outcomes.

Hence, the main challenge proposed in this work is knowing *how to design high-quality GGs in an easy and intuitive manner, considering the relationship between game elements and foundations while being effective in achieving their goals, especially in terms of learning or emotional outcomes.* It is important to notice that this challenge is not exclusive to SGs and GBL practices but also related to purely entertainment games, since they also must balance their learning outcomes (related to the game rules and player expertise) and emotional outcomes (the "fun" aspect of the game). Rather than a specific role or fixed process, design here follows Schell [83] definition, being considered as an umbrella term for any activity that is related to creating and modifying games, including brainstorming phases, tests with players, and active technical development. Similar challenges and aspects of this problem have already been proposed in the literature, like the exploratory survey of SGs design conducted by Dimitriadou et al. [22]. However, these proposals tend to favor one facet of the problem (e. g. learning) and/or a particular role (e. g. educators) rather than tackling it in an integrated manner. The challenge proposed in this work differentiates from such studies by stating that not only hedonic and utilitarian aspects of games should be considered equally but, given the multidisciplinary nature of this challenge, such aspects must be tackled by professionals from different backgrounds, from artists and game designers to psychologists and educators. To address this challenge, discuss its details and proposed actions aimed at solving it, this work is divided as follows: Sect. 2 further details the proposed challenge and its implications in research; Sect. 3 discuss some game design definitions and reviews recent academic studies involving game foundations, especially affective and sociocultural ones; Sect. 4 proposes a research agenda and actions for the next decade, tackling the proposed challenge through various different perspectives. Section 5 concludes this chapter with final remarks, potential issues and additional opportunities related to the proposed challenge.

2   The Challenge

In order to effectively address the challenge of creating high-quality games with a full understanding of its foundations and elements it is necessary to integrate several definitions and even conflicting views about each one of the terms related to it. Even this process in itself presents a very serious problem since several definitions have been proposed to what constitutes a game, what is a high-quality game, and what constitutes a game element. Aggregated definitions, such as a combination of game elements that could be used to classify a particular game in a game genre (e. g. puzzle, action), are also a topic of debate [18].

Games can be defined from several perspectives, from philosophical to sociocultural. Huizinga [37] defines a game "as a non-serious, free, voluntary activity consciously taken outside the boundaries of the "real world" and defined by its own space, time, and rules"; Callois [13] separates the ludic concept of play structured by rules and goal (*ludus*) from the free-form, expressive and more unstructured form of play (*paidia*). Similarly, Klabbers [42] defines games as forms of play, where its rules and resources define three classes of games: rule-based, where the rules are not questioned, only followed; principle-based, where rules exist but the actors involved (e. g. players) have the freedom to interpret them; and free-form games, where "only a few ground rules or "rules of nature" exist, such as the time of the beginning, the stop rule, the role of the facilitator, and the location in which the game takes place" [42]. Mayra [53] proposes an interesting definition by stating that games are interactive cultural systems, with "a specific emphasis on meaning-making through playful action (*ludosis*), as contrasted with meaning-making as decoding of messages or media representations (*semiosis*)" [53]. Stenros [90] takes a different approach and identify 10 topics of discussion about games in research by reviewing over 60 game definitions from various schools of thought. These topics are: rules, purpose and function, activity vs. artifact nature, the boundary with reality, the role of the player, the outcomes of a game, competition and conflict, goals and end state, structural coherence, game definition boundaries (i. e. what is not a game) [90].

However accurate, these definitions are used to either describe a comprehensive taxonomy for studying the subject or to provide a more practical perspective and aid designers in creating new games [90]. This work takes the latter approach to describe the proposed challenge, and based on authors' previous works and on widely known game definitions [39,82,83] defines a game as a *"system focused on affective outcomes in which players engage in a learning challenge designed to overcome a problem, with a playful attitude"* [61]. This definition is inspired by the notion that every game has an implicit learning goal: to understand and master its rules and dynamics, with tools provided by the game mechanics. Gee [26], a prominent researcher of games and education, shares a similar view by stating that good games have inherent properties that make them suitable for educational purposes [26], being even considered as distributed learning systems [25]. What differentiates SGs and GBL practices from traditional games is that the former have additional learning goals. One could argue against this definition by stating that in SGs and GBL the learning goals take precedence and are more important than the emotional outcomes. However, in line with recent studies associating the important role of emotions in learning (e. g. [14, 47, 48]), we state that the role of affective outcomes is as important as the learning outcomes in games, regardless their intended purpose. Therefore, both players' emotions and learning should be equally considered during game design. Inspired by the perspective of GGs, high-quality games related to the challenge are defined simply as a GG that implements and effectively produces emotional and learning outcomes as an integral part of the player experience. To that end, several characteristics of high-quality games have been proposed in the literature either through models, empirical reviews or design guidelines. Based on a series of game industry development reports (*postmortems*), Ullmann et al. [96] describe several environmental and design factors that lead to high-quality games, such as team size, marketing and production aspects. Finally, works such as Desurvire and Wiberg [20] propose a series of heuristics/game design principles that leads to high-quality games. For the challenge proposed in this study, we abstain from benefiting from one view over another in terms of what defines a high-quality game. Rather, a formal definition and discussion involving multiple perspectives in order to precisely define this quality is also a fundamental part of the challenge.

Similarly, even the broad concept of a game element, defined here as a cornerstone component of a game and related primarily to its mechanics, aesthetics and narrative, should also be further discussed and detailed considering both industry and academic perspectives. While some game elements may seem straightforward, their definition has yet to be integrated into the design and research vocabulary. Elements such as core mechanics, as well concept of game loop, which is a relatively known concept in the game design practice [87], have yet to make their way as an analytical framework for researchers to frame their projects (and games) on so that a common language is drawn for cross-disciplinary studies and to improve the communication between educators, researchers and game design practitioners.

Hence, even the challenge proposition must involve further discussion, definition and integration of concepts that are utilized and proposed in industry and academia. Therefore to tackle this massive challenge of creating high-quality GGs and mapping the nature and relationship of their elements and foundations, this work suggests an integration of various research topics, summarized as follows:

i) Establish the relationship between specific game elements with learning theories;

ii) Understand the connection between affect, cognition, motivation and socio-cultural foundations in games, and how they influence both player's experience and learning;

iii) Create intuitive and effective tools, models and frameworks for designing and assessing GGs, based on both empirical practices/industry standards in game design and academic research, that can be used by educators and designers with various backgrounds.

These research topics relate directly with the steps aimed at answering questions like: "*Which game genre is better suited for fostering a specific skill?*" (items *i* and *ii*); "*What emotions can we evoke in the player to aid knowledge acquisition?*" (item *ii*); "*Which game mechanic (jump, shoot, collect, etc.) a designer should employ to evoke a particular emotion?*" (item *ii*); and "*How can a designer/educator create a successful, high-quality game?*" (item *iii*). As simple as they may be, these questions have only recently begun to be even considered in research.

3   Contextualizing the Challenge

Given the huge proportions and complexity of the proposed challenge, several studies and tentative solutions have been proposed throughout the years. For each game foundation related to the challenge, there are entire fields of study and specialized scholars stemming from fields such as Psychology, Education and Design. In this context, rather than being a fully comprehensive description of each foundation, this section is focused on discussing the previously defined research topics with particular attention to cognitive-affective and sociocultural game foundations, as well as educational aspects, given the importance and novelty of these topics in research.

3.1   Games and Education

The relationship between GGs and pedagogical theories and elements is not a new topic. However, this inherent connection between learning and games has yet to be tackled effectively both in research and practice, due to several reasons. One reason that can be attributed to this complexity of connecting pedagogy and games is the clustered nature of game research itself: researchers either come from an educational-focused perspective, heavily relying on pedagogy and psychology to create SGs and GBL practices that are effective in learning outcomes but lacking in entertainment value, or they come from a more empirical-oriented nature, focused on creating entertainment experiences with games without relying extensively on validated theories from other fields (such as education or psychology). While many guidelines, patterns and games from the first type of research have been proposed in the literature, they lack further empirical support and comparison among other game design models, as well as a standardized way to measure their efficacy. In general, little is known about the acceptance and usage of this type of research by practitioners/academics other than the ones that created these guidelines. An example of those models is the RETAIN model [29]. While being extensively used for the design and evaluation of SGs, it has yet to be compared to other GGs design models in terms of intuitiveness and easy-of-use, and even with other specific SGs design models in terms of design efficacy. A common framework proposed and utilized by the second type of research, and perhaps the most widely used GGs design tool is the Mechanics, Dynamics and Aesthetics (MDA) framework. While extensively used, MDA lacks further theoretical integration with game foundations (e. g. affective, sociocultural, cognitive) and presents several limitations [99], which were used as a basis for the development and understanding of game elements and related frameworks [99,101]. MDA also lacks further comparison with alternative GG design models and practices, especially in terms of its design efficacy.

Another reason that can explain the problem in relating learning and games is the inherent complexity of game elements themselves. As an example, Plass et al. [70] define learning mechanics as design patterns or meta-mechanics that adapt the moment-to-moment activity of a game mechanic to create a meaningful learning activity, grounded on learning sciences/theories such as constructivism [103]. Being a set of meta-mechanics, learning mechanics must be instantiated and adapted into traditional game mechanics in order to be effective. They must be fully integrated as an important part of the game in order to be useful, to avoid the so-called "chocolate-covered broccoli" game design [16]. Arnab et al. [4] propose the Learning Mechanics-Game Mechanics (LM-GM) model that relates learning mechanics with their game counterparts. Some examples of learning mechanics present in LM-GM are instructional guidance, tutorials, feedback, discussions, repetition, and experimentation [4]. Plass et al. [70] describe an additional type of mechanic called assessment mechanics. Assessment mechanics are design patterns grounded on test theory and focused on learners' assessment. One example of this type of mechanic is the concept of letting the apply game rules to solve puzzles [70]. The number of rules utilized and time spend to solve a particular puzzle can inform the design about the player's learning progress. In this context, applying a simple game element such as a mechanic involves knowing a full list of available learning and assessment mechanics, their context of application and efficacy, and well as possible interactions with other game elements and foundations. Hence this inherent complexity can be drawn as a major obstacle towards integrating games and learning.

Furthermore, while works connecting game attributes with educational practices in higher education [45], games with player/learner types and behavioral traits [31,43,86], and game genres with learning styles/outcomes [41] have been proposed in the literature, they need further empirical validation and connection with other game foundations, such as affective and sociocultural ones. Particularly, future research should be oriented towards bridging educational theories, game elements involving learning (e. g. learning and assessment mechanics) and behavioral/psychological traits, such as the work proposed by Paulin et al. [65].

Research involving games and educational theories must go beyond these obstacles by providing a comprehensive view of educational factors in games, weighing entertainment and learning values equally and studying learning in games regardless of their original focus (e. g. commercial game, SG). Besides, educational game research must be expanded from the traditional pedagogical axis of instructional design, constructivism, and constructionism [2], which are historically grounded on children's education, and looking for new ways of teaching and learning to new audiences. One way of doing that is by focusing on andragogical and heutagogical schools of thought. Andragogy is a field stemmed from pedagogy, but focused on adult and self-directed education [9], while Heutagogy goes one step further and proposes full learner agency and self-determined learning, focusing on developing capabilities, lifelong learning skills, and metacognition rather than on knowledge acquisition [9]. Research involving games and these relatively new educational perspectives have started to be proposed in the literature, such as the E.M.O.T.I.O.N framework, which bridges SG design, andragogy and emotional outcomes [49]. However, in order to effectively tackle new educational demands going forward into the 21st century, it is necessary to increase the number of studies and results that shows the effect of self-directed learning and focuses on lifelong learning skill acquisition.

3.2 Emotions and Games

Research in recent years has shown that learning and performance cannot be understood through a cognitive or sociocultural perspective alone [74]. One key component missing in understanding these human phenomena is affective elements such as emotions and mood. This is particularly true in the GGs' context since player experiences are a combination of emotions, thoughts and sensations during play [46]. Emotions are essential in GGs to maintain player focus, make decisions, learn and enjoy the process of play [46].

However, the study of affect is a difficult endeavour, especially considering whether or not certain emotions are universal across cultures. Perhaps the most popular and widely known study of emotions is the one proposed by Ekman and Friesen [24], which proposes the occurrence of 6 universal emotions drawn from the analysis of facial expressions across cultures. This work is a prototypical one in describing emotions as a discrete set. Another way of understanding emotions is by considering them a set of continuous values along a predefined axis, which is particularly useful for creating computational models to understand and replicate emotions, a field known as Affective Computing [68]. One example of such dimensional perspectives on emotion is the Hourglass model, where emotions are continuously defined along four axes: Pleasantness, Attention, Sensitivity, and Aptitude [15]. Another way of understanding affective states that is being increasingly studied is through appraisal processes. An appraisal can be defined as a person's subjective evaluation and the resulting outcomes from unconscious strategies devised for coping with a particular situation [84], which will then leads to a particular emotions elicitation. These appraisal processes go beyond affective states and also take into account motivational and cognitive-behavioral factors. Following this view, Roseman [81] defines emotions as discrete syndromes characterized by five response types: phenomenological (thoughts and feelings), physiological (e. g. heart rate), expressive (manifestations in face, voice and posture), behavioral (action tendencies), and motivational (goals). Appraisals in this view guide and integrate these emotional responses [81].

Given the previous definition of game, which involves learning challenges and problem-solving, a particularly useful affective theory that can be applied to GG's context is the Control-value Theory of Achievement Emotions (CVT) [66], which describe emotions that arise in achievement activities (e. g. studying) and outcomes (success/failure). Positive-valued emotions in CVT (e. g. joy) have been linked to higher learning outcomes [14], while negative-valued emotions (e. g. anxiety) have been shown as detrimental for learning [47]. The use of CVT and similar models go beyond player outcomes in GGs, and can be utilized as a tool to design affective experiences. This emotional design process is based on a set of design features that positively impact the player's emotions in order to achieve a desired goal. Norman [62] details three levels of emotional design: reflective (cognitive thinking), behavioral, and visceral (i. e. quick reactions related to external stimuli). These emotional design principles and overall affective models have been utilized to design GGs (e. g. [5,12,85]). Particular attention has been dedicated to color and anthropomorphism [72,97] with positive results in terms of learning outcomes [11], which are linked with the visceral level of design. However, studies involving the behavioral and reflective levels remain to be carried out, as well as studies involving the impact of certain types of mechanics (e. g. jump, shoot) on players' emotional outcomes. Furthermore, emotional models such as CVT utilized as a basis to conduct such studies must also be further explored under the scope of sociocultural foundations. While CVT shows great potential at being a universal account of achievement emotions, it also presents some degree of cultural variation, especially within physiological and expressive response types [91], which could impact emotional assessments in GG involving these two responses (e. g. facial imagery, heart rate monitoring, skin conductance level).

Furthermore, the role of emotions in GGs must also be analysed from a non-achievement and purely entertainment-oriented perspective, looking for particular emotions that are simultaneously easy to evoke through emotional design principles and effective in increasing players' motivation. For instance, while anxiety in CVT is a negative-valued emotion, a GG may evoke it coupled with other emotions (such as fear) in order to create an entertaining experience related to a particular genre (e. g. horror). Hence emotional design principles must also be expanded in such a way that allows designers to create experiences that are focused on evoking a particular emotion, so that the designed GG may relate to a particular genre or attract a certain type of player.

3.3 Sociocultural Processes

Culture can be defined as a collective set of thoughts and beliefs that distinguishes members of one group from others [34]. In other words, it is a collective system of meaning [53] that depends on societal relationships to take place. Several models have been proposed to address the study of culture and its influence on behavior and decision-making. The most utilized approach in this context is the Hofstede model, which evaluates culture across six dimensions: power distance (solutions to human inequality), uncertainty avoidance (society's level of stress when faced with an unknown future), individualism/collectivism (degree in which a society is integrated into groups), masculinity/femininity (distribution of values between genders), short-term/long-term orientation (choice of focus for people's efforts: present or future), and indulgence/restraint (degree of gratification vs. control of basic desires) [34].

Cultural analysis has been utilized as a way to direct efforts and shift user perspectives towards a particular value/goal, given that culture influences what people pay attention to and what they ignore [67]. In games, the design implications of cultural values have recently begun to be explored. Meershoek et al. [54] proposed the Culture-driven Game Design Method (CDGDM), which relates player cultural values with game elements. Ratan et al. [78] explored the cross-cultural gaming motivations of Singaporean, German, and American players. Similarly, Bialas et al. [7] evaluated player styles by comparing cultures from 8 different countries. Jossan et al. [38] studied the acceptability of GBL practices according to cultural dimensions, indicating differences in Eastern and Western cultural affinities regarding this practice.

However, the sociocultural foundations of GGs invite further investigation. Several issues remain open regarding this direction: i) while the number of studies relating culture and GGs is increasing, cross-cultural comparisons remain dominant in developed countries. Studies focused on developing countries such as the ones located in Latin America (e. g. [100]) and Africa have yet to be conducted in a more expressive manner; ii) most studies proposed in the literature, such as the ones previously illustrated, are based on Hofstede's dimensions. While being the most used perspective on culture to this date, Hofstede's theory has been severely critiqued in recent years, especially due to its reliance on nations as a proxy for culture [54], replicability and internal reliability issues [57]. Furthermore, culture is typically considered through a static and homogeneous lens within countries, which can be a fallacious assumption. Intra-national differences can be as significant as cross-national comparisons [95]. These intra-cultural considerations may even be more relevant for the design of GGs, since they are commonly designed for a particular group regardless of a nation's borders. Additionally, since cultural models such as Hofstede's present a collective behavioral pattern, researchers and practitioners must be careful in utilizing these cultural patterns at the individual level, a mistake that is often referred to as an ecological fallacy [28]. Even though there seems to be a relationship between cultural values and individual psychological/behavioral traits (e. g. [35]), further research and empirical validation is warranted on when to use collective (cultural) or individual (personality) analysis in the process of designing GGs, and whether these measurements are complementary or redundant.

3.4   Cognitive-Affective Processes

One of the most prominent theories in the literature regarding cognition is the Cognitive Load Theory (CLT). CLT is an instructional theory primarily based on the relationships between working (short-term) memory and long-term memory, and how they impact learning [92]. CLT considers an evolutionary view of human cognitive architecture, which divides the knowledge into biologically primary knowledge, which refers to skills acquired and evolved over several generations (such as listening and speaking), and biologically secondary knowledge, referring to information that needs to be acquired due to cultural and social significance, like reading and writing. CLT is based on the concept of cognitive load, where learning and general cognition takes up space and processing power from different types of memories. In particular, CLT divides the working memory cognitive load into three different categories: i) intrinsic load, associated with the complexity of the information being processed [92]; ii) extrinsic load, related to how the information is presented and what the learner has to do to understand it [93]; and iii) germane load, related to the load that is required to learn new information and store it in long-term memory. Although extensively used and researched in the last decade, CLT has received some criticism and updates in recent years. In recent definitions, it is assumed that germane load redistributes resources in working memory from extraneous to intrinsic load during learning [93], thus being called germane processing [88]. One major consequence of this change is that an increased germane load is no longer believed to increase the overall cognitive load, which could lead to a detrimental learning performance [88].

CLT was further enhanced to account for more modern ways of learning, particularly those involving multimedia resources. Mayer [50] proposed a new Cognitive Theory of Multimedia Learning (CTML); in this context, multimedia learning is defined as the process of building a mental representation from words (text and spoken) and pictures (animated or static). Unlike CLT, CTML distinguishes the processes of *information acquisition* and *knowledge construction* in multimedia learning, focusing on the latter. Information acquisition is defined as simply committing information to memory (i. e. transfer from working to long-term memory), whereas knowledge construction refers to building a coherent cognitive structure [50]. CTML focuses on knowledge construction, focusing on the learner as an active information processor. Its goal is to understand and provide guidelines for fostering *meaningful learning* (organized and integrated knowledge that provides good retention and transfer) [50].

Unlike CLT, which proposes only two memory stores, CTML proposed a three-structured memory process, composed by i) *sensory memory*, an unlimited storage that briefly holds copies of incoming words and pictures (sensory information), ii) *working memory*, a limited and short-lived storage for processing incoming information, as defined in the CLT, and iii) *long-term memory*, an unlimited and permanent storage that holds all mental representations and prior knowledge. [51]. However, cognitive load types in CTLM are analogous to the ones in CLT. In CTML these load are divided into *extraneous processing* (i. e. extraneous load from CLT), *essential processing* related to selecting relevant information (i. e. intrinsic load from CLT), and *generative processing* (akin to germane load from CLT). The latter is related to organizing and integrating incoming information with prior knowledge, and is related to metacognition and the student's motivation to learn. However, CTML follows the old version of CLT, claiming that the sum of extraneous, essential, and generative contributes to the total cognitive capacity of an individual [51]. Hence the goals of CTML in instructional design are: i) reduce extraneous processing, since it does not contribute to learning but affects the total cognitive capacity available, ii) manage essential processing, since a piece of very complex information may also overload the total cognitive capacity, and iii) foster generative processing, stimulating the learner to take an active role in knowledge acquisition. CTLM was further expanded to include both affective and motivational components, given the importance of these two elements in learning. The resulting Cognitive-Affective Theory of learning with media (CATLM) expands on CTLM by adding not only the role of emotions, metacognition and motivation as key factors in multimedia learning, but also increasing its application to environments that are composed by other elements besides words and pictures, such as games, virtual reality and agent-based simulations [59]. CATLM also proposes that: i) motivational factors mediate learning by increasing or decreasing cognitive engagement; ii) metacognitive factors mediate learning by regulating cognitive processing and affect; and iii) individual differences such as learner's prior knowledge, cognitive styles and abilities also mediate how much is learned in a particular intervention [58,59].

Additionally, CATLM divides long-term memory into two common processes found in neurocognition: episodic and semantic knowledge. Semantic knowledge refers to a person's storage of general and conceptual knowledge, schematic representations retrieved independently from their original spatial and temporal contexts. Episodic knowledge refers to the collection of personally experienced events, with specific spatial and temporal contexts. Typically this knowledge is formed as a result of engaging with an event, as it is experienced [79]. A full schematic of CATLM is illustrated in Fig. 1.

Another model that has been proposed in the literature involving cognitive-affective aspects is the Integrated Cognitive-Affective Model of Learning with Multimedia (ICALM). ICALM is based on CATLM's assumptions and processes of selecting/organizing/integrating verbal and visual information [73]. ICALM proposes that affective considerations are intertwined and inseparable from cognitive processes, providing a more detailed notion of the information processing flow when compared to CATLM. Differently from CATLM, ICALM states that the multimedia environment itself induces affective responses, constituting a *core affect* that is perceived simultaneously with the sensorial memory. As learners organize the incoming information in their working memory, affective appraisal processes help organize the information through mental schemas. These appraisal processes are experienced in terms of interest and motivation. Finally, the resulting experienced affect is integrated with visual and verbal representations, creating emotion schemas that are stored in the long-term memory [73]. Thus, rather than simply serving as a mental filter as in CATLM, affective processes

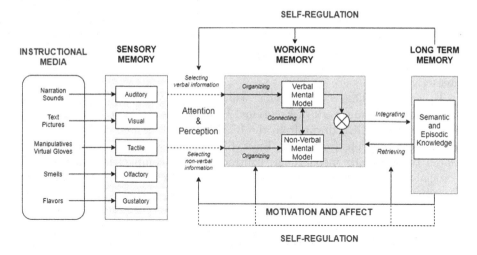

Fig. 1. Cognitive-Affective Theory of Learning with Media (CATLM). Based on Moreno [58].

in ICALM are also stored as part of the learner's memory and retrieved for future information processing. Additionally, just as the previous models suggest that one must minimize the cognitive load associated with non-essential processing, ICALM suggests that a learning design should evoke a balanced and efficient emotional experience. The full schema of ICALM is shown in Fig. 2.

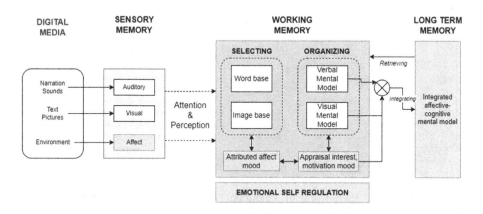

Fig. 2. Integrated Cognitive-Affective Model of Learning with Multimedia (ICALM). Based on Plass and Kaplan [73].

Even though the models discussed above can be utilized as a foundation for understanding GG's impact on players, they are not specific to game design practices, being more applicable to traditional multimedia interventions using videos and/or animations. The inherent nature of GGs also leads to a higher importance of affective outcomes either in the long-term (e. g. GG's impressions after playing it) or in the short-term. This short-term emotional impact is referred to in the literature as the concept of *game feel*, the affective aspect of real-time interactivity [69].

To address these GGs specific aspects, Loderer et al. [48] proposed the Integrative Framework of Emotional Foundations in Game-based Learning (EmoGBL). EmoGBL draws from the ICALM model, as well as CVT. Besides achievement emotions from CVT, EmoGBL encompasses i) epistemic emotions, related to processing incongruent, contradictory or complex information [98]; ii) social emotions, related to appraisals of others' actions; iii) topic emotions, related to individual interest towards a particular topic [33]; iv) aesthetic emotions, describing the intrinsic pleasantness of an object [55]; and finally v) technology emotions, describing control and value appraisals of technological devices and environment (e. g. [47]). EmoGBL also accounts for emotional transmission processes, such as empathy and contagion (i. e. unconscious process of reading and imitating emotional cues from others/environment) [48]. Its main difference from previous models are its foundation on the latest research involving digital learning environments as well as the description of specific game elements, such as game mechanics, visually aesthetic design, music score, narrative and incentive systems [71]. These elements in EmoGBL trigger emotional appraisals in a constant feedback loop that is mediated by the player's own beliefs, culture, gender and other factors such as motivation and metacognition. The full EmoGBL model is shown in Fig. 3.

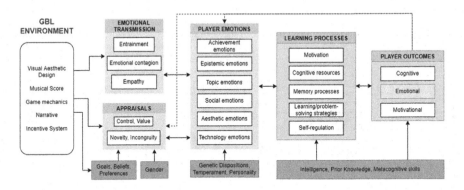

Fig. 3. Integrative framework of emotional foundations in game-based learning (EmoGBL). Based on Loderer et al. [48].

However comprehensive these models may be, they are far from representing the whole complexity of game-player interactions and their impact on player outcomes. Many models like the ones discussed above are complementary rather than mutually exclusive views, drawing from different theoretical backgrounds. There is also a need for a more comprehensive empirical validation of the model's implications and relationships, especially when taking emotions into account. Studies of GG design in terms of color, shape, dimension and anthropomorphism [72, 97] have already been proposed in the literature, but are specific to a particular sociocultural environment and focus on small changes in a controlled game design setting. Another issue related to these models is to identify the exact nature and temporal disposition of emotions being evoked in games: studies concerning the interactions between emotions over time just recently began to be proposed. One study that goes in this direction discovered that emotions such as boredom and frustration have a delayed effect on learning and overall game experience [80]. Finally, some effects predicted by the aforementioned models must be adapted for the GG environment and rigorously validated through empirical studies. To illustrate this matter, one ongoing debate involving these models that need further empirical examination is whether or not the addition of purely aesthetical elements to GGs can foster learning outcomes or shift the players' attention to these elements, a phenomenon called the seductive details effect [63]. Furthermore, while these models provide an interesting view from a theoretical standpoint, their complexity can prevent their use by designers and educators as an effective GG design tool. Even more straightforward proposals that offer practical guidelines and cognitive effects for the design of multimedia experiences, such as CLT/CTML, must be reevaluated in light of GG's context. For instance, Mayer [52] showed that while some CTML concepts and principles are effective in game design, others need further validation within the game design domain, such as the *immersion principle* (i. e. people learn better when realism is increased), which so far has been invalidated in GGs [52].

Hence, in order to address the challenge of creating high-quality GGs, these models must be further researched and effectively integrated into the game design practice, considering both theoretical and empirical approaches, providing intuitive guidelines to help designers and educators, and considering the temporal nature of emotions in player's experience.

3.5 Game Design Practices and Tools

Game design research and design research as a whole are based on both empirical and theoretical foundations, where typically the understanding of a problem is achieved by building and testing a designed solution [32]. Due to this dual nature, several conferences and organizations related to games attempt to bridge industry practices with academic research, like the IEEE Conference on Games[1], and the Brazilian SBGAMES[2]. However, these industry-academic tracks are more focused on academic approaches to industry-related problems than on industry practices that could be utilized by various audiences, such as educators and researchers. Given that very few educators and stakeholders present all the required skills to create quality GGs [22], new approaches that bridge the gap between academia and industry design practices are needed.

---

[1] https://ieee-cog.org/.

[2] https://www.sbgames.org/.

In this context, the challenge of how to create GGs relies not only on structuring game elements and foundations but also on creating tools, models and frameworks that can support their design. While frameworks such as MDA, RETAIN and LM-GM have been proposed in the literature, they lack further empirical validation and feedback from experienced industry practitioners. Various game authoring tools such as the ones reviewed by Metikaridis and Xinogalos [56] have also been proposed in the literature as an alternative way of designing and developing games without the need for advanced technical skills. While these tools offer a pathway to solving the challenge, such proposals tend to be more concerned with the modelling capability of their solutions (can this tool help the design of a game for a specific purpose/audience?) than with embedding design guidelines and theories that could lead to a more meaningful player experience (can this tool help the design of *a high quality* game?). Furthermore, the utilization of lessons learned from industry (e. g. *postmortems*, experience reports) must be a common practice in academic studies as a basis for proposing new tools and models related to game design. Politowski et al. [75] have conducted promising studies in this direction by analysing industry reports and *postmortems* on past game design projects, summarizing common problems found in design and how to avoid them.

Another practical way to include industry guidelines in academic environments (and vice-versa), is through the proposal of design patterns, describing general guidelines and artifacts focused on creating games [8]. Several approaches have been elaborated in this direction.Žavcer et al. [105] focused on educational aspects of games by proposing a unifying canvas for describing SGs patterns. Authors such as Dormann et al. [23] and Argasiński and Węgrzyn [3] focused on proposing patterns that are related to affective foundations. Even the authors of this work recently devised a meta-structure for proposing new patterns in game design, connecting all foundations and educational perspectives [60]. However, these studies lack empirical evaluation of their usefulness, which could come more easily with a closer relationship with industry designers and practitioners. Inspired by Passarelli et al. [64] and Greenwood et al. [27], to close this gap between academia and industry it is necessary to: i) exchange empirical practices among game designers and researchers, in the form of joint initiatives, consulting projects and shared libraries/resources (e. g. patterns, development assets); ii) promote the dissemination and creation of gray literature (e. g. blog posts) by researchers, helping them keep an open and ubiquitous channel of communication with practitioners; iii) promote workshops and action-oriented events (e. g. game jams), where researchers can interact with practical issues and approaches to game design; iv) promote joint studies and partnerships with selected game studios, where researchers can access a larger cohort population and designers can experiment with state-of-the-art design practices.

4   Research Agenda for the Challenge

The proposed challenge warrants more than just short-term actions or studies based on a single research area. Rather, it involves several different fields (e. g. communication, design, psychology) and their integration/collaboration over long-term studies regarding each aspect of the challenge: what is a game element (and how many of them exist), how can one measure a game's quality, what is the impact of elements in game's foundations and player experience, and so on. Hence, this work puts forth the following actions required for analyzing and proposing solutions in this context:

1. Proposal and application of a unified taxonomy of game elements and their collective manifestations (i. e. genre) that can be used and understood by industry practitioners, educators and researchers. This can be started by reviewing existing definitions and taxonomies from the literature, as well as validating them through an empirical analysis of how well these taxonomies fit with existing games on platforms such as Steam;
2. Integration of several models and theories stemming from fields such as social sciences, information systems and design that can simultaneously provide a basis for conducting game studies and describing dimensions of players' outcomes and games' foundations. That means improvements over models such as EmoGBL, proposing accompanying measurement techniques of game foundations so that research can be compared at an international level in a reproducible way;
3. Creation of a unified open repository of empirical evidence concerning the use of game elements and their incremental impact on all GGs' foundations (cognitive-affective, motivational, and sociocultural), as well as including design experiences and lessons learned. This repository should integrate both academic studies (especially meta-analyses and studies that rely heavily on statistical validation) and industry practices (e. g. *postmortems*). Ways to start such repositories include the analysis of success factors in existing games in the industry, as well as proposing studies related to GGs' foundations that incrementally add changes to the game during interventions, an approach known as Value-added research [52];
4. Proposal of easy-to-use tools, models and frameworks that can support practitioners, researchers, and professional designers in game design activities. This also means reviewing existing models from both theoretical and empirical standpoints (such as MDA), assessing their usefulness based on researchers' and practitioners' opinions, as well as thoroughly testing them by organizing experiments that involve the creation of games (e. g. game jams);
5. Validation of GGs' design through empirical evidence and feedback from a series of stakeholders: educators, game design experts, and players. This includes the proposal of comprehensive methods for evaluating and experimenting with games, as well as utilizing assessment methods that evaluate motivational, cognitive and affective foundations simultaneously, such as the Player Experience Inventory [1].

To properly evaluate research aimed at following these directions and its progress over the years, this work proposes a series of follow-up/feedback actions: i) periodically assessing game research and gray literature (e. g. game releases, blog posts from industry experts) in an attempt to create and update a unified taxonomy of game elements and genre. This assessment should identify new trends, compile research and industry directions; ii) monitoring game research and studies in academia through literature reviews, listing and integrating identified research methods and approaches that could form a foundation for research in games and enable reproducible results across studies. Additionally, monitoring the number of studies in peer-reviewed journals and conferences that employ empirical research to propose and/or validate GGs. iii) periodically conducting systematic reviews and meta-analysis of studies that relates specific game elements and/or foundations and providing a summary of their results and impact on design. Similarly, studying and proposing gray literature related to game design elements and their foundations, especially with practical design considerations. One initiative that goes in this direction is the *Museum of Mechanics: Lockpicking*[3] release on Steam, a compilation of games related to lockpicking mechanics with designer comments and considerations for this genre. iv) monitoring the acceptance of design artifacts both in academia and industry, through usage metrics and heuristic evaluations, as well as monitoring research that considers the impact of specific game elements in the learning environment. This acceptance must be evaluated from the player and the design perspective. That is, besides knowing which GG element and/or practice is more effective to players, it is also necessary to evaluate whether or not proposed design models and tools are being utilized by researchers and practitioners, avoiding works that create models which are only utilized by the ones who proposed it; and v) periodically organizing workshops between academics and game designers, along with conducting industry censuses related to the use of GG design practices and artifacts. This would allow a cross-pollination of ideas between practitioners and researchers, reinforcing any utilized game design terminology and models. Furthermore, these workshops can take a more theoretical perspective (e. g. lectures, experience reports) or a more practical one. An example of the latter is the proposal of specific game jams where teams are composed of academic researchers and industry practitioners.

5   Conclusion

Even though the use and efficacy of GGs in learning and entertainment have been established in the literature, there is a knowledge gap regarding the relationship between specific game elements and player outcomes, especially considering cognitive-affective and sociocultural foundations. Based on the majority of research studies concerning this gap, this work proposes that the process of

---

[3] https://store.steampowered.com/app/1735110/Museum_of_Mechanics_ Lockpicking/.

designing games in their various forms (e. g. serious, entertainment, GBL practices) and a more general understanding of the incremental role of game elements (e.g. mechanics, aesthetics, narrative), learning, and game foundations (affective, cognitive, cultural, motivational) has the potential to be a major challenge in game research during the next decade.

To address this challenge, this work puts forth some actions to support future research: create a unifying perspective of game elements (e. g. mechanics); integrate existing theories from different fields related to game foundations; understand GGs and their relationship with these foundations; proposing intuitive tools for game design drawn from the game industry. The progress of this challenge must be evaluated by monitoring studies based on empirical evidence and/or industry collaboration, in the form of recurrent censuses, workshops, interviews and grounded research. This work is just a first step in tackling the challenge and its ramifications in industry and academia, warranting further investigation. Future research should also propose and integrate empirical results in a unified repository to inform game design practices and their influence on learning and entertainment.

Acknowledgments. This study was financed in part by the Coordenação de Aperfeiçoamento de Pessoal de Nível Superior - Brasil (CAPES) - Finance Code 001.

References

1. Abeele, V.V., Spiel, K., Nacke, L., Johnson, D., Gerling, K.: Development and validation of the player experience inventory: a scale to measure player experiences at the level of functional and psychosocial consequences. Int. J. Hum.-Comput. Stud. **135**, 102370 (2020)
2. Ackermann, E.: Piaget's constructivism, Papert's constructionism: what's the difference? Future Learn. Group Publ. **5**(3), 11 (2001)
3. Argasiński, J.K., Węgrzyn, P.: Affective patterns in serious games. Futur. Gener. Comput. Syst. **92**, 526–538 (2019)
4. Arnab, S., et al.: Mapping learning and game mechanics for serious games analysis. Br. J. Educ. Technol. **46**(2), 391–411 (2015)
5. Baharom, S.N., Tan, W.H., Idris, M.Z.: Emotional design for games: the roles of emotion and perception in game design process. In: Proceedings of the Serious Games Conference 2014, pp. 19–25. Research Publishing Services (2014)
6. Bakan, U., Bakan, U.: Game-based learning studies in education journals: a systematic review of recent trends. Actualidades Pedagógicas **72**, 119–145 (2018)
7. Bialas, M., Tekofsky, S., Spronck, P.: Cultural influences on play style. In: 2014 IEEE Conference on Computational Intelligence and Games, pp. 1–7 (2014). iSSN 2325-4289
8. Bjork, S., Holopainen, J.: Patterns in Game Design. Charles River Media Game Development Series, 1st edn. Charles River Media, Hingham (2005)
9. Blaschke, L.M.: The pedagogy–andragogy–heutagogy continuum and technology-supported personal learning environments. In: Jung, I. (ed.) Open and Distance Education Theory Revisited. SE, pp. 75–84. Springer, Singapore (2019). https://doi.org/10.1007/978-981-13-7740-2_9

10. Boyle, E.A., et al.: An update to the systematic literature review of empirical evidence of the impacts and outcomes of computer games and serious games. Comput. Educ. **94**, 178–192 (2016)
11. Brom, C., Stárková, T., D'Mello, S.K.: How effective is emotional design? A meta-analysis on facial anthropomorphisms and pleasant colors during multimedia learning. Educ. Res. Rev. **25**, 100–119 (2018)
12. de Byl, P.: A conceptual affective design framework for the use of emotions in computer game design. Cyberpsychology **9** (2015)
13. Caillois, R.: Man, Play, and Games. University of Illinois Press (2001)
14. Camacho-Morles, J., Slemp, G.R., Pekrun, R., Loderer, K., Hou, H., Oades, L.G.: Activity achievement emotions and academic performance: a meta-analysis. Educ. Psychol. Rev. **33**, 1051–1095 (2021)
15. Cambria, E., Livingstone, A., Hussain, A.: The hourglass of emotions. In: Esposito, A., Esposito, A.M., Vinciarelli, A., Hoffmann, R., Müller, V.C. (eds.) Cognitive Behavioural Systems. LNCS, vol. 7403, pp. 144–157. Springer, Heidelberg (2012). https://doi.org/10.1007/978-3-642-34584-5_11
16. Camps-Ortueta, I., González-Calero, P.A., Quiroga, M.A., Gómez-Martín, P.P.: Measuring preferences in game mechanics: towards personalized chocolate-covered broccoli. In: van der Spek, E., Göbel, S., Do, E.Y.-L., Clua, E., Baalsrud Hauge, J. (eds.) ICEC-JCSG 2019. LNCS, vol. 11863, pp. 15–27. Springer, Cham (2019). https://doi.org/10.1007/978-3-030-34644-7_2
17. Chalki, P., Mikropoulos, T.A., Tsiara, A.: A delphi study on the design of digital educational games. In: Antona, M., Stephanidis, C. (eds.) HCII 2019. LNCS, vol. 11572, pp. 433–444. Springer, Cham (2019). https://doi.org/10.1007/978-3-030-23560-4_32
18. Clarke, R.I., Lee, J.H., Clark, N.: Why video game genres fail: a classificatory analysis. Games Cult. **12**(5), 445–465 (2017)
19. De Troyer, O.: Towards effective serious games. In: 2017 9th International Conference on Virtual Worlds and Games for Serious Applications (VS-Games), pp. 284–289 (2017). iSSN 2474-0489
20. Desurvire, H., Wiberg, C.: Game usability heuristics (PLAY) for evaluating and designing better games: the next iteration. In: Ozok, A.A., Zaphiris, P. (eds.) OCSC 2009. LNCS, vol. 5621, pp. 557–566. Springer, Heidelberg (2009). https://doi.org/10.1007/978-3-642-02774-1_60
21. Deterding, S., Dixon, D., Khaled, R., Nacke, L.: From game design elements to gamefulness: defining gamification, vol. 11, pp. 9–15 (2011)
22. Dimitriadou, A., Djafarova, N., Turetken, O., Verkuyl, M., Ferworn, A.: Challenges in serious game design and development: educators' experiences. Simul. Gaming **52**(2), 132–152 (2021)
23. Dormann, C., Whitson, J.R., Neuvians, M.: Once more with feeling: game design patterns for learning in the affective domain. Games Cult. **8**(4), 215–237 (2013)
24. Ekman, P., Friesen, W.V.: Constants across cultures in the face and emotion. J. Pers. Soc. Psychol. **17**(2), 124–129 (1971). http://doi.apa.org/getdoi.cfm?doi=10.1037/h0030377
25. Gee, E., Gee, J.P.: Games as distributed teaching and learning systems. Teach. Coll. Rec. 22 (2017)
26. Gee, J.P.: Learning by design: good video games as learning machines. E-Learn. Digit. Media **2**(1), 5–16 (2005)
27. Greenwood, J., Achterbosch, L., Stranieri, A., Meredith, G.: Understanding the gap between academics and game developers: an analysis of gamasutra blogs, p. 8 (2021)

28. Grenness, T.: Hofstede revisited: is making the ecological fallacy when using Hofstede's instrument on individual behavior really unavoidable? Int. J. Bus. Manage. **7**(7) (2012)

29. Gunter, G.A., Kenny, R.F., Vick, E.H.: Taking educational games seriously: using the RETAIN model to design endogenous fantasy into standalone educational games. Educ. Tech. Research Dev. **56**(5), 511–537 (2008)

30. Hamari, J., Keronen, L.: Why do people play games? A meta-analysis. Int. J. Inf. Manage. **37**, 125–141 (2017)

31. Hamdaoui, N., Khalidi Idrissi, M., Bennani, S.: Modeling learners in educational games: relationship between playing and learning styles. Simul. Gaming **49**(6), 675–699 (2018)

32. Hevner, A.R., March, S.T., Park, J., Ram, S.: Design science in information systems research. MIS Q. **28**(1), 75–105 (2004)

33. Hidi, S., Renninger, K.A.: The four-phase model of interest development. Educ. Psychol. **41**(2), 111–127 (2006)

34. Hofstede, G.: Dimensionalizing cultures: the hofstede model in context. Online Read. Psychol. Cult. **2**(1) (2011)

35. Hofstede, G., McCrae, R.R.: Personality and culture revisited: linking traits and dimensions of culture. Cross-Cult. Res. **38**(1), 52–88 (2004)

36. Hookham, G., Nesbitt, K.: A systematic review of the definition and measurement of engagement in serious games. In: Proceedings of the Australasian Computer Science Week Multiconference, ACSW 2019, pp. 1–10. Association for Computing Machinery, Sydney (2019)

37. Huizinga, J.: Homo Ludens: a study of the play-element in culture. Am. Sociol. Rev. **16**(2), 274 (1951)

38. Jossan, K.S., Gauthier, A., Jenkinson, J.: Cultural implications in the acceptability of game-based learning. Comput. Educ. **174**, 104305 (2021)

39. Juul, J.: The game, the player, the world: looking for a heart of gameness, pp. 30–45. Utrecht University (2003)

40. Kailani, S., Newton, R., Pedersen, S.: Game-based learning and problem-solving skills: a systematic review of the literature. In: EdMedia+ Innovate Learning, pp. 1127–1137. Association for the Advancement of Computing in Education (AACE) (2019)

41. Khenissi, M.A., Essalmi, F., Jemni, M., Kinshuk, Graf, S., Chen, N.S.: Relationship between learning styles and genres of games. Comput. Educ. **101**, 1–14 (2016)

42. Klabbers, J.H.G.: The magic circle: principles of gaming & simulation. BRILL (2009)

43. Konert, J., Göbel, S., Steinmetz, R.: Modeling the player, learner and personality: independency of the models of Bartle, Kolb and NEO-FFI (Big5) and the implications for game based learning. In: European Conference on Games Based Learning, pp. 329–335. Academic Conferences International Limited, Reading (2013). iSSN 2049-0992

44. Lamb, R.L., Annetta, L., Firestone, J., Etopio, E.: A meta-analysis with examination of moderators of student cognition, affect, and learning outcomes while using serious educational games, serious games, and simulations. Comput. Hum. Behav. **80**, 158–167 (2018)

45. Lameras, P., Arnab, S., Dunwell, I., Stewart, C., Clarke, S., Petridis, P.: Essential features of serious games design in higher education: linking learning attributes to game mechanics. Br. J. Edu. Technol. **48**(4), 972–994 (2017)

46. Lazzaro, N.: Why we play: affect and the fun of games. Hum.-Comput. Interact.: Designing Diverse Users Domains **155**, 679–700 (2009)
47. Loderer, K., Pekrun, R., Lester, J.C.: Beyond cold technology: a systematic review and meta-analysis on emotions in technology-based learning environments. Learn. Instruct. **70**, 101162 (2020)
48. Loderer, K., Pekrun, R., Plass, J.: Emotional foundations of game-based learning. In: Handbook of Game-Based Learning, 1st edn. The MIT Press, Cambridge (2019)
49. Malliarakis, C., Tomos, F., Shabalina, O., Mozelius, P.: Andragogy and E.M.O.T.I.O.N.: 7 key factors of successful serious games (2018)
50. Mayer, R.E.: Multimedia learning. In: Psychology of Learning and Motivation, vol. 41, pp. 85–139. Academic Press (2002)
51. Mayer, R.E.: Cognitive theory of multimedia learning. In: The Cambridge Handbook of Multimedia Learning. Cambridge Handbooks in Psychology, 2nd edn., pp. 43–71. Cambridge University Press, Cambridge (2014)
52. Mayer, R.E.: Cognitive foundations of game-based learning. In: Handbook of Game-Based Learning, pp. 83–110. The MIT Press, Cambridge (2020)
53. Mayra, F.: An Introduction to Game Studies. Sage Publications Ltd. (2008)
54. Meershoek, C.J., Kortmann, R., Meijer, S.A., Subrahmanian, E., Verbraeck, A.: The culture driven game design method: adapting serious games to the players' culture. In: Dignum, V., Dignum, F. (eds.) Perspectives on Culture and Agent-based Simulations. SPS, vol. 3, pp. 231–249. Springer, Cham (2014). https://doi.org/10.1007/978-3-319-01952-9_13
55. Menninghaus, W., et al.: What are aesthetic emotions? Psychol. Rev. **126**, 171 (2019)
56. Metikaridis, D., Xinogalos, S.: A comparative analysis of tools for developing location based games. Entertain. Comput. **37**, 100403 (2021). https://www.sciencedirect.com/science/article/pii/S1875952120301117
57. Minkov, M.: A revision of Hofstede's model of national culture: old evidence and new data from 56 countries. Cross Cult. Strategic Manage. **25**(2), 231–256 (2018)
58. Moreno, R.: Does the modality principle hold for different media? A test of the method-affects-learning hypothesis: modality principle. J. Comput. Assist. Learn. **22**(3), 149–158 (2006)
59. Moreno, R., Mayer, R.: Interactive multimodal learning environments. Educ. Psychol. Rev. **19**(3), 309–326 (2007)
60. Natucci, G., Borges, M.: Bridging emotional design and serious games: towards affective learning design patterns (2021)
61. Natucci, G.C., Borges, M.A.F.: The experience, dynamics and artifacts framework: towards a holistic model for designing serious and entertainment games. In: 2021 IEEE Conference on Games (CoG), pp. 1–8 (2021). iSSN 2325-4289
62. Norman, D.A.: Emotional design: people and things (2005)
63. Park, B., Flowerday, T., Brünken, R.: Cognitive and affective effects of seductive details in multimedia learning. Comput. Hum. Behav. **44**, 267–278 (2015)
64. Passarelli, M., et al.: Library not found - the disconnect between gaming research and development, pp. 134–141 (2021)
65. Paulin, R.E., Battaiola, A.L., Alves, M.M.: The study of the relations between the *BrainHex* player profiles, MBTI psychological types and emotions as means to enhance user experience. In: Marcus, A. (ed.) DUXU 2014. LNCS, vol. 8518, pp. 732–741. Springer, Cham (2014). https://doi.org/10.1007/978-3-319-07626-3_69

66. Pekrun, R., Stephens, E.J.: Achievement emotions: a control-value approach. Soc. Pers. Psychol. Compass **4**(4), 238–255 (2010)
67. Pereira, R., Cecília Calani Baranauskas, M.: A value-oriented and culturally informed approach to the design of interactive systems. Int. J. Hum. Comput. Stud. **80**, 66–82 (2015)
68. Picard, R.W.: Affective Computing. MIT Press, Cambridge (1997)
69. Pichlmair, M., Johansen, M.: Designing game feel. A survey. IEEE Trans. Games **14**, 138–152 (2021)
70. Plass, J.L., Homer, B.D., Kinzer, C., Frye, J., Perlin, K.: Learning mechanics and assessment mechanics for games for learning. G4LI White Paper. Games for Learning Institute (2011). http://rgdoi.net/10.13140/2.1.3127.1201
71. Plass, J.L., Homer, B.D., Kinzer, C.K.: Foundations of game-based learning. Educ. Psychol. **50**(4), 258–283 (2015)
72. Plass, J.L., et al.: Emotional design for digital games for learning: the effect of expression, color, shape, and dimensionality on the affective quality of game characters. Learn. Instruct. **70**, 101194 (2020)
73. Plass, J.L., Kaplan, U.: Emotional design in digital media for learning. In: Emotions, Technology, Design, and Learning, pp. 131–161. Emotions and Technology, Academic Press, San Diego (2016)
74. Plass, J.L., Kaplan, U.: Emotional design in digital media for learning. In: Emotions, Technology, Design, and Learning, pp. 131–161. Elsevier (2016)
75. Politowski, C., Petrillo, F., Ullmann, G.C., Guéhéneuc, Y.G.: Game industry problems: an extensive analysis of the gray literature. Inf. Softw. Technol. **134**, 106538 (2021)
76. Qian, M., Clark, K.R.: Game-based learning and 21st century skills: a review of recent research. Comput. Hum. Behav. **63**, 50–58 (2016)
77. Ralph, P., Monu, K.: Toward a unified theory of digital games. Comput. Games J. **4**(1–2), 81–100 (2015)
78. Ratan, R.A., Chen, V.H.H., Degrove, F., Breuer, J., Quandt, T., Williams, P.: Gender, gaming motives, and genre: comparing Singaporean, German, and American Players. IEEE Trans. Games **14**, 456–465 (2021)
79. Renoult, L., Irish, M., Moscovitch, M., Rugg, M.D.: From knowing to remembering: the semantic-episodic distinction. Trends Cogn. Sci. **23**(12), 1041–1057 (2019)
80. Riemer, V., Schrader, C.: Mental model development in multimedia learning: interrelated effects of emotions and self-monitoring. Front. Psychol. **10**, 899 (2019)
81. Roseman, I.: Appraisal in the emotion system: coherence in strategies for coping. Emot. Rev. **5**, 141–149 (2013)
82. Salen, K., Zimmerman, E.: Rules of Play: Game Design Fundamentals. MIT Press, Cambridge (2004)
83. Schell, J.: The Art of Game Design: A Book of Lenses. Elsevier/Morgan Kaufmann, Amsterdam/Boston (2008)
84. Scherer, K.R.: Appraisal theory. In: Handbook of Cognition and Emotion, pp. 637–663. Wiley, Chichester (2005)
85. Schorer, A., Protopsaltis, A.: Effects of Serious Games and game-based learning on learners' achievement emotions (2020)
86. Shabihi, N., Taghiyareh, F., Abdoli, M.H.: Analyzing the effect of game-elements in e-learning environments through MBTI-based personalization. In: 2016 8th International Symposium on Telecommunications (IST), pp. 612–618 (2016)
87. Sicart, M.: Loops and metagames: understanding game design structures. In: FDG (2015)

88. Skulmowski, A., Xu, K.M.: Understanding cognitive load in digital and online learning: a new perspective on extraneous cognitive load. Educ. Psychol. Rev. **34**, 171–196 (2021)
89. Sousa, C., Costa, C.: Videogames as a learning tool: is game-based learning more effective? Rev. Lusófona Educ. **40**, 199–210 (2018)
90. Stenros, J.: The game definition game: a review. Games Cult. **12**(6), 499–520 (2017)
91. Stockinger, K., et al.: Are concepts of achievement-related emotions universal across cultures? A semantic profiling approach. Cogn. Emot. **34**, 1–10 (2020)
92. Sweller, J.: Cognitive load theory. In: Psychology of Learning and Motivation, vol. 55, pp. 37–76. Elsevier (2011)
93. Sweller, J., van Merriënboer, J.J.G., Paas, F.: Cognitive architecture and instructional design: 20 years later. Educ. Psychol. Rev. **31**(2), 261–292 (2019)
94. Theodosiou, S., Karasavvidis, I.: Serious games design: a mapping of the problems novice game designers experience in designing games. J. e-Learn. Knowl. Soc. **11**(3) (2015)
95. Tung, R.L.: The cross-cultural research imperative: the need to balance cross-national and intra-national diversity. J. Int. Bus. Stud. **39**(1), 41–46 (2008)
96. Ullmann, G., Politowski, C., Petrillo, F., Guéhéneuc, Y.G.: Aspects of high-rated games. arXiv:2105.14137 [cs] (2021)
97. Uzun, A.M., Yıldırım, Z.: Exploring the effect of using different levels of emotional design features in multimedia science learning. Comput. Educ. **119**, 112–128 (2018)
98. Vogl, E., Pekrun, R., Murayama, K., Loderer, K.: Surprised-curious-confused: epistemic emotions and knowledge exploration. Emotion **20**(4), 625–641 (2020)
99. Walk, W., Görlich, D., Barrett, M.: Design, dynamics, experience (DDE): an advancement of the MDA framework for game design. In: Korn, O., Lee, N. (eds.) Game Dynamics, pp. 27–45. Springer, Cham (2017). https://doi.org/10.1007/978-3-319-53088-8_3
100. Wanick, V., Dunn, R., Ranchhod, A., Wills, G.: Analysing cross-cultural design in advergames: a comparison between the UK and Brazil. EAI Endors. Trans. Game-Based Learn. **5**(17) (2019)
101. Winn, B.M.: The design, play, and experience framework. In: Handbook of Research on Effective Electronic Gaming in Education, p. 19 (2009)
102. Wouters, P., Van Nimwegen, C., Van Oostendorp, H., Van Der Spek, E.D.: A meta-analysis of the cognitive and motivational effects of serious games. J. Educ. Psychol. **105**(2), 249 (2013)
103. Wu, W.H., Hsiao, H.C., Wu, P.L., Lin, C.H., Huang, S.H.: Investigating the learning-theory foundations of game-based learning: a meta-analysis. J. Comput. Assist. Learn. **28**(3), 265–279 (2012)
104. Yu, Z.: A meta-analysis of use of serious games in education over a decade. Int. J. Comput. Games Technol. **2019**, 1–8 (2019)
105. Žavcer, G., Mayr, S., Petta, P.: Design pattern canvas: an introduction to unified serious game design patterns. Interdisc. Description Complex Syst. INDECS **12**(4), 280–292 (2014)

Enhancing Students' Learning Experience Through Gamification: Perspectives and Challenges

Paula Palomino[1,2](✉)(iD), Luiz Rodrigues[3](iD), Armando Toda[3,4](iD), and Seiji Isotani[5](iD)

[1] NEES, Federal University of Alagoas, Maceio, Brazil
paula.palomino@nees.ufal.br
[2] HCI Games Group, University of Waterloo, Stratford, ON, Canada
[3] ICMC, University of São Paulo, São Carlos, Brazil
[4] Durham University, Durham, UK
[5] Harvard Graduate School of Education, Cambridge, MA, USA

Abstract. One of the main challenges we face in the educational domain nowadays is the lack of student engagement in traditional teaching methods. One way to address this challenge is through gamification strategies, especially in educational systems. In this chapter, we address some difficulties and possible solutions, discussing high-impact studies in the area, whose methods together comprise frameworks and guidelines that assist in developing, implementing, and evaluating gamified strategies both from the developers' point of view, the teachers' and the students themselves.

Keywords: Gamification · Gamified educational systems · Computers and education · Learning experience · Users' experience

1 Introduction

Gamification, defined as "the use of game elements in non-game contexts" [10], is an approach widely used to engage and motivate users, to perfect or create a desired behaviour in the learning process, and to improve users' experiences in digital systems [20]. In the educational domain, one of the biggest problems educators face nowadays is the students' lack of engagement [5]. This occurs due to the rapid advances in Information Technologies (IT) services that are not assembled or tied to the traditional teaching approaches [40]. Consequently, traditional models are not effective enough to maintain the interest and attention of these students [63]. This situation became even more prominent since the beginning of the COVID-19 pandemic in early 2020, when the traditional educational system had to be quickly migrated to the remote system, bringing a series

The authors are thankful for the financial support from CNPq (141859/2019-9; 163932/2020-4; 308458/2020-6), and CAPES (Finance Code - 001).

of new challenges for teachers, students, and school administrations [53]. In the specific case of Brazil, the problems were emphasized due to the pandemic, since part of the population lack access to the internet or technological resources, and the teachers also have no training in the use of digital technologies, therefore exposing the enormous gap in equity.

Gamification has been widely explored within the educational domain [30], mainly through digital environments. Nevertheless, it is also possible to apply it in non-technological environments through the use of unplugged strategies [67]. The application of gamification in education has overall positive results in terms of motivational, behavioural, and cognitive learning outcomes [8,60]. However some studies show uncertain and negative findings (*e.g.*, demotivation and disengagement) [22,71], with gamification designs often blamed for these undesired outcomes [34,39,65]. Henceforth, the main challenge we pose in this chapter is:

How to increase students' engagement in the learning process through the use of cutting-edge research on gamification design?

Based on recent reviews in the field of gamification in education [27,38,58], we summarized two topics that must be addressed in order to implement the best gamified strategies to enhance students' motivation and engagement:

(i) Provide tools to support teachers to design and implement gamification properly (within virtual or unplugged environments);
(ii) Understand, design and implement ways to keep the student immersed within the content with the help of the game elements, where their user experience is of utmost importance.

To address these challenges, we propose a connection of multiple research directions that scholars have been exploring recently, which we summarize as follows: *i) To create personalized contents, through automatic generation, that drive learners towards motivation and engagement* [54,79]; *with the goal of ii) delivering a clear and effective framework that can be used by any educator, even by those without knowledge in gamification, to create instructional designs* [70]; *iii) featuring gamified contents to be experienced in a subtle way, guiding the students to an enhanced learning process by means of immersive experiences* [47].

Next, we elaborate on how to address these challenges through the lens of the three proposed research directions. Section 2 discusses research on tailoring gamification. Section 3 discusses how to design gamification based on insights from empirical data. Section 4 discusses how those techniques can contribute to students' learning experience. Finally, Sect. 5 presents our final considerations, summarizes the challenges we proposed, and provides considerations on how to address them.

2   Tailoring Gamification

One size does not fit all. For gamified systems, that claim holds as well. Strong empirical evidence has demonstrated that gamification's effectiveness varies from one user to another [57,78]. Accordingly, tailored gamification has attracted the attention of several researchers interested in mitigating the limitations of the one-size-fits-all approach [14,58]. Whereas tailored gamification is a recent research field with several challenges to be addressed [27], we have witnessed promising empirical evidence on the benefits it might bring [13,55,74]. Thus, this section discusses the various challenges involved in designing and applying tailored gamification to improve student motivation, after providing background information on it.

2.1   Understanding Tailored Gamification

Broadly speaking, tailoring gamification refers to designing it so that it equally suits the many users of a given gamified system in a given context [27]. Nevertheless, we can further understand it in terms of *who*, *when*, and *how* it happens.

Tailoring gamification involves both personalization and customization of gamified systems, definitions which concern *who* is in charge of the tailoring. On one hand, *customization* concerns situations wherein the final users are in charge [77], an approach previously referred to as user-initiated personalization [44]. On the other hand, *personalization* attributes that responsibility to designers or the system itself [77], an approach that has been referred to as system-initiated personalization [44] and static adaptation [14] as well.

Additionally, personalization can also refer to *when* the tailoring happens. For instance, personalization refers to when the gamification design changes (right) before usage. Such an approach is specially valuable to address the cold-start problem, wherein there is little to no information about the users, allowing the system to provide a tailored design since one's first interaction with the gamified system [75]. In contrast, *adaptive* gamification (or dynamic adaptation) refers to having a system change its gamification design as usage occurs [14,28]. For instance, that can be used to adapt the gamification design when the user is returning to the system after a first-time experience or going from one page to another.

Furthermore, *how* to tailor can be accomplished through two alternatives [14]. One of them is to change *which game elements are available*. For instance, research has widely explored this approach, seeking to understand which game elements suit a user better (e.g., [6]) to turn elements on or off when a person uses a gamified system (e.g., [37]). Differently, one might change *how game elements work*. For instance, that can be implemented by changing the criteria for completing a goal or leveling up.

In light of that overview, we highlight those are not exclusive properties. For instance, one can employ tailoring by changing both the game elements available as well as their functioning. Similarly, a system can personalize its gamification design at one's first usage and, then, adapt it as new usages occurs. Regardless of how the tailoring is characterized, that process often relies on a three-step process: i) acquiring user and contextual information, ii) passing it to a tailoring model, and iii) using the model to define the tailored gamification design aiming to improve users' experiences; often, student motivation in educational domains

[27,80]. Thus, we discuss what information to consider, how to create tailoring models from those, and tailoring's effectiveness next.

2.2 What Information to Tailor For?

The main driver for research on tailored gamification is the fact that people are different. For instance, empirical research demonstrates that students using the same gamified educational system can have significantly different experiences [57,78]. Accordingly, empirical evidence demonstrates that one's preference for one game element or another significantly changes depending on their characteristics (e.g., gender, gaming preferences, and behavioural profiles) [65,76]. Hence, characterizing a moderator of one's preference. Thus, considering personal characteristics can explain differences in users' preferences, researchers sought to tailor gamification designs accordingly, aiming to mitigate situations wherein gamification is positive for some but negative for others.

Based on that assumption, research has examined several factors that might moderate one's preference and, consequently, gamification's success. Predominantly, such studies have relied on surveys [58]. That is, they design a survey, collect user feedback on how much they prefer some game elements, and then analyze whether each game element's score changes depending on respondents' characteristics. For instance, if *males prefer competition more than females*, gender would be a moderator. Those studies have provided valuable contributions by offering empirical evidence that factors such as demographics, gaming habits, and behavioural profile (e.g., [6,73]). However, they have two main limitations: i) they are based on potential experiences and ii) they often ignore context's role in gamification's success [39,41].

In contrast, some experimental studies have sought to identify moderators of gamification's effect based on true usage. For instance, [52] explored how gamification's effect differed for gamers compared to non-gamers. Additionally, few studies have analyzed how contextual factors moderate gamification's success. For instance, [57] compared how gamification's effect on students' motivations differed depending on their prior familiarity with the task to be done. Given that such task is a central part of the context [64], analyzing attributes related to it contributes to understanding the role of context-related moderators.

Moreover, one must note that most studies examine the moderator role of a single factor at a time [27]. In contrast, the literature provides strong evidence that there are several moderators (e.g., see [26]). Consequently, examining those in isolation provides limited contribution to achieving a full understanding of what (and how those) factors affect gamification's success. While studies started to address that gap, both in terms of potential [59] and real [56] usage, research remains needed to understand what are the moderators of gamification's effect [60]. Thus, given the need for identifying such moderators so they can be used in designing tailoring models, we have the following challenge:

What user and contextual information should be considered when tailoring gamified educational interventions?

2.3   How to Create Effective User Models?

Once we know what factors to consider when tailoring gamification designs, we have to create a model (such as a mathematical function) that receives them as input and provides design recommendations as outputs. For instance, such recommendations might be in terms of what game elements to turn on/off or how each game element should behave (or both), as discussed in Sect. 2.1. To create such model, one might adopt two main approaches: preference-based or data-driven.

Developing *preference-based models* is the approach used the most [58]. In those cases, researchers rely on preference data, often captured through surveys, to create a model that is based on potential experiences. Accordingly, that strategy naturally fits within the idea of personalization: it is independent of usage data, providing a starting point to address the cold-start problem. Despite several such approaches have been published (e.g., [43,75]), they have a limitation similar to research on moderators of gamification's effect: they are mostly focused on users' characteristics, whilst considering only one or few of the several information relevant to tailoring gamification [27].

Differently, *data-driven models* are those built upon real usage data [36]. Those models fit both adaptive and personalization strategies. However, to be used in the latter case, tailoring for one's first-time experience requires generalizing data from one user to another. Data-driven approaches (e.g., [13]) are promising because they reflect true user behaviours, hence, implicitly encompassing user and contextual factors, unlike preference-based ones (see [58]). On the other hand, they are dependent on usage data collected from several users, interacting with varied game elements within a number of contexts. Thereby, limiting their effectiveness to address cold starts. Additionally, in contrast to preference-based strategies, data-driven models have only begun to be researched [27].

From one perspective, we believe preference-based and data-driven approaches can and should be used together, combining their strengths and weaknesses to accurately inform the design of tailored gamification. However, in common for both of them, there is a lack of empirical evidence on whether their recommendations lead to effective gamification designs when compared to standard gamification designs [58], such as the widely used points, badges, and leaderboard triad [3]. Thus, considering accurately modeling users is a prominent step towards achieving effective tailored gamification design and the lack of empirically validated models, we pose the following challenge:

What is a model that accurately guides on how to tailor gamified educational interventions?

2.4   Testing

Intuitively, once we accurately model relevant user and contextual information, as well as their interactions, we expect tailored gamification leads to better student motivation than the standard approach. That is what research has sought for: testing whether the experiences of those who used personalized/customized gamification suppresses those of people who used the one-size-fits-all approach (e.g., [33,37]). Empirical support for that expectation, however, is inconclusive [58], as empirical studies have reported mixed results [13,37,55] (i.e., both positive and nonsignificant differences).

Nevertheless, there is a perspective we believe has not been addressed yet. Recall that tailoring gamification aims to cope with variations of gamification's effect by making it suitable for each user. Therefore, it would be reasonable to expect that tailoring gamification reduces gamification's effects variations, rather than, for instance, increasing students' overall motivation. For example, that could be observed in practice by reducing the number of moderators of gamification's effect when it's tailored, or the degree to which outcomes vary (e.g., reduced homogeneity in a dependent variable's measure). Studying such issues is especially important because tailored gamification is a recent field study [27,75]. However, according to our best knowledge, the single research inspecting moderators of tailored gamification's effect focused outside the educational domain [13]. Hence, understanding what to expect from it could reliably drive research efforts and inform practitioners' expectations. Thus, we pose the following challenge:

How does tailored gamification improve the one-size-fits-all approach, if so, in the context of gamified educational interventions?

2.5 Summary

This section discussed tailored gamification as a means to improve student motivation by mitigating the drawbacks of the one-size-fits-all approach. First, we introduced tailored gamification in terms of *who* is in charge of it, *when* it can act, and *how* to implement it. Then, we discussed relevant issues that must be addressed to better understand it, such as identifying *what to consider* in tailoring, *how to model* relevant inputs into tailored designs, and *what one might expect* from tailoring gamification. In doing so, we presented open research questions that must be addressed to reliably and effectively take advantage of tailored gamification to improve student learning. Thus, in summary, we challenge our community to i) **identify what information moderates gamification's success and ii) develop models that accurately inform the most motivating gamification design for a given user and context iii) to empirically support how tailored gamification improves student motivation by addressing limitations of the one-size-fits-all approach.**

3 Data-Driven Gamification Design in Education to Support Teachers and Instructors

Designing and implementing gamification in real education scenarios is not a trivial task [12] since teachers need to deal with their current overload of tasks as well as design and manage gamified strategies, which can take a lot of their time. In most cases, teachers are not prepared to design effective and meaningful gamified strategies [62], which can lead to poor students performance and engagement during their interactions with learning environments (both virtual and non-virtual) [71].

When considering virtual learning scenarios, such as Massive Online Open Courses (MOOCs) or Learning Management Systems (LMS), the interactions between students and the gamified strategies can generate a lot of data that can be difficult to read and interpret, specially for teachers and instructors that are not familiarized with the concepts covered within gamification [62]. One possible solution for this problem is the use of data-driven design to help teachers to pick the most suitable gamified strategies for their educational contexts, or to automate the design process, tailoring the gamified system to their students' needs [36].

3.1   Understanding Data-Driven Gamification Design (DDGD)

According to Meder [36], data-driven gamification design is a recent field that addresses the use of artificial intelligence (mainly machine learning) algorithms to support gamification design. In this sense, we can use unsupervised and supervised learning algorithms [65]. Briefly speaking, supervised learning is used when the researcher/teacher knows the variables (which can be students' demographic characteristics, gaming profile or preferences, gamification preferences, etc.) and they know how these variables influence in the outcome (e.g. students' from a given player profile, tend to have better learning performance when exposed to a certain group of gamification elements).

One example can be seen in the study of Knutas et al. [29] where the authors proposed a machine learning algorithm to personalize the students' experience based on content selection. The authors used a CN2 rule induction algorithm to model a set of rules that would distinguish between a variety of scenarios (based on students' player profiles). These generated recommendations of gamified strategies to support computer-support collaborative learning (CSCL) scenarios.

As for unsupervised learning, it is usually used when the teacher/researcher knows the variables (e.g. again related to students' characteristics which can be demographic or behavioural data) but does not know exactly what is the outcome. So, they can be used explicitly for design and test purposes [21].

An example can be seen in the work of Toda et al. [66] where the authors collected users' perceptions on gamification usage and identified patterns and relations between their intention to use gamification in learning environments. For instance, when the person knows about gamification, and has a routine of playing games, they are more likely to be positive towards the use of gamification in learning environments. This kind of information can be used by teachers to guide them when or not to gamify a certain learning environment.

Broadly speaking, data-driven algorithms can be powerful tools to support the gamification design process in its early phase (planning) and after it is onboarding phase (implementation). It can improve students' experience by supporting the tailoring process, e.g. using the students' interaction data to adapt and modify the gamified interface to match their needs automatically.

3.2 Implications and Impacts of DDGD

Although being a very promising approach, it is important to understand and recommend that DDGD should not be used to promote a One-Size-Fits-All approach. Data should be used to guide and support gamification design but should not be used irresponsibly since it tackles directly students' motivation and engagement.

The data obtained to support planning should support teachers and instructors to design better gamified scenarios, e.g., by presenting possible choices of gamified strategies that are similar to the context the teacher is in [68]. One practical example would be to use data mining techniques to identify gamified strategies that have been used in Biology courses. Those gamified strategies would be presented to the teacher/instructor that has an interest in gamifying their courses and then this teacher would adapt the strategies in a way that suits their students' needs and using resources that are available. Besides, it is of utmost importance to also train these teachers to use these tools in order to achieve the desired positive effects of gamification. Understanding that these teachers have limited time and, sometimes, technological resources, capacitating these professionals pose as a difficult challenge and research problem:

> **How can we capacitate the teacher and instructors to use and interpret data-driven algorithms, to help them generate gamified strategies in the planning phase?**

Post-implementation data can support the teacher/instructor to tailor the gamified strategies to their needs, and also be useful to others that have a similar context. The teacher/instructor can also provide feedback on the gamified strategies that were used and which ones did not attend their students, so other teachers/instructors can use this information to help them during the planning phase [17]. Based on this premise, we can propose the following research problem:

> **How can we support teachers to evaluate and analyze data obtained from the data-driven gamified designs, post-implementation phase?**

Regarding possible impacts, it is important to state again that DDGD should not be used to promote OSFA approaches. Interpretation of data is important and tailored to specific contexts. In addition, this interpretation should avoid generating possible stereotypes in the gamified strategies, e.g., competition-based strategies for boys or market-based strategies for girls. The reinforcement of existing stereotypes substantially harms students' motivation, which is the exact opposite of what gamification aims to provide [25]. Based on this statement, we propose the following research problem:

How can we use data-driven gamification design to promote equity and equality in learning scenarios?

Furthermore, this is still a new field of study and much more research needs to be done to understand the best ways DDGD can support the planning and implementation phase. It can help to understand personalized gamification by supporting student modeling in grouping some elements tied to different students' characteristics as well as analyzing associations between the students' interactions in the system and gamification elements to improve their experience [58]. This statement can be tied to the previous gaps exposed in the previous section.

3.3   Summary

This section discussed some of the key concepts related to data-driven gamification design. First, we contextualize presenting one existing problem which is the huge amount of data that teachers have access when considering existing virtual learning systems, such as MOOCs and LMSs. Next, we explain the concept of data-driven gamification design, which is the use of data-driven algorithms to support gamification planning phase, and how this concept has been used in literature to promote the design of better gamified scenarios. Next, we discuss some of the structural and practical challenges related to DDGD. Then, we expose those challenges to our community, in i) **find ways to train and support teachers to use data-driven algorithms and analyze the data obtained, and ii) identify how can we use this data to promote equity and equality in learning scenarios?**

4   Exploring the User Experience Through Gamification

As discussed in the previous sections, there is evidence of gamification's positive [59] and negative [71] effects, depending on how the gamification strategies are designed and applied. However, when comparing education with other areas that study gamification, such as marketing, psychology, and medicine, the primary purpose of engaging and motivating users in a particular action or set of specific tasks acquire an additional layer of complexity. That happens because gamification should not over-engage and distract the student from the content to be assimilated, which can end up harming their learning experiences [3,56].

In this sense, recent research deepens the look at more subjective game elements, such as narrative, storytelling, and sensations [69]. According to Kapp [24], most gamification frameworks developed are structural (e.g. aggregating scoring systems, ranking), with few content-based frameworks (where elements and concepts of games are applied to the content) [15]. This happens partly because of the difficulty of embedding these subjective elements on a platform other than a game. However, the high potential for engagement existing in different types of narrative and storytelling, and the fact that these elements can be worked directly in the content to be taught, explains the importance of further researching this area [47]. Therefore, this section seeks to define some concepts, provide background information on the area, and discuss the various challenges involved in creating and applying different gamified strategies based on subjective game elements to improve student motivation and focus on the subjects taught.

4.1   Gameful Experiences, Gameful Systems, Gameful Design

Based on the recent studies by Hodent [18], the part of UX that is most relevant for a user to want to use a system and to continue using it (*i.e.*, its retention rate) is the "engagement capacity," or "game flow," a well-known term that, despite representing some aspects of engagement, does not encompass everything essential to engage these users (or players) and keep them in that state. For the author, the term expresses the ability of an application or game to engage its user. The variables behind usability and engagement ability are not working independently; they interact with each other [18]. She also describes the capacity for engagement divided into three aspects: motivation, which is the origin of all human behaviour, the emotions that serve the motivation in the sense that they help to choose the correct behaviour (for example, to escape when one is afraid) and the game flow, a state of deep focus and immersion, which is a concept derived from Theory of the Flow [9], and which functions as a connection between all other aspects.

Also, according to Pink's motivational theory [49], the motivation of the individual is influenced by three predominant factors: Autonomy, Mastery and Purpose. The first refers to the control of the individual about their actions, the second deals with their abilities that are improved, and the latter is represented by the intrinsic need of the individual to perform a particular action. These three pillars can be observed in digital games since the player can control their actions (autonomy) and hone their skills (mastery) voluntarily (purpose).

Recent research sought to refine these concepts to help design these game-like systems. According to Landers *et al.* [32], gamefulness is commonly cited as the primary goal of gamification, encompassing engagement, motivation and behaviour changes; however, the term is not well defined across the literature, hampering the definition of what to expect from gamification strategies. Therefore, the authors presented a theory that divided gamefulness into three different constructs. First, **gameful experience** is a psychological state resulting from three characteristics: having non-trivial and attainable goals to pursue; being motivated to pursue them according to a set of rules; and willing to accept those rules because they make such activity possible. Second, a **gameful system** is any system that provides its users a gameful experience. Third, **gameful design** is a process to design systems with characteristics that can provide users with gameful experiences. This process, according to Toda *et al.* [72], consists of a series of events that result in a gamified strategy; that is, a specific action related to game elements. The success of a gamification strategy can be hindered by the absence or inadequate implementation of a gameful design. For example, an inadequate gamification strategy in education can lead to the loss of motivation and engagement and the impairment of the learning process [11,71]. However, according to the literature, frameworks can support the design process, ensuring that all steps and elements of the gameful design are present [1]. Hence, understanding how users deal with gamification, what they expect, how they feel, and what they consider useful in the design can drive further research efforts. Thus, we pose the following challenge:

How to consider the user a key agent in the gamification design process, within the education scope, while taking into account their learning gains (in the case of students) or their routines (in the case of teachers)?

4.2   Narrative and Storytelling for Gamification

To discuss narrative in gamification, it is essential to observe the role of the narrative as it is lived through a game. In this sense, the narrative begins to unfold from the moment the player reads the title of the game or interacts with the options menu, the visual representation of the game and its interaction mechanics. Everything is an element that contributes directly and uniquely to this narrative experience in games [46]. Bellow, we present three base narrative definitions in digital media, especially in games.

Manovich *et al.* [35] discusses what the new media would be and how this new language or digital code affects the narrative. For them, the changes in the media have triggered transformations in the cultural body, promoting new communication, language, behavioural, and representative strategies. The narrative, in turn, is established as a modality within a broader aspect, which is the way human being experiences their existence and how they choose to represent it in the digital age. Manovich *et al.* [35] verifies its basic elements can be found in the fundamentals of programming. Data, elements, goals, descriptions, problems and possibilities of reaching solutions are common features of the traditional plot and a simple algorithm. In addition, as novels and movies favoured the narrative as a crucial piece of cultural expression, the computing age exhibits its equivalent correlate: *the database.*

As for Salen *et al.* [61], narrative is defined as a composition of rules that are experienced through play, so the player interacts in the space of possible actions within a game, allowing them to explore, discover, manipulate and activate the game's universe. They further stress that it is essential not to rely only on comparison with narrative in other media and not to be distracted from essential elements such as rules, objectives, the player's participation and the impact of their actions in the game universe. To the authors, there is no genre or cultural form that is not understood by the concept of narrative [61].

This can occur in two distinct ways. The first one is called by Salen *et al.* [61] of *embedded narrative* and defined as pre-generated content that exists prior to the interaction of the player. This kind of narrative is designed to motivate playing the game, the game's story, for example, because it gives a sense of purpose to actions. The embedded narrative aims to give a significant stake to the player through the plot, as a premise to story, characters and sequence of events, which give a dramatic unity to the player's interactions and journey.

The second possibility is called *emergent narrative*, configuring itself in the story created from the player's interactive experience. The game designer also plans its base, but its unfolding is often not. This is due to the events created as an organic consequence of the player's freedom of choice in the face of the game mechanics and their meaningful experience as a user [46,51,61].

By this logic, the emergent narrative is only possible because it is directly connected to the chain of mechanisms that make up the game system and the meaningful participation of the player who is able to interfere. Thus, a change in the system from the player's actions can result in another modification of the narrative patterns of the game and affect the experience as a whole. The emergent narrative depends not only on the player's action but also on what is happening in the system at that very moment. Thus, the same actions may result in different outcomes since the changes that occurred in the systems are not necessarily the same. The emphasis of narrative is how the player interacts with the game system and creates their own, and unique sequence of events [47,51]. In addition, Salen *et al.* [61] believe that the two narrative types should balance each other when well worked. This balance allows unique narrative experiences, only possible in games.

In the same field, Bissell [4] also explored narrative in digital games. According to the author, games with narrative structure usually have two ways of telling stories. One is the framed narrative of the game, what happens in the "fictional present" of the game, in the animation films, and usually occurs independently and beyond the player's control. The other modality would be the "ludo-narrative". In other words, the narration of the sequence of events triggered and occurred due to the decisions and participation of the player in that fictional universe [4]. This contrast between the two forms of narrative - which are similar to the definitions of embedded and emergent narrative proposed by Salen *et al.* [61] - gives rise to great difficulty for the management of stories in games. After all, one model is rigid and unchanging, while the other is fluid and free. This is known as ludo-narrative dissonance. Still, they coexist in a game or interactive system and are both parts of the narrative. The author also criticizes how the framed narrative aims to bring meaning and relevance to the events witnessed by the player, while the ludo-narrative is only concerned with creating exciting situations for the player. Finally, he points out that without communication between the two narrative modalities, it is not possible to overcome the contrast between them and the strangeness that arises from it [4].

As we can see from these three main definitions, narrative in digital media is intrinsically connected to the system from which it derives. In this aspect, we found it essential to consider the Human-Computer Interaction (HCI) concepts such as user experience [41]. From this point in the work, what can be stated is that narrative (either embedded or emergent) in interactive digital systems depends heavily on the user experience [47]. Based on these premises, to design a narrative project, one should answer the following questions: *Where do narratives in a game reside? How can one design games as narrative experiences? What kinds of narrative experiences do games make possible? What is the role of narrative in the design of meaningful play?"* [61].

As such, Palomino *et al.* defined **Narrative** in gamification for education as **"the process in which the users build their own experience through a given content, exercising their freedom of choice in a given space and time, bounded by the system's logic."** and **Storytelling** as **"how the context is presented and the plot developed (the story is told) in a particular environment"** [47]. Considering these definitions, and their subjective and complex ways of use, we believe more in-depth research is needed to bring to light systematic methods to use these kind of game elements. Thus, we propose the following challenge:

How to embed and control Narrative and Storytelling in learning contents, so that the student is, at the same time, engaged in gamification but also focused on learning?

4.3   Content Gamification Frameworks

In the context of this research, frameworks are defined as a set of steps and tools aimed at specific results (in this case, a gameful design) [1]. According to recent research, the number of frameworks for gamification significantly increased in the last years [38]. These can be categorized as *structural frameworks* (based on structural game elements such as ranking, points, badges and leaderboards) or *content frameworks* (based on subjective game elements applied directly to the content such as narrative, storytelling and sensation) [23].

Currently, one of the most accepted frameworks for the digital game and gamification design by academia and the market is the Mechanics-Dynamics-Aesthetics, or MDA [19]. *Mechanics* are understood to be base components of the game - its rules, each main action that the player can take in the game, algorithms and data structures of the game engine, *dynamics* is the run-time behaviour of mechanics that acts on the player's input and cooperates with other mechanics, and *aesthetics* are the emotional responses evoked in the player.

According to Hamari *et al.*, [16], most of the frameworks for gamification developed are structural (*i.e.* aggregating scoring systems, ranking), with few content frameworks (where you apply elements and concepts of games in the content to be explained itself, aiming to make it more like a game). This view is confirmed by the recent systematic review by Mora *et al.* [38], where 40 unique works that addressed the development of frameworks for gamification were studied and cataloged. However, most of these frameworks were developed based on MDA, and very few have a content approach, such as experimenting with applying story to quizzes with positive results [31] or researching "Storyfication" as a recent pedagogical technique to change the story, add gamified elements and adapt the content independently from the visual medium used [2].

Furthermore, among the few existing content approaches, there is only one research that created a full Narrative Gamification Framework for Education [48], which is based on the "Hero's Journey", a template derived from various categories of tales and lore that involves a hero who goes on an adventure, and after dealing with a decisive crisis wins a victory, returning home changed or transformed [7]. In their research, she related Narrative and User Experience, Storytelling and Learning Experience, creating a full gamification journey to be followed by the student. However, the framework is difficult to apply in existing gamified educational systems, benefiting from platforms more focused on storytelling such as Storium[1] and Classcraft[2]. Also, for unplugged applications, the burden for the teachers, who would need to restructure their pedagogical content to embed the gamification journey still needs to be addressed. Thus, we propose the following challenge:

How to design content gamification frameworks that are simple and straightforward to apply in different instructional designs?

4.4 Summary

This section discussed different research and strategies to consider the user experience in gamification designs and the use of subjective game elements to mitigate the problem of engagement versus learning focus. First, we introduced user experience in games and gamification and how gamification design can consider the users as its central pillar. Next, we approached complex game elements such as Narrative and Storytelling, defining their characteristics in game-related environments and exposing their definition versions for gamification purposes. Then, we discussed structural and content-based gamification frameworks, demonstrating examples of each and its strengths and weaknesses. In doing so, we presented open research questions that must be addressed to facilitate applying user experience approaches for gamification. In short, we challenge our community to **i) develop strategies to keep the user (students or even teachers) as their primary focus in gamification designs for education; ii) find other ways to use subjective game elements better to improve the learning experience and equity in education, and iii) think about reducing the workload on teachers to empower them to use gamification strategies.**

5 Final Remarks

Brazil is a country with several problems in the area of education [42], which were further accentuated by the global pandemic of COVID-19 [53]. There is still much to be researched and developed regarding the transition from traditional teaching methods to the digital environment. Gamification in this context is very relevant, as it is one of the forms of engagement most accepted by the younger generations,

---

[1] https://storium.com/.
[2] https://www.classcraft.com/.

born after the internet and digital games [50]. This chapter presented high-impact research in gamification developed by Brazilian researchers that obtained international recognition, which lead to raising several research challenges to be addressed in the future. As summarized by Table 1, these challenges concern three pillars: tailoring gamification, exploring data-driven gamification design, and maximizing students' user experience with gamified educational systems.

In summary, all of the pillars presented in this chapter are related to themselves and aim to tackle a wider scope of motivation and engagement gaps in education. Each pillar works as a gear, which together seeks to provide a complete framework that can be socially useful as it is concerned with everyone involved in gamified learning, bringing equity in education a step closer to reality. The results of these studies will possibly bring in the next decade new specific frameworks, systems and guidelines that can effectively be used in classrooms and gamified digital environments. Also, as an area that draws more attention each year, we expect to see other new challenges and research to tackle them.

Table 1. Challenges in gamification for education.

Challenge	Call for action
Tailoring	
What user and contextual information should be considered when tailoring gamified educational interventions?	Identify what information moderates gamification's success
What is a model that accurately guides how to tailor gamified educational interventions?	Develop models that accurately inform the most motivating gamification design for a given user and context
How does tailored gamification improve the one-size-fits-all approach, if so, in the context of gamified educational interventions?	Empirically support how tailored gamification improves student motivation by addressing limitations of the one-size-fits-all approach
Data-driven gamification design	
How can we capacitate the teacher and instructors to use and interpret data-driven algorithms, to help them generate gamified strategies in the planning phase?	Develop methods to support teachers and instructors to use these algorithms and analyze their results.
How can we support teachers in evaluating and analyzing data obtained from the data-driven gamified designs, in the post-implementation phase?	Design approaches to evaluate gamification and make it easy-to-understand guidelines for teachers and instructors

(continued)

Table 1. (*continued*)

Challenge	Call for Action
How can we use data-driven gamification design to promote equity and equality in learning scenarios?	Use the data obtained from studies to create approaches that consider students' needs and characteristics
User experience in gamified systems	
How to consider the user a key agent in the gamification design process, within the education scope, while taking into account their learning gains (in the case of students) or their routines (in the case of teachers)?	Develop strategies to keep the user (students or teachers) as the primary focus in gamification designs for education
How to embed and control Narrative and Storytelling in learning contents, so that the student is, at the same time, engaged in gamification but also focused on learning?	Find other ways to use subjective game elements better to improve the learning experience and equity in education
How to design content gamification frameworks that are simple and straightforward to apply in different instructional designs?	Think about how to reduce the workload on teachers to empower them to use gamification strategies

Acknowledgements. A previous version of this chapter was published as a short paper at the Brazilian Symposium on Games and Digital Entertainment (SBGames) [45].

References

1. An, Y., Zhu, M., Bonk, C.J., Lin, L.: Exploring instructors' perspectives, practices, and perceived support needs and barriers related to the gamification of moocs. J. Comput. High. Educ. **33**(1), 64–84 (2021). https://doi.org/10.1007/s12528-020-09256-w
2. Aura, I., Hassan, L., Hamari, J.: Teaching within a story: understanding storification of pedagogy. Int. J. Educ. Res. **106**, 101728 (2021)
3. Bai, S., Hew, K.F., Huang, B.: Is gamification "bullshit"? Evidence from a meta-analysis and synthesis of qualitative data in educational contexts. Educ. Res. Rev. **100322** (2020)
4. Bissell, T.: Extra Lives: Why Video Games Matter. Vintage, New York (2011)
5. Boruchovitch, E.: A motivação do aluno: contribuição da psicologia contemporânea. Vozes (2001)
6. Bovermann, K., Bastiaens, T.J.: Towards a motivational design? Connecting gamification user types and online learning activities. Res. Pract. Technol. Enhanced Learn. **15**(1), 1–18 (2020). https://doi.org/10.1186/s41039-019-0121-4
7. Campbell, J.: The Hero with a Thousand Faces, vol. 17. New World Library, Novato (2008)

8. Campillo-Ferrer, J.M., Miralles-Martínez, P., Sánchez-Ibáñez, R.: Gamification in higher education: impact on student motivation and the acquisition of social and civic key competencies. Sustainability **12**(12), 4822 (2020)

9. Csikszentmihalyi, M., Csikszentmihalyi, I.S.: Optimal Experience: Psychological Studies of Flow in Consciousness. Cambridge University Press, Cambridge (1992)

10. Deterding, S., Dixon, D., Khaled, R., Nacke, L.: From game design elements to gamefulness: defining gamification. In: Proceedings of the 15th International Academic MindTrek Conference: Envisioning Future Media Environments, pp. 9–15. ACM (2011). https://doi.org/10.1145/2181037.2181040

11. Dichev, C., Dicheva, D.: Gamifying education: what is known, what is believed and what remains uncertain: a critical review. Int. J. Educ. Technol. High. Educ. **14**(1), 1–36 (2017). https://doi.org/10.1186/s41239-017-0042-5

12. Dichev, C., Dicheva, D., Irwin, K.: Towards activity-centered gamification design. In: Proceedings of the IEEE International Conference on Teaching, Assessment, and Learning for Engineering (TALE 2019) (2019)

13. Hajarian, M., Bastanfard, A., Mohammadzadeh, J., Khalilian, M.: A personalized gamification method for increasing user engagement in social networks. Soc. Netw. Anal. Min. **9**(1), 1–14 (2019). https://doi.org/10.1007/s13278-019-0589-3

14. Hallifax, S., Serna, A., Marty, J.-C., Lavoué, É.: Adaptive gamification in education: a literature review of current trends and developments. In: Scheffel, M., Broisin, J., Pammer-Schindler, V., Ioannou, A., Schneider, J. (eds.) EC-TEL 2019. LNCS, vol. 11722, pp. 294–307. Springer, Cham (2019). https://doi.org/10.1007/978-3-030-29736-7_22

15. Hamari, J., Koivisto, J., Sarsa, H.: Does gamification work? - A literature review of empirical studies on gamification. In: 2014 47th Hawaii International Conference on System Sciences (2014)

16. Hamari, J., Koivisto, J., Sarsa, H.: Does gamification work?-a literature review of empirical studies on gamification. In: HICSS, vol. 14, pp. 3025–3034 (2014)

17. Heilbrunn, B., Herzig, P., Schill, A.: Tools for gamification analytics: a survey. In: 2014 IEEE/ACM 7th International Conference on Utility and Cloud Computing, pp. 603–608. IEEE, December 2014. https://doi.org/10.1109/UCC.2014.93, https://dl.acm.org/citation.cfm?id=2759989.2759996

18. Hodent, C.: The Gamer's Brain: How Neuroscience and UX Can Impact Video Game Design. CRC Press, Boca Raton (2017)

19. Hunicke, R., LeBlanc, M., Zubek, R.: MDA: a formal approach to game design and game research. In: Proceedings of the AAAI Workshop on Challenges in Game AI, vol. 4, p. 1722 (2004)

20. Huotari, K., Hamari, J.: Defining gamification: a service marketing perspective. In: Proceeding of the 16th International Academic MindTrek Conference, pp. 17–22 (2012). https://dl.acm.org/citation.cfm?id=2393137

21. Hussain, S., Atallah, R., Kamsin, A., Hazarika, J.: Classification, clustering and association rule mining in educational datasets using data mining tools: a case study. In: Silhavy, R. (ed.) CSOC2018 2018. AISC, vol. 765, pp. 196–211. Springer, Cham (2019). https://doi.org/10.1007/978-3-319-91192-2_21

22. Hyrynsalmi, S., Smed, J., Kimppa, K.: The dark side of gamification: how we should stop worrying and study also the negative impacts of bringing game design elements to everywhere. In: GamiFIN, pp. 96–104 (2017)

23. Kapp, K.M.: The Gamification of Learning and Instruction. Wiley, San Francisco (2012)

24. Kapp, K.M.: The gamification of learning and instruction: game-based methods and strategies for training and education (2012). https://dl.acm.org/citation.cfm?id=2378737

25. Kim, T.W., Werbach, K.: More than just a game: ethical issues in gamification. Ethics Inf. Technol. **18**(2), 157–173 (2016). https://doi.org/10.1007/s10676-016-9401-5

26. Klock, A.C.T., Gasparini, I., Pimenta, M.S.: Designing, developing and evaluating gamification: an overview and conceptual approach. In: Tlili, A., Chang, M. (eds.) Data Analytics Approaches in Educational Games and Gamification Systems. SCI, pp. 227–246. Springer, Singapore (2019). https://doi.org/10.1007/978-981-32-9335-9_12

27. Klock, A.C.T., Gasparini, I., Pimenta, M.S., Hamari, J.: Tailored gamification: a review of literature. Int. J. Hum Comput Stud. **144**, 102495 (2020)

28. Klock, A.C.T., Pimenta, M.S., Gasparini, I.: A systematic mapping of the customization of game elements in gamified systems. Anais do Simpósio Brasileiro de Jogos e Entretenimento Digital (2018)

29. Knutas, A., van Roy, R., Hynninen, T., Granato, M., Kasurinen, J., Ikonen, J.: A process for designing algorithm-based personalized gamification. Multimedia Tools Appl. **78**(10), 13593–13612 (2018). https://doi.org/10.1007/s11042-018-6913-5

30. Koivisto, J., Hamari, J.: The rise of motivational information systems: a review of gamification research. Int. J. Inf. Manage. **45**, 191–210 (2019). https://doi.org/10.1016/j.ijinfomgt.2018.10.013

31. Landers, R.N., Collmus, A.B.: Gamifying a personality measure by converting it into a story: convergence, incremental prediction, faking, and reactions. Int. J. Sel. Assess. **30**(1), 145–156 (2022)

32. Landers, R.N., Tondello, G.F., Kappen, D.L., Collmus, A.B., Mekler, E.D., Nacke, L.E.: Defining gameful experience as a psychological state caused by gameplay: replacing the term 'Gamefulness' with three distinct constructs. Int. J. Hum Comput Stud. **127**, 81–94 (2019). https://doi.org/10.1016/j.ijhcs.2018.08.003

33. Lopez, C.E., Tucker, C.S.: Adaptive gamification and its impact on performance. In: Fang, X. (ed.) HCII 2021. LNCS, vol. 12789, pp. 327–341. Springer, Cham (2021). https://doi.org/10.1007/978-3-030-77277-2_25

34. Loughrey, K., Broin, D.: Are we having fun yet? Misapplying motivation to gamification. In: 2018 IEEE Games, Entertainment, Media Conference (GEM), pp. 1–9. IEEE (2018). https://doi.org/10.1109/GEM.2018.8516535

35. Manovich, L., Malina, R.F., Cubitt, S.: The Language of New Media. MIT press, Cambridge (2001)

36. Meder, M., Plumbaum, T., Albayrak, S.: A primer on data-driven gamification design. In: Proceedings of the Data-Driven Gamification Design Workshop, pp. 12–17. CEUR-WS.org (2017)

37. Mora, A., Tondello, G.F., Nacke, L.E., Arnedo-Moreno, J.: Effect of personalized gameful design on student engagement. In: 2018 IEEE Global Engineering Education Conference (EDUCON), pp. 1925–1933, April 2018. https://doi.org/10.1109/EDUCON.2018.8363471

38. Mora, A., Riera, D., González, C., Arnedo-Moreno, J.: Gamification: a systematic review of design frameworks. J. Comput. High. Educ. **29**, 516–548 (2017). https://doi.org/10.1007/s12528-017-9150-4

39. Morschheuser, B., Hassan, L., Werder, K., Hamari, J.: How to design gamification? A method for engineering gamified software. Inf. Softw. Technol. **95**, 219–237 (2018). https://doi.org/10.1016/j.infsof.2017.10.015

40. Neto, E.B.: O ensino híbrido: processo de ensino mediado por ferramentas tecnológicas. Ponto-e-Vírgula: Revista de Ciências Sociais (22), 59–72 (2017)
41. Norman, D.A.: Emotional Design: Why We Love (or Hate) Everyday Things. Basic Civitas Books, New York (2004)
42. OECD.: PISA 2018 Assessment and Analytical Framework. OECD publishing (2019)
43. Orji, R., Nacke, L.E., Di Marco, C.: Towards personality-driven persuasive health games and gamified systems. In: Proceedings of the 2017 CHI Conference on Human Factors in Computing Systems, pp. 1015–1027 (2017)
44. Orji, R., Oyibo, K., Tondello, G.F.: A comparison of system-controlled and user-controlled personalization approaches. In: Adjunct Publication of the 25th Conference on User Modeling, Adaptation and Personalization, pp. 413–418. UMAP 2017, ACM, New York (2017). https://doi.org/10.1145/3099023.3099116
45. Palomino, P., Toda, A., Rodrigues, L., Oliveira, W., Isotani, S.: From the lack of engagement to motivation: gamification strategies to enhance users learning experiences. In: 19th Brazilian Symposium on Computer Games and Digital Entertainment (SBGames)-GranDGames BR Forum, pp. 1127–1130 (2020)
46. Palomino, P.T.: We will hold the line: O Fandom como forma de participação dos fãs no desenvolvimento do universo transmidiático do jogo Mass Effect (2015)
47. Palomino, P.T., Toda, A.M., Oliveira, W., Cristea, A.I., Isotani, S.: Narrative for gamification in education : why should you care ? In: International Conference of Advanced Learning Techniques - ICALT 2019 (2019)
48. Palomino, P.T.: Gamification of virtual learning environments: a narrative and user experience approach. Ph.D. thesis, University of Sao Paulo (2022)
49. Pink, D.H.: Drive: The Surprising Truth About What Motivates Us. Penguin, Westminster (2011)
50. Prensky, M.: Digital Game-Based Learning, vol. 1. McGraw-Hill, New York (2003). https://doi.org/10.1145/950566.950596
51. Protásio, A.: Jogando histórias: refletindo sobre a narrativa dos jogos eletrônicos (2014)
52. Recabarren, M., Corvalán, B., Villegas, M.: Exploring the differences between gamer and non-gamer students in the effects of gamification on their motivation and learning. Interact. Learn. Environ., 1–14 (2021)
53. Reimers, F.M., Schleicher, A.: A framework to guide an education response to the COVID-19 pandemic of 2020. OECD (2020). Accessed 14 Apr 2020
54. Rodrigues, L., Oliveira, W., Toda, A., Palomino, P., Isotani, S.: Thinking inside the box: how to tailor gamified educational systems based on learning activities types. In: Proceedings of the Brazilian Symposium of Computers on Education, pp. 823–832. SBC (2019). https://doi.org/10.5753/cbie.sbie.2019.823
55. Rodrigues, L., et al.: Personalization improves gamification: evidence from a mixed-methods study. Proc. ACM Hum. -Comput. Interact. 5(CHI PLAY), 1–25 (2021). https://doi.org/10.1145/3474714
56. Rodrigues, L., et al.: Are they learning or playing? Moderator conditions of gamification's success in programming classrooms. ACM Trans. Comput. Educ. (TOCE) 3, 1–27 (2022)
57. Rodrigues, L., Toda, A.M., Oliveira, W., Palomino, P.T., Isotani, S.: Just beat it: exploring the influences of competition and task-related factors in gamified learning environments. In: Anais do XXXI Simpósio Brasileiro de Informática na Educação, pp. 461–470. SBC (2020)

58. Rodrigues, L., Toda, A.M., Palomino, P.T., Oliveira, W., Isotani, S.: Personalized gamification: a literature review of outcomes, experiments, and approaches. In: García-Peñalvo, F.J. (ed.) Proceedings of the 8th International Conference on Technological Ecosystems for Enhancing Multiculturality (TEEM 2020), Salamanca, Spain, 21–23 October 2020, October 2020

59. Rodrigues, L., Toda, A.M., dos Santos, W.O., Palomino, P.T., Vassileva, J., Isotani, S.: Automating gamification personalization to the user and beyond. IEEE Trans. Learn. Technol. **15**, 199–212 (2022)

60. Sailer, M., Homner, L.: The gamification of learning: a meta-analysis. Educ. Psychol. Rev. **32**, 77–112 (2020). https://doi.org/10.1007/s10648-019-09498-w

61. Salen, K., Tekinbaş, K.S., Zimmerman, E.: Rules of Play: Game Design Fundamentals. MIT press, Cambridge (2004)

62. Sánchez-Mena, A., Martí-Parreño, J.: Gamification in higher education: teachers' drivers and barriers. In: Proceedings of the International Conference of The Future of Education, July 2016

63. dos Santos, W.O., Bittencourt, I.I., Vassileva, J.: Gamification design to tailor gamified educational systems based on gamer types. Anais dos Workshops do Congresso Brasileiro de Informática na Educação 2018 **7**(1), 42 (2018). https://doi.org/10.5753/cbie.wcbie.2018.42

64. Savard, I., Mizoguchi, R.: Context or culture: what is the difference? Res. Pract. Technol. Enhanc. Learn. **14**(1), 1–12 (2019). https://doi.org/10.1186/s41039-019-0112-5

65. Toda, A., Oliveira, W., Shi, L., Bittencourt, I., Isotani, S., Cristea, A.: Planning gamification strategies based on user characteristics and DM: a gender-based case study. In: 12th International Conference on Educational Data Mining, pp. 438–443, July 2019

66. Toda, A., et al: For whom should we gamify? Insights on the users intentions and context towards gamification in education (CBIE), pp. 471–480 (2020). https://doi.org/10.5753/cbie.sbie.2020.471

67. Toda, A., Rafael, Y., Cruz, W., Xavier, L., Isotani, S.: Um processo de gamificação para o ensino superior: Experiências em um módulo de bioquímica. In: Anais do Workshop de Informática na Escola, vol. 22, p. 495 (2016)

68. Toda, A.M., do Carmo, R.M., da Silva, A.P., Bittencourt, I.I., Isotani, S.: An approach for planning and deploying gamification concepts with social networks within educational contexts. Int. J. Inf. Manage. **46**, 294–303 (2019). https://doi.org/10.1016/j.ijinfomgt.2018.10.001

69. Toda, A.M., et al.: Analysing gamification elements in educational environments using an existing gamification taxonomy. Smart Learn. Environ. **6**(1), 16 (2019). https://doi.org/10.1186/s40561-019-0106-1

70. Toda, A.M., et al.: How to gamify learning systems? An experience report using the design sprint method and a taxonomy for gamification elements in education. J. Educ. Technol. Soc. **22**(3), 47–60 (2019)

71. Toda, A.M., Valle, P.H.D., Isotani, S.: The dark side of gamification: an overview of negative effects of gamification in education. In: Cristea, A.I., Bittencourt, I.I., Lima, F. (eds.) HEFA 2017. CCIS, vol. 832, pp. 143–156. Springer, Cham (2018). https://doi.org/10.1007/978-3-319-97934-2_9

72. Toda, A.M., Toda, A.M., da Silva, A.P., Isotani, S.: Desafios para o Planejamento e Implantação da Gamificação no Contexto Educacional. RENOTE **15**(2), January 2017. https://doi.org/10.22456/1679-1916.79263, https://seer.ufrgs.br/index.php/renote/article/view/79263

73. Tondello, G.F., Mora, A., Nacke, L.E.: Elements of gameful design emerging from user preferences. In: Proceedings of the Annual Symposium on Computer-Human Interaction in Play, pp. 129–142. ACM (2017). https://doi.org/10.1145/3116595.3116627

74. Tondello, G.F., Nacke, L.E.: Validation of user preferences and effects of personalized gamification on task performance. Front. Comput. Sci. **2**, 29 (2020)

75. Tondello, G.F., Orji, R., Nacke, L.E.: Recommender systems for personalized gamification. In: Adjunct Publication of the 25th Conference on User Modeling, Adaptation and Personalization, pp. 425–430. ACM (2017). https://doi.org/10.1145/3099023.3099114

76. Tondello, G.F., Wehbe, R.R., Diamond, L., Busch, M., Marczewski, A., Nacke, L.E.: The gamification user types Hexad scale. In: Proceedings of the 2016 Annual Symposium on Computer-human Interaction in Play, pp. 229–243. ACM (2016). https://doi.org/10.1145/2967934.2968082

77. Tondello, G.F.: Dynamic Personalization of Gameful Interactive Systems. Ph.D. thesis, University of Waterloo (2019)

78. Van Roy, R., Zaman, B.: Need-supporting gamification in education: an assessment of motivational effects over time. Comput. Educ. **127**, 283–297 (2018). https://doi.org/10.1016/j.compedu.2018.08.018

79. Yannakakis, G.N., Togelius, J.: Experience-driven procedural content generation. IEEE Trans. Affect. Comput. **2**(3), 147–161 (2011). https://doi.org/10.1109/T-AFFC.2011.6

80. Zainuddin, Z., Chu, S.K.W., Shujahat, M., Perera, C.J.: The impact of gamification on learning and instruction: a systematic review of empirical evidence. Educ. Res. Rev. **30**, 100326 (2020)

Ethics and Games, Ethical Games and Ethics in Game

Luiz Paulo Carvalho[1]([envelope]) [ORCID], Flávia Maria Santoro[2], Jonice Oliveira[1],
and Rosa Maria M. Costa[2]

[1] PPGI, UFRJ, Rio de Janeiro, Brazil
luiz.paulo.carvalho@ppgi.ufrj.br, jonice@dcc.ufrj.br
[2] DICC, UERJ, Rio de Janeiro, Brazil
{flavia,rcosta}@ime.uerj.br

Abstract. In the 2020s, we perceive complexity unique to the 20th century with issues such as younger and younger children playing on cell phones; the rise of e-Sports; with virtual reality, a player can role-play acts with near-real proximity; gamification invading areas such as Education and Business; less demanding and more popular technical components, allowing more and more interested parties to develop games. This plurality of factors leads us to think: are we thinking about the Brazilian gaming scenario, including research, from foundations and principles in Ethics? Are academic-scientific researches considering Research Ethics? Do the game design and production consider ethical aspects? We propose the challenge of elevating the thinking and doing of Games in Brazil to also encompass ethical reflection. That is, it is not reduced to the mere analysis of "good" or "bad", it is about elaborating, analyzing, evaluating, and reflecting on complex and compound ethical dilemmas.

Keywords: Computational ethics · Ethics · Digital games · Great challenges · Metascience

1 Level 1. Starting with Ethics

This section introduces the core of this present work and the heart of this great challenge. Ethics is one of the traditional branches of Philosophy that studies actions through the values of customs, habits, and conduct, known as Moral Philosophy [34]. It encompasses the Theory of Value [12] together with Aesthetics, known as the Philosophy of Art [33]. While Ethics encompasses practices, Aesthetics encompasses, *lato sensu*, beauty and taste through emotional or sensory values.

There are several lines of thought associated with Ethics. We dialogue with the knowledge and definitions in [11, 12, 34, 37]. The subject of Ethics is Morality. Despite being commonly associated with "good" and "bad", "right" and "wrong",

---

Supported in part by CNPq/CAPES.

R. P. d. Santos and M. d. S. Hounsell (Eds.): GranDGamesBR 2020/2021, CCIS 1702, pp. 134–158, 2023.
https://doi.org/10.1007/978-3-031-27639-2_7

or concepts linked to Justice or Virtue, its scope overflows these socially constructed concepts in different times and spaces. A society without any of these constructs is still subject to scrutiny by Ethics.

We soon return to Ancient Greece. Plato elaborated on metaphysical analyses dealing with the human soul, dividing it in a structuralist way into three hierarchical parts that guide us. **Desire**, instincts and impulses; **emotion**, subjectivity and feelings; **reason**, objectivity, facts, and arguments. One of the seminal philosophers of Ethics, Aristotle, extended this concept to the Theory of Value. This framework is considered the dominant paradigm for Ethics to this day. Plato proposes a hierarchical perception of the human soul. The incessant search would reach the full human essence for reason and rationality in its actions, Ethics.

Aristotle places Ethics at the *tripartite* apex, in reason. The study of Ethics has its foundations in reason, i.e., rational analyses. At recent moments in history, thinkers questioned the positioning of Ethics as strictly rational. Hume links Reason to Emotion, rethinking this whole structure of philosophical thought as a maturing fuel for other ethical principles in the 20th century, such as the Ethics of Care. Science is categorically and objectively guided by Reason [18], as well as its practices. However, Ethics does not always guide Science.

The Moral is subject to subjective perception. We are all endowed with morals, manifested through our actions, consciously or unconsciously. On the other hand, ethics is objective. It operates at the extremes between particular and relative, balancing subjectivity and objectivity in negotiation between individual and collective interests without giving up rationality. Furthermore, ethical consideration respects the self-immanence of being, preventing self-annulment or going against itself. Decision-making guided by reason is considered ethical, moral, or immoral depending on its context.

Ethics deals with plausible, rational, and open **dilemmas**. For example, a game of tag between children is an action; eventually, children may quarrel, argue, develop some frustration, and get upset - a psychosocial phenomenon of a game with people involving disputes, winners, and losers. If a strange adult, let us consider a man, gets involved in the game, this game of tag dialogues with different values. From this new scenario, ethical dilemmas can be raised, varying with the moral parameters of the environment.

1.1   Bonus Stage. Terminology, Definitions, and Examples

Several definitions and concepts are available in the literature from different periods. In this section, we present these concepts, their definitions, and examples to situate better and contextualize them. It is necessary to announce with whom we dialogue the objective of this Section. We will delve into the three central foundations, **Ethics, Morals, Value**, and **ethical principles or theories**. Other concepts will be announced as needed and emerge throughout this work.

Starting with ethics:

"Ethics is the theory, investigation or explanation of a type of human experience or form of human behavior, of morality, but considered in its totality, diversity and variety.

[...]
The value of ethics as a theory lies in what it explains, not in prescribing or recommending action in concrete situations.
[...]
Like other sciences, ethics is faced with facts. Because they are human, this in turn implies that they are facts of value. But this in no way detracts from the demands of an objective or rational study. Ethics studies a form of human behavior that men deem valuable and, moreover, obligatory and inescapable. But none of this in the least alters the truth that ethics must provide a rational understanding of a real, effective aspect of human behavior.
[...]
Ethics is the theory or science of the moral behavior of men in society.
In other words, it is the science of a specific form of human behavior.
[...]
According to this approach, ethics is concerned with an object of its own: the sector of human reality that we call moral, constituted - as we have already said - by a peculiar type of human facts or acts. As a science, ethics starts from a certain type of facts in order to discover their general principles. In this sense, although it starts from empirical data, that is, from the existence of an effective moral behavior, it cannot remain at the level of a simple description or record of them, but transcends them with its concepts, hypotheses and theories. As scientific knowledge, ethics must aspire to more complete rationality and objectivity, at the same time, it must provide systematic, methodical and, as far as possible, verifiable knowledge." [37] [our translation]

In this sense, we move Ethics away from a strictly or essentially speculative area of knowledge, as traditionally defined [22,37], bringing it closer to science, as the study of moral behavior. It takes place in an interdisciplinary dialogue with areas such as Sociology, Anthropology, Psychology, and Law Studies [37].

Ethical consideration or scrutiny depends on two factors, conscious motive and voluntary act, which brings us back to the perspective of self-preservation.

On motivation and consciousness, the Loot Box (LB) system in digital games is an example [9,35]. These systems are similar to the mechanics of *gacha* games[1]. Considering its potential to arouse or promote addictive behavior in games [35], individuals negatively influenced by these mechanisms have impaired motivational consciousness. That is, their moral act is beyond the ethical sphere. In the Brazilian context, [9] reinforces the categorization of the LB phenomenon as a game of chance, and to be regularized, they need to move away from this. A person addicted to gambling acts subconsciously or unconsciously, harming himself. Without the rational or conscious perception of its actions, it consumes *loot boxes* indiscriminately, either until reaching its goal or extending this behavior to subsequent events.

Regarding voluntary acts, we can analyze game development and the psychosocial influence of games. Design choices, primarily aesthetic, are moral acts by game designers. Despite the absence of scientific consensus on the degree to which digital games psycho-socially influence their players, it is absurd to think

---

[1] https://en.wikipedia.org/wiki/Gacha_game. Accessed on 07/07/2022.

that, on the other hand, the influence is null. We could bring here extensive literature on this topic. However, our focus is on voluntary acts associated with designers' freedom of design. That is, when a designer materializes an idea and makes it a functional or non-functional requirement of a digital game, he does so through a voluntary act. Even if it did and culminated in an "illegal" outcome, like a game with Nazi propaganda, it would still do it voluntarily. Moreover, it culminates in the conclusion in [14]:

> "Results demonstrated that female characters within video games are unevenly represented compared with male characters, with female characters mostly shown as subordinate to the male hero of the game, objectified, and hypersexualized with disproportionate body parts. The review also uncovered the propensity for men exposed to objectified and sexualized female characters within video games to hold sexist attitudes toward women in a real-life setting, and being more lenient to accept cultural rape myths." [14]

Then, we perceive negligence on the part of designers of digital games regarding this scientifically structured reality[2]. Despite several works indicating the adverse effects and consequences, the design of female characters persists in the same way. They carry out an ethical reflection; consciously, this is the moral act chosen by those involved.

Consider, at a superstructure level, phenomena such as machismo, hegemonic masculinity, and patriarchy combined with digital game design. From an ethical perspective guided by rationality, the intention and motivation behind a particular graphic design choice must be analyzed if the argument is "female bodies outside the hegemonic paradigm of excluding beauty, without elements of sensuality, or without graphic artifices of sexual appeal, do not sell or not are commercially appealing", and also think that the female body or images are a product and that its primary intention is to remain a fetish so that it can be commercialized. Through trivial and simple ethical reasoning, we can conclude that this ideology, which will underlie the moral act behind the design, is both not beneficial and potentially harmful, initially on a symbolic level, to people who identify themselves as female.

We move on to morals:

> "Morality is a system of norms, principles and values, according to which the mutual relations between individuals or between them and the community are regulated, in such a way that these norms, endowed with a historical and social character, are freely accepted. Consciously, out of an inner conviction, and not in a mechanical, external, or impersonal way.
> [...]
> But, both in the way the individual conscience reacts to them and asserts itself, and in the way in which the personal and the collective relate to each other in moral behavior, the influence of dominant social conditions and relationships is

---

[2] In this specific passage, we avoid the debate about "how to represent the female gender in digital games graphically", the focus is on the epistemic responsibility of the influence of games through their design.

evidenced. Strictly speaking, as the individual does not exist in isolation, but as a social being, there is also no strictly personal morality. The agents of moral acts are only concrete individuals, whether they act separately or in social groups, and their moral acts - by virtue of the social nature of individuals - always have a social character.

[...]

Morality tends to transform itself into morality due to the demand for fulfillment that is in the essence of the normative itself; morality is morality in action, practical and practiced morality.

[...]

But even when the individual thinks that he is acting in exclusive obedience to his conscience, to a supposed "inner voice", which in each case tells him what he should do, that is, even when he thinks he decides alone in the holy recess of his conscience, the individual does not fail to accuse the influence of the social world of which he is a part and, from his interiority, he does not fail to speak to the social community to which he belongs.

[...]

The moral act, as a conscious and voluntary act, presupposes a free participation of the subject in its performance, which, although incompatible with the forced imposition of norms, is not compatible with the historical-social necessity that conditions it." [37] [our translation]

The moral is an ideology [37], which occurs in both subjective and objective scopes. Subjective refers to individuals and their sensations, experiences, paths, and perspectives; objective, because we formalize and structure this subjectivity in the form of negotiating it and living with others. An example of the objectivity of morality is norms or laws; we judge subjectivity as "good" or "bad". From subjection, an objective disruption emerges that influences norms and laws morally. It is a dialectical or dialogic relationship.

We can cite aspects of morality in two examples associated with digital games. The first deals with the phenomenon of toxic meritocracy in e-Sports: "In esports women are trained to support sexist structures and focus on their flaws as individuals, similar to what is occurring in games culture more broadly as well as television and film, which prohibits feminist alternatives of success and failure." [8]. As mentioned above, concerning the superstructures that favor the masculine gender and their characteristics, the current morality about the context of playing, mainly professionally as an athlete, is favorable to *cis* men and harmful to other identities [29]. This scenario worsens when it involves gender militancy. Players actively engaged in feminist causes may suffer even more discrimination, and reprisals, for clashing with the dominant moral *status quo*.

The second is related to age rating and games. There is an indicative age rating for digital games in several places worldwide, such as Brazil, Brazilian advisory rating system[3]; United States of America, Entertainment Software Rating

---

[3] https://en.wikipedia.org/wiki/Brazilian_advisory_rating_system. Accessed on 07/07/2022.

Board[4] (ESRB); and Europe, Pan European Game Information[5] (PEGI). These institutional entities define "appropriate ages" for children or young people to consume cultural artifacts with moral content that is appropriate and healthy for their respective age groups.

For each of these entities, the minimum age related to the game *Counter-Strike: Global Offensive* (CS:GO) is different, ranging from 16, Brazil; 17 (Mature), ESRB; 18, PEGI. As an **indicative** recommendation only, several child prodigies are listed, ranging in age from 14 to 17 years old [24]. Moreover, a 16-year-old player, Lizhi "Starry" Ye, announced a temporary "retirement" from the game after anti-addiction rules by China's video game regulator drastically limited the playing time of under-18s [26].

In a broader scope, through cyberspace itself, the perception of the minimum age to play CS:GO is divergent, as shown in Fig. 1. While experts indicate minimum age of 16 years, adults and kids indicate 12 years, according to data extracted from the *common sense media* forum[6]. Interestingly, adults, mainly parents or guardians, are more concerned with toxic, vulgar, or profane interactions between players than explicit game violence.

Parent reviews for Counter-Strike: Global Offensive

Common Sense says	Parents say	Kids say
☑ age 16+	age 12+	age 12+
★★☆☆☆	★★★★☆	★★★★☆
Based on our expert review	Based on 25 reviews	Based on 88 reviews

Fig. 1. Different perceptions about CS:GO age rating

Ethics has Morals as its object of study, and related to these two Values arise:

"[...] value is the preferential abstract quality attributed by the subject raised by the inherent characteristics of a given object that satisfy the needs and interests of that object.
With this definition, we consider the ideal nature of value, however, rooted in the material existence of the object, a reality from which the subject starts and which is not indifferent to him. For this very reason, in our view, this definition also emphasizes the relational nature of value, simultaneously objective and subjective, which constitutes the indelibly axiological mark of the subject in relation to other existing beings (ontological).
[...]

---

[4] https://pt.wikipedia.org/wiki/Entertainment_Software_Rating_Board. Accessed on 07/07/2022.
[5] https://pt.wikipedia.org/wiki/Pan_European_Game_Information. Accessed on 07/07/2022.
[6] https://www.commonsensemedia.org. Accessed on 07/07/2022.

It does not follow, however, that values are only subjective, since the valuation comes from a concrete and real object, or only objective, since their appreciation is made according to the subject's interest, a fact that denotes a certain ambivalence in the characterization of values because they present, at the same time, an objective and subjective dimension." [22] [our translation]

As far as we can see, Ethics is objective; Morality and values are objective and subjective. It is wrong to reduce Ethics to values [22]; the study of values is the nature of Axiology. [13] presents an extensive work dedicated to the intersection between values and games: "Decisions about game mechanics, which dictate how players may and may not function in a game world, and narrative content, which sets the rule system within a coherent framework, may reflect designers' conscious and unconscious considerations of values and their beliefs about 'how the world works', even when that world is fictional.".

Digital games are cultural artifacts that shape reality, intentionally or accidentally. Values are projected into games through their owners, based on morality. Game design can, consciously or not, be influenced by ethical considerations.

In the circumstances of software engineering, it is impossible to say that either creator, designers, or developers (or other members of operational sectors) transmit their values to the respective games conceived for reasons. First, depending on the organizational model, entities alien to the *de facto* engineering of the game may determine restrictions or obligations, depending on privilege and power, where not always who "builds" the game is who conveys its values to it. For example, when shareholders, executives, or producers make operational decisions related to games. Second, huge teams can design games, so it is implausible that the values of all team members influence or are transmitted to the game. For example, a vegan developer gets involved in a cooking game with ingredients and recipes involving animals. Third, legal or organizational norms may affect the game's design, and even if this does not concretely and materially impede the transmission of values, it mitigates.

Regarding the third item in the list above, a real example is the game *Wild Rift* (WR). WR is "the mobile version" of *League of Legends* (LoL). While LoL features excess sexism and graphic discrepancy in gender representation [5], WR has mitigated much of this inequality or representative fetish. In this sense, one can assume that Riot Games, the company responsible for both games, became aware of the excess of sexism and adjusted the graphic design of its characters, for example, covering the body of the female characters. However, the real and concrete intent concerns the greater reach of players, far from morals improvement or values revision. In order to lower the age rating in several countries, the company had to adapt the game to specific design restrictions. If the company insisted on the original graphic design, they would have to increase the age rating, which could cause regulatory problems in certain countries that are stricter in this regard; for example, preventing children from finding the game by configuring parental control mechanisms.

In Fig. 2 we separate certain arts from both LoL and WR. Some aspects are inconsistent, like the belly exposure when comparing Miss Fortune to Jinx

Fig. 2. Skins comparison between League of Legends (LoL) and Wild Rift (WR)

in both games. Although both depict women, only the first had her belly covered. In the case of Lux, the same skin in WR features greater clothing coverage. Thresh case is quite specific, and they stated its design change between games in an official communication [21]: "*To meet the requirements of Wild Rift's mobile platforms, and in order for us to maintain our current age rating (which is important because we want to make sure players of nearly all ages can play Wild Rift), we needed to make some adjustments to Thresh's existing design.*". The graphic design of the characters, part of the non-functional aesthetic requirements of the game, indirectly composes and transmits its values.

Another example of values, analyzed by [10], is the game *Rape Day* [39]. Briefly, its focus is heinous crimes such as rape and murder, including infanticide. The game's creator advertised the same as a niche game-oriented and dedicated to sociopaths, identifying himself as one. The game was banned from being broadcast on the *Steam* platform and would be considered a crime in Brazil, as it broadcasts heinous crimes. This example exposes a clash of values, both those important to the creator and those framed as immorality.

However, other games with an apology for rape and sexual harassment remain or have remained for a long time, aired on *Steam*, such as *Leanna's Slice of Life* [10]. Despite framing both games' values as part of immoral behavior, only *Rape*

Day has achieved extensive publicity and popularity, to the point of garnering immense amounts of negative ratings, both by the media and on Steam's recommendation systems. In the case of *Leanna's Slice of Life*, no, remaining on the platform[7]. In this sense, we can reflect on how *Steam* deals with values widely considered immoral, such as sexual violence/harassment, and makes decisions about the products present on its platform. For example, driven by financial losses, a flood of negative evaluations, following a utilitarian perspective, and legal determination, among others.

Concluding, throughout this work, we mention ethical principles and theories several times. However, given its complexity and extensiveness, we will keep this explanation brief.

As it is traditional in the academic-scientific practice of an area of knowledge, the domain of Ethics presents theories, concepts, principles, traditions, and renowned authors. For example, the construction of the conceptual perception of reality about the "good" object of study by several authors of Moral Philosophy, such as Aristotle, Kant, Epicurus, Aristippus, Bentham, Stuart Mill, and Marquis de Sade, among others [37].

Ethical principles and theories seek to structurally, formally, and adequately analyze human practices, morals, and values. When dealing with Computing, certain equivalences are limited, precarious, or impossible, which led several authors to think about other perspectives for Ethics, explicitly thinking about Computing, such as Floridi [1]. For example, analyzing an AI under the auspices of Ethics. Assign a value to AI practices. Analyze whether to attribute the benefits generated by AI to it or its author. Furthermore, if there are harms or risks, think about its author (e.g., an academic-scientist or engineer), who takes advantage of it (e.g., a company or organization), and who uses it (e.g., its users or customers), and who is subject to its reach (e.g., citizens indirectly affected by the influence or impact).

Despite these limitations and difficulties, theories and ethical principles can still be the basis for several reflections in the universe of computer games and digital entertainment. For example, [17] brings an interpretation of ethics in games through the bias of Aristotle, Saint Augustine, and Kant. It is customary in the epistemology of Moral Philosophy to refer to authors, endorsing their line of thought and their specific theories or principles.

Famous ethical constructs are, for example, Virtue Ethics, Consequentialism, Deontology, Utilitarianism, Communitarianism, Contractualism, Categorical Imperatives, Business Ethics, Feminist Ethics, Ethics of Care, Relativism [1,11,37]. It is already a starting point to think about specific elements, such as benefits, losses, risks, advantages, conflicts, consequences or impacts, and justice, among others; for a perspective more intertwined with Ethics, a step forward is also to incorporate ethical principles or theories.

---

[7] Up to the moment of publication of this present work, the game remains broadcast, marketed, and available on the platform.

2   Level 2. Heading to Games

Now that we have dealt with ethics, in this section, we will bring some of the complexities of games that might arise ethical or moral concerns. To start, we present some contemporary, current, and notorious examples related to ethics and morals in games. These examples can also serve as a foundation of concern for academic research or reflections on game design or projects.

We resort to the proceedings of digital games-related events. In the Brazilian context, it includes the Brazilian Symposium on Computer Games and Digital Entertainment (SBGames). Internationally, it encompasses events such as the Foundations of Digital Games (FDG) and the Digital Games Research Association (DiGRA) conferences. Emphasizing that these can be primarily related to games, rather than the artifacts themselves; secondarily, its development, project, idea, sponsorship, financing, art, among others; indirectly, its effects, influences, implications, consequences, impacts, among others.

1. Are firearms present? If so, are they realistic?
2. Can the Player Character (PC) have the possibility of drastically violating a Non-Player Character (NPC)? For example, beating, raping, dismembering, among others;
3. Will the NPCs react according to the PC's actions? For example, if an NPC notices the player acting violently, he will initiate a "call the police" action or even intervene in the PC's actions;
4. Will the game dynamics reward or punish the PC's actions? For example, is there a different reward between saving or killing an NPC? Shouldn't some of these two options bring rewards? Should he be rewarded just for solving challenges or problems by resorting to violence? Can he/she be rewarded as well, if not more, by choosing paths without violence? At first, do these paths just exist?
5. Can PCs engage in non-heterosexual romantic and emotional relationships with NPCs? Is it possible to express affection in non-traditional ways?
6. Can the player build a PC with identity plurality? For example, playing with a wheelchair user;
7. If the game's setting is Rio de Janeiro city, will the *favelas* be represented in a fetishist way as "dens of crime and poverty"? Is the *favela* a geographic location in the game associated only with negative elements, such as poverty, sadness, hunger, misery?
8. As a game developed in Brazil by Brazilians, should the game's setting be located in Brazil? Considering the specifics of the Brazilian context? That is, without "Americanization";
9. If the project involves only one category of hegemonic identity, will they be able to represent and convey symbolic elements alien to their identity? For example, in a project where the entire team is made up of men or where men dictate all effective and conclusive decisions, they will represent women of different body types without appeal to sexual or sensual elements?

10. Should the missions and objectives of the game consider an educational or instructional aspect? Two examples: first, on a realistic map, when the character arrives at a location, navigation resources indicate historical facts there; second, when the PC attacks or tries to attack an NPC, the game either prevents him or exposes an anti-violence message or, through narrative immersion, generates a negative consequence for it and makes clear the association between the two.

11. If there are morally controversial relationships between characters, how can you represent them graphically? For example, sexual intercourse;

12. Can the game allow mods indiscriminately? For example, a mod where you "play as Hitler" and get rewarded for "killing Jewish NPCs"?

13. Should the project prioritize financial returns first and moral lessons second? For example, perhaps the "rape" functionality brings greater financial return or excluding firearms culminates in loss;

14. How should the project team interact with suggestions and criticisms from the external community? For example, thousands of players requesting the implementation of firearms, if not;

15. Let us consider (i) games, (ii) stakeholders involved in their design or production, and (iii) their implications or influences; are they separable? For example, if a game condones rape or non-consensual sex, who conceives or produces it is in favor of rape or non-consensual sex? If a player who consumes this game commits a rape, is there influence of the game? How to analyze the causal relationship between these three items without an explicit and objective testimony about this relationship (for example, the player explicitly announces that the game taught or motivated him)?

16. Should the Government intervene, in addition to defining age ratings, determining restrictive norms for digital games in Brazilian cyberspace?

17. Is it the responsibility of the distribution platform (e.g., *Steam*) to determine value prerequisites for the games on it? For example, reject that its catalog contains a game with graphic and excessive gratuitous violence?

18. Games that were developed at the expense of over exploitation and poor working conditions of the respective developers should be boycotted? Regardless of its intrinsic technical quality?

19. Regarding Intellectual Property (IP), should stakeholders involved in game engineering be considered co-owners of their creations? Or should only producers or proprietary companies, who have borne most of the expenses and costs, own this IP?

20. Considering the current moral values of the most famous and popular games in the e-sports scene, can they be included as Olympic sports? Or included in any official sports competitions? Or, in greater abstraction, to be considered whatsoever a sport? For example, First Person Shooter (FPS) depicting explosives, melee weapons and firearms are used to achieve the objective or Multiplayer Online Battle Arena (MOBA) in which the ultimate objective is achieved through destruction or violence, whether magical or realistic.

The practice of playing is older than the idea of Culture [16]. "Play", the act systematized and structured as a game, is older than the formal conception of

Ethics or Morals. The body, character, and mind go through a process similar to education through play, developing attitudes, even if disconnected from facts of reality [4], our character being constituted primarily by morals, reverberated by attitudes. Huizinga and Caillois, mentioned in this paragraph, are two authors who are fundamental to the epistemology of games, digital or not. However, their reflections are limited to the resources and time of their intellectual immanence, both of whom died before 1980. We believe that Huizinga and Caillois would perceive games, as in the 2020 s, differently. Let us consider the dynamics where a "player" can abuse the graphic power of immersive virtual reality technology to commit the most violent and immoral acts possible and the motivations that lead game designers to develop these features. Closing his seminal book, [16] announces:

> "Whenever we are seized with vertigo at the ceaseless shuttlings and spinnings in our mind of the thought: What is play? What is serious? we shall find the fixed, unmoving point that logic denies us, once more in the sphere of ethics. Play, we began by saying, lies outside morals. In itself it is neither good nor bad. But if we have to decide whether an action to which our will impels us is a serious duty or is licit as play, our moral conscience will at once provide the touchstone. As soon as truth and justice, compassion and forgiveness have part in our resolve to act, our anxious question loses all meaning. One drop of pity is enough to lift our doing beyond intellectual distinctions. Springing as it does from a belief in justice and divine grace, conscience, which is moral awareness, will always whelm the question that eludes and deludes us to the end, in a lasting silence."

Huizinga makes us reflect on whether playing is within the scope of morality. However, if the game allows explicit unethical or immoral acts in its context, the values spread to the parties involved beyond the respective game. And although this text appears to attack freedom of expression or ideas and creativity, our intention is not, *a priori*, to censor or abolish games. Ethical scrutiny is associated with them, which we hardly notice or even find in their *design rationale*. Alternatively, in some instances, even if perceived or found, it exposes a selfish view, with selfishness being an ethical position [12]; categorized as "amoral".

3   Level 3. The *wombo Combo*, ethics + games

After dealing with ethics and digital games, we are now going to link these two domains in this section, paving the way for thinking about the great challenges.

In the 2020 s, we perceive reality in a complexity unique to the 20th century. Younger and younger children are playing games on cell phones; age ratings do not prevent them from playing the overwhelming majority of games widely available on the Internet, such as *Counter Strike*; with the rise of *e-Sports*, many young people dream of a professional career, like *League of Legends*, with championships distributing prizes of hundreds of thousands of dollars; new studios and production companies are emerging on the Brazilian scene, with a dialogic relationship with the growth of digital game courses; digital migrants, such as adults and seniors, are occupying the gaming space, whether with *Candy Crush* or *Cartola FC*; while on the console and on the keyboard the player simulated, distantly, symbolic violence, today with virtual reality he can stage this act with almost real proximity, e.g., sticking a knife in the head of his enemies; the phenomenon of *gamification* has been invading, in a myopic and poorly founded way, areas involved with computational solutions, such as Education and Business; *engines* and other technical components are less demanding and more popular, allowing more and more interested parties to develop and produce games; governments, such as Korean and Chinese, and public institutions are increasingly involved with games and their requirements, functional or non-functional. These phenomena have been well recorded and structured in works by the SBGames.

As one of the possibilities to guide these challenges, we propose three structures for reflection on the combination of games and ethics. Ethics and games as a field of traditional knowledge; ethics and games as engineering or pragmatics, artifacts; research involving games and ethics. They can unfold at other levels.

Initially, we can think of **Ethics in games at a conceptual, theoretical and abstract level**. That is, thinking about the "idea" of a game, of playing, of entertainment, of the function of a game; aimed at digital games. Examples of topics for reflection are, but are not limited to, categorizing and validating the Blue Whale Challenge or Round 6 series dynamics as a game; if the interaction with Non-Fungible Tokens (NFT) is leisure, work or a disruptive way to merge these two concepts; think about the dynamics of "playing anything for money" and its moral interaction with the classical and traditional idea of playing; to weigh ethically between the distinction between serious play and "non-serious" play and how effectively "serious" a game must be to be considered a serious game; ethically ponder Chinese sesame credit as a game [27]; or, a conceptual classic in [16], to think of war as a game.

For example, a considerable portion of the world's population consumes digital games fueled by easy access to smartphones. Some digital games have greater critical mass compared to traditional sports. About this new conjuncture, we bring some questions for reflection. What remains for e-Sports to be part of more significant sporting competitions, such as the Olympics? Are the values and morality around the most famous games, like CS:GO or LoL, an obstacle? Should digital games have their competition like their own Olympics? Does framing these games as "Olympic sports" harm their leisure and entertainment character? Traditional sports are independent and dissociable from companies or organizations (football is not the intellectual property of any company). If Riot Games discontinues LoL after it is elevated to an Olympic sport, how to deal with this hypothesis?

In this sense, we can think of game ethics as an area and a concept. For example, instead of thinking about the human graphical representation aspects of a game, think about the idea of graphically representing humans in games based on ethical, moral, and value considerations. We can briefly sketch with the example of the inequality of gender representation in the LoL game, present in several other games.

When we choose to represent characters, there is a level of dialogue between reality and fantasy. As in [5,30], we perceive that the practice of representing female characters is the target of daydreams and fetishes that exceed their ideas and are mechanically repeated game after game. For example, female warriors wearing high heels, or *boobplates*, or with an amount of clothing incompatible with their final concept. High heels are a trivial example to analyze, being an object initially designed for men, and by men, by way of history, it was "pushed" to women only.

Regarding high heels, we noticed that they "choose" to ignore that men, in a given time and historical space, saw high heels as status symbols and valid or interesting footwear. Just as they choose to represent female combatants using them, when analyzing games in historical contexts[8] where male characters would wear high heels, they do not. On the other hand, high heels are "forced" in the design of female characters regardless of time, space, or impediment [30]. Not because these games are committed to "educating" or "conveying historical truth" to their audience, there is a choice of values behind them. Moreover, it is not unconscious or involuntary, so it is an ethical choice grounded in a particular morality.

For the perception of many people, the idea of women in high heels indicates sexuality, attractiveness, and status [38]. Digital games reinforce this fetish instead of stressing or questioning it. And then, we can stress this topic from a functionalist perspective and think if games should reinforce things as they are. Alternatively, from a conflict perspective, they should combat elements of discrimination. Furthermore, this reflection of games' conceptual or theoretical universe extends to secondary elements, such as price, access and availability, age rating, art, and goals, among others.

Leaving the level of thinking about games in an abstract way, at a conceptual and logical level, we go to the level of pragmatics. The second category is aimed at **"making" games considering ethical aspects**, while the first is "thinking" games. Here we treat games as artifacts in fact, in their applications, influences and impacts. Whether materialized games, projects or in production.

Here we can reflect on the engineering of games and their technical components, such as programming languages, data storage, graphics processing, among others. Moving to a more "down to earth" level, an example of an ethical aspect involving a game is the developers work conditions. A famous case involves the producer *Naughty Dog* and the game franchise *The Last of Us* [32]. We can ethically ponder the acceptability to exceed the limit of healthy workload to develop excellent games. Thinking about organizational responsibility, whether it is valid to boycott products from companies that over exploit their developers. Or, also, to think if the moral quality of the work is separated from its production, or is the former compromised by the latter. How would the developer feel if the entire result of their time, effort, and dedication (even more, through over exploitation) were ostracized because they boycotted the game and company in question.

---

[8] Either with characters set in these historical periods or with no formal historical allegiance commitment.

This analysis also includes organizations, whether public or private; players, marketing distribution platforms, among others. That is, it is not limited to the development team. Returning to the case of *Rape Day*, the creator explicitly announced that it is a niche game, dedicated and oriented "for sociopaths" like himself. And at first, a naive analyst may consider the proposal "unethical", which is epistemologically false, because the proposal was, indeed, ethically considered. The creator voluntarily, consciously and with moral responsibility included baby murders and rape in the game. And despite how monstrous some consider the game to be, it's undeniable that it was ethically thoughtful. Now, if games are supposed to make an apology for rape and infanticide, exposing these acts graphically and explicitly, allowing the player to perform them, this is a reflection on the previous point, about games as an abstraction.

We can think of the responsibilities of game distribution and marketing platforms in relation to their products [9]. Here we can think of some concerns for further reflection. If they allow games involving rape, will they be conniving with these values? Should these cases be resolved by massively negative interaction from community members? Because from this perspective, many immoral games would not have been de-indexed from searches on the platform, considering its positive reviews. Should this be resolved by legal norm or is the ideal an ethical self-regulation of the community itself?

From these two previous points we find most of the works published in SBGames; the third presents greater deficiency, ethics in the research of games and involving games. Analyzing ethical aspects through the SBGames proceedings, we found very few considerations about research in general or about the research in question [7].

What we perceive is a lack of seriousness or formality in research involving games regarding ethical aspects. That is, if we consider the traditional scientific aspects, the panorama is highly deficient [7].

Three are the central elements of this analysis. The first deals with ethical considerations when carrying out the research, such as the Ethics Committee or Free and Informed Consent; concerns about participants and their participation; treatment of the research protocol; transparency of research data, such as funding and databases involved; explicit communication about the research paradigm, approach, methodology and methods.

The second element involves consideration of the influence, impact, and consequence of the research, as well as proposed artifacts, if any. That is, what ethical, moral, or value interventions are expected, whether positively or negatively. Again returning to the case of *Rape Day*, its creator developed the game with ethically clear intentions, if we could consider the hypothesis that playing *Rape Day* would improve the well-being of sociopaths and keep them away from the intention of committing heinous acts, the influence of the game would be beneficial. But another setback is the uncontrolled distribution. Just as not every person can buy any prescription drug, if Rape Day (considered the aforementioned well-being improvement) could be distributed in a controlled and managed way to specific sociopaths, it would exponentially mitigate the moral consequence. Especially because to sociopaths the hideous specifics of the game would be "neutral".

The third, and most complex, element is the researcher's self-reflection on their game research. For example, a female researcher suffered from sexual violence and decided to develop her research around a game to make girls aware of sexual violence. This element also invites the game researcher to ask themselves "why am I doing this?" or "what improvements does this bring to my significant others?".

Here, the researcher must seek to distance himself as much as possible from a contribution, result or purpose that is particular to him. Because in this case, the neutral essence expected of the research is lost [37], however, the researcher can take a moral or political position when declaring his motivations and intentions, reiterating that his final proposal is collective, not self-centered. It is ethically plausible for the researcher to conduct a study that improves his life, as long as also considers the collective, i.e., not exclusively self-centered.

4   The Brazilian Special Level. *Punhos de Repúdio.*

In this Section, we analyze the Brazilian game *Punhos de Repúdio* (PdR)[9] from the perspective of ethics, morals and values. The game is featured on its Steam page:

"Fists of Rejection is a satirical 2D beat'em up game with classic arcade influences and a modern look.
The game tells the fictional story of a pandemic that has spread across the world and is being ignored by fanatics who do not believe that the disease is real, making the 4 unnamed protagonists, ordinary citizens adequately protected with gloves and mask, deal with these fanatics and resolve the situation with the force of their own fists." [our translation]

About the description, the developers announce: "Foul language, insults and profanity. Blood and cartoon violence", age rating 16.

The beat'em up style was quite famous in arcades and old games, considering the technical simple design and mechanics. Games with a "gratuitous violence" perspective, without explicit political appeal, or fantasy-themed, such as defeating a supernatural threat, stand out. Unlike these, PdR has a political appeal based on the extreme outrage of certain citizens against denialists or other morally dubious profiles implemented in the game as enemies.

The game has a clear political connotation. As mentioned above, Ethics deals with dilemmas. In addition to the values related to violence, the game concern is about the exemplary symbolism of dealing with denialist profiles during the COVID-19 pandemic. Using physical violence to interact with possible denialist vectors of COVID-19 that violate health guidelines and, in this way, expose both the protagonists of PdR and the other fictional characters (Brazilians) in danger.

---

[9] https://store.steampowered.com/app/1425760/Punhos_de_Repdio/. Accessed on 07/07/2022.

Unlike the morally dominant "pacifist" institutional paradigm, the developers also express their indignation and anger by dialoguing with a scenario extremely close to real danger, with a contemporary theme, with a real threat, in the Brazilian context. Concerning symbolic interactionism, even if the game's message is not objectively "beat the negationists" this is the moral result.

The ethical conflict revolves around principles versus consequences. In this case, we can cite the Tolerance Paradox through the "benevolent despotism" [25]. The "good citizen" must be parsimonious and tolerant of intolerance or use institutional means and channels to resolve this same intolerance. Nevertheless, there is a scenario of generalized moral and sanitary rot, where these members of the executive powers, who should enforce the use of masks and other official hygiene determinations, fail to comply with their basic sanitary practices, for example, neglecting the use of masks [28]. In this sense, it is controversial to think about how to be tolerant when the allegedly paladins are negligent and circumvent the established hygiene regulations; the same ones that are supposed to be the moral examples of the values they claim to defend and reinforce.

So the game goes against the principled idea of peace, peaceful education, and infinite tolerance, appealing to the consequence that violence is a possible way out in a maladjusted, immoral ecosystem with inconsistent or distorted values.

On the other hand, resorting to violence ignores the concrete resolution of the problem at a systemic or structural level. At this point, violence boils down to just that, violence. Drawing a parallel with concrete reality, beating someone will not make that person wear a mask or hand sanitize; in the game, this opponent will disappear when defeated. Thus, the game fails as an educational initiative because it uses an ineffective practical mechanism. It is effective in the short term but is a useless and morally reprehensible resource in the medium or more prolonged-term.

Together, other political elements are present. There is criticism of specific sociopolitical groups, such as religious fanatics, extremist nationalists, patrons of bars neglecting the pandemic, disinformation vectors, denialists, and exclusionary elitists, among others. It promotes values related to public goods, such as the Unified Health System (*Sistema Único de Saúde* – SUS) (in the game represented by a similar pseudonym) and partnership with application providers, as an operator of "essential services", for example, an *iFood* biker. In addition to the enemies representing the profiles already mentioned, NPCs transit through the game, acting following health standards peacefully, indicating that the PC can only interact negatively with its enemies.

The game deals with values such as violence, indignation, rebellion, corruption, health negligence, praise of the Brazilian public health system, realistic Brazilian culture, respect for essential services operating during the pandemic, and active militancy; supporting or repudiating them. In the moral aspect, there is an appeal to violence as a means of combating irresponsible intolerant people; as the reflection that is resorting to violence solves the symptom and not the cause; agenda oriented towards collusion with health measures. Ethically, dilemmas and reflections are easily perceptible. For example, following the reasoning of specific contributions, the game can assuage the repressed indignation, anger, and disgust of those who sympathize with the game's scenario, symbolically enabling them to resort to the fetish of cartoon violence as a way out. That is, compensating for the negative feeling experienced in reality through the game as an escape valve, without explicitly and directly expressing "resort to violence against these individuals who neglect health standards and offer danger to other Brazilians".

In this case, we can see in PdR a maturity associated with ethical aspects. The moral intention and the expression of values are intentional, explicit, and straightforward. It appeals to an immoral element in principle, violence; to an ineffective end, to solve the health neglect of selfish and perverse citizens through satirical tropes. However, it expresses an honest intention of indignation and discontent with the corrupt Brazilian ecosystem of the COVID-19 pandemic. It resorts abundantly to political elements, bringing a progressive and constructive agenda aligned with "left" aspects.

We can make an association with another game, also with clearly political aspects, published on the Steam platform and in a 2D beat'em up style; *Bolsomito 2K18* [2,15]. In the game *Bolsomito 2K18*, the then-presidential Jair Bolsonaro is represented attacking individuals with profiles considered "left", such as LGBTQIA+ people, blacks, and women, among others; and renowned political figures on the Brazilian scene, such as another presidential candidate, Fernando Haddad, his political opponent.

Unlike PdR, the protagonist does not resort to violence as a reaction to other objective violence. As announced by the game, the objective is to face "enemies who intend to establish a criminal ideological dictatorship in the country". The protagonist, Bolsonaro, takes to the streets, intending to beat enemies of the supposed "red army", who turn into feces when defeated.

In this comparison, a cold and superficial analysis can lead to an erroneous assessment that the two are "the same". Assertively, both resort to violence and share several values, such as political indignation[10], violence, satire through sociocultural tropes, and Brazilian elements.

However, other perceptions emerge when we delve more deeply through the bias of ethical aspects. Furthermore, these insights expose the differences. All PdR characters are fictional. In *Bolsomito 2K18* the image of Jair Bolsonaro is used without his formal consent or authorization, the same for other NPCs with highly faithful representations of personalities from concrete reality.

Bolsomito 2K18 promotes aggression against profiles of minority social representations, symbolically feeding the phenomenon of violence against them. PdR resorts to fictitious tropes of identities in a situation of privilege and power,

---

[10] It is imperative to emphasize, despite the two games dealing with political indignation, the epistemological difference of this item. Both are indignation in the political sphere, but in *Bolsomito 2K18* there is a socio-material void. In PdR, there is a concrete, observable and factual indignation; in *Bolsomito 2K18* there is a fanciful symbolic conspiracy that "left-wing minorities" are actively seeking to destroy Brazil through an affront to traditionalist and conservative values.

neutral or advantageous, using effectively real elements associated with facts. For example, religious fanatics: "Under the shield of faith, evangelical leaders across the country have encouraged the flock to disregard sanitary measures and pierce quarantines decreed by mayors and governors.", with disregard for social distancing, and the use of masks [3]. That is, there is a rational basis in the design of the satirical profiles of these characters.

Looking at principles, means, and ends, *Bolsomito 2K18* goes beyond the perspective of gratuitous violence, encouraging a targeted violence agenda. The simple act of attacking minorities for the sake of attacking, based on an unreal and illusory crusade, boils down to hatred, which also conveys indignation, only oriented to nullify and destroy others.

Finally, when we think about *Bolsomito 2K18* in the broad context, there is a relationship with the Brazilian presidential elections of 2018; in PdR, it is related to the COVID-19 pandemic. The first symbolically influences, through violence and hatred, the already polarized and decisive scenario for the country's future. The second encourages indignation at non-compliance with health standards without a political agenda that interacts with political decision-making events, influencing the panorama of privilege and power.

In this sense, we reflect on PdR, and *Bolsomito 2K18* games ethical aspects in the descriptive sphere, indicating the possibility of this practice without deep or complex specifications, such as Ethics theories or concepts. We could, equally, think in the normative sphere and reflect on ethical aspects, whether ethics, morals, or values, that brought improvements to both games. Complex or simple reflections are welcome, as long as they are well-founded and articulated.

5   Final Battle. With Great Importance Comes Great Challenges

This complexity mentioned in Sect. 3 is just the top of the iceberg. In this section, we will present the great challenges intersecting ethics and games as the central contribution of this work. Do we think about the Brazilian gaming scenario, including research in this domain, based on foundations and principles in Ethics? Are academic-scientific researches considering Research Ethics? Do game design and production consider ethical aspects in their practice? Whether they are Brazilian or international, operating in Brazil. What we perceive when analyzing the production of the largest academic event dedicated to the production of formal and structured knowledge of games in Brazil, SBGames, lacks this analysis and presents a fruitful and inviting gap for research on this topic, mainly inter/transdisciplinary.

We propose the challenge of elevating the thinking and doing of Games in Brazil to encompass ethical reflection. Regarding ethical reflection, we embrace all the elements exposed in Sect. 1. Not reducing to an axiological reduction of Ethics, e.g., the mere analysis of "good" or "bad". It is about elaborating, analyzing, evaluating, and reflecting on complex and compound ethical dilemmas.

Based on ethical principles and theories, to structure the reflection on morally sanitized games, coerced to adapt to certain norms, legal or not.

Other ethical elements are viable and in line with contemporary dilemmas. For example, when we say that, during ethical reflection, the person preserves himself and does not cancel himself, we can extend this weighting to the social discrimination perceived by the discriminated social entities by phenomenology. In the Games domain, when authors question sexism against women, symbolically, e.g., represented as a fetish, sexual objects, or tropes [5,30]; concretely, e.g., despised and violated in the games industry [6]. Like Arabs or Muslims routinely portrayed as terrorists, or other harmful tropes, in games produced in the United States [20]. As well as the interest of indigenous populations to enter the universe of game design to, from their vision and voice, communicate their culture to the world in a playful way[11], tired of perceiving the image and culture of their nation stereotyped in the hegemonic mainstream media.

Extending, Ethics values rational reflection, i.e., based on consolidated data, plural and sustainable visions, reliable references, and structured arguments. We can not disregard the context and setting, as moral and ethical precepts are a social, historical, and cultural construction. Freedom of expression and human rights and freedoms are linked, such as dignity, image, and self-preservation. Even if all analysis and evaluation are hostages to human bias, it is necessary to expand the rational horizon for dialogue and negotiation with other elements of reality. For example, they are representing LGBT+ people as exaggerated, e.g., absurdly feminized tropes, while a rational analysis and evaluation of reality expose that this discriminatory generalization is false. Thus, reducing this practice to depreciate the identity of others symbolically.

5.1   The Great Challenges

Limited to our knowledge, the combination of Ethics and Games is incipient in Brazilian research. Not only well-delineated issues follow this work. Regarding our interpretation, we will point out deficiencies and guidelines.

An Ethics for Games. Ensuring moral or ethical value to artifacts and games can be a path and a challenge. As Tavani problematizes Computational Ethics [36], we extend it to Ethics in Games. As noted in the SBGames proceedings, we can also contemplate ethical aspects, those involved in the design, and active or passive users (we will extend this topic in Sect. 5.1). When we say "involved in design" it is not just the designers. We also encompass entities in the engineering process, such as shareholders who make indirect decisions about game design. When we say "active or passive users" we mean those who effectively interact with the game and its values and those who do so passively, such as political entities that have never played a digital game but define age ratings, for example.

---

[11] http://www.gamehunikuin.com.br. Accessed in 07/07/2022.

Compartmentalization of Complexity. Dealing with the multivariate heterogeneity of reality [19]. When dealing with design, designer, artifact, and users, a rational ethical analysis must seek to encompass "the whole". So having a plural vision with composite elements is a priority. For example, they are analyzing the involvement of the value of designers and the responsible organization, considering a game that objectifies the representation of the female gender? Do the designers involved have the power and sociopolitical capital to define design requirements? Or are the entire top management, board, and executives headed by misogynistic and discriminating individuals? Even if there is diversity in that same organization, there is still hierarchical oppression. Therefore, the cause and effect relationship, condition, and consequence are not so simple to be analyzed only through the bias of the artifact alone. This complexity extends not only to the parties but also to space and time, e.g., (i) games with transnational reach and that cross different nations and cultures; (ii) a game that is morally accepted and promoted in the 20th century may no longer be perceived in this way in the 2020 s, regarding time and also the ethical and moral paradigm advances.

Ethics and Aesthetics. This field is open and little discussed in the gaming domain, whether as differentiation, intersection, or complement. Even if some philosophers, like Wittgenstein [40] in 1994, point to Ethics and Aesthetics as only one concept, this is not the consensus in the area [31]. While computing solutions mainly focus on informativeness and not beauty, this structuring is less objective and clearly expressed in the gaming domain. Not just for software, the physical design of video games (hardware) is an example of a gray zone in this challenge.

Social Sustainability. In gaming, do organizations have a moral duty to hire employees with social and cultural diversity in mind? Are all-male organizations necessarily misogynistic organizations? If a person of color participated in the design of a game that is widely considered racist, does that person's participation exempt from criticism? Do users have an epistemic responsibility to boycott or sabotage games that express explicitly immoral values? Should gamers be concerned about the moral values and working conditions of designers and developers involved in games they are fond of?

These ethical or moral dilemmas do not present easy or objectively correct answers. Both these and similar discussions are fortuitous and little discussed in the Brazilian context.

Moral Values, Their Influences and Impacts. Finally, we will explain based on a scenario of violence. Violent games make children violent? What values do these games convey? Do they serve as an "escape valve" from others' internalized violence, or encourage mass shootings, or are they developed by people alienated from ethics? Currently, there is a debate about the aspects of symbolic interactionism that games bring to the other elements that touch them.

If the game violence is limited to the symbolic field, why should it be evaluated by a concreteness approach?

Moreover, even if there is no objective measurement and classification, is there a way to escape the paradigm of violent games as we observe today? Is it a game that teaches, for example, how to faithfully build a lethal weapon supported by freedom of expression and ideas? Constructive and positive games, by reverse reasoning, will influence their users to better actions?

Anti-colonialism and Political-Cultural Sovereignty. Most games, physical or digital, consumed by the most considerable portion of the Brazilian population are not controlled, managed, maintained, or controlled by Brazilians. We find in popular and informal communications, even daily, statements such as "Brazilian games are bad", "Brazilians do not know how to play games", or "Brazil does not have producers, developers, or good games" . Most games, physical or digital, consumed by the most Brazilian population are not controlled, managed, maintained, or controlled by Brazilians. This phenomenon can be associated with the colonization and depreciation of Brazilian sovereignty: (i) cultural, most games do not present any Brazilian aspects, like history or culture; (ii) economic, even if the games consider the Brazilian culture, they do not maintain income or profit in Brazil; (iii) professional, where Brazilian specialists, e.g., historians, could apply their specialized knowledge in Brazil in games about Brazil; or (iv) technical, developing computer solutions native to Brazil, for use in Brazilian projects, such as the Lua language, developed by PUC-Rio.

We are constantly bombarded and encouraged to consume games that bring aspects and universes different from ours, while Brazil offers us many options. It is worth reflecting on what we symbolically consume, how much we encourage and value Brazilian elements, and how to think about a domain of Games in Brazil aimed at the Brazilian universe. These mentioned aspects are just a few in the context of anti-colonialism and political-cultural sovereignty.

As presented in Sect. 1, this ethical analysis must be reasonable and rational, i.e., avoiding "damn everything that comes from outside" or "playing games about Vikings is wrong and harmful to the cultural formation of Brazilians". At the same time, no Brazilian or Brazil enthusiast should play a game because it is considered "100% Brazilian".

Gamification from/to Everything. With the pandemic and related events, such as quarantine and social isolation, the Brazilian Digital Transformation process accelerated, easily noticeable. The translation of several services to a totally or partially digital way has sharpened the discussion about the phenomenon of Gamification. A striking example is in Education, as [23] points out, driven by the explosion of data, available platforms, and evaluative functionality. What, in the future, will not be "gamified"? Can everything be "gamified"? Is there any limit? Are the implementation cases of these initiatives ethically pondering positive and negative aspects? Or is it easier to pass grade students as if they "pass a stage" and paste grades as if they "beat a game"?

Considering that Gamification is here and will stay, how to implement it ethically? Thinking about its principles, values, consequences, and, most importantly, even disregarding it if the context indicates so?

6   Epilogue. Final Remarks

Ethical aspects, or Ethics alone, are complex of objective monitoring and measurement, that is, being "assessed as strongly structured indicators". In this sense, we forward the proposal to accompany thinking, research and studies; and doing, design, and project, routinely. In this sense, the following analytic examples can help in the evolution tracking of this great challenge: the quantity and quality progress of ethical aspects in scientific communications, e.g., the occurrence of an Ethics Committee and Free and Informed Consent; track if games produced follow ethical considerations about themselves, as their values and possible consequences; considering ethical foundations and principles, follow up if there will be a rise in the debate of moral values. This short, non-exhaustive list brings some examples of issues that can guide the follow-up and advancement of the topic over time. As a future referral, Sect. 5 elements can be condensed as a good or better practices guide, with adequate formatting and examples.

These are just a few examples of challenges that SBGames adequately conveys, concerning Ethics and Morals, in its published scientific communications. Even so, the domain of Brazilian games is not limited to SBGames, and the domain of Ethics is a fruitful and inviting field for reflection.

References

1. Barger, R.: Computer Ethics: A Case-Based Approach. Cambridge University Press, Cambridge (2008)
2. Borges, D., Câmara, M.: Bolsomito 2K18: Jair Bolsonaro é tema de jogo na Steam que agride mulheres, gays e negros (2018). https://www.techtudo.com.br/noticias/2018/10/bolsonaro-ganha-jogo-polemico-contra-oponentes-politicos.ghtml Accessed 07 July 2022
3. Bruno, C., Sampaio, J.: No pior momento da pandemia, as igrejas evangélicas permanecem lotadas (2021). https://veja.abril.com.br/brasil/no-pior-momento-da-pandemia-as-igrejas-evangelicas-permanecem-lotadas/ Accessed 07 July 2022
4. Caillois, R., Barash, M.: Man, Play, and Games. University of Illinois Press, Champaign (2001)
5. Carvalho, L.P., Cappelli, C.: Sexism and league of legends: NFR aesthetic analyses. In: Anais da V Escola Regional de Sistemas de Informação do Rio de Janeiro, pp. 38–45. SBC, Porto Alegre, RS, Brasil (2018)
6. Carvalho, L.P., Oliveira, J.: Subjectivities in software development from an STS and social institution perspective, a riot games case study. In: Anais do V WASHES, pp. 61–70. SBC, Porto Alegre, RS, Brasil (2020)
7. Carvalho, L.P., Suzano, J.A., Santoro, F.M., Oliveira, J., Costa, R.M.M.: Ética: Qual o Panorama de Pesquisa no Simpósio Brasileiro SBGames? In: Anais do XX SBGames. SBC, Porto Alegre, RS, Brasil (2021)

8. Cullen, A.L.L.: "I play to win!": Geguri as a (post) feminist icon in esports. Feminist Media Stud. **18**(5), 948–952 (2018). https://doi.org/10.1080/14680777.2018.1498112

9. Fantini, L.M., Fantini, E., Garrocho, L.F.: A regulamentac, ao das loot boxes no brasil: consideracÿoes eticas e legais acerca das microtransacÿ toes e dos jogos de azar. In: Anais do XVIII SBGAMES. SBGAMES '19, Rio de Janeiro, Rio de Janeiro, Brasil (2019)

10. Farbiarz, J.L., Valadares, V.H.D.P.R.: Nós não temos culpa, só conectamos pessoas: analisando a responsabilidade legal da plataforma de games steam no brasil nos crimes sexuais presentes em jogos adultos. In: Anais do XIX SBGAMES. SBGAMES '20, Recife, Pernambuco, Brasil (2020)

11. Ferraz, C.A.: Ética Elementos Básicos. NEPFIL online, Pelotas (2014)

12. Fieser, J.: Ethics. In: The Internet Encyclopedia of Philosophy (2020). https://iep.utm.edu/ethics/ Accessed 07 July 2022

13. Flanagan, M., Nissenbaum, H.: Values at Play in Digital Games. MIT Press, Cambridge (2014)

14. Gestos, M., Smith-Merry, J., Campbell, A.: Representation of women in video games: a systematic review of literature in consideration of adult female wellbeing. Cyberpsychol. Behav. Soc. Netw. **21**(9), 535–541 (2018). https://doi.org/10.1089/cyber.2017.0376

15. Gomes, H.S.: Passando vergonha! Jogo "Bolsomito 2k18" expõe Brasil no exterior, diz MP (2018). https://www.uol.com.br/start/ultimas-noticias/2018/12/05/passando-vergonha-jogo-bolsomito-2k18-expoe-brasil-no-exterior-diz-mp.htm Accessed 07 July 2022

16. Huizinga, J.: Homo ludens: o jogo como elemento da cultura. Editora da Universidade de S. Paulo, Editora Perspectiva, Coleção estudos (1971)

17. Joselli, M.: A ética e os games: "morais, imorais ou amorais?". um estudo sobre a ética em games segundo aristóteles, santo agostinho e kant. In: Anais do XIII SBGAMES. SBGAMES '14, Porto Alegre, Rio Grande do Sul (2014)

18. Lakatos, E., de Andrade Marconi, M.: Metodologia científica. Atlas (2017)

19. Luca Casali, G., Perano, M.: Forty years of research on factors influencing ethical decision making: establishing a future research agenda. J. Bus. Res. **132**, 614–630 (2020)

20. Machado, E.A.M.: Jogos digitais, guerra e identidade: a reprodução de temáticas securitizadas em jogos que envolvem a temática bélica. In: Anais do XIV SBGAMES. SBGAMES'26, Teresina, Piauí, Brasil (2015)

21. Moore, A., Forbes, B.: /Dev: thresh Re-fleshed and the viego no-go (2021). https://wildrift.leagueoflegends.com/en-us/news/dev/dev-thresh-re-fleshed-and-the-viego-no-go/. Accessed 07 July 2022

22. Pedro, A.P.: Ética, moral, axiologia e valores: confusões e ambiguidades em torno de um conceito comum. Kriterion **55**(130) (2014). https://doi.org/10.1590/S0100-512X2014000200002

23. Pimentel, M., Carvalho, F.: As máquinas (digitais em rede) de ensinar, a instrução (re)programada e a pedagogia (ciber)tecnicista (2021). https://horizontes.sbc.org.br/index.php/2020/06/02/maquinas-de-ensinar Accessed 07 July 2022

24. Popat, M.: The young prodigies of CSGO (2019). https://www.talkesport.com/news/the-young-prodigies-of-csgo/. Accessed 07 July 2022

25. Popper, K.: The Open Society and Its Enemies: New One-Volume Edition. Princeton University Press, Princeton (2013)

26. Rawat, A.S.: Breakout CS:GO talent starry might retire due to China's anti-addiction rules (2021). https://afkgaming.com/csgo/news/breakout-csgo-talent-starry-might-retire-due-to-chinas-anti-addiction-rules. Accessed 07 July 2022
27. dos Reis, A.V., Press, L.T.: Sesame credit and the social compliance gamification in china. In: Anais do XVIII SBGAMES. SBGAMES'19, Rio de Janeiro, Rio de Janeiro, Brasil (2019)
28. Rodrigues, G.: Policiais burlam uso da máscara contra a Covid-19 nas ruas de Goiânia (2021), https://www.metropoles.com/brasil/policiais-burlam-uso-da-mascara-contra-a-covid-19-nas-ruas-de-goiania. Accessed 07 July 2022
29. Rogstad, E.T.: Gender in esports research: a literature review. Eur. J. Sport Soc. **19**, 1–19 (2021). https://doi.org/10.1080/16138171.2021.1930941
30. Saláfia, J.S., Ferreira, N.B., Nesteriuk, S.: Os estereótipos em jogos de luta: da indumentária á hipersexualização de personagens femininas. In: Anais do XVII SBGAMES. SBGAMES'18, Foz do Iguaçu, Paraná, Brasil (2018)
31. Schellekens, E.: Aesthetics and Morality. Bloomsbury Aesthetics, Bloomsbury Academic, London (2008)
32. Schreier, J.: As naughty dog crunches on the last Of US II, developers wonder how much longer this approach can last (2020). https://kotaku.com/as-naughty-dog-crunches-on-the-last-of-us-ii-developer-1842289962. Accessed 07 July 2022
33. Schroeder, M.: Value Theory. In: The Internet encyclopedia of philosophy (2021). https://plato.stanford.edu/archives/spr2021/entries/value-theory/. Accessed 07 July 2022
34. Schwemmer, O.: Ethik. In: Mittelstraß, J. (ed.) Enzyklopädie Philosophie und Wissenschaftstheorie: Band 2: C-F, pp. 404–411. Metzler (2005)
35. Spicer, S.G., Nicklin, L.L., Uther, M., Lloyd, J., Lloyd, H., Close, J.: Loot boxes, problem gambling and problem video gaming: a systematic review and meta-synthesis. New Media Soc. **24**(4), 1001–1022 (2021). https://doi.org/10.1177/14614448211027175
36. Tavani, H.: The uniqueness debate in computer ethics: what exactly is at issue, and why does it matter? Ethics and Information Technology **4** (2002). https://doi.org/10.1023/A:1015283808882
37. Vázquez, A.S.: Ética. Civilização Brasileira, 39th (edn.) (2018)
38. Wade, T.J., Burch, R., Fisher, M.L., Casper, H.: On a pedestal: high heels and the perceived attractiveness and evolutionary fitness of women. Pers. Individ. Differ. **188**, 111456 (2022). https://doi.org/10.1016/j.paid.2021.111456
39. Wilde, T., Lahti, E., Brown, F.: Steam is currently listing a game called Rape Day in which you play as a 'serial killer rapist' (Updated) (2019). https://www.pcgamer.com/steam-is-currently-listing-a-game-called-rape-day-in-which-you-play-as-a-serial-killer-rapist/. Accessed 07 July 2022
40. Wittgenstein, L.: Tractatus logico-philosophicus. EDUSP (1994)

Challenges for XR in Games

Esteban W. G. Clua[1]([✉]), Daniela G. Trevisan[1], Thiago Porcino[2][iD],
Bruno A. D. Marques[3][iD], Eder Oliveira[1][iD], Lucas D. Barbosa[1][iD],
Thallys Lisboa[1], Victor Ferrari[1][iD], and Victor Peres[1][iD]

[1] Universidade Federal Fluminense, Niterói, Brazil
`esteban@ic.uff.br`
[2] Dalhousie University, Halifax, NS, Canada
[3] Universidade Federal do ABC, Santo André, Brazil

Abstract. Extended Reality as a consolidated game platform was always a dream for both final consumers and game producers. If for one side this technology had enchanted and called the attention due its possibilities, for other side many challenges and difficulties had delayed its proliferation and massification. This paper intends to rise and discuss aspects and considerations related to these challenges and solutions. We try to bring some of the most relevant research topics and try to guess how XR games should look in the near future. We divide the challenges into 7 topics, based on extensive literature reviews: Cybersickness, User Experience, Displays, Rendering, Movements, Body Tracking and External World Information. We believe that this topics are a Grand Challenge, since the next generation of entertainment depends on adequately solving them in the near future.

Keywords: Extended reality · Virtual reality · Digital entertainment · Head-mounted displays · UX

1 Introduction

Extended Reality (XR) platform can be considered as an increment of Virtual Reality in relation to immersion and interaction aspects. While VR platforms are mostly dedicated to visual issues and AR uses real scenes as the main stage, XR includes more external elements and senses, such as movements, tactile, haptics and the usage of the real environment as the application stage [116]. According to the Milgram Continuum, the virtual immersion is a result that comes not only from accurate visual aspects, but mostly from a precise combination of all human senses, orchestrated in such a way that all of them enhances each other. While many progresses had been achieved in graphics, audio, tracking and interfaces issues, there are still many remaining challenges, mostly related to a correct combination on adaption to recent XR hardware devices. In this paper we propose a division of areas for these challenges. We believe that for a real consolidation for games within this platform it is necessary to have robust

R. P. d. Santos and M. d. S. Hounsell (Eds.): GranDGamesBR 2020/2021, CCIS 1702, pp. 159–186, 2023.
https://doi.org/10.1007/978-3-031-27639-2_8

solutions in each field. We divide the challenges into 7 topics: cybersickness (CS), user experience and design guidelines, display and fovea, image quality and rendering, movements and redirect walking, body tracking and finally external world information and acquisition.

2   Cybersickness

Motion sickness (MS) is defined as the discomfort felt during a forced visual movement (without the same body movement), which typically happens in airplane trips, boats, or land vehicles. Such discomfort is also experienced in virtual environments and is called VIMS (Visually Induced Motion Sickness). MS can be split into two subcategories [53]: transportation sickness, which is tied to the real world and simulator sickness, which is associated to the virtual world and includes CS, as shown in Fig. 1. XR environments that use head-mounted displays (HMDs) are strongly related to common indications of discomfort [59]. Among the potential causes, CS deserves special attention as it is the most common and is usually associated to long exposures to HMDs. Additionally, more than 60% of HMDs usability problems are considerably related to discomfort [59]. The most persistent symptoms caused by CS are general discomfort, headache, stomach awareness, nausea, vomiting, sweating, fatigue, drowsiness, disorientation, and apathy [30].

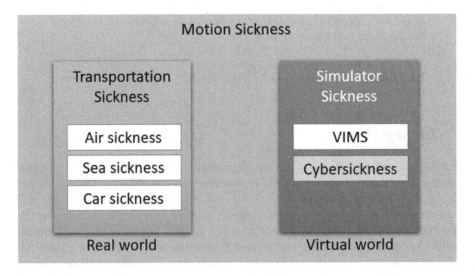

Fig. 1. Motion sickness and its subcategories according to environments and trigger mechanisms.

These symptoms influence the user experience and impact the profit and coverage of XR game manufacturing. In addition, discomfort symptoms can vary over people and tasks, where some individuals are more susceptible than others.

Several studies have been conducted using deep learning models to predict and mitigate CS, such as convolutional neural network (CNNs) and recurrent neural networks (RNNs) [47,57]. Although deep learning classifiers are the most suitable approach for CS prediction, deep neural networks are black boxes that are very difficult to grasp. In contrast, a recent approach apply techniques to make deep learning models explainable [121], although the literature is still scarce in the topic.

Furthermore, symbolic machine learning algorithms enable a straight understanding of decision paths [93]. Another critical problem in CS researching is associated with data labeling. In general, researchers collect verbal, haptic, or brain signal feedback to construct the ground truth of sickness. While verbal feedback is highly subjective and different from each participant, collecting haptic feedback when participants are under discomfort can often be corrupted by the delay associated with participant feedback. A straightforward challenge is related to gender differences tied to XR tasks.

Some works [28,37] pointed out that specific tasks can produce different results of CS for different user-profiles and groups. Additionally, Porcino et al. [92] suggested the importance of a better understanding of the correlation between profile attributes (such as gender, age, XR experience, and other individual characteristics) and gameplay elements, and also how outcomes obtained from profile attributes can be used to tag XR experiences according to distinct groups of users.

In this context, studies involving machine learning models combined with an evaluation of individual tasks associated with CS causes in XR games may produce a more profound study isolating any other XR possible influences on CS results. Overcoming these issues will help designers to produce better XR content and improves the user experience and retain users for longer XR exposures.

2.1   Review of CS Causes

Several factors can cause pain and discomfort when using HMD [126]. Manifestations of CS can lead to more intense symptoms, such as nausea, eye fatigue, neuralgia, and dizziness [54]. According to the literature [31,59,69,109], it is possible to highlight the main factors that contribute to the manifestation of CS symptoms.

1. **Locomotion** - According to Rebenitsch [99], locomotion can be correlated to CS. When the participant travels and has greater control of his movements and is close to natural movements, he will experience less CS. However, when the user experiences continuous visual movement stimulation while resting (also known as vection), it can induce painful sensations. Moreover, this problem reduces the time limit of using virtual reality in a comfortable state.

2. **Acceleration** - Visual accelerations without generating any response in the corresponding vestibular organs cause uncomfortable sensations that result in CS symptoms. High accelerations during movements produce higher degrees of CS [66,110]. An example of this report is considered by Laviola [66] using a virtual reality driving simulator as example. High-frequency acceleration movements contribute more to the CS. In contrast, the lower ones generate more comfortable experiences. This fact occurs because, during the acceleration increase, sensory conflicts can occur. Such conflicts make the body manifest discomfort information. However, the critical issue is the constant deceleration and acceleration. In other words, the duration of the acceleration change, not its magnitude, which makes people feel CS symptoms. An instantaneous acceleration from 0 to 100, instantaneous displacement, does not cause much discomfort than accelerations that frequently occur [1].

3. **Field of view** - In VR environments, a wide field of view generates a great sense of immersion. However, a wide field of view contributes to the CS manifestation. In contrast, a narrow field of view creates a more comfortable experience in VR but decrease the user's immersion [31,126].

4. **Depth of field** - Inadequate simulation of focus on stereoscopic HMDs with flow tracking devices creates unbelievable images and, consequently, causes discomfort. In the human eye, focus forces blur effects naturally that depend on the depth of field (DoF) and distance range of objects in the observed area. Due to ocular convergence, objects outside this range, located behind or in front of the eyes, are blurred [94].

5. **Degree of control** - According to Stanney and Keneddy [110], interactions and movements that are not being controlled by the user may cause CS.

6. **Duration use time** - Many works have showed that time exposure to VR experiences might raise discomfort in a proportional way [74,91,110].

7. **Latency-lag**, has persisted for years as an obstacle in the previous generations of HMDs [82]. Latency is the delay between action and reaction latency is the time difference between the time of input given and the corresponding action to take place in a virtual scenario. High latency may drastically increase CS levels.

8. **Static rest frame** - The lack of a static frame of reference (static rest frame) can cause sensory conflicts and, ultimately, CS [21]. According to Cao et al. [21] most users are able to better tolerate virtual environments created by projectors such as cave automatic virtual environments (CAVEs) [27] compared to HMDs devices.

9. **Camera rotation** - Rotations in virtual environments with HMDs increase the chances of sensory conflicts. The feeling of vection is greater in rotations when two axes are used in comparison to just one axis [13].

2.2   Review of CS Measurements

CS measuring is not trivial. The first problem is that the lack of a unique variable for discomfort level. VR users may experience multiple symptoms and some adverse effects that may not be described in the literature. Another difficulty is the considerable variation of CS susceptibility. Some users are more susceptible to CS symptoms than others. Meanwhile, research shows several ways to capture data for CS quantification. Such data can be classified as subjective, bio-signal and profile data (biological or behavioral profile).

1. **Subjective Data** - The best-known way to measure CS in VR is through subjective data captured from users by applying questionnaires. Such a methodology is simple and has been historically used. However, the results can be very subjective and dependent directly on the participants' responses.

   The Kennedy Questionnaire (Simulator Sickness Questionnaire - SSQ) [54] is the most cited tool for measuring manifestations reflecting most VR disease problems. In the SSQ, 16 symptoms of discomfort were grouped into three categories: oculomotor, disorientation, and nausea. The oculomotor assembly includes eye fatigue, trouble concentrating, blurred vision, and headache. The disorientation group comprises dizziness and vertigo. The nausea set covers upset stomach, increased salivation, and vomiting urges. When taking the questionnaire, participants classified each of the 16 symptoms on the following scale of discomfort: none (none), mild (mild), moderate (moderate), or severe (severe). The results of the SSQ are calculated and presented on four score scales: total disease (overall) and three sub-punctuations, i.e., oculomotor, disorientation, and nausea. To date, SSQ is the most widely used tool to detect symptoms of CS-associated discomfort [18, 22].

   Moreover, each individual has a different CS susceptibility level. The Motion Sickness Susceptibility Questionnaire (MSSQ) [36, 97] was not created for VR but it is sometimes used in VR studies [98]. The MSSQ can be used to determine the time taken by VR users to manifest MS symptoms in VR. This survey contains questions about the frequency with which individuals experience feelings of discomfort similar to those of MS. In MSSQ, the following scale is used: never, rarely, occasionally, and frequently. The issues are grouped into two phases of an individual's life: childhood and last "decade." This census made it possible to account for significant individual differences in MS levels. Kim H. et al. [56] revised and modified the traditional SSQ, proposing the Virtual Reality Sickness Questionnaire (VRSQ). The New VRSQ has nine items split in two classes of symptoms called "oculomotor" and "disorientation." Some recent research [123] has adhered to VRSQ use. Sevinc et al. [106] state that SSQ is not suitable for VR applications, given the psychometric quality issues. It also states as a disadvantage the fact that tests were conducted on 32 individuals only, which is an insufficient sample of all VR users.

2. **Bio-signal Data** - Electrical activity of the brain is bio-signal data that often helps detect illness and behavioral body symptoms. Electroencephalography (EEG) is a monitoring methodology used to record the human brain's electrical activity. Many diseases and brain problems are diagnosed through the evaluation of such devices' data. In adults and healthy people, signs vary depending on different states, for example, awake, aware, or asleep. The characteristics of brain waves also vary according to an individual's age. Brain

waves can be distinguished and separated into five different groups of frequency bands. These waves range from low to high frequencies. These are known as alpha, theta, beta, delta, and gamma waves [9,105].

According to studies [24,77], it is possible to capture (delta, theta, and alpha) from certain regions of the human brain. Such regions exhibit an Motion Sickness (MS) level. Lin et al. [68] found that 9–10 Hz values in the brain's parietal and motor regions are linked to MS levels. These values increased to 18–20 Hz in individuals exposed to MS. Other studies reported an increase in theta signal in situations similar to MS [46,79].

An individual's exposure to VR environments can induce stomach reactions. Studies used electrogastrogram (EGG) information to evaluate MS. According to Hu et al. [45] and Xu et al. [122], gastric myoelectric activities are MS indicators. Wink movements are linked to MS emergence [29]. Blinking and eye movement were observed in the work of Kim et al. [58]. Eye-tracking systems can collect information in VR environments (eye movement, pupil diameter, winks quantity, etc.) [89]. Unnatural eye movements can contribute to CS emergence. Eye fixation can minimize the effect of discomfort [125].

Through the body's electrodermic activity, also known as galvanic skin response (GSR), it is possible to obtain information about actions within the autonomic parasympathetic nervous system, which indicate alterations associated with cognition, emotion, and attention levels. [88]. Nalivaiko et al. [78] experimented with rats that were exposed to MS triggering situations. According to the authors, thermoregulation (sweating) disturbance plays a role in the pathophysiology of nausea. Despite testing on rats, similarities with human symptoms are verifiable. The work of Nalivaiko et al. concludes that nausea is part of the body's natural defense against poisoning and so validating the poison theory presented earlier in this review. Body cooling after "toxin" detection possibly represents a beneficial evolutionary "defensive hypothermia." This type of defensive hypothermia occurs in both humans and animals. Therefore, it is possible to conclude that visual or vestibular disorders can trigger the same type of defensive action by the human body. Studies have pointed out that the cardiac rate can significantly increase during experiments that cause MS [58]. According to Sugita et al. [111], cardiac frequency can be considered a strong indicator of MS or CS. In VR environments, Yang et al. [124] report that heart disease rates are even higher compared with other environments. Such cardiac elevation can induce visual discomfort [26].

3. **Profile Data** - VR user profile data such as gender, age, health condition, experience, and visual fatigue are associated with manifestations of discomfort.

   With respect to gender, women and men see in different ways [3]. According to Biocca et al. [10], women are more inclined to MS manifestations than men. According to Kolasinski et al. [59], this is due to a gender difference in the peripheral view. Women usually have wider FoVs than men. A wide FoV increases the likelihood of discomfort. Age is another factor that can increase CS or MS sensitivity.

According to Reason [96], susceptibility is a product of an individual's experience as a whole and relates to MS. This theory states that older people have less susceptibility to MS than children, for example. However, several studies [17,32,86] showed that older participants were more susceptible to MS than younger ones. According to Arns et al. [7], assuming that CS follows the same pattern as MS may lead to erroneous conclusions.

Previous studies show, for example, that MS is more prevalent in younger groups. However, the study by Arns et al. demonstrated that the opposite happens in the case of CS. This difference may also be because although MS shares some similarities with CS, it does not occur in virtually simulated environments. The theory of Reason et al. [97] treats experience as a whole, that is, life experience (from an individual's birth to one's present). The younger the individual, the less chance one would have to be exposed to such a situation. At the time of those publications, 1975 and 1978, driving and navigating would be experiences children would not normally experience. Nowadays, however, children can be exposed to CS symptoms through VR environments.

Moreover, health conditions can contribute to increased susceptibility to MS or CS once individuals are exposed to favorable environments. According to Frank et al. [35] and Laviola et al. [66], any symptoms, such as stomach pain, flu, stress, hangover, headache, visual fatigue, lack of sleep, or respiratory illnesses, can lead to increased susceptibility to visual discomfort.

Furthermore, flicker is a phenomenon of visual physical discomfort. Such a phenomenon causes physical and psychic fatigue [104]. Flicker sensitivity varies from person to person. An environment with high fps rates will possibly contribute to the user not noticing the flicker [10].

Eye dominance is an important information and has been described as the inherent tendency of the human visual system to prefer scene perception from one eye over the other [90]. According to Meng et al. [76], the eye dominance information can be used as a guide to produce less complex VR scenes without user perception loss based on foveated rendering. An efficient render produces high fps rates. Consequently, a high fps average contributes to avoid virtual reality discomfort.

Previous exposure to MS experiences are key in terms of discomfort susceptibility [63,96]. Individuals that are more frequently exposed to MS activities (e.g., driving, playing electronics games, etc.) are less susceptible to discomfort. This is most probably due to their ability to predict scenarios and situations in these environments [39].

3   Designing the Player Experience for XR Interactions

Since XR (including VR, AR and MR technologies) is a new technology and there are many people experiencing it for the first time, it is important that XR designers make their experiences as intuitive and memorable as possible. The gaming UX accounts for the whole experience players have with a game, from first hearing about it to navigating menus and progressing in the game. The question is: How to make a better game user experience (UX)?

It is not a novelty that the first issue prohibiting good evaluation of entertainment technologies is the inability to define what makes a system successful [101]. Differently from traditional user interfaces where the user is interacting to accomplish real tasks (for instance shopping, e-mailing, text editing and so on) in general during the game interaction the player is usually performing unreal tasks assuming be characters with some kind of special super power immersed in some fantasy world. On the other hand, similarly to traditional user interfaces, the player still needs to know how to interact efficiently and properly in order to be engaged as fast as possible with the game experience.

Celia Hodent [44] says UX is about understanding the gamer's brain: understanding human capabilities and limitations to anticipate how a game will be perceived, the emotions it will elicit, how players will interact with it, and how engaging the experience will be. In that way, looking to provide memorable and effective XR experiences, designers should be aware of how to deal with the following challenges while considering immersives interactions: confort [33] and cybersickness issues (see Sect. 2), design of appropriate scaling (size of virtual controls, buttons and font size), constraints, feedbacks, modalities of interactions (poses, gestures, gazing, voicing, typing [34]), guidance and instructions, locomotion and spatial affordance [107]. Besides that, ethical design principles in games, including gender representation, ethinicities, cultural aspects as well ethics of multiplayer games from an industry perspective [2] are timely and warranted.

Additionally, techniques commonly applied in the game user research with the goal to better understand the UX and provide very concrete and easy-to-use guidelines to anticipate and even solve UX design problems are those based on the user centered design approach as well on the cognitive and behavioral psychology. Examples of using such mixed methods are user interviews, surveys embedded into the own XR experience [84], usability heuristics for VR [50], usability testing, analysis of physiological signals [40], wizardOz [83], game analytics and quantitative behavioral telemetry. Finally, as other UX researchers [16], we believe by combining qualitative observation of issues, quantitative measures of player's emotions and analytics capturing player behavior in game can help tackle the game designer's intent, distinguish between intended and accidental difficulty, and identify only unintended challenges.

4 Displays and Foveated Rendering

The advent of wider Field of View HMDs with higher resolutions have increased shading complexities in rendering [5]. These advances brought a bottleneck of computing power, requiring some sort of optimizations for keeping the target frame rates, as conventional VR rendering is cost-full since two images have to be rendered. Trying to leverage the workload on rendering, some studies have suggested to create non regular pixel distribution (Foveated Rendering), knowing that the human eye has a non regular distribution of cones and rods.

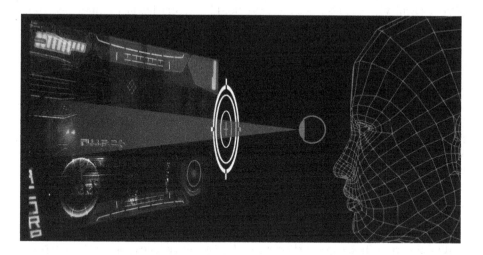

Fig. 2. Foveated rendering simulation. Source: [119]

Foveated Rendering refers to a technique that exploits the way the human eye works to render exclusively what is essential in a three-dimensional scene. According to Swafford et al. [114], usually the entire screen is rendered at the same resolution, regardless of where the user is looking. Since the human eye only perceives details in the center of vision, this uniformity in resolution, anyway of the user's focus, is a waste of valuable resources such as computing power. This technique uses an eye-tracker to determine where the user's gaze is and then, renders the peripheral parts of the vision at a lower quality, keeping the maximal quality possible only in the center of gaze. An illustration of this is found in Fig. 2. As human eyes have an inability to detect details outside its central field of view, the image generated by this optimization would still look the same even if it is rendered differently.

The first implementation of a computer generated image dependent of user gaze was made in 1973 by Reder [100]. He studied human attention by means of on-line monitoring of eye-position signals. Rendering aspects were not explored in the study. Only in 1989, Foveated Rendering was introduced by Levoy et al. [67] and applied to speed up rendering. They used the technique to ray tracing in 1989 to see how it could speed up the visualization of volumetric data. Their work had constraints on pursue lossless image quality feature because of high hardware latency used at that time, which made the transition of better-to-lower quality (or lower-to-better) on saccades visible to users.

Just in 2012, Foveated Rendering showed a more promising result for a general tridimensional scenario with the paper of Guenter et al. [38]. They designed a foveated renderer based on three layers of image quality and an anti-aliasing solution to minimize artifacts in lower resolution layers. The layer's radius, or foveated areas, around the gaze point were defined using a simple linear psychophysical model based on Minimal Angle of Resolution (MAR, the reciprocal of visual acuity), which is the commonly used linear mathematical model to compute visual acuity. They showed a performance improvement of 5–6x on desktop displays.

Since 2012, the field gained more strength in real-time rendering. Patney et al. [87] developed a rasterization Foveated Renderer with a smaller Fovea radius than Guenter et al., different pixel granularities and a modified temporal anti-aliasing based on TAA [60] that considers eye saccades as a variable of the algorithm's weights. Their two-layer foveated rendering design solved Guenter's problem of tunneling vision with the use of a contrast preserving peripheral blur. Weier et al. [120] and Koskela et al. [61] applied Foveated Rendering to real-time ray-tracing and path-tracing respectively. Instead of Guenter et al's work, VR displays were used in Patney et al. [87], Weier et al. [120] and koskela et al. [61], showing that foveated rendering could be used in VR scenarios.

While Foveated Rendering is already being implemented by some rendering engines, there are still many challenges for optimizing and customizing it. Besides finding a correct balance for the foveated areas, challenges such as understanding how this impacts human perception, color distortions and dynamic factors according with the game scene (games with constant colors in large areas naturally requires less pixels to be rendered and enhances the foveated optimizations). It is also important to create robust factors for measuring and better calibrating rendering parameters. Finally, we believe that this concept can also be transposed for different refresh rates for each foveated area, taking into consideration that rods are more dense at the peripheral human vision area.

5   Image Quality and Rendering

Increasing image quality and rendering in Virtual Reality is a demanding challenge, mainly for computational performance, and it requires sophisticated methods for rendering and simulating reality.

Path-tracing was first introduced by Kajiya via the rendering equation [51], as an integral equation that approximates optical reflection, and its numerical solution via Monte Carlo integration methods. It is currently the state-of-the-art in interactive and real-time rendering, since it is able to achieve a higher degree of realism needed for demanding graphical applications such as movies and games. It can faithfully simulate graphical effects such as soft shadows, indirect lighting, reflectance and others. This is mostly due to the nature of the method, which makes the light bounces to a random direction when it reaches an object, calculating the color contribution until it reaches the camera - or the backwards path, depending on the implemented method.

It does so for every pixel in a scene at least once (1 sample per pixel), making the performance directly proportional to the number of pixels of the target

Fig. 3. Path traced image in dual screens using foveation, before denoiser.

resolution. In HMDs, the resolution can range from $1{,}440 \times 1{,}600$ up to $2{,}880 \times 2{,}720$ per eye. Furthering the challenge, add to this the need to render it at least 90 times per second.

Hardware optimizations were made both in CPU and GPU, Nvidia recently released the RTX architecture [55], access to GPUs capable of optimizing the intersection calculation of a ray with a polygon, having BVH optimization features and, thus, accelerating realistic rendering became available for the mass market.

Approaches such as hybrid rendering combines both rasterization and path-tracing in different stages of the rendering pipeline [8], and have the advantage of reducing the amount of samples per pixel and per frame while achieving high-quality results for real-time rendering.

For HMDs with eye-tracking technology, we can further reduce the total number of samples per pixel using foveated rendering techniques. By using the properties of vision such as the concentration of cone distribution in the fovea and devices that allow tracking of the user's gaze, we can avoid rendering parts of the screen with such sharp details or rendering at a reduced spatial sampling frequency. Previous studies have experimented based on user studies to define what an optimal distribution would be, with probabilistic selection of which pixels will be selected by rays, thus decreasing the amount of traced rays and optimizing the algorithm [120]. Similarly, other studies use a fixed texture for ray selection.

Path-traced images requires a high number of samples per pixel to achieve a high fidelity rendered frame. By using fewer samples, the image is left with a high variance also known as noise. Reconstruction algorithms known as denoisers are already commonly used in path-tracing rendering, lowering the variance left in the lighting step with fewer samples per pixel, and thus increasing the performance of the rendering pipeline. Current algorithms for denoising apply different techniques, such as frequency analysis, nonlinear filters, sampling techniques, and deep learning, to name the most important [129].

Using denoisers in combination with foveated rendering techniques is further required since such an optimization haves even fewer samples than the conventional path-tracing, as shown in Fig. 3.

Reconstruction algorithms known as denoisers, which are already commonly used in path tracing rendering, are even more relevant with the fovea distributions, as shown in Fig. 3. It can achieve a lower variance with few samples per pixels, increasing the performance of the rendering pipeline.

In VR, it is possible to use log-polar space rendering and adapt reconstruction to be compatible to it in the early stages of rendering [61], making it possible to obtain a distribution close to the cone distribution of the fovea, with a higher concentration in the center.

6   Real and Virtual Movements

Moving is another form of people unconsciously and continuously interacting with their surroundings daily. Locomotion techniques are one way to change the user's state from a passive to an active character in the environment, creating a deep sense of existence and enhancing the experience [64]. However, there are challenges for each type of locomotion [25, 64]. Albert summed them up into three fundamental challenges: sickness, presence, and fatigue [4]. This section will present the types of locomotion and the problems attached to movement in XR.

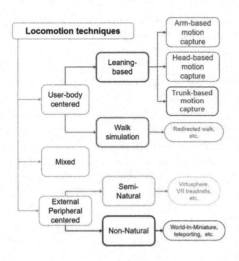

Fig. 4. Virtual reality locomotion techniques taxonomy. Source: [25]

Several researchers proposed classifications for all locomotion techniques [4,6,12,15,25,112]. Cherni proposes a taxonomy of locomotion techniques in virtual reality based on whether the input is body-centered, external peripheral centered, or both [25]. Figure 4 shows visually how the techniques are separated. The three main groups' names are User-body centered, Mixed, and External Peripheral centered. User-body centered are techniques based on the user's movement such as leaning the head [43,128], swinging arms [19,75], or even natural walking as inputs [49,62,73]. External Peripheral-centered techniques are hardware-based inputs such as omnidirectional mills [19,118], teleportation (Fig. 5), and the use of a joystick [43,65,102]. The mixed types are techniques that apply both categories simultaneously, such as holding a controller button while swinging an arm or using the joystick to move in the virtual space while the rotation is done by rotating the head [43,102].

Fig. 5. Teleport locomotion technique. Source: [25]

Even though there are several solutions for creating a way to move in a VR environment, there is not yet one better solution for every application [4,12, 25]. Each method has its pros and cons, but there are typical problems in all techniques, as mentioned before. The first one, and already seen in this work, is sickness, caused by dissonance between the motion visualized in the virtual environment and the motion felt in the real world [4]. A problem common in the External Peripheral centered class since the ones which reduce motion sickness are the body-centered self-motion techniques [25].

The next challenge is presence, better described as the sense of presence. Slater defines it as the user's sense of being in a virtual world, which enhances immersion, that is, the technical description of the virtual environment capable of producing the sense of presence [4,108]. Techniques based on natural walking are considered the most presence-enhancing form of locomotion [12,64,80,95,112]. However, unlike the other challenges, any technique can break the immersion since its use may create a more profound or shallower interaction depending on the design of the experience [15,25].

The last main challenge is fatigue. This ergonomic issue is less known than the others since it appears after continued use of the HMD. Although, while developing an application evaluating this problem can be determined its success. It is worst in walk base techniques and treadmills. In other words, techniques where the user needs to move [4,81].

There are specific challenges for specific solutions, besides the three main problems mentioned by Albert [4], that are worth mentioning. Most external peripheral-centered semi-natural techniques are expensive and challenging to use and maintain, therefore not considered a viable option to implement [19,25]. However, researchers are working on them because it can be an option in the future to solve the main three problems [11,41]. Another locomotion technique recognized as promising to solve three main problems is Redirect Walking [20].

This solution aims to create, in the user, the feeling of mimicking his movement by misleading his senses [49]. Redirect walking tricks the user's perception and makes him feel that he is walking forward, but he is walking on a curved path. The main problem with this is how to shift the virtual environment without triggering the user's perception, which can cause cybersickness and break the immersion. Instead of only diverting the player's movement or turning the whole scenery, researchers use devices, tools, and methods to improve Redirect Walking. Methods such as pointed out by Sun [113] recognize when there is saccade movement of the eye and shifts the scene simultaneously. Redirect walking is the least used method of movement in VR applications mainly because of the necessity of bigger spaces to fully reach its potential of making the user unaware of the reorientation of his movement. Matsumoto [73] experimented that a circular arc of 22 m is necessary to avoid perception, but Rietzler [103] managed to constrain the movements to an area of 6 m × 6 m. Even though there are advances in this topic, it is still necessary to develop more efficient methods for inferring the smaller required spaces for each situation (Fig. 6).

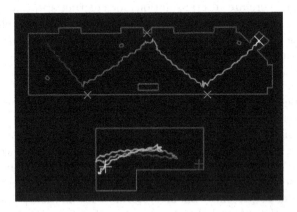

Fig. 6. Redirect walking. The blue region shows the virtual environment, and the blue wiggled line is the virtual path the users chose to move. The red area is the real-life area and the red line is the user's path made imperceptibly. Source: [49] (Color figure online)

As said by Qi and supported by other authors, locomotion is one of the most critical forms of interaction in VR [64,95,113]. Therefore, choosing which method to implement is crucial. It is a choice based on the use of the application and analyzing which problems are worst to the experience and should be solved. Cherni even adds a table to his work, showing the better techniques depending on which body parts the user will dedicate to the locomotion [25]. Hence the technique should be a design-driven choice.

7 Body Tracking

XR games must provide users with an immersive experience with a sense of presence and satisfying natural interaction. Body tracking allows reconstruction of the body movement needed to achieve a satisfying natural interaction [52], especially in multiplayer games [48], enabling users to observe other players' movements.

A virtual body is crucial for a good level of immersion, and when the user identifies himself with this virtual body, we can see the feeling of presence [108]. Although there are many important works related to the subject [23], most are related to showing only floating hands or VR controllers due to the lack of movement data.

In the application domain, XR in Games, vision-based body tracking remains a challenge because of sudden object motion changes, cluttered background, partial occlusion, and camera motion. The hands are the most used body parts in XR in games, as they provide a robust form of interaction. Consequently, vision-based hand-tracking is a topic of interest for several researchers. Most work on hands-tracking focuses on the use of depth cameras [115] or RGB [83]. Depth-based approaches present results that are superior to RGB-based approaches. A depth camera provides hand geometry in terms of a 2.5D point cloud, and the model-based approaches can reliably fit a hand mesh to the reconstructed point cloud [115].

Using hand tracking input with mobile technology is a problem mainly due to the high energy consumption. Han et al. [42] present a real-time tracking system that uses four egocentric monochrome fisheye cameras to produce 3D hand pose estimates and run not only on PC but also on mobile processors. On PC runs 60 Hz and 30 Hz on a mobile processor (Fig. 7).

The detection-by-tracking method of Han et al. [42] utilizes neural network architectures for detecting hands and leverages tracking history to produce spatially and temporally consistent poses. Besides, the system supports a large working volume for a diverse set of users and runs in various real-world environments.

The method mentioned presents failures under complicated hand-hand interactions (Fig. 8a), an uncommon view of the hand for egocentric cameras (Fig. 8b) and hand-object interactions (Fig. 8c and 8d), showing that grasping objects and training data generation are still open issues in mobile hand tracking interactions.

Fig. 7. A real-time hand-tracking system using four monochrome cameras mounted on a VR headset. Source: [42]

8   External World Information

Acquiring and processing the external world information is an essential and challenging aspect of XR applications. Real-world data acquisition for XR applications comes from different sources such as motion sensors, cameras, depth sensors, and other hardware. Aggregating and incorporating this data into meaningful information for XR games is not a trivial task.

Considering the visual features of XR applications, one crucial aspect is the consistent appearance between virtual and real-world objects. One of the main characteristics that drive the consistent appearance is the lighting between virtual and real-world objects. In this context, the external world information is the real-world lighting.

One possible approach to solving this problem is to relight a real object into a particular lighting setting around this object. This solution is usually applied to well-known objects, such as faces [85] and architectural entities [14]. This approach works by bringing the real-world domain to the virtual-world domain. It implies that the real world is adjusted to match the virtual world. It works well for inserting a few objects into the virtual scene, like an object viewer in augmented virtuality, where one real-world object is centered in the user's view. However, this is not a realistic scenario for general XR applications where a scene contains hundreds to thousands of objects from the real-world domain. Relighting the whole real-world environment in real-time is still an open challenge.

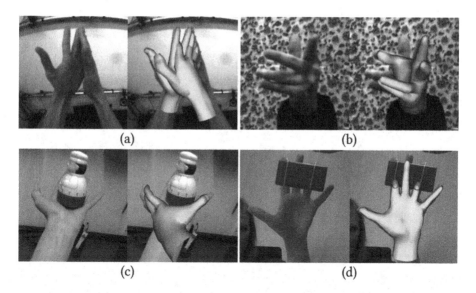

Fig. 8. The system usually fails under complicated hand-hand interactions (a), uncommon view of the hand for egocentric cameras (b) and hand-object interactions (c), (d). Source: [42]

Another way around is to bring the virtual-world domain to the real-world domain. This can be accomplished by getting the lighting information from the real-world scene and using this information to render the virtual objects. Usually, in XR applications, all the lighting information is estimated from pictures of the environment. A common source of information is the frames of real-time videos captured from cameras in the user's HMD.

An approach that uses this perspective to solve the problem can be easily extended to all the virtual objects, hence, relight all the virtual objects in the XR scene (Fig. 9).

Some works have been developed to estimate a global environment lighting of the real-world [70, 71]. Using global environment lighting to relight virtual objects implies that all places in the scene receive the same global illumination. Thus the environment lighting is spatially invariant. This is a reasonable approach for straightforward scenarios with a limited field of view and without objects obstructing the view or casting shadows in the localized spots in the scene. For instance, a fixed camera pointing at an unobstructed surface would be a good example.

Recently, methods that consider spatial variance have been developed [127] [72]. These methods use special representations of the lighting and distinctively crafted datasets that allow a neural network to learn the spatial information from the data. The rendering of virtual objects using the estimation from those methods produces plausible and high-quality XR environments. The spatially varying feature of those methods enables each object to have particular lighting

Fig. 9. Left: rendering of XR scene with inconsistent lighting. Right: relighting of XR scene with consistent environment lighting.

based on the spatial localization of the object in the scene. Thus an object in a shadowed area would not receive the same lighting as the object in a bright spot at the scene.

Figure 10 depicts a global and a spatially varying environment rendering of an XR scene. In the global lighting setting, on top, all of the bunnies are rendered using the same lighting, thus sharing the same appearance independent of the placement in the scene. In the spatially varying rendering, the bunnies have different lighting settings for each position in the scene, producing a natural appearance for every instance of the virtual object in the scene.

The methods mentioned in this section share a common characteristic. All of them use deep learning techniques to estimate the lighting information. A characteristic of deep learning methods is the dependence of an enormous quantity of data to produce outstanding results. In the previously mentioned work of Marques et al. [71], the training data were created through the generation of synthetic samples using computer graphics due to scarcity of datasets portraiting environment and real-world measured lighting. There is a trend in using synthetic data for training neural networks where real-world data is unavailable.

The usage of real-world data mixed with synthetic data can significantly improve neural network estimations by providing a rich context for the neural network by combining the advantage of creating a high quantity of data while maintaining the features of the real-world samples. This element can be explored to allow improvements in the lighting estimation characteristics, such as color consistency [72].

(a) Global lighting

(b) Spatially-varying lighting

Fig. 10. Top: rendering of an XR scene using global lighting estimation. Bottom: rendering of an XR scene using a spatially varying lighting estimation. Source [72].

The challenge for lighting estimation still resides in creating a suitable method for real-time applications to estimate lighting in a time-consistent manner. Time consistency is an essential feature for XR applications since abrupt changes in lighting can potentially worsen the user's immersion. The state-of-art has solved the problem regarding the spatial variance of the lighting and color consistency [127] [72]. However, those methods use the information of one frame at a time to produce the results, hence having limitations with time consistency on real applications.

As the writing of this paper, there is no publicly available dataset from real-world measurement that can capture all the features necessary for creating knowledge for lighting estimation considering time, spatial, and color consistency. Furthermore, acquiring such a dataset is not a trivial task. Progress in training neural networks using natural and synthetic data seems a promising step to achieve a complete solution for XR lighting estimation. The usage of Generative Adversarial Network [117] to generate such a dataset has demonstrated excellence in other tasks and could be explored for external world data estimation and further improve the XR experience regarding visual fidelity.

Extracting and estimating external world information is still considered a difficult task. Developments regarding the representation of the information, including the recent advancements in computer vision methods, can dramatically improve XR environments by allowing new forms of interaction between the virtual and the real world.

9   Conclusion

Extended Reality as a game platform has an incredible potential, due its high immersive conditions. However, it is a totally new computational and ubiquitous environment and brings many challenges and problems, some of them not trivial. In this work we categorize these issues in 7 different topics, although there can be many others: cybersickness (CS), user experience and design guidelines, display and fovea, image quality and rendering, movements and redirect walking, body tracking and finally external world information and acquisition. This classification is not exhaustive and there are many other aspects that could also be included, such as audio, new interface devices and collaborative environments.

References

1. Oculus Founder Palmer Luckey on What It Will Take to Make Virtual Reality Really Big (2020). https://www.technologyreview.com/2016/03/17/161530/. Accessed 10 Dec 2020
2. Sparrow, A.L., Gibbs, M., Arnold, M.: The ethics of multiplayer game design and community management: industry perspectives and challenges. In: Proceedings of the 2021 CHI Conference on Human Factors in Computing Systems. CHI 2021, Association for Computing Machinery, New York, NY, USA (2021). https://doi.org/10.1145/3411764.3445363
3. Abramov, I., Gordon, J., Feldman, O., Chavarga, A.: Sex and vision ii: color appearance of monochromatic lights. Biol. Sex Differ. 3(1), 21 (2012). https://doi.org/10.1186/2042-6410-3-21
4. Albert, J.: User-Centric Classification of Virtual Reality Locomotion Methods. Master's thesis, University of Washington (2018)
5. Albert, R., Patney, A., Luebke, D., Kim, J.: Latency requirements for foveated rendering in virtual reality. ACM Trans. Appl. Percept. (TAP) 14(4), 1–13 (2017)
6. Ams, L.L., Bernard, J., Vance, J., Lutz, R., Prabhu, G.: A new taxonomy for locomotion in virtual environments. Ph.D. thesis, Iowa State University (2002)

7. Arns, L.L., Cerney, M.M.: The relationship between age and incidence of cyber-sickness among immersive environment users. In: IEEE Proceedings. VR 2005. Virtual Reality, 2005, pp. 267–268. IEEE (2005)
8. Barré-Brisebois, C., et al.: Hybrid rendering for real-time ray tracing. In: Ray Tracing Gems, pp. 437–473. Apress, Berkeley, CA (2019). https://doi.org/10.1007/978-1-4842-4427-2_25
9. Berger, H.: Über das elektrenkephalogramm des menschen. Eur. Arch. Psychiatry Clin. Neurosci. 87(1), 527–570 (1929)
10. Biocca, F.: Will simulation sickness slow down the diffusion of virtual environment technology? Presence: Teleoperators Virtual Environ. 1(3), 334–343 (1992)
11. Birnstiel, S., Oberdörfer, S., Latoschik, M.E.: Stay safe! safety precautions for walking on a conventional treadmill in VR. In: 2022 IEEE Conference on Virtual Reality and 3D User Interfaces Abstracts and Workshops (VRW), pp. 732–733 (2022). https://doi.org/10.1109/VRW55335.2022.00217
12. Boletsis, C.: The new era of virtual reality locomotion: a systematic literature review of techniques and a proposed typology. Multimodal Technol. Interact. 1, 24 (2017). https://doi.org/10.3390/mti1040024
13. Bonato, F., Bubka, A., Palmisano, S.: Combined pitch and roll and cybersickness in a virtual environment. Aviat. Space Environ. Med. 80(11), 941–945 (2009)
14. Boss, M., Braun, R., Jampani, V., Barron, J.T., Liu, C., Lensch, H.P.: Nerd: neural reflectance decomposition from image collections. In: IEEE International Conference on Computer Vision (ICCV) (2021)
15. Bowman, D.A., Koller, D., Hodges, L.F.: A methodology for the evaluation of travel techniques for immersive virtual environments (1998)
16. Bromley, T.: How To Be A Games User Researcher: Run better playtests, reveal usability and UX issues, and make videogames better. Independently Published (2021)
17. Brooks, J.O., et al.: Simulator sickness during driving simulation studies. Accid. Anal. Prev. 42(3), 788–796 (2010)
18. Bruck, S., Watters, P.A., et al.: Cybersickness and anxiety during simulated motion: Implications for VRET. Annu. Rev. Cybertherapy Telemedicine 144, 169–173 (2009)
19. Calandra, D., Billi, M., Lamberti, F., Sanna, A., Borchiellini, R.: Arm swinging vs treadmill: a comparison between two techniques for locomotion in virtual reality, pp. 53–56. The Eurographics Association (2018). https://doi.org/10.2312/egs.20181043
20. Cannavò, A., Calandra, D., Prattico, F.G., Gatteschi, V., Lamberti, F.: An evaluation testbed for locomotion in virtual reality. IEEE Trans. Vis. Comput. Graph. 27(3), 1871–1889 (2021). https://doi.org/10.1109/TVCG.2020.3032440
21. Cao, Z., Jerald, J., Kopper, R.: Visually-induced motion sickness reduction via static and dynamic rest frames. In: 2018 IEEE Conference on Virtual Reality and 3D User Interfaces (VR), pp. 105–112. IEEE (2018)
22. Carnegie, K., Rhee, T.: Reducing visual discomfort with HMDs using dynamic depth of field. IEEE Comput. Graph. Appl. 35(5), 34–41 (2015)
23. Caserman, P., Garcia-Agundez, A., Göbel, S.: A survey of full-body motion reconstruction in immersive virtual reality applications. IEEE Trans. Vis. Comput. Graph. 26(10), 3089–3108 (2019)
24. Chelen, W., Kabrisky, M., Rogers, S.: Spectral analysis of the electroencephalographic response to motion sickness. Aviat. Space Environ. Med. 64(1), 24–29 (1993)

25. Cherni, H., Métayer, N., Souliman, N.: Literature review of locomotion techniques in virtual reality. Int. J. Virtual Reality **20**, 1–20 (2020). https://doi.org/10.20870/ijvr.2020.20.1.3183

26. Cheung, B., Hofer, K., Heskin, R., Smith, A.: Physiological and behavioral responses to an exposure of pitch illusion in the simulator. Aviat. Space Environ. Med. **75**(8), 657–665 (2004)

27. Cruz-Neira, C., Sandin, D.J., DeFanti, T.A., Kenyon, R.V., Hart, J.C.: The cave: audio visual experience automatic virtual environment. Commun. ACM **35**(6), 64–73 (1992)

28. Curry, C., Li, R., Peterson, N., Stoffregen, T.A.: Cybersickness in virtual reality head-mounted displays: examining the influence of sex differences and vehicle control. Int. J. Hum.-Comput. Interact. **36**(12), 1–7 (2020)

29. Dennison, M.S., Wisti, A.Z., D'Zmura, M.: Use of physiological signals to predict cybersickness. Displays **44**, 42–52 (2016)

30. Dennison, M.S., D'Zmura, M.: Cybersickness without the wobble: experimental results speak against postural instability theory. Appl. Ergonomics **58**, 215–223 (2017)

31. Draper, M.H., Viirre, E.S., Furness, T.A., Gawron, V.J.: Effects of image scale and system time delay on simulator sickness within head-coupled virtual environments. Hum. Factors: J. Hum. Factors Ergon. Soc. **43**(1), 129–146 (2001)

32. Edwards, C., Creaser, J., Caird, J., Lamsdale, A., Chisholm, S.: Older and younger driver performance at complex intersections: Implications for using perception-response time and driving simulation (2003)

33. Evangelista Belo, J.a.M., Feit, A.M., Feuchtner, T., Grønbæk, K.: Xrgonomics: Facilitating the creation of ergonomic 3d interfaces. In: Proceedings of the 2021 CHI Conference on Human Factors in Computing Systems. CHI 2021, Association for Computing Machinery, New York, NY, USA (2021). https://doi.org/10.1145/3411764.3445349

34. Foy, C.R., Dudley, J.J., Gupta, A., Benko, H., Kristensson, P.O.: Understanding, detecting and mitigating the effects of coactivations in ten-finger mid-air typing in virtual reality. In: Proceedings of the 2021 CHI Conference on Human Factors in Computing Systems. CHI 2021, Association for Computing Machinery, New York, NY, USA (2021). https://doi.org/10.1145/3411764.3445671

35. Frank, L.H., Kennedy, R.S., McCauley, M., Root, R., Kellogg, R.: Simulator sickness: Sensorimotor disturbances induced in flight simulators. Technical report, Naval Training Equipment Center Orlando FL (1984)

36. Golding, J.F.: Motion sickness susceptibility questionnaire revised and its relationship to other forms of sickness. Brain Res. Bull. **47**(5), 507–516 (1998)

37. Grassini, S., Laumann, K.: Are modern head-mounted displays sexist? a systematic review on gender differences in HMD-mediated virtual reality. Front. Psychol. **11**, 1604 (2020)

38. Guenter, B., Finch, M., Drucker, S., Tan, D., Snyder, J.: Foveated 3d graphics. ACM Trans. Graph. (TOG) **31**(6), 1–10 (2012)

39. Guo, C., Tsoi, C.W., Wong, Y.L., Yu, K.C., So, R.: Visually induced motion sickness during computer game playing. Contemp. Ergon. Hum. Factors **51**(58), 51–58 (2013). ROUTLEDGE in association with GSE Research (2013)

40. Halbig, A., Latoschik, M.E.: A systematic review of physiological measurements, factors, methods, and applications in virtual reality. Front. Virtual Reality **25**(2) (2021). https://doi.org/10.3389/frvir.2021.694567

41. Han, S., Yoon, P., Ha, M., Kim, K.: VR wayfinding training for people with visual impairment using VR treadmill and VR tracker. In: 2022 IEEE Conference on Virtual Reality and 3D User Interfaces Abstracts and Workshops (VRW), pp. 596–597 (2022). https://doi.org/10.1109/VRW55335.2022.00149

42. Han, S., et al.: Megatrack: monochrome egocentric articulated hand-tracking for virtual reality. ACM Trans. Graph. **39**(4), 87 (2020)

43. Hashemian, A.M., Kruijff, E., Adhikari, A., Heyde, M.V.D., Aguilar, I., Riecke, B.E.: Is walking necessary for effective locomotion and interaction in VR? pp. 395–396. Institute of Electrical and Electronics Engineers Inc. (2021). https://doi.org/10.1109/VRW52623.2021.00084

44. Hodent, C.: The Gamer's Brain: How Neuroscience and UX Can Impact Video Game Design. CRC Press, Boca Raton (2017). https://books.google.com.br/books?id=JzyhDwAAQBAJ

45. Hu, S., McChesney, K.A., Player, K.A., Bahl, A.M., Buchanan, J.B., Scozzafava, J.E.: Systematic investigation of physiological correlates of motion sickness induced by viewing an optokinetic rotating drum. Aviat. Space Environ. Med. (1999)

46. Hu, S., Stern, R.M., Vasey, M.W., Koch, K.L.: Motion sickness and gastric myoelectric activity as a function of speed of rotation of a circular vection drum. Aviat. Space Environ. Med. (1989)

47. Jeong, D., Yoo, S., Yun, J.: Cybersickness analysis with EEG using deep learning algorithms. In: 2019 IEEE Conference on Virtual Reality and 3D User Interfaces (VR), pp. 827–835. IEEE (2019)

48. Jiang, F., Yang, X., Feng, L.: Real-time full-body motion reconstruction and recognition for off-the-shelf VR devices. In: Proceedings of the 15th ACM SIGGRAPH Conference on Virtual-Reality Continuum and Its Applications in Industry, vol. 1, pp. 309–318 (2016)

49. Jonathan, E., Roberts, C., Presentation, S., Razzaque, S., Kohn, Z., Whitton, M.: Redirected walking. In: Proceedings of Eurographics (2001)

50. Joyce, A.: 10 usability heuristics applied to virtual reality (2021)

51. Kajiya, J.T.: The rendering equation. In: Proceedings of the 13th Annual Conference on Computer Graphics and Interactive Techniques, pp. 143–150 (1986)

52. Kasahara, S., et al.: Malleable embodiment: changing sense of embodiment by spatial-temporal deformation of virtual human body. In: Proceedings of the 2017 CHI Conference on Human Factors in Computing Systems, pp. 6438–6448 (2017)

53. Kemeny, A., Chardonnet, J.R., Colombet, F.: Getting Rid of Cybersickness: In Virtual Reality Augmented Reality, and Simulators. Springer, Cham (2020)

54. Kennedy, R.S., Lane, N.E., Berbaum, K.S., Lilienthal, M.G.: Simulator sickness questionnaire: an enhanced method for quantifying simulator sickness. Int. J. Aviat. Psychol. **3**(3), 203–220 (1993)

55. Kilgariff, E., Moreton, H., Stam, N., Bell, B.: Nvidia turing architecture in-depth (2018). https://developer.nvidia.com/blog/nvidia-turing-architecture-in-depth/

56. Kim, H.K., Park, J., Choi, Y., Choe, M.: Virtual reality sickness questionnaire (VRSQ): motion sickness measurement index in a virtual reality environment. Appl. Ergon. **69**, 66–73 (2018)

57. Kim, J., Kim, W., Oh, H., Lee, S., Lee, S.: A deep cybersickness predictor based on brain signal analysis for virtual reality contents. In: Proceedings of the IEEE International Conference on Computer Vision, pp. 10580–10589 (2019)

58. Kim, Y.Y., Kim, H.J., Kim, E.N., Ko, H.D., Kim, H.T.: Characteristic changes in the physiological components of cybersickness. Psychophysiology **42**(5), 616–625 (2005)

59. Kolasinski, E.M.: Simulator sickness in virtual environments. Technical report, DTIC Document (1995)

60. Korein, J., Badler, N.: Temporal anti-aliasing in computer generated animation. In: Proceedings of the 10th Annual Conference on Computer Graphics and Interactive Techniques, pp. 377–388 (1983)

61. Koskela, M., Lotvonen, A., Mäkitalo, M., Kivi, P., Viitanen, T., Jääskeläinen, P.: Foveated real-time path tracing in visual-polar space. In: Proceedings of 30th Eurographics Symposium on Rendering. The Eurographics Association (2019)

62. Kunz, A., Zank, M., Kunz, A.: Using locomotion models for estimating walking targets in immersive virtual environments (2015). https://doi.org/10.3929/ethz-a-010530701

63. Lackner, J.: Human orientation, adaptation, and movement control. Motion Sickness Vis. Displays Armored Veh. Des. 28–50 (1990)

64. Langbehn, E.: Walking in Virtual Reality: Perceptually-inspired Interaction Techniques for Locomotion in Immersive Environments. Ph.D. thesis, Hamburg University (2019)

65. Langbehn, E., Lubos, P., Steinicke, F.: Evaluation of locomotion techniques for room-scale VR: joystick, teleportation, and redirected walking. In: Proceedings of the Virtual Reality International Conference-Laval Virtual, p. 4. ACM (2018)

66. LaViola, J.J., Jr.: A discussion of cybersickness in virtual environments. ACM SIGCHI Bull. **32**(1), 47–56 (2000)

67. Levoy, M., Whitaker, R.: Gaze-directed volume rendering. In: Proceedings of the 1990 Symposium on Interactive 3D Graphics, pp. 217–223 (1990)

68. Lin, C.T., Chuang, S.W., Chen, Y.C., Ko, L.W., Liang, S.F., Jung, T.P.: EEG effects of motion sickness induced in a dynamic virtual reality environment. In: 2007 29th Annual International Conference of the IEEE Engineering in Medicine and Biology Society, pp. 3872–3875. IEEE (2007)

69. Lin, J.J., Abi-Rached, H., Lahav, M.: Virtual guiding avatar: an effective procedure to reduce simulator sickness in virtual environments. In: Proceedings of the SIGCHI Conference on Human Factors in Computing Systems, pp. 719–726. ACM (2004)

70. Marques, B.A., Drumond, R.R., Vasconcelos, C.N., Clua, E.: Deep light source estimation for mixed reality. In: Visigrapp (1: grapp), pp. 303–311 (2018)

71. Marques, B.A.D., Clua, E.W.G., Vasconcelos, C.N.: Deep spherical harmonics light probe estimator for mixed reality games. Comput. Graph. **76**, 96–106 (2018). https://doi.org/10.1016/j.cag.2018.09.003

72. Marques, B.A.D., Gonzalez Clua, E.W., Montenegro, A.A., Nader Vasconcelos, C.: Spatially and color consistent environment lighting estimation using deep neural networks for mixed reality. Comput. Graph. **102**, 257–268 (2022). https://doi.org/10.1016/j.cag.2021.08.007. https://www.sciencedirect.com/science/article/pii/S0097849321001710

73. Matsumoto, K., Ban, Y., Narumi, T., Yanase, Y., Tanikawa, T., Hirose, M.: Unlimited corridor: redirected walking techniques using visuo haptic interaction. In: ACM SIGGRAPH 2016 Emerging Technologies. SIGGRAPH 2016, Association for Computing Machinery, New York, NY, USA (2016). https://doi.org/10.1145/2929464.2929482

74. McCauley, M.E., Sharkey, T.J.: Cybersickness: perception of self-motion in virtual environments. Presence: Teleoperators Virtual Environ. **1**(3), 311–318 (1992)

75. McCullough, M., et al.: Myo arm: swinging to explore a VE. In: Proceedings of the ACM SIGGRAPH Symposium on Applied Perception, pp. 107–113. SAP 2015,

Association for Computing Machinery, New York, NY, USA (2015). https://doi. org/10.1145/2804408.2804416

76. Meng, X., Du, R., Varshney, A.: Eye-dominance-guided foveated rendering. IEEE Trans. Visual Comput. Graph. **26**(5), 1972–1980 (2020)

77. Morales, R., Chelen, W., Kabrisky, M.: Electroencephalographic theta band changes during motion sickness. Aviat. Space Environ. Med. **61**, 507 (1990)

78. Nalivaiko, E., Rudd, J.A., So, R.H.: Motion sickness, nausea and thermoregulation: the "toxic" hypothesis. Temperature **1**(3), 164–171 (2014)

79. Naqvi, S.A.A., Badruddin, N., Jatoi, M.A., Malik, A.S., Hazabbah, W., Abdullah, B.: EEG based time and frequency dynamics analysis of visually induced motion sickness (VIMS). Australas. Phys. Eng. Sci. Med. **38**(4), 721–729 (2015)

80. Nguyen, A.: Identification of Redirected Walking in Immersive Virtual Enviroments. Ph.D. thesis, ETH Zurich (2021)

81. Nichols, S.: Physical ergonomics of virtual environment use. Appl. Ergon. **30**(1), 79–90 (1999). https://doi.org/10.1016/S0003-6870(98)00045-3, https://www.sciencedirect.com/science/article/pii/S0003687098000453

82. Olano, M., Cohen, J., Mine, M., Bishop, G.: Combatting rendering latency. In: Proceedings of the 1995 Symposium on Interactive 3D graphics. pp. 19-ff. ACM (1995)

83. de Oliveira, E., Clua, E.W.G., Vasconcelos, C.N., Marques, B.A.D., Trevisan, D.G., de Castro Salgado, L.C.: FPVRGame: deep learning for hand pose recognition in real-time using low-end HMD. In: van der Spek, E., Göbel, S., Do, E.Y.-L., Clua, E., Baalsrud Hauge, J. (eds.) ICEC-JCSG 2019. LNCS, vol. 11863, pp. 70–84. Springer, Cham (2019). https://doi.org/10.1007/978-3-030-34644-7_6

84. Oliveira, W., Tizuka, M., Clua, E., Trevisan, D., Salgado, L.: Virtual and real body representation in mixed reality: an analysis of self-presence and immersive environments. In: van der Spek, E., Göbel, S., Do, E.Y.-L., Clua, E., Baalsrud Hauge, J. (eds.) ICEC-JCSG 2019. LNCS, vol. 11863, pp. 42–54. Springer, Cham (2019). https://doi.org/10.1007/978-3-030-34644-7_4

85. Pandey, R., et al.: Total relighting: learning to relight portraits for background replacement. ACM Trans. Graph. **40**(4) (2021). https://doi.org/10.1145/3450626. 3459872

86. Park, G., Rosenthal, T.J., Allen, R.W., Cook, M.L., Fiorentino, D., Viirre, E.: Simulator sickness results obtainted during a novice driver training study. In: Proceedings of the Human Factors and Ergonomics Society Annual Meeting, vol. 48, pp. 2652–2655. SAGE Publications Sage CA, Los Angeles, CA (2004)

87. Patney, A., et al.: Towards foveated rendering for gaze-tracked virtual reality. ACM Trans. Graph. (TOG) **35**(6), 1–12 (2016)

88. Poh, M.Z., Swenson, N.C., Picard, R.W.: A wearable sensor for unobtrusive, long-term assessment of electrodermal activity. IEEE Trans. Biomed. Eng. **57**(5), 1243–1252 (2010)

89. Poole, A., Ball, L.J.: Eye tracking in HCI and usability research. In: Encyclopedia of Human Computer Interaction, pp. 211–219. IGI Global (2006)

90. Porac, C., Coren, S.: The dominant eye. Psychol. Bull. **83**(5), 880 (1976)

91. Porcino, T., Clua, E., Vasconcelos, C., Trevisan, D.: Dynamic focus selection for first-person navigation with head mounted displays. SBGames (2016)

92. Porcino, T., Rodrigues, E.O., Bernardini, F., Trevisan, D., Clua, E.: Identifying cybersickness causes in virtual reality games using symbolic machine learning algorithms. Entertainment Comput. **41**, 100473 (2022)

93. Porcino, T., Rodrigues, E.O., Silva, A., Clua, E., Trevisan, D.: Using the gameplay and user data to predict and identify causes of cybersickness manifestation in virtual reality games. In: 2020 IEEE 8th International Conference on Serious Games and Applications for Health (SeGAH), pp. 1–8. IEEE (2020)

94. Porcino, T.M., Clua, E., Trevisan, D., Vasconcelos, C.N., Valente, L.: Minimizing cyber sickness in head mounted display systems: design guidelines and applications. In: 2017 IEEE 5th International Conference on Serious Games and Applications for Health (SeGAH), pp. 1–6. IEEE (2017)

95. Qi, M., Liu, Y., Cui, J.: A novel redirected walking algorithm for VR navigation in small tracking area, pp. 518–519. Institute of Electrical and Electronics Engineers Inc. (2021). https://doi.org/10.1109/VRW52623.2021.00141

96. Reason, J.T.: Motion sickness adaptation: a neural mismatch model. J. R. Soc. Med. 71(11), 819–829 (1978)

97. Reason, J.T., Brand, J.J.: Motion Sickness. Academic press, Cambridge (1975)

98. Rebenitsch, L., Owen, C.: Review on cybersickness in applications and visual displays. Virtual Reality 20(2), 101–125 (2016). https://doi.org/10.1007/s10055-016-0285-9

99. Rebenitsch, L.R.: Cybersickness Prioritization and Modeling. Michigan State University, Michigan (2015)

100. Reder, S.M.: On-line monitoring of eye-position signals in contingent and non-contingent paradigms. Behav. Res. Methods Instrum. 5(2), 218–228 (1973)

101. Regan, L., Mandryk, K.M.I., Calvert, T.W.: Using psychophysiological techniques to measure user experience with entertainment technologies. Behav. Inf. Technol. 25(2), 141–158 (2006). https://doi.org/10.1080/01449290500331156

102. Riecke, B.E., LaViola, J.J., Kruijff, E.: 3D user interfaces for virtual reality and games: 3D selection, manipulation, and spatial navigation. In: ACM SIGGRAPH 2018 Courses. SIGGRAPH 2018, Association for Computing Machinery, New York, NY, USA (2018). https://doi.org/10.1145/3214834.3214869

103. Rietzler, M., Gugenheimer, J., Hirzle, T., Deubzer, M., Langbehn, E., Rukzio, E.: Rethinking redirected walking: on the use of curvature gains beyond perceptual limitations and revisiting bending gains. In: 2018 IEEE International Symposium on Mixed and Augmented Reality (ISMAR), pp. 115–122 (2018). https://doi.org/10.1109/ISMAR.2018.00041

104. Riva, G.: Virtual Reality in Neuro-psycho-physiology: Cognitive, Clinical and Methodological Issues in Assessment and Rehabilitation, vol. 44. IOS press, Amsterdam (1997)

105. Sanei, S., Chambers, J.A.: EEG signal processing (2007)

106. Sevinc, V., Berkman, M.I.: Psychometric evaluation of simulator sickness questionnaire and its variants as a measure of cybersickness in consumer virtual environments. Appl. Ergon. 82, 102958 (2020)

107. Shin, J.E., Yoon, B., Kim, D., Woo, W.: A user-oriented approach to space-adaptive augmentation: the effects of spatial affordance on narrative experience in an augmented reality detective game. In: Proceedings of the 2021 CHI Conference on Human Factors in Computing Systems. CHI 2021, Association for Computing Machinery, New York, NY, USA (2021). https://doi.org/10.1145/3411764.3445675

108. Slater, M., Wilbur, S.: A framework for immersive virtual environments (five): speculations on the role of presence in virtual environments. Presence: Teleoperators Virtual Environ. 6(6), 603–616 (1997)

109. So, R.H., Lo, W., Ho, A.T.: Effects of navigation speed on motion sickness caused by an immersive virtual environment. Hum. Factors: J. Hum. Factors Ergon. Soc. **43**(3), 452–461 (2001)

110. Stanney, K.M., Kennedy, R.S., Drexler, J.M.: Cybersickness is not simulator sickness. In: Proceedings of the Human Factors and Ergonomics Society Annual Meeting, vol. 41, pp. 1138–1142. SAGE Publications Sage CA, Los Angeles, CA (1997)

111. Sugita, N., et al.: Quantitative evaluation of effects of visually-induced motion sickness based on causal coherence functions between blood pressure and heart rate. Displays **29**(2), 167–175 (2008)

112. Suma, E.A., Bruder, G., Steinicke, F., Krum, D.M., Bolas, M.: A taxonomy for deploying redirection techniques in immersive virtual environments (2012)

113. Sun, Q., et al.: Towards virtual reality infinite walking: dynamic saccadic redirection. ACM Trans. Graph. **37**(4) (2018). https://doi.org/10.1145/3197517.3201294

114. Swafford, N.T., Iglesias-Guitian, J.A., Koniaris, C., Moon, B., Cosker, D., Mitchell, K.: User, metric, and computational evaluation of foveated rendering methods. In: Proceedings of the ACM Symposium on Applied Perception, pp. 7–14 (2016)

115. Taylor, J., et al.: Articulated distance fields for ultra-fast tracking of hands interacting. ACM Trans. Graph. (TOG) **36**(6), 1–12 (2017)

116. Valente, L., Feijó, B., do Prado Leite, J.C.S., Clua, E.: A method to assess pervasive qualities in mobile games. Pers. Ubiquit. Comput. **22**(4), 647–670 (2018)

117. Wang, L., Chen, W., Yang, W., Bi, F., Yu, F.R.: A state-of-the-art review on image synthesis with generative adversarial networks. IEEE Access **8**, 63514–63537 (2020). https://doi.org/10.1109/ACCESS.2020.2982224

118. Warren, L.E., Bowman, D.A.: User experience with semi-natural locomotion techniques in virtual reality: the case of the virtuix omni. In: Proceedings of the 5th Symposium on Spatial User Interaction, p. 163. SUI 2017, Association for Computing Machinery, New York, NY, USA (2017). https://doi.org/10.1145/3131277.3134359

119. Web, T.N.: Fove's $250,000 kickstarter campaign wants to bring eye-tracking control to virtual reality (2021). https://thenextweb.com/news/foves-250000-kickstarter-campaign-wants-to-bring-eye-tracking-control-to-virtual-reality. Accessed 28 July 2021

120. Weier, M., et al.: Foveated real-time ray tracing for head-mounted displays. Comput. Graph. Forum **35**(7), 289–298 (2016)

121. Xie, N., Ras, G., van Gerven, M., Doran, D.: Explainable deep learning: A field guide for the uninitiated. arXiv:2004.14545 (2020)

122. Xu, L., et al.: Hypothalamic and gastric myoelectrical responses during vection-induced nausea in healthy Chinese subjects. Am. J. Physiol.-Endocrinol. Metab. **265**(4), E578–E584 (1993)

123. Yan, Y., Chen, K., Xie, Yu., Song, Y., Liu, Y.: The effects of weight on comfort of virtual reality devices. In: Rebelo, F., Soares, M.M. (eds.) AHFE 2018. AISC, vol. 777, pp. 239–248. Springer, Cham (2019). https://doi.org/10.1007/978-3-319-94706-8_27

124. Yang, J., Guo, C., So, R., Cheung, R.: Effects of eye fixation on visually induced motion sickness: are they caused by changes in retinal slip velocity? In: Proceedings of the Human Factors and Ergonomics Society Annual Meeting, vol. 55, pp. 1220–1224. SAGE Publications Sage CA, Los Angeles, CA (2011)

125. Yang, X., Wang, D., Hu, H., Yue, K.: P-31: visual fatigue assessment and modeling based on ECG and EOG caused by 2D and 3D displays. SID Symp. Digest Tech. Pap. **47**(1), 1237–1240 (2016)

126. Yao, R., Heath, T., Davies, A., Forsyth, T., Mitchell, N., Hoberman, P.: Oculus VR best practices guide

127. Zhan, F., et al.: Sparse needlets for lighting estimation with spherical transport loss. In: Proceedings of the IEEE/CVF International Conference on Computer Vision (ICCV), pp. 12830–12839 (2021)

128. Zielasko, D., Horn, S., Freitag, S., Weyers, B., Kuhlen, T.W.: Evaluation of hands-free HMD-based navigation techniques for immersive data analysis. In: 2016 IEEE Symposium on 3D User Interfaces (3DUI), pp. 113–119 (2016). https://doi.org/10.1109/3DUI.2016.7460040

129. Zwicker, M., et al.: Recent advances in adaptive sampling and reconstruction for Monte Carlo rendering. Comput. Graph. Forum (Proceedings of Eurographics - State of the Art Reports) **34**(2), 667–681 (2015). https://doi.org/10/f7k6kj

Stimulation of the Executive Functions Mediated by Digital Games: Current Challenges in the School Context

Bernardo Benites de Cerqueira$^{(\boxtimes)}$ (ID), Débora Nice Ferrari Barbosa (ID),
and João Batista Mossmann (ID)

Feevale University, Novo Hamburgo, RS 93525-075, Brazil
{bernardo,deboranice,mossmann}@feevale.br

Abstract. Executive Functions are a group of cognitive abilities that guide the behavior of individuals towards achieving goals, regulation and control of thoughts, emotions, and inhibition of behavioral tendencies. The healthy development of the executive components are predictors of several aspects in the life of individuals, such as success in professional life, academic performance, and socio-affective relationships. Studies indicate that impairments in the Executive Functions are directly related to several known clinical conditions, e.g., depression and attention-deficit/hyperactivity disorder. Investigations show that it is possible to foster the components of Executive Functions, so that individuals can obtain cognitive gains, promoting benefits in several aspects of one's life, especially when it occurs during childhood and adolescenthood. Digital games are a cultural artifact present in the lives of children and adolescents and have been increasingly used in educational settings. Therefore, investigations based on robust evidence are needed about cognitive stimulation using digital games in the school context. This chapter presents five challenges in the field, and how to evaluate them: (I) Development of Digital Games for Cognitive Stimulation and Assessment; (II) Methodologies using Digital Games; (III) Applications within the School Environment and Brazilian Scope; (IV) Difficulty Curves in Digital Games; (V) Cognitive Stimulation in the School Context after Social Isolation by COVID-19.

Keywords: Executive functions · Digital games · Cognitive stimulation · Neuropsychological intervention · School setting

1 Introduction

Executive Functions (EF) [30, 39] are cognitive components that develop and mature at different times, from birth to adulthood. Research in the area shows that it is possible to work specifically with their stimulation, so that individuals can obtain gains in their EF, as well as have benefits in life [28]. Studies indicate that the EF are essential for a good school performance [26, 34, 80], as well as for proper development of socio-affective, professional, academic, and planning skills of individuals [5, 22, 45]. They are also fundamental for success in marital harmony, health and quality of life [28]. Thus, the

R. P. d. Santos and M. d. S. Hounsell (Eds.): GranDGamesBR 2020/2021, CCIS 1702, pp. 187–206, 2023.
https://doi.org/10.1007/978-3-031-27639-2_9

healthy development and maturation of these cognitive functions in individuals are considered extremely important, since they are the cognitive basis on which other cognitive functions are built, such as reasoning, emotional control, planning capacity, task management, among others. Different theoretical models seek to clarify the organization and functioning of EF. Miyake and colleagues [60] carried out investigations on theoretical constructs, in which they reported that the three-factor model is the most suitable [39, 60].

In this context, the model widely accepted in the field of neuropsychology is the one proposed by Diamond [30], in which EF consist of a family of three central, interrelated abilities, which are the necessary basis for the functioning of other cognitive processes of an individual:

1) *Working Memory* (WM), responsible for managing, preserving, relating, connecting and treating current information with previously acquired information. They are essential for the reasoning, problem solving and creative thinking of individuals. In addition, WM is responsible for keeping transient information in mind while performing one or more mental operations, a component without which the latter would not be possible [26, 28, 30, 39, 45];

2) *Inhibitory Control* (IC), responsible for stopping and inhibiting inappropriate or distracting impulses or behaviors, emotions and thoughts, enabling self-control and unusual responses according to the demands of each situation faced by the individual. The IC is related to the individual's ability to wait, as well as to respond in a thoughtful way rather than reactively or impulsively, without being at the mercy of uncomfortable social situations. Hence, an individual would not have the ability to act in an unusual or non-impulsive manner without the existence of this executive component [26, 28, 30, 39, 45].

3) *Cognitive Flexibility* (CF), responsible for changing the focus of attention between different tasks, as well as for adapting to changing environments and being able to change perspectives. In addition, CF is necessary at times when the individual is faced with unexpected or new situations, events or challenges. This enables individuals to adapt to environments, in different contexts, as well as in the different ways of solving problems [26, 28, 30, 39, 45].

1.1 Developmental Aspects of the Executive Functions

In studies with typically developing children, good EF performance can be correlated with other skills, including adequate academic performance and appropriate socio-affective functioning, as previously mentioned [7, 56]. Although, other investigations carried out with children with atypical development, who have some neurodevelopmental, neurological or psychiatric disorder, may present significant impairment in these executive components [25, 47]. Such findings are presented in different investigations: Levin e Hanten [53] researched children with traumatic brain injury; Chiang e Gau [17] investigated children with Attention-Deficit/Hyperactivity Disorder (ADHD); Varvara et al. [85] investigated patients with dyslexia. In addition, studies with children who were abused or who were subjected to adverse environmental conditions, such as early care deprivation, showed a deficit in their EF [20, 21].

Furthermore, several clinical conditions have already known relationships with EF [88]. Among the clinical conditions, we can mention Conduct Disorder [36], Obsessive Compulsive Disorder [68] and Depression [82]. Investigations also report that IC deficits, for example, are correlated with Autism Spectrum Disorder (ASD) [18]. It is known that children with ADHD have problems controlling or maintaining attention [38], which are factors linked to IC [75]. Thus, strategies or interventions that can provide the stimulation of EF components can have beneficial effects on the life cycle of the subjects, accompanying them throughout their lives [24].

In the academic area, educators have recognized the importance of EF for the educational performance of students [89], due to investigations that analyze the reasons why students cannot fully develop their potential during school activities [41]. Studies show that EF-related deficiencies are often associated with academic difficulties, such as reading, writing and math skills [19, 62, 84]. Investigations suggest the need to invest and promote programs aimed at the exercise of EF still in childhood, in an early-preventive way, aiming to mitigate the effects of the low development of these skills and their consequences throughout the life of the individuals [8, 34].

Among the evidence found regarding the subject, Miller et al. [59] found that young people who had lower development of EF, specifically in the behavioral aspect, were exponentially more likely to have adverse health conditions. Another longitudinal study [61] shows that adults with lower self-control in childhood were more likely to be drug addicts, single parents, or commit more crimes than those with better IC as children. According to Diamond and Ling [28], research also suggests that EF stimulated earlier in life can reduce the aforementioned problems, as well as antisocial or inappropriate behaviors, and that improving executive development early in life is fundamental to the trajectory of children.

1.2 Is it Possible to Improve One's Executive Functions?

Given the relevance of these skills in childhood, researchers have been interested in understanding and proposing interventions that promote and improve executive functions [3, 12, 31, 48, 54, 64, 83]. These interventions can take place in diverse contexts and involve different methods, including computerized cognitive training, non-computerized and computerized games, aerobic exercise, martial arts and mindfulness practice, as well as complementary curriculum programs within the school setting [26].

Therefore, the importance of ecological approximation in research and investigation with study participants, such as children, is an important factor [28]. The ecological approach considers the daily tasks that individuals perform, or the context and environment in which they are inserted and which, if not properly attended or observed, can lead to inaccurate results in assessments or interventions focused on the development of individuals [66].

Among the available tools seeking to improve EF, the category of computerized programs includes digital games aimed at the context of cognitive stimulation, instead of focused on entertainment [26]. The presence of technology in the daily lives of individuals is an aspect that adheres to the issue of promoting the benefits of using digital games, since it can reduce the need for human resources in applications aimed at stimulating, as well as motivating participants [23]. For example, a computer program on mobile devices with the purpose of cognitive stimulation can be used with several people in the same environment while having a small team of applicators, or even applications made without their presence, although the importance and impact of the presence of applicators/monitors/tutors on the results of interventions with study participants is still being discussed [28].

The scalability of this type of application, with the use of digital games, which seeks the cognitive stimulation of individuals, after properly investigated and validated in their potential, would be possible through the technology currently available in everyday life. Also, as an advantage of the use of computerized programs, they may be able to automatically adapt to the performance of individuals during the applications, in relation to the level of difficulty of the tasks presented [11, 48].

However, in the literature, authors indicate the existence of contradictions in the evidence presented about the effectiveness of the EF approach through computerized programs and digital games [26, 28, 80]. Some studies have shown that these programs are effective for typically developing preschool children [83]. However, the benefits of this type of intervention are not yet well established, with regard to the transfer effect, as well as the generalization of gains obtained during the performance of cognitive stimulation programs [27, 57]. In this context, many different methodologies are used [55], which demands a behavioral investigation before and after the applications, in order to identify the adaptive issues addressed by the interventions focused on cognitive stimulation.

Thus, questions still pertinent to the field of neuropsychology are raised, which, despite continuing to be extensively studied and scientifically scrutinized, remain unanswered. In this sense, what would be the best means to apply, measure and define the impact or potential of programs that use digital games on study participants? Would it be possible to reproduce the effects of studies in different social contexts, or even different cultures or countries? Furthermore, how would it be more appropriate to select the cognitive evaluation battery and psychometric measures to assess and affirm the effect of studies aimed at cognitive stimulation? Finally, when it comes to digital games, which types of activities presented and promoted in these games could have the desired effects, to a greater or lesser extent, for the stimulation of the proposed cognitive functions?

As important as all the issues raised, is the assessment of cognitive impacts, as well as the cognitive stimulation of children in a school environment. In this context, how can the cognitive improvements resulting from cognitive stimulation programs be verified in other aspects of individuals' lives, in the daily lives of participants of these studies?

This chapter seeks to raise the main points related to the research area of EF and digital games as mediators of their stimulation, with emphasis on the school environment. Thus, through discussion with different authors, provide guidelines with which to think and direct academic research in this field to Brazilian researchers. To this end, five main challenges are proposed for this research field, as well as possible ways to promote and evaluate the results and the evolution of investigations within the time window of the next 10 years in the Brazilian scenario.

2   Stimulation of the Executive Functions

Studies in the field of neuropsychology associate EF with the behaviors of everyday life in children with typical development, in which the correlations found include issues such as school success and socio-affective functioning [56]. Other investigations in this context corroborate the finding and demonstrate that a good development of these executive components is imperative to ensure good development at school, at work and in various daily aspects [45].

In the context of the development of EF, studies also show that the maturation of these skills occurs from early childhood [5] in a long course to adulthood [22], being each of the components established at different moments of the development of individuals. Although, the maturation process is significantly strengthened during childhood and adolescence [6].

Results from different investigations emphasize that executive abilities are essential in the context of learning and also for social interactions [13, 14, 29, 43]. For instance, these functions help children to maintain attention during a class, and are also fundamental for moral, social and emotional development in this context [69]. When a child is stressed, lonely, sad or physically unfit, skills that are related to EF are negatively affected. Likewise, when the physical, social or emotional needs of these individuals are neglected, EF are also affected, and, as a consequence, so is the persons' academic performance [30].

Currently, it is known that it is possible to help children to develop and improve executive skills through ludic tasks and activities that work on cognitive aspects, such as reasoning, planning and self-control [27, 52]. Studies show that high levels of EF in childhood are directly related to greater ability to control impulses, creativity and flexibility between tasks [14, 43].

Exercising EF can be beneficial in different activities, such as reading, writing and in mathematics teaching issues [10, 19, 62, 84, 87]. Investigations demonstrate the urgency of investing in programs aimed at stimulating EF, especially in the context of childhood. However, despite the large number of researchers involved in this search for programs that enable the stimulation of these functions, there remain several questions related to scientific rigor, the methodologies used and the effects of stimulation on the lives of participants in such programs, especially in the area of technology [27, 28].

Most computer programs, including digital games, available in the literature so far, work with the category of working memory stimulation [11, 81]. School-based interventions that aim to stimulate and focus other components of EF, such as inhibitory control or cognitive flexibility [81] through digital games, need further investigation [4, 28, 81], since most of these types of computerized intervention are aimed for memory components [11, 28].

It is important to highlight, within the stimulation environment, questions that remain unanswered: what would be the types of computer programs that could offer the most appropriate challenge to the participants? Also, which application format could be most beneficial to participants? In this research context, some programs focus on the realization of controlled paradigms when approaching the stimulation of EF, while others target activities or programs within a specific context.

Baniqued and colleagues [2], for example, argue that casual digital games demand, through a contextualized and integrated environment, the execution of a variety of cognitive skills, complex rules, and challenging objectives. In this sense, the authors exemplify a game that simulates the daily life of a restaurant, and that demands multitasking skills and working memory by challenging the player to order ingredients, clean tables and keep the business running. In contrast, paradigm-based computer programs such as dual *N-back* require participants to remember pairs of auditory and visual stimuli in sequence in a predictable order, as well as the timing and type of the stimulus. In the latter case, the participant ends up performing the most controlled and sterile tasks, while digital games enable the demand to perform tasks in a more externally valid environment [2].

In a series of meta-analyses carried out by Takacs and Kassai [81], investigations were assessed with several games used for the purpose of stimulating children, as well as the evidence found in the studies. The games included in the investigation were *Cogmed, Braingame Brian, Memory Booster, Jungle Memory, Mate Marote* and *LocuTour Multimedia Cognitive Rehabilitation.* Among the studies, significant effects on Working Memory were found in comparison with Inhibitory Control and Cognitive Flexibility, although the authors emphasize that this is due to the fact that most studies seek explicit Working Memory training with Cogmed. Furthermore, the analysis noted that the effects on Working Memory were sustained over time, compared to the other executive components. Another interesting result is that explicit training effects were significantly lower in the group of children with atypical development compared to children with typical development. The authors propose that interventions using implicit training, i.e. involving the use of new and different strategies of self-regulation, can provide similar or more effective benefits for nontypically children than explicitly training executive functions tasks with typically development children.

Diamond and Ling [28] carried out a systematic review in search of evidence found in the context of EF stimulation in all age groups. Among the categories examined by the study, the most promising were practices involving conscious (mindful) movement (which include practices such as *Tai Chi, Taekwondo,* traditional Chinese mind-body exercises, and *Quadrato*). The authors suggest, in this context, the need for more longitudinal investigations and a greater number of measures to determine the gains at the EF level of these practices. Apart from the mindful movement category, the school programs category showed more consistent results than the other categories analyzed, with improvements in the overall EF indices analyzed.

In the context of improving Inhibitory Control, of all the studies analyzed, Diamond and Ling [28] state that those with school programs involving children from preschool to 4th grade (*MindUP, PATHS, Tools of the Mind*) were the most successful. In this context, the researchers argue that programs integrated into the school curriculum have several advantages, such as the possibility of reaching most children, in an economic and fair way, in terms of accessibility. Thus, it is possible to reach all the targeted children, and not only those who would be able to pay to participate in programs carried out outside the school context, and this includes: the possibility of a greater number and duration of applications, as well as the frequency in the programs, in relation to other types of interventions or forms of training of EF outside school setting. In addition, there is the ability to train EF in different circumstances, including the issue of transfer to other activities.

With regard to the use of computerized training in the school setting, a literature review carried out by Cardoso et al. [11] demonstrated that most computer programs available used in school interventions with children aimed to stimulate working memory. In addition to *Cogmed*, a non-commercial computer game that was reported in the investigations, *Braingame Brian* [71], which aims to stimulate EF in children with ADHD and impaired cognitive control. No transfer effect to untrained domains was found in studies with these computer games.

Although there are controversies regarding the effectiveness of stimulation through computerized programs, as well as the methodologies used [55] and the reproduction of results in other studies [42], authors indicate that such contradictions are evidenced in adaptive issues that are usually forgotten in cognitive stimulation programs. This aspect is called "Transfer Effect", in which the benefits obtained by stimulating an executive ability in a given scenario must also be observed in other environments, in addition to the trained one.

In this context, a meta-analysis by Kassai et al. [46] investigated the topic of near and far-transfer effect in neuropsychological interventions with children. However, no strong evidence was found that training a specific EF would be effectively transferred to untrained executive components. Furthermore, the results of investigations by Melby-Lervåg and Hulme [57] and Sala and Gobet [74] found no significant transfer effect from Working Memory training to Inhibitory Control in participating children, whereas Volckaert and Noël [86] showed preliminary results of marginal transfer effect between Inhibitory Control and Cognitive Flexibility. Kassai et al. [46] highlighted that the results of their investigation studies could have been impacted due to the similarity between the measures used and the game activities practiced by the participating children.

Therefore, a behavioral investigation before and after the execution of the proposed task must be carried out, and the gains in skills must also appear in the performance of other skills or untrained tasks. However, to search for such evidence, investigations must also evaluate the effect of training on tasks unrelated to those trained. In this context, the development of stimulation programs, especially in terms of digital games, must be aligned with the promotion of the adaptive functioning of individuals as a whole, and not just applied to the activities practiced and evaluated [27].

Regarding the transfer effect of computerized working memory programs, Melby-Lervåg and Hulme [57] and Melby-Lervåg, Redick and Hulme [58] demonstrated that training with Cogmed had significant immediate effects on verbal working memory and visuospatial in children. However, the benefits of interventions with computer programs, specifically with regard to transfer effects and generalization gains, have yet to be established [27, 57].

As mentioned earlier, EF are essential for school preparation, academic performance, career success, socio-affective functioning, marital harmony, good health and quality of life [28]. However, an investigation by Miller et al. [59] found evidence that young people who had low development of EF, specifically Inhibitory Control, were exponentially more likely to suffer from adverse health conditions. Seabra et al. [77] also pointed out that children and adolescents with the development of adequate inhibitory skills, and who exercised this component, tended to be less involved in crimes, to abuse less of illicit substances, to have a lower rate of school dropout and greater professional success in adult life.

Furthermore, Diamond and Ling [28] promote the importance of stimulating and improving the IC, relating it to aspects such as the temptation to resist completing complex tasks, avoiding saying or doing actions that may generate later regret, presence of mind to wait before speaking or acting, being able to resist impulsive reactions, as well as creative problem solving and even seizing unexpected opportunities.

Thus, IC is an ability that operates in the behavioral aspect of the individual. It is a capacity that is possessed to control and stop inappropriate actions, allowing the subject to choose between different behaviors and reactions in the face of certain situations or objectives. In the clinical context, Salum et al. [75] sustain that impairments in relation to IC are presented by children diagnosed with ADHD. Thus, investigations related to the stimulation of this cognitive component in children with typical development are needed, also bringing improvements to children in the context of impairment of this component.

3 Challenges

We propose as the main challenge in the interface of digital games and neuropsychology the definition of the impact of the use of digital games for the stimulation and evaluation of the cognition of children and adolescents in the school environment. As mentioned, investigations on this topic have shown contradictory results about the potential of games to stimulate EF.

The discussion in the area [4, 11, 27, 28, 55, 81] brings up questions that are still open in the methodological context, application, evaluation and sampling, for example. Therefore, the proposed challenges seek to address the issues through an overview of what is debated in the research field, bringing studies and some of the results obtained by researchers within each aspect addressed.

In the first challenge, points already discussed and best practices pointed out by different peers are brought up in the context of the development of digital games, seeking to stimulate and evaluate executive functions in children and adolescents.

The second challenge addresses the design of methodologies and the guidelines indicated among researchers in the field to attain results in order to obtain, including for the purpose of comparison between studies, the impacts in the area of stimulation with the use of digital games.

The third point discusses carrying out investigations within the school setting, as a common means for the study of the different realities that are concentrated within the classroom, in the school environment, in terms of participants in the national sector.

The fourth challenge concerns the employment and use of means to assess and quantify the challenges proposed in the digital games under development by researchers, with the game difficulty and design being the guiding thread of the participants' playing experience.

Finally, the fifth challenge brings to the discussion the use of games in the context of the consequences of social isolation and confinement resulting from the world pandemic of Covid-19, since 2020. In this context, the need to conduct research within a possible time window to study the cognitive impacts on children and adolescents in the school setting is discussed.

Therefore, the challenges arising from the discussion around the use of digital games in cognitive stimulation from the perspective of neuropsychology and game development are addressed below:

3.1 Development of Digital Games for Cognitive Stimulation and Assessment in Children and Adolescents

In the context of digital games, different types of games have been used in the search for evidence of cognitive stimulation [4, 27, 28, 33, 42, 50, 57, 70, 80, 81]. To this end, games developed specifically for assessment and stimulation are used, as well as commercial entertainment games that have elements and mechanics related to EF components, such as selective attention, among others [4, 11, 26, 28, 57, 81]. However, while these developed games usually cover general EF skills – in research and educational context – others are used in a commercial model [50], largely aimed at the adult audience or the clinical context of atypical development [15, 16, 50, 73]. Despite the fact that commercial games demand the improvement of cognition and reflexes of the players, they often have as a setback the fact that they have not been developed under the scrutiny of specialists in the area of stimulation along with game designers, before its use in stimulation studies.

Furthermore, Krause et al. [50] demonstrated that the application of digital games for the development of EFs is commonly focused on the adult and elderly public, in comparison to children and adolescents, possibly because the first group is more prone to diseases with greater damage to EF.

In terms of EF assessment, according to Seabra and colleagues [9, 77, 78], there are few studies that use validated neuropsychological tests for the Brazilian population, contemplating the different stages of development and the subjects' school learning.

Research involving cognitive digital games for mobile devices for children [44] are still incipient [15, 16, 44]. Therefore, research on digital games for neuropsychological assessment and cognitive stimulation with mobile technologies can also contribute to this field of knowledge, especially in the Brazilian context. The need for investigations in the area of cognitive stimulation and assessment through digital games [28] is highlighted, especially with mobile devices in children [44], applicable in the educational setting in order to verify the impact in teaching and learning.

Although games developed for stimulation and assessment require resources for their production, the challenge of developing these games with a focus on evidence-based EF stimulation has the potential to bring benefits to study participants. These benefits come from the multidisciplinary collaboration required for the product development, which may include games, health, and behavioral specialists on the team.

The challenge in the area lies in investigating the best way to develop and apply these games, especially in terms of paradigms used and narrative elements that contribute to the participants' experience and positive impacts [4, 11, 23, 26–28, 48, 55, 57, 80, 81]. Investigations are also needed on the combinations of game mechanics and behavior change processes to maximize behavior changes, with the least possible side effects on participants, such as lack of motivation or disinterest during applications.

3.2 Methodologies - Design of the Studies Using Digital Games

The topic of methodological design of the investigations is central to stimulation with the use of digital games [28]. It is known that there are controversies in the area, especially regarding the application format, as well as in the observation of investigation results and in the attempt to reproduce stimulation benefits reported by other researchers [42]. The great variety in the methodologies used [55, 81] to verify the participants' cognitive stimulation mediated by digital games is also noteworthy.

Thus, another challenge relevant to the theme is the search for evidence through a common approach in the design of studies by researchers in the area, especially in the question of evaluating the effect of the training on tasks unrelated to those trained [35]. In this context, the development of stimulation programs and the assessment of their impacts must be aligned with the promotion of the adaptive functioning of individuals, and not just applied to the activities practiced and evaluated [27].

3.3 Applications Within the School Environment and Brazil's Scope

Considering the various complexities that the use of digital games involves in the school environment, in addition to the need for the availability of technologies by schools or by the group of researchers, another relevant challenge is the investigation of moderators of cognitive improvement in the school environment [4, 11, 28].

In this context, it is necessary to clarify, especially in the national context, what are the cultural and socioeconomic impacts on the benefits of cognitive stimulation through digital games within the school context. In other words, it is necessary to investigate regional and socioeconomic differences as a factor related or not to the ability of a digital game to stimulate, as well as in the reproduction of results in different regions/populations of the same country, or between countries. Therefore, there is an urgent need for collaboration between research groups for the application and reproduction of interventions mediated by digital games for the cognitive stimulation of participants, especially with children and adolescents within the school setting [11].

In the context of regional differences, Pazeto et al. [67] reinforce the importance of identifying skills and variables even in the context of preschool education, such as EF, oral language, initial literacy and writing skills, in children as precursors for the later performance of students in Elementary School. The authors state that the identification of these elements provides information so that early-preventive interventions can be provided with the objective of minimizing future difficulties in the school environment.

Dias and Seabra [32] show evidence that cognitive skills such as oral language and EF have a great contribution to student performance at the end of Elementary School, indicating that children with greater phonological skills, vocabulary and cognitive flexibility are associated with better school performance and better grades. Thus, the importance of investigations in this subject is highlighted.

Cardoso et al. [11] point to the need for investments in intervention programs with preventive approaches within the school environment, aimed at caring for cognitive impairments and promoting the cognitive health of children in the early years. In addition, they indicate that for a greater generalization of preventive applicability, the knowledge of different neurocognitive stimulation strategies, general and EF, should be aligned with mediators, such as professionals in the fields of neuropsychology and education.

However, the discussion at the national level of Brazil on the theme of EF stimulation combined with the use of digital games with children in the school environment has taken shape [1, 4, 11, 32, 72, 79], but it is still incipient considering children and adolescents with typical and atypical development, with an emphasis on scientific rigor to support the evidences. Thus, the challenge lies in the need for more studies in the area involving children within the school environment. In particular, considering the national profile of both children and school development, in which it is necessary to consider the cultural and economic diversity of the country.

3.4   Use of Difficulty Curves in Digital Games

Another challenge in the context of improvements in EF are studies on the impact of difficulty curves adopted in digital games aimed at cognitive stimulation [63]. In this sense, the difficulty curves have a direct impact on the game experience and the stimulation potential mediated by the digital game with the participants. It is through the difficulty designed for the game that players can feel more or less challenged and motivated to carry out the activities proposed in the games, therefore, influencing the experience of playing.

Schell [76] indicates the need to progressively increase the difficulty, as the player succeeds in the activities proposed during the levels of a game, seeking to maintain the player's interest in the game. Hence, players exercise their skills within the game and overcome levels, while being required to perform different and more complex challenges, represented by levels with their own difficulties. On the other hand, if the difficulty does not progress throughout the game, it becomes boring and uninteresting for players. However, how to modulate the difficulty of a digital game aimed at the cognitive stimulation of players?

Krause and colleagues [49] discuss and propose a cognitive model aimed at the interaction between the game and the player, which approaches elements of digital games, such as game mechanics and level design, and EF. Other studies have investigated this aspect of digital games through static difficulty curves modelling [63], as well as incremental difficulty curves adaptive to the user [11], or even without increasing the difficulty of the digital game used (placebo effect) [33] in order to comprehend the relationship between the game difficulty and cognitive stimulation. Although, more studies in the area are needed on the different strategies and models for adapting the difficulty curves to the user, in the context of a game proposed activity and cognitive stimulation.

To meet this challenge, it is necessary to call for a greater collaboration between game designers, neuropsychologists, health and behavior professionals so that techniques aimed at behavioral changes, based on evidence, are guaranteed. Therefore, to investigate the best combinations between game mechanics and behavior change processes, to maximize behavior changes, with the least possible side effects on the participating individuals, in this case, children [44].

Finally, the modulation of difficulty curves of a digital game to create an experience that demands more or less effort from players needs to be addressed. In the relationship and context of the classroom, the interaction between students also takes place while carrying out their activities, something that may not be foreseen in the use of digital games, since they have strictly pre-defined rules for carrying out the activities and completing the proposed levels and the interactions extrapolate the game platform. In this context, would it be possible to use the particularities of social interaction present in the classroom within the difficulty curve of a digital game?

3.5 Cognitive Stimulation in the School Context After Social Isolation by COVID-19

Finally, we consider it urgent and a challenge from the research perspective to investigate the impacts on the cognitive development of children and adolescents in relation to social isolation resulting from the COVID-19 pandemic. Also, physical distancing from the school environment, a situation that still has a psychological effect not fully known among different age groups [37].

As mentioned earlier, given that the maturation process of EF is significantly strengthened in childhood and adolescence [6], and that their healthy development is associated with individuals' cognitive, socio-affective, emotional, behavioral and moral competencies, it is necessary to assess whether there was cognitive impairment and, if so, the extent of the impairment resulting from social isolation, confinement and closure period of the schools.

Hence it is necessary, concomitantly with stimulation studies, to assess the participants' cognitive components as attentional issues, school performance (reading, writing and arithmetic), planning, self-control, quality of life, as well as phonological, vocabulary and motor development skills. Few exploratory studies so far have addressed the relationship between the development of EF and the situation of confinement with children and adolescents with typical development [51], with atypical development [65], in addition to the cognitive consequences of COVID infection [40].

It is also important to focus on understanding the cognitive consequences in participants, children and adolescents previously affected with COVID-19, to understand the impacts both in terms of stimulation and in comparison with their peers in the school environment. Thus, the challenge lies in the investigation of EF stimulation mediated by digital games with children and adolescents in the possible time window at school age, at different levels of schooling – in Elementary School (I and II) and High School.

Therefore, we propose the need for the investigation of cognitive stimulation in children and adolescents who went through the isolation resulting from COVID-19 during school age, in the search for the reduction of any losses arising from social isolation in these stages of development. From this, we indicate the need for EF stimulation programs that can act as a means to reduce and mitigate such cognitive losses.

4 Evaluation

As ways of evaluating progress in the area of digital games to stimulate EF in children and adolescents within the school context, we highlight the growth of publications involving research in the national context, and the monitoring of the impacts of interventions on participants' lives.

We point to a need for studies involving the stimulation of EF and components, with emphasis on Inhibitory Control and Cognitive Flexibility, within the school environment in participants with typical and atypical development. To this end, we indicate the urge for the assessment of behavioral, cognitive and emotional aspects of individuals in such studies, moving beyond the evaluations of tasks trained by digital games or exclusively qualitative – specifically with regard to the effects of transfer and generalization gains, which still need to be established [27, 28, 57, 81].

The challenge encompasses the development of interdisciplinary research, involving areas such as digital games, education and neuropsychology, aimed at more integrative and longitudinal solutions, involving evaluation and stimulation of EF in various stages of school development. To assess the progress in the field of cognitive stimulation and digital games within the school environment, we propose the following:

- Increase in the number of digital games aimed at stimulating and assessing Executive Functions in the Brazilian context.

    - Evaluation is required in quantitative and qualitative terms. The development of more games for the purpose of stimulating or evaluating Executive Functions, within the scientific rigor brought in the 5 proposed challenges, is essential for outlining the potential impact of this type of initiative. Added to this topic is the need for greater financial investment, public and/or private for the development of such games, especially in the educational context.

- Increase in the number of applications evaluating the impacts of the use of stimulation games with quantitative psychometric batteries and also qualitative methods – such as interviews with parents and teachers about the impacts of the studies on the participants;

    - Evaluation is also necessary in both quantitative and qualitative terms, although it is not possible to establish an exact measure. Previous studies demonstrate the development of non-technological interventions, but in the current context, children have a significant interest in digital games. It is suggested that this type of intervention is a potential resource that can contribute to engagement and greater adherence to the proposed interventions. Field research remains necessary and arises from the need for partner groups to apply studies using digital games in various locations, nationally and internationally, aimed at the use of similar application methodologies with digital games produced for this purpose.

- Scientific publications with documentation about the development steps and processes – design, development, validation with expert judges and target audience, application, and analysis of data to verify impacts.

    - This type of qualitative evaluation is necessary, seeking to provide the research field with the knowledge and tools necessary for the development of games with the greatest potential for beneficial impacts on the participants. Thus, with greater evidence of the processes of developing applications for the stimulation of EF through digital games in the school context, future studies can be developed with children with different clinical and neurodevelopmental conditions.

- Formation of research groups integrating the multidisciplinary domains involved in the production of digital games aimed at stimulation, such as, specialists in game development, neuropsychology, education, and health.

  - The involvement of different areas of knowledge is essential for the success of initiatives involving the development of digital games. The growth of groups focused on this purpose has the potential to generate and share knowledge, ensuring better results from the different fields of knowledge involved in the production of this type of application.

- Investigations of the stimulation potential in different social contexts, such as public and private schools.

  - The replication of results obtained in interventions in different contexts is necessary to elucidate the potential impact of digital games aimed at cognitive stimulation, as well as the survey of socioeconomic and cultural variables that may restrict or benefit this type of intervention.

- Growth of investigations and publications involving applications inserted in the daily lives of children and adolescents, such as within the school setting.

  - The evaluation in quantitative terms of interventions with ecological approaches aimed for children and adolescents are necessary, given the urgency of inserting current academic knowledge of the Executive Functions in applied research. Incipient in Brazil, this ecological approach to the development and usage of digital games is urgent when observing the developmental consequences in individuals caused by social isolation from the school environment as a result of COVID-19.

- Alignment between teams of researchers to create early preventive protocols, seeking to obtain positive and measurable impacts from a cognitive point of view mediated by digital games.

  - Develop partnerships for interventions in different regions of the country due to variables related to socioeconomic and cultural factors that may interfere with both applicability and results. From the initial data collected and shared, better proposals for interventions can be elaborated. E.g., in terms of gameplay of games aimed for interventions, application time, number of sessions, or even if there is a difference in theoretical types and categories of games to be developed for the stimulation of the different components of the Executive Functions.

- Definitions about the different mechanics and rules of the game that are most appropriate and directed to the cognitive stimulation of players from different groups, *i.e.* children and adolescents with typical development and atypical development.

  - Alignment between practice and game theory, their categorization, and better strategies for the purpose of stimulation or assessment of Executive Functions with children and adolescents.

- Increase of investigations directed to the impact of interventions using digital games in children and adolescents with clinical diagnoses in ecological approaches, such as Learning Disabilities or Attention-Deficit/Hyperactivity Disorder (ADHD), in the school environment.

  - A great potential is observed within applications in ecological environment using digital games, in the perspective of different approaches and clinical groups.

Acknowledgements. The present work was carried out with the support of the Coordination for the Improvement of Higher Education Personnel - Brazil (CAPES) - Financing Code 001. The authors also thank the National Council for Scientific and Technological Development (CNPQ), Research Support Foundation of Rio Grande do Sul (FAPERGS), Secretary of Innovation, Science and Technology of Rio Grande do Sul (SICT/RS) and Feevale University for their support for this research.

References

1. Alves, L.: Jogos Digitais e Funções Executivas: Desenvolvimento, Pesquisas e Aprendizagens Mediadas Pelo Gamebook Guardiões da Floresta, 1st edn. EDUFBA, Salvador (2021)
2. Baniqued, P.L., et al.: Cognitive training with casual video games: points to consider. Front. Psychol. **4**, 1010 (2014). https://doi.org/10.3389/fpsyg.2013.01010
3. Barnett, W.S., et al.: Educational effects of the tool of the mind curriculum: a randomized trial. Early Child. Res. Q. **23**(3), 299–313 (2008). https://doi.org/10.1016/j.ecresq.2008.03.001
4. Benites Cerqueira, B., Barbosa, D.N.F., Mossmann, J.B., Cardoso, C.D.O., Barbosa, J.L.V.: Inhibitory control stimulation in elementary school children through digital games: a systematic mapping study. Appl. Neuropsychol. Child **11**(3), 541–552 (2022). https://doi.org/10.1080/21622965.2020.1843040
5. Bernier, A., Carlson, S.M., Whipple, N.: From external regulation to self-regulation: early parenting precursors of young children's executive functioning. Child Dev. **81**(1), 326–339 (2010)
6. Best, J.R., Miller, P.H.: A developmental perspective on executive function. Child Dev. **81**(6), 1641–1660 (2010)
7. Blair, C., Razza, R.P.: Relating effortful control, executive function, and false belief understanding to emerging math and literacy ability in kindergarten. Child Dev. **78**(2), 647–663 (2007)
8. Borella, E., Carretti, B., Pelegrina, S.: The specific role of inhibition in reading comprehension in good and poor comprehenders. J. Learn. Disabil. **43**(6), 541–552 (2010)

9. Brito, G.R., Maia, S.A.Á., Seabra, A.G.: Teste de fluência em leitura (TFL): desenvolvimento, evidências de validade e precisão. Neuropsicología Latinoamericana **13**(2), 11–22 (2021)

10. Bull, R., Espy, K.A., Wiebe, S.A.: Short-term memory, working memory, and executive functioning in preschoolers: Longitudinal predictors of mathematical achievement at age 7 years. Dev. Neuropsychol. **33**(3), 205–228 (2008). https://doi.org/10.1080/87565640801982312

11. Cardoso, C.D.O., Dias, N., Senger, J., Colling, A.P.C., Seabra, A.G., Fonseca, R.P.: Neuropsychological stimulation of executive functions in children with typical development: a systematic review. Appl. Neuropsychol. Child **7**(1), 61–81 (2018). https://doi.org/10.1080/21622965.2016.1241950

12. Cardoso, C.D.O., Seabra, A.G., Gomes, C.M.A., Fonseca, R.P.: Program for the neuropsychological stimulation of cognition in students: impact, effectiveness, and transfer effects on student cognitive performance. Front. Psychol. **10**, 1784 (2019). https://doi.org/10.3389/fpsyg.2019.01784

13. Cardoso, C.O.: Programas de intervenção neuropsicológica precoce-preventiva: estimulação das funções executivas em escolares. PhD Dissertation — Pontifícia Universidade Católica do Rio Grande do Sul (PUCRS), Porto Alegre – Brazil (2017)

14. Carlson, S.M., Moses, L.J., Claxton, L.J.: Individual differences in executive functioning and theory of mind: an investigation of inhibitory control and planning ability. J. Exp. Child Psychol. **87**(4), 299–319 (2004). https://doi.org/10.1016/j.jecp.2004.01.002

15. Cerqueira, B.B., Barbosa, D.N.F., Mossmann, J.B.: Revisão exploratória de literatura em jogos digitais voltados para estimulação do controle inibitório em crianças do ensino fundamental. Revista Conhecimento Online **3**, 28–40 (2018)

16. Cerqueira, B.B., Barbosa, D.N.F., Mossmann, J.B., Barbosa, J.L.V.: Adaptation of an educational exergame to mobile platforms: a development process. Commun. Comput. Inf. Sci. **1**, 287–298 (2018)

17. Chiang, H.L., Gau, S.S.F.: Impact of executive functions on school and peer functions in youths with ADHD. Res. Dev. Disabil. **35**(5), 963–972 (2014). https://doi.org/10.1016/j.ridd.2014.02.010

18. Christ, S.E., Holt, D.D., White, D.A., Green, L.: Inhibitory control in children with autism spectrum disorder. J. Autism Dev. Disord. **37**(6), 1155–1165 (2007). https://doi.org/10.1007/s10803-006-0259-y

19. Christopher, M.E., et al.: Predicting word reading and comprehension with executive function and speed measures across development: a latent variable analysis. J. Exp. Psychol. Gen. **141**(3), 470 (2012). https://doi.org/10.1037/a0027375

20. Cicchetti, D.: The impact of social experience on neurobiological systems: illustration from a constructivist view of child maltreatment. Cogn. Dev. **17**(3–4), 1407–1428 (2002). https://doi.org/10.1016/S0885-2014(02)00121-1

21. Colvert, E., et al.: Do theory of mind and executive function deficits underlie the adverse outcomes associated with profound early deprivation?: findings from the English and Romanian adoptees study. J. Abnorm. Child Psychol. **36**(7), 1057–1068 (2008). https://doi.org/10.1007/s10802-008-9232-x

22. Conklin, H.M., Luciana, M., Hooper, C.J., Yarger, R.S.: Working memory performance in typically developing children and adolescents: behavioral evidence of protracted frontal lobe development. Dev. Neuropsychol. **31**(1), 103–128 (2007). https://doi.org/10.1207/s15326942dn3101_6

23. Cruz, V.T., et al.: A rehabilitation tool designed for intensive web-based cognitive training: description and usability study. JMIR Res. Protoc. **2**(2), e59 (2013). https://doi.org/10.2196/resprot.2899

24. Dalsgaard, S., Østergaard, S.D., Leckman, J.F., Mortensen, P.B., Pedersen, M.G.: Mortality in children, adolescents, and adults with attention deficit hyperactivity disorder: a nationwide cohort study. Lancet **385**(9983), 2190–2196 (2015). https://doi.org/10.1016/S0140-673 6(14)61684-6

25. Dexter, D.D., Park, Y.J., Hughes, C.A.: A meta-analytic review of graphic organizers and science instruction for adolescents with learning disabilities: implications for the intermediate and secondary science classroom. Learn. Disabil. Res. Pract. **26**(4), 204–213 (2011)

26. Diamond, A., Lee, K.: Interventions shown to aid executive function development in children 4 to 12 years old. Science **333**(6045), 959–964 (2011). https://doi.org/10.1126/science.120 4529

27. Diamond, A., Ling, D.S.: Conclusions about interventions, programs, and approaches for improving executive functions that appear justified and those that, despite much hype, do not. Dev. Cogn. Neurosci. **18**, 34–48 (2015). https://doi.org/10.1016/j.dcn.2015.11.005

28. Diamond, A., Ling, D.: Review of the evidence on, and fundamental questions about, efforts to improve executive functions, including working memory. In: Novick, J., et al. (eds.) Cognitive and Working Memory Training: Perspectives from Psychology, Neuroscience, and Human Development, pp. 143–431. Oxford University Press, New York (2020)

29. Diamond, A.: Activities and programs that improve children's executive functions. Curr. Dir. Psychol. Sci. **21**(5), 335–341 (2012). https://doi.org/10.1177/0963721412453722

30. Diamond, A.: Executive functions. Annu. Rev. Psychol. **64**, 135–168 (2013). https://doi.org/ 10.1146/annurev-psych-113011-143750

31. Dias, N.M., Seabra, A.G.: Is it possible to promote executive functions in preschoolers? A case study in Brazil. Int. J. Child Care Educ. Policy **9**(1), 1–18 (2015). https://doi.org/10. 1186/s40723-015-0010-2

32. Dias, N.M., Seabra, A.G.: Intervention for executive functions development in early elementary school children: effects on learning and behaviour, and follow-up maintenance. Educ. Psychol. **37**(4), 468–486 (2017). https://doi.org/10.1080/01443410.2016.1214686

33. Dovis, S., Van der Oord, S., Wiers, R.W., Prins, P.J.: Improving executive functioning in children with ADHD: training multiple executive functions within the context of a computer game. A randomized double-blind placebo-controlled trial. PloS ONE **10**(4), e0121651 (2015). https://doi.org/10.1371/journal.pone.0121651

34. Duncan, G.J., et al.: School readiness and later achievement. Dev. Psychol. **43**(6), 1428 (2007)

35. Eichenbaum, A., Bavelier, D., Green, C.S.: Fundamental questions surrounding efforts to improve cognitive function through video game training. In: Novick, J., et al. (eds.) Cognitive and Working Memory Training: Perspectives from Psychology, Neuroscience, and Human Development, pp. 432–454. Oxford University Press, New York (2020)

36. Fairchild, G., et al.: Decision making and executive function in male adolescents with early-onset or adolescence-onset conduct disorder and control subjects. Biol. Psychiatry **66**(2), 162–168 (2009)

37. Fonseca, R.P., Sganzerla, G.C., Enéas, L.V.: Fechamento das escolas na pandemia de COVID-19: impacto socioemocional, cognitivo e de aprendizagem. Debates em Psiquiatria **10**(4), 28–37 (2020)

38. Fosco, W.D., Kofler, M.J., Alderson, R.M., Tarle, S.J., Raiker, J.S., Sarver, D.E.: Inhibitory control and information processing in ADHD: comparing the dual task and performance adjustment hypotheses. J. Abnorm. Child Psychol. **47**(6), 961–974 (2019)

39. Friedman, N.P., Miyake, A.: Unity and diversity of executive functions: individual differences as a window on cognitive structure. Cortex **86**, 186–204 (2017). https://doi.org/10.1016/j.cor tex.2016.04.023

40. Frolli, A., et al.: The impact of COVID-19 on cognitive development and executive functioning in adolescents: a first exploratory investigation. Brain Sci. **11**(9), 1222 (2021). https://doi.org/ 10.3390/brainsci11091222

41. Gonçalves, H.A., Viapiana, V.F., Sartori, M.S., Giacomoni, C.H., Stein, L.M., Fonseca, R.P.: Funções executivas predizem o processamento de habilidades básicas de leitura, escrita e matemática? Neuropsicologia Latinoamericana 9(3) (2017)

42. Holmes, J., Gathercole, S.E., Dunning, D.L.: Adaptive training leads to sustained enhancement of poor working memory in children. Dev. Sci. 12(4), F9–F15 (2009)

43. Hughes, C., Ensor, R.: Executive function and theory of mind: predictive relations from ages 2 to 4. Dev. Psychol. 43(6), 1447 (2007). https://doi.org/10.1037/0012-1649.43.6.1447

44. Institute of Digital Media and Child Development Working Group on Games for Health, Baranowski, T., Blumberg, F., Buday, R., DeSmet, A., Fiellin, L.E., Young, K.: Games for health for children—current status and needed research. Games Health J. 5(1), 1–12 (2016)

45. Jurado, M.B., Rosselli, M.: The elusive nature of executive functions: a review of our current understanding. Neuropsychol. Rev. 17(3), 213–233 (2007). https://doi.org/10.1007/s11065-007-9040-z

46. Kassai, R., Futo, J., Demetrovics, Z., Takacs, Z.K.: A meta-analysis of the experimental evidence on the near-and far-transfer effects among children's executive function skills. Psychol. Bull. 145(2), 165 (2019)

47. Kenworthy, L., Yerys, B.E., Anthony, L.G., Wallace, G.L.: Understanding executive control in autism spectrum disorders in the lab and in the real world. Neuropsychol. Rev. 18(4), 320–338 (2008)

48. Klingberg, T., et al.: Computerized training of working memory in children with ADHD - a randomized, controlled trial. J. Am. Acad. Child Adolesc. Psychiatry 44(2), 177–186 (2005)

49. Krause, K.K.G., Hounsell, M.S., Gasparini, I.: A model for the interrelationship between executive functions and elements of digital games. Braz. J. Comput. Educ. 28, 596–625 (2020). https://doi.org/10.5753/RBIE.2020.28.0.596

50. Krause, K.K.G., Hounsell, M.S., Gasparini, I.: Aplicações dos jogos digitais nas funções executivas: um mapeamento sistemático da literatura. In: XVII Brazilian Symposium on Computer Games and Digital Entertainment (SBGames), pp. 54–62. SBC, Foz do Iguaçu (2018)

51. Lavigne-Cerván, R., Costa-López, B., Juárez-Ruiz de Mier, R., Real-Fernández, M., Sánchez-Muñoz de León, M., Navarro-Soria, I.: Consequences of COVID-19 confinement on anxiety, sleep and executive functions of children and adolescents in Spain. Front. Psychol. 12, 334 (2021). https://doi.org/10.3389/fpsyg.2021.565516

52. León, C.B.R., Rodrigues, C.C., Seabra, A.G., Dias, N.M.: Funções executivas e desempenho escolar em crianças de 6 a 9 anos de idade. Revista Psicopedagogia 30(92), 113–120 (2013)

53. Levin, H.S., Hanten, G.: Executive functions after traumatic brain injury in children. Pediatr. Neurol. 33(2), 79–93 (2005). https://doi.org/10.1016/j.pediatrneurol.2005.02.002

54. Mackey, A.P., Hill, S.S., Stone, S.I., Bunge, S.A.: Differential effects of reasoning and speed training in children. Dev. Sci. 14(3), 582–590 (2011). https://doi.org/10.1111/j.1467-7687.2010.01005.x

55. Mansur-Alves, M., Saldanha-Silva, R.: Does working memory training promote changes in fluid intelligence? Temas em Psicologia 25(2), 787–807 (2017). https://doi.org/10.9788/TP2017.2-19En

56. McClelland, M.M., Cameron, C.E., Connor, C.M., Farris, C.L., Jewkes, A.M., Morrison, F.J.: Links between behavioral regulation and preschoolers' literacy, vocabulary, and math skills. Dev. Psychol. 43(4), 947 (2007). https://doi.org/10.1037/0012-1649.43.4.947

57. Melby-Lervåg, M., Hulme, C.: Is working memory training effective? A meta-analytic review. Dev. Psychol. 49(2), 270–291 (2013). https://doi.org/10.1037/a0028228

58. Melby-Lervåg, M., Redick, T.S., Hulme, C.: Working memory training does not improve performance on measures of intelligence or other measures of "far transfer" evidence from a meta-analytic review. Perspect. Psychol. Sci. 11(4), 512–534 (2016). https://doi.org/10.1177/1745691616635612

59. Miller, H.V., Barnes, J.C., Beaver, K.M.: Self-control and health outcomes in a nationally representative sample. Am. J. Health Behav. **35**(1), 15–27 (2011). https://doi.org/10.5993/ajhb.35.1.2

60. Miyake, A., Friedman, N.P., Emerson, M.J., Witzki, A.H., Howerter, A., Wager, T.D.: The unity and diversity of executive functions and their contributions to complex "frontal lobe" tasks: a latent variable analysis. Cogn. Psychol. **41**(1), 49–100 (2000). https://doi.org/10.1006/cogp.1999.0734

61. Moffitt, T.E., et al.: A gradient of childhood self-control predicts health, wealth, and public safety. Proc. Natl. Acad. Sci. **108**(7), 2693–2698 (2011). https://doi.org/10.1073/pnas.1010076108

62. Monette, S., Bigras, M., Guay, M.C.: The role of the executive functions in school achievement at the end of Grade 1. J. Exp. Child Psychol. **109**(2), 158–173 (2011). https://doi.org/10.1016/j.jecp.2011.01.008

63. Mossmann, J.B., Cerqueira, B.B., Barbosa, D.N., Fonseca, R.P., Reategui, E.B.: The planning of difficulty curves in an exergame for inhibitory control stimulation in a school intervention program: a pilot study. Front. Psychol. **10**, 2271 (2019). https://doi.org/10.3389/fpsyg.2019.02271

64. Mossmann, J.: Exergames Como Mediadores Da Estimulação De Componentes Das Funções Executivas Em Crianças Do Ensino Fundamental I. 261 p. PhD Dissertation, Doutorado em Informática na Educação. PPGIE/UFRGS, Brasil (2018)

65. Navarro-Soria, I., Real-Fernández, M., Juárez-Ruiz de Mier, R., Costa-López, B., Sánchez, M., Lavigne, R.: Consequences of confinement due to COVID-19 in Spain on anxiety, sleep and executive functioning of children and adolescents with ADHD. Sustainability **13**(5), 2487 (2021). https://doi.org/10.3389/fpsyg.2021.565516

66. Parsons, T.D.: Virtual reality for enhanced ecological validity and experimental control in the clinical, affective and social neurosciences. Front. Hum. Neurosci. **9**, 660 (2015). https://doi.org/10.3389/fnhum.2015.00660

67. Pazeto, T.D.C.B., Dias, N.M., Gomes, C.M.A., Seabra, A.G.: Prediction of reading and writing in elementary education through early childhood education. Psicologia: Ciência e Profissão **40** (2020). https://doi.org/10.1590/1982-3703003205497

68. Penades, R., Catalan, R., Rubia, K., Andres, S., Salamero, M., Gasto, C.: Impaired response inhibition in obsessive compulsive disorder. Eur. Psychiatry **22**(6), 404–410 (2007). https://doi.org/10.1016/j.eurpsy.2006.05.001

69. Pinto, A.B.: Desenvolvimento das funções executivas em crianças dos 6 aos 11 anos de idade. PhD Dissertation, Universidade do Porto, Porto (2008)

70. Pires, E.U., Landeira-Fenandez, J.: Development of a computerized tool to assess executive skills in children: O Jogo das Cartas Mágicas. PhD Dissertation, Pontifícia Universidade Católica do Rio de Janeiro, Rio de Janeiro (2014)

71. Prins, P.J.M., et al.: Braingame brian: toward an executive function training program with game elements for children with ADHD and cognitive control problems. Games Health J. **2**, 44–49 (2013). https://doi.org/10.1089/g4h.2013.0004

72. Ramos, D.K., Melo, H.M.: Can digital games in school improve attention? A study of Brazilian elementary school students. J. Comput. Educ. **6**(1), 5–19 (2018). https://doi.org/10.1007/s40692-018-0111-3

73. Ramos, D.K., Garcia, F.: Jogos digitais e aprimoramento do controle inibitório: um estudo com crianças do atendimento educacional especializado. Revista Brasileira de Educação Especial **25**(1), 37–54 (2019). https://doi.org/10.1590/s1413-65382519000100003

74. Sala, G., Gobet, F.: Working memory training in typically developing children: a meta-analysis of the available evidence. Dev. Psychol. **53**(4), 671 (2017). https://doi.org/10.1037/dev0000265

75. Salum, G.A., et al.: Specificity of basic information processing and inhibitory control in attention deficit hyperactivity disorder. Psychol. Med. **44**(3), 617–631 (2014). https://doi.org/10.1017/S0033291713000639

76. Schell, J.: The Art of Game Design: A Book of Lenses. CRC Press, Florida (2008)

77. Seabra, A.G., Laros, J.A., Macedo, E.C., Abreu, N.: Inteligência e funções executivas: avanços e desafios para a avaliação neuropsicológica, pp. 39–50. Memnon, São Paulo (2014)

78. Seabra, A., Dias, N.: Avaliação Neuropsicológica Cognitiva: Atenção e Funções Executivas. Memnon, São Paulo, SP (2012)

79. Spaniol, M.M., Shalev, L., Kossyvaki, L., Mevorach, C.: Attention training in autism as a potential approach to improving academic performance: a school-based pilot study. J. Autism Dev. Disord. **48**(2), 592–610 (2017). https://doi.org/10.1007/s10803-017-3371-2

80. Staiano, A.E., Calvert, S.L.: Exergames for physical education courses: physical, social, and cognitive benefits. Child Dev. Perspect. **5**(2), 93–98 (2011). https://doi.org/10.1111/j.1750-8606.2011.00162.x

81. Takacs, Z.K., Kassai, R.: The efficacy of different interventions to foster children's executive function skills: a series of meta-analyses. Psychol. Bull. **145**(7), 653 (2019). https://doi.org/10.1037/bul0000195

82. Tavares, J.V.T., Clark, L., Cannon, D.M., Erickson, K., Drevets, W.C., Sahakian, B.J.: Distinct profiles of neurocognitive function in unmedicated unipolar depression and bipolar II depression. Biol. Psychiatry **62**(8), 917–924 (2007). https://doi.org/10.1016/j.biopsych.2007.05.034

83. Thorell, L.B., Lindqvist, S., Bergman Nutley, S., Bohlin, G., Klingberg, T.: Training and transfer effects of executive functions in preschool children. Dev. Sci. **12**(1), 106–113 (2009). https://doi.org/10.1111/j.1467-7687.2008.00745.x

84. Toll, S.W., Van der Ven, S.H., Kroesbergen, E.H., Van Luit, J.E.: Executive functions as predictors of math learning disabilities. J. Learn. Disabil. **44**(6), 521–532 (2011). https://doi.org/10.1177/0022219410387302

85. Varvara, P., Varuzza, C., Padovano Sorrentino, A.C., Vicari, S., Menghini, D.: Executive functions in developmental dyslexia. Front. Hum. Neurosci. **8**, 120 (2014). https://doi.org/10.3389/fnhum.2014.00120

86. Volckaert, A.M.S., Noël, M.P.: Training executive function in preschoolers reduce externalizing behaviors. Trends Neurosci. Educ. **4**(1–2), 37–47 (2015). https://doi.org/10.1016/j.tine.2015.02.001

87. Welsh, J.A., Nix, R.L., Blair, C., Bierman, K.L., Nelson, K.E.: The development of cognitive skills and gains in academic school readiness for children from low-income families. J. Educ. Psychol. **102**(1), 43–53 (2010). https://doi.org/10.1037/a0016738

88. Zelazo, P.D.: Executive function and psychopathology: a neurodevelopmental perspective. Annu. Rev. Clin. Psychol. **16**(1), 431–454 (2020)

89. Zelazo, P.D., Blair, C.B., Willoughby, M.T.: Executive Function: Implications for Education. NCER 2017-2000. National Center for Education Research (2016)

Perceptual Analysis of Computer Graphics Characters in Digital Entertainment

Soraia Raupp Musse[1], Greice Pinho Dal Molin[1],
Victor Flávio de Andrade Araujo[1(✉)], Diogo Hartmann Muller Schaffer[1],
and Angelo Costa Brandelli[2]

[1] School of Technology, Pontifical Catholic University of Rio Grande do Sul,
Porto Alegre, Brazil
soraia.musse@pucrs.br,
{greice.pinho,victor.flavio,diogo.schaffer}@acad.pucrs.br
[2] School of Health and Life Sciences,
Pontifical Catholic University of Rio Grande do Sul, Porto Alegre, Brazil
angelo.costa@pucrs.br

Abstract. This chapter presents a discussion regarding the area of perceptual analysis in Computer Graphics (CG) characters. This discussion is focused on presenting one challenge area in Digital Entertainment. Many issues in the area of perception analysis have been researched in last years, in particular with respect to the theory of Uncanny Valley (UV) proposed by Masahiro Mori in 1970. Indeed, it is known that realistic characters from movies and games can cause strangeness and involuntary feelings in viewers, what can affect the acceptance of audience in games and movies. This chapter aims to present concepts and discuss issues in this area. For this, we present two case studies: *i)* The first one is related to perceptual analysis, in which we use characters in groups with different skin colors and different levels of realism; *ii)* The second one is related to computational analysis and aims to estimate the perceived comfort by human beings automatically.

Keywords: Computer graphics · Comfort · Charisma · Uncanny valley · Perception · Emotion

1 Introduction

In recent years, advances in Computer Graphics (CG) have allowed the entertainment industry to create very realistic virtual humans [18] in terms of animation of their bodies and faces [25]. In some movies, real actors have been replaced by CG characters (such as Disney's 2016 Rogue One movie, 2019 Aladdin movie, and 2020 The Mandalorian series), and often this substitution is not even perceived by the public; however, there are still some perceived artifacts, such as the movement of the mouth and eyes [29]. In some cases, those artifacts or other distortions and images characteristics can cause strangeness and negative feelings

R. P. d. Santos and M. d. S. Hounsell (Eds.): GranDGamesBR 2020/2021, CCIS 1702, pp. 207–232, 2023.
https://doi.org/10.1007/978-3-031-27639-2_10

in viewers, what can affect the acceptance of audience. Knowing how humans perceive and understand virtual characters can be important to help mitigate these oddities to generate a CG character more similar to a human being, making the experience of watching a movie, a game, or interacting with a character more fluid.

Perception comes from the Latin word with the same spelling that means "to apprehend" or "to understand". According to Zell et al. [46], the brain processes information from the senses and interprets its relevance to the organism. The first process of transforming information driven by the senses is called the ascending process. The second process is based on information acquired about the world through learning and provides a context for meaning information to be interpreted, known as the top-down process. Therefore, when looking at a person or a character, for example, a perception is created about what is being seen and represented by the face of the other.

The roboticist Masahiro Mori [28] conducted an analysis of the emotional reaction of humans when exposed to artificial beings. According to his theory, artificial beings (robots, CG characters, etc) with a high degree of realism next to real humans may fall into the Uncanny Valley (UV), causing a strange impression on the viewer. The UV theory analyzes human perception in an emotional context for artificial beings. According to Mori, artificial beings with a high level of realism (high similarity to humans) and without a common characteristic can cause strange sensations to those who watch them. This feeling is intensified when artificial beings give signs of life, as a movement, thereby changing the shape of the valley. Moreover, this feeling can also be caused by lack of familiarity with being artificial or other characteristics that can cause discomfort.

The perception area is essential for CG since many techniques developed in the past were based on knowledge of how the human visual system interprets visual stimuli [46]. Human perception is also a theme present in many pieces of research in CG [45,46], and it is considered very relevant when discussing the evolution of virtual humans and realistic faces. According to Mori [28], robots made to appear too similar to real humans can fall into the UV, where sometimes a high degree of human realism evokes an eerie feeling in the viewer. According to Tinwell et al. [41], the technological advancements that help developing realistic characters is accompanied over the years by people's discernment about this content. With that, Tinwell and colleagues believed that the UV would never be surpassed since discernment can help people to observe the technical tricks better. The UV hypothesis on CG characters has become increasingly influential in scientific studies [19,38], but some questions are still unanswered.

Based on these concepts, we carried out two case studies presented next. In Sects. 3) we present a perceptual study in relation to groups of characters with different skin colors (concepts better explained in the section); and in Sect. 4 we describe a methodology we propose to estimate the perceived comfort by human beings automatically. Therefore, this chapter is organized as follows: Sect. 2 presents the related work; Sect. 3 discusses our first case-study (perceptual analysis), while Sect. 4 describes our second case-study (computational analysis). Finally, Sect. 5 addresses final discussions about the results and indications from these results.

2 Related Work

In this section we present some specific problems that have been discussed in literature with respect to perceptual analysis in CG characters.

Concerning the perception of CG characters, many papers have proposed various ways to evaluate humans perception. For example, the work of Zell et al. [46] was essential to understand the perception process (i.e., how to create a stimulus, how to measure and evaluate perceptual data, etc.). They analyzed two traits of appearance: shape and material, and with the help of artists, they designed stimuli consisting of different stylization levels for both parameters. They analyzed how different combinations affect the perceived realism, appeal, eeriness, and familiarity. Also, the authors investigated how such combinations affect the perceived intensity of different facial expressions, and concluded that the shape of a character is relevant to its realism and expression. Chaminade et al. [9] investigated how the appearance of animated characters can influence the perception of their actions. The authors presented different animated characters with movement data captured from human actors or by interpolation between poses and asked the participants to categorize movement as biological or artificial. The results showed that the more anthropomorphic, the less biological bias the character had.

The effect of the UV theory on human perceptions of 3D models also has been investigated by the CG community. MacDorman and Chattopadhyay [27] aimed to determine whether reducing realism in visual characteristics would increase the uncanny effect. The authors based themselves on the theory of inconsistency in realism, which states that an entity can cause the Valley without some characteristic of an anthropomorphic being. Schwind [37] conducted nine studies that examined the effects of UV on human perception, how it affects interaction with computer systems, what cognitive processes are involved, and the causes that may be responsible for the phenomenon. Hyde et al. [17] conducted two experiments showing how exaggerated facial movement influences the impressions of cartoons and more realistic characters, and stated that an essential factor in diminishing the sensation of strangeness is the attempt to replicate human expressions (body and facial) in CG characters. Ruhland et al. [35] used algorithms to synthesize real-time motion capture of human expressions with animation data created by designers. To validate synthesized animations, they conducted a perceptual study, and results indicated that the animations had an expressive similarity to animations made by hand.

Flach et al. [12] investigated the UV theory to evaluate its effects on the perception of CG characters used in movies, games, and computational simulations. The authors evaluated the human perceptions about these characters through a questionnaire containing images and videos of these characters. Araujo et al. [2] revisited Flach experiment, in 2021, with the same questionnaire tested in 2012, and also the same images and videos of CG characters, in addition to more recent ones. Some of Araujo's findings include: *i)* the perceived comfort increased over time when comparing the characters of 2012 and 2020. However, it did not change significantly for the perceived comfort of 2012 characters. It means that the perceived comfort of people in 2012 and 2020 remain very similar in relation to 2012 characters. In addition, they found a correlation between perceived charisma and familiarity about tested CG characters, and between charisma and comfort. Interestingly, more charisma was perceived in videos than in images, and unrealistic characters were also perceived as more charismatic.

Regarding the perceived charisma, MacDorman [26] has hypothesized that an uncanny robot can cause innate fear of death and create culturally supported defenses to deal with the inevitability of death. Concerning charisma, in one of the experiments, the author showed speeches by two politicians, one charismatic and one relationship-oriented, and asked participants which candidate they would vote. Participants who previously saw uncanny robots preferred more charismatic speeches than participants who previously saw a human being. Rosenthal-von der Pütten and Krämer [31] provided an overview and categorization of explanatory approaches to the UV effect. The authors presented images and videos of humanoid robots and uncanny androids to participants to explore their evaluations of robots, their attitudes about these robots, and their emotional reactions towards these robots. The results showed that the appearance of robots was important for participants since some characteristics matched specific skills. For example, participants described charisma as a human characteristic.

With regard to characters that can generate charisma, according to West and Armstrong [44], one of the ways to study the complexities of charisma is through fiction. Goethals and Allison [13] related charismatic characters to their appearances, citing as examples that Obi-Wan "Ben" Kenobi from Star Wars and Dumbledore from Harry Potter had archetypes of sages, which could increase the emotional impact on viewers. In terms of charismatic leadership, Awamleh and Gardner [4] reported the importance of vocal variety, eye contact, relaxed posture, and lively facial expressions. Riggio [33] already described charismatic individuals as animated, charged with emotion, and full of life.

Specifically concerning CG characters, Araujo et al. [1] recently presented a discussion about following questions: i) How does the comfort perceived by people of both tested genders (female and male) relate to the genders of the characters? and ii) Is the charisma influenced by the realism of the characters, considering the subjects and genders of the characters? Authors conducted perceptual studies on characters created using CG in images and videos through questionnaires. Their results indicated that the gender of the subjects and characters affected comfort, charisma and perceived realism. In addition, they also revisited the aspect of the UV theory (perception of comfort and human likeness), and found coherent curves compared to many works in the literature.

The CG field is also involved in studies with animated characters, concerning macro and micro expressions. Several authors have already developed methods that sought to imitate and respond to the emotions presented by humans ([30]). The research developed in this work is inspired by the work of Queiroz et al. [32] and based on three psychological studies that deal with the perceptions of micro expressions. The first study is proposed by Bornemann et al. [8], in which micro expressions are displayed briefly enough (between 10 and 20 milliseconds) to ensure that people do not consciously perceive them. In the second study, Shen et al. [39] applied two experiments based on two methodologies, BART (*Brief Affect Recognition Test*) and METT (*Microexpression Training Tool*), also based on Ekman's studies. The BART condition consists of showing the six universal expressions after a fixed point. In the METT paradigm, the universal expressions are displayed between two sequences of neutral faces. This study investigated a possible upper limit of time for the perception of micro expressions, concluding that from 160 milliseconds on, the accuracy of the participants' responses began to stabilize. The third and last study used as the basis for our research is the work of Li et al. [23].

3   Case-Study: Perceptual Analysis

CG has evolved a lot in recent years [18]. Several media have taken advantage of this evolution, such as games, movies, animations, simulations. In movies and games, real actors are constantly replaced by characters created with CG. However, as shown in Kim's Siggraph 2021 presentation[1], and in the work of Kim et al. [21], most of time, the scientific community chooses to show CG advances based on 3D models with white skin colors. In addition, the work of Kim and his colleagues also shows that in games where the user can choose character attributes, both black skin tones and afro-descendant hair appear in the last choice options. Regarding characters created with CG, the user experience (movie viewers, video game players, etc) often requires that the character be charismatic and not fall into the UV [28]. In this sense, this section aims to present a case study to assess the perception of comfort, charisma and realism in relation to characters with black and white skin colors in groups. For this, we used the dataset from the work of Araujo et al. [3], that contains CG characters with black and white skin colors, and that also contains perceptual data (obtained from people's answers) about realism, comfort and charisma.

In this case, the concepts of realism and comfort are based on UV theory [28], which was created by roboticist Mori, and used in the work of Araujo et al. [3]. The UV theory says that an artificial being very similar to a human being tends to fall into a perceptual valley that causes feelings of discomfort in those who observe it. The UV is represented by a chart: *i)* the x-axis represents the Human Likeness, the farther to the right, the more similar to a human being. In our case, artificial beings are CG characters, and the most realistic ones are to the right of the x-axis; and *ii)* the y-axis represents perceived comfort.

3.1   Data Obtained

First, to follow the Ensemble Coding concept, we used the dataset from the Work of Araujo et al. [3], which has perceptual data on realism, comfort and charisma about characters from different media (movies, games, animations and

---

[1] www.youtube.com/watch?v=ROuE8xYLpX8.

simulations). In addition, the dataset has characters in three realism groups (unrealistic, moderately realistic, and very realistic), having both black and white skin colors in all three groups. To obtain the perceptual data, we used the questions used in the work of Araujo et al. [3]: *i)* Realism, having answers in three Likert-Scales to know what level of realism perceived by the participant about the presented character. Therefore, each character had an average of realism between 1 and 3; *ii)* Discomfort, having answers "Yes" or "No" to know if the participant felt uncomfortable with the presented character. In this case, the authors counted the percentages of "No" answers (i.e., comfort percentage) for each character; *iii)* Charisma, having "Charismatic" and "Non Charismatic" answers to obtain the perceived charisma in relation to the presented character. Therefore, the authors counted the percentages of "Charismatic" answers. Thus, we used the average values of perceived realism, and the percentage values of comfort and charisma perceived for each character used in this present section (for more information about the dataset, please read the work by Araujo et al. [3]). In this case study, these values are used for generating the realism, comfort and charisma averaged scores of each group of characters in the images used as stimuli presented to the participants, which is explained in Sect. 3.3.

3.2   Characters

To include different skin colors in our case study, we chose three characters for both black and white skin colors from the dataset of the work of Araujo et al. [3] (only image data). Figure 1 presents all the characters in the dataset of the work by Araujo et al. Each of these groups had an unrealistic character, a moderately realistic character, and a very realistic character, guaranteeing the three levels of realism presented in Araujo's work. We chose the only three characters with black skin color in the dataset. While the characters with white skin color were chosen based on the similarities between their values of realism, comfort and charisma (for example, moderately realistic characters who had similar realism values), again using information from a previous work [3]. The characters used in our work are shown in Table 1, where the first column shows the id of each character, the second column presents the figures of the characters, the third column the average values of perceived realism, the fourth and fifth columns present the percentages of perceived comfort and charisma, according to [3]. The first two characters ("m", and "s") in Table 1 represent the unrealistic group of characters, the "e" and "a" characters represent the moderately realistic group, and the last two represent the very realistic ("v", and "r") characters. In addition, we did not use female characters with black skin colors, as the dataset did not contain such characters.

3.3   Creation of Stimuli

Group perception is important as it allows people to assess patterns of groups directly and quickly, without requiring complex inspections and comparisons [22]. In an Ensemble Coding, the summarized representations of a set of

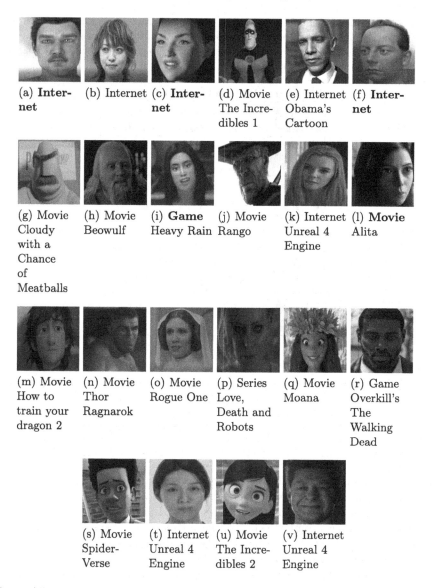

Fig. 1. All characters of the work of Araujo et al. [3] and the work of Flach et al. [12]. Note: The identifications of all characters used in this chapter follow the identification used in this figure. In addition, highlighted in bold, the characters that caused discomfort in accordance with our method that is shown in Sect. 4.

objects can be obtained through simple statistics, such as average and standard deviation, in a short period of time [22].

Based on Ensemble Coding (the work of Goldenberg et al. [14] and the work of Lamer et al. [22]), we created images with groups of 12 faces of the characters

Table 1. The table presents the id and figure of each character presented in the work by Araujo et al. [3], and used in our work. In addition, the table also presents the average values of perceived realism, and the values of percentages of comfort and charisma perceived in relation to the characters.

Id	Figure	Realism	Comfort	Charisma
m		1.39	88.23%	84.87%
s		1.43	89.07%	78.99%
e		1.75	65.54%	63.86%
a		2.08	41.17%	39.49%
v		2.6	79.83%	47.89%
r		2.72	81.51%	21.84%

presented in Sect. 3.2, varying the realism and skin color. Each of these images had two characters (six faces of each character), one or two levels of realism, and one or two skin color type. In addition, based on the values in Table 1, each image also had an average realism value, a charisma percentage and a comfort percentage. Therefore, the image could have six faces of an unrealistic character with white skin color and six faces of a very realistic character with black skin color, as shown in Fig. 2. With respect to the values in Fig. 2, the average realism was 2.05 (obtained by the average of the two realism values of the two characters), and the comfort and charisma percentages were 84.87% (obtained by the average percentage of the two comfort values of the two characters) and 53.35% (obtained by the average percentage of the two charisma values of the two characters). With that, we created 15 images with all possible combinations.

Following the Ensemble Coding concept that people can summarize features in short periods of time, we showed each image to the participants for 500 milliseconds. After that, the image disappeared, and then we presented the three questions (about realism, comfort, and charisma) to the participants. In these three questions, we presented three sliders (one for each question) with values between 0 and 100, and we asked participants to mark values that represented the realism of the image, the comfort perceived by the participant, and the charisma transmitted by the characters in the image.

First, participants viewed images with a single realism, from less realistic to more realistic, and images of different skin colors. For example, the first image presented contained the characters "m" and "s", the second image contained the characters "e" and "a", the third contained the characters "v" and "r", etc. After that, we presented images without repeating characters from the previous image, and without repeating a level of realism more than twice (for example, it could not have three images in a row containing an unrealistic character). All these processes were carried out to try to avoid realism and skin color biases.

The images and questions were presented through a form created on the JotForm[2] platform, written in Portuguese, distributed to Brazilian respondents through social networks (groups of WhatsApp, Facebook and Instagram). Before the questions we presented a consent form approved by an ethics committee, we asked the participants to answer demographic questions (gender, race, educational level, age, and familiarity with CG), and we explained that the images would appear only for 500 milliseconds and would be followed by three questions about them. The experiment (project number - 46571721.6.0000.5336) was conducted with ethics approval from the Research Ethics Committee (Comitê de Ética em Pesquisa - CEP) of Pontifical Catholic University of Rio Grande do Sul, Brazil. In the consent form, it was informed that the participants could withdraw from the research at any time, and if they felt uncomfortable. Demographic questions had multiple choice answers (except for the age question, since it was an open field for the participant to inform age), and were distributed as follows: *i)* For Educational Level, the question was "Inform the level of education" and the answer options were "Incomplete high school", "Complete high school", "Complete higher education", and "Postgraduate"; *ii)* For Gender, the question was "How do you identify with your gender?" and the options were "Female", "Male", "I prefer not to inform", and "Other" (having a free field of answer); *iii)* Regarding Race, the question was "How do you identify with your color or race?", and the answer options were "Black", "Indigenous", "Yellow", "Brown", "White", "Other" (having a free field of answer), "I prefer not to inform", and "I don't know"; *iv)* Regarding Familiarity with CG, the question was "Do you have any familiarity with Computer Graphics (examples, watched movies with characters created with computer graphics, played electronic games, simulations, among others)?" and the response options were "Yes", "No" and "I don't know". In relation to the questions *ii)* and *iii)* and its answer options, we based on the IBGE (Brazilian Institute of Geography and Statistics). In addition, no financial compensation was provided, meaning we only collected data from volunteer participants.

3.4 Results of Perceptual Analysis

Regarding the results, 32 volunteer participants answered the questionnaire (all agreed with the consent form), mean age was 24.34 years, 81% were men and 19% women, 88% were white people, 53% had completed high school, and only two people were unfamiliar with CG. As most demographic features did not have balanced responses, except for Educational Level, so we did not evaluate separate responses for women, men, people who considered themselves white, etc. Therefore, all analyzes were performed without "demographic filters". Initially,

---

[2] www.jotform.com.

Fig. 2. One of 15 images created with 12 character faces. In this case, six faces of character "m" and six of character "r". These images were created as a stimulus for using Ensemble Coding.

with the objective of ordering in levels of realism the images created with the CG characters (presented in Sect. 3.3, and in Fig. 2), we used as a basis the comfort chart presented in the work by Araujo et al. [3], and the UV chart presented in the work by Mori [28]. In these two charts, the x-axis represents Human Likeness, that is, the farther to the right is the image with characters, the more it is considered realistic. The x-axis in Fig. 3 shows the ordering of the images according to the values of the average realism of the characters shown in Table 1 and the y-axis represents the perceived comfort percentage values. In addition, the blue line in Fig. 3(a) represents the comfort percentage values (obtained in Table 1), and the orange line represents the values of comfort obtained by Ensemble Coding. The blue line in (b) represents the charisma percentage values, and the orange line represents the values of charisma obtained by Ensemble Coding.

Regarding realism, we performed a Spearman's rank test to compare the ordering of images between the average realism values obtained by Table 1 and the realism values obtained by Ensemble Coding. First, we separated the images into two groups, the first contained characters with black and white skin colors in each of the images, while the second each image contained characters with the same skin color (that is, a group with only black skin color, and a group with only white skin color). This was done to assess whether realism could be influenced by skin color separation. Overall (all 15 images), we found a strong correlation (0.91) between the order of realism averages and the realism value obtained by Ensemble Coding, that is, the perception of a group of characters when compared to the individual perception did not impact the perceived realism. The same happened when we separated the images into two groups, being 0.917 for the

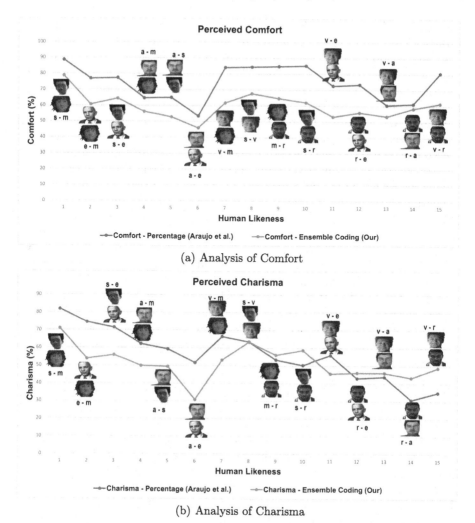

(a) Analysis of Comfort

(b) Analysis of Charisma

Fig. 3. Charts representing comfort and realism in (a), and charisma and realism in (b). (Color figure online)

group of images that contained black and white skin colors, and 1.0 for the group of images containing characters with the same skin color. It means the skin color of characters does not affect the perceived realism.

Regarding perceived comfort, comparing the comfort percentages presented in the blue line (percentages of the values obtained in the work by Araujo et al. [3], and shown in Table 1) with the comfort perceived through the Ensemble Coding presented in the orange line in Fig. 3(a), we can notice that the comfort perceived individually behaves in a similar way to the comfort perceived globally (in a group of characters), even if the images have characters with different skin colors. If we look individually, the two characters with comfort below 70% (one with black skin color and one with white skin color, as shown in Table 1) had increased comfort values when paired with other characters. In addition, we used the T-test to compare the average perceived comfort individually (74.22) and the average perceived comfort globally (59.82), and we found a significant p-value (0.0002). With that, **we can say that the feeling of discomfort increases when there is more than one CG character in an image.** As was done in the realism analysis, we separated the character images into two groups, and performed further analysis using the T-test in relation to these groups. We found significant results in the comparisons between the average comfort perceived individually and the average comfort perceived globally, both in relation to the group of images that had characters with different skin colors (individually average = 74.22, globally average = 60.40, and p-value = 0.01) and in the group of images that had characters with the same skin colors (individually average = 74.22, globally average = 58.95, and p-value = 0.006). Therefore, **we can say that, looking at the means and at the significant p-values, the difference between the perceptions of individual and global comfort was greater for the images that had characters with the same skin color.** However, looking at the global perception, we did not find a significant result in the comparison of the averages of perceived comfort of the two groups of images, even though the average was a little higher for the images that had characters with different skin colors.

Comparing the percentages of perceived charisma in Table 1 presented in the blue line with the charisma perceived through the Ensemble Coding presented in the orange line in Fig. 3(b), we can note that, as well as the perceived comfort, the charisma perceived individually also behaves similarly to globally perceived charisma. Furthermore, there was a tendency that the greater the realism (higher values in x-axis), the greater the similarity between the lines. Using the T-test, we did not find significant results either in the comparisons between individual (average of group of characters with different skin colors = 56.16 and average of group of characters with same skin colors = 56.16) and global perceptions (average of group of characters with different skin colors = 51.32 and average of group of characters with same skin colors = 51.62), or between the two groups of images (group of characters with different skin colors and group of characters with the same skin color). Therefore, **we can say that the charisma perceived globally was similar to the charisma perceived individually, that is, the addition in the amount of CG characters with and without skin color difference did not affect the perception of charisma.**

4 Case-Study: Computational Analysis

This section aims to present a regression model proposed in this research with the goal to estimate the perceived comfort discussed in last sections. This model proposes a method we called CCS (Computed Comfort Score) that calculates a percentage of estimated strangeness for a certain character's face. We present the proposed pre-processing phase, feature extraction and, finally, information about the proposed training, testing and validation process.

4.1   Dataset

Our selection of characters is based on the work of Araujo et al. [3] and Flach et al. [12], who analyzed, with subjects, the perception of comfort obtained when watching characters created with CG (films, games and computer simulations). Therefore, we use images and videos of the same 10 characters as Flach, as shown in Fig. 1 from (a) to (j). Besides the characters from Flach's work, we included more recent CG characters, as proposed by Araujo et al. [3] shown in Fig. 1 from (k) to (v). In the literature of virtual humans related to Uncanny Valley [3,12,28], the definition of "unrealism" is based on cartoon characters. Following the work of Katsyri et al. [19], this level of realism is positioned before the valley. Furthermore, still in the work by Katsyri et al., the authors defined that virtual humans with high levels of realism tend to go beyond the valley. With this, following the definitions of Araujo et al. [3] and of Flach et al. [12], to guarantee the variation of human similarity present in the UV, some of chosen characters represent a human being in a cartoonish way (q), (s) and (u), and other are more realistic, as (m), (n), (v), (r), (k) in Fig. 1.

To obtain human perceptions of realism and comfort (variables necessary to build the X and Y axes of the UV chart [28]), we used the survey from previous work [1]: *i)* Q1 - "How realistic is this character?", having three scales Likert's answers ("Unrealistic", "Moderately realistic" and "Very realistic") to perceived realism; *ii)* Q2 - "Do you feel some discomfort (strangeness) looking at this character?", with answers "YES" and "NO" to perceived comfort; and *iii)* Q3 - "In which parts of the face do you feel more strangeness?", having multiple choice ("eyes", "mouth", "nose", "hair", "others" and "I do not feel discomfort").

In addition, we also used the 19 videos (one short movie for each character illustrated in Fig. 1) and removed those frames which did not contain the face of the character to be analyzed. This process resulted in 5730 images. In our ground truth processing, we consider the answer of Q1 to determine the perceived level of realism, Q2 is used to determine the percentage of perceived comfort, and Q3 answers are used to evaluate the parts of the face which generate more strangeness. To categorize the characters in different levels of realism, we used the averages of scores of Q1 answers, so each character has an average value of realism. We used the same groups and definitions of realism that were used in the work by Araujo et al., that is, unrealistic, moderately and very realistic characters.

4.2   Computed Comfort Score (*CCS*)

As mentioned before, we propose the Computed Confort Score (*CCS*) which aims to estimate the perceived comfort by human beings, automatically. Next sections detail the methods.

Pre-processing Data. The overview of our method, illustrated in Fig. 4, is inspired on proposed by Liu et al. in [24] for natural photographic images. In order to verify whether CG images contain pixels that exhibit strong dependencies in space and frequency, which carry relevant information about an image, we implemented a model that could extract characteristics from spatial and spectral entropy.

We performed three main processes in order to prepare data to be used in our method: *A)* the face detection, *B)* the extraction of image Entropy features, and *C)* the features pooling. After the pre-processing phase, we perform the Computed Comfort Score (*CCS*) to estimate the face comfort. We implemented our method using OpenCV [16], scikit-learn [43] and dlib [34].

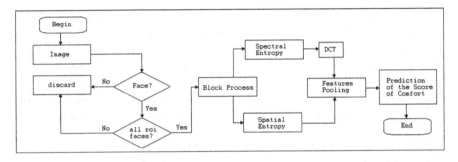

Fig. 4. The overview of our model described in Sect. 4.2.

(A) Face Detection. The method used for face detection is proposed by Paul Viola and Michael Jones [42]. This method detects a face and also parts of the face. In the latter case, there are eight parts: mouth, middle of the mouth, right and left eyes, right and left eyebrows, nose, and jaw.

For our model, we consider that if no face is detected, or if the face is detected and the eight parts are not, the image is discarded. We do not use the middle mouth region for our model because it is already inside the mouth, and the jaw is not used because it already evaluated the entire face. After the discarded images, we have a total of 5730 images.

(B) Features Extraction. In this step, we proceed with the features extraction. First, it resized each image to be a multiple of 2 and partitioned into 8×8 blocks. This block size is based on the work proposed by Liu et al. [24], who performed several experiments until setting M = 8 as a good block size value. We compute the spatial and spectral entropy characteristics locally for each block of pixels and each region of interest, i.e., the whole face and its parts. According to the definition of entropy of the image [40], its main function is to describe the amount of information contained in an image. In the image quality assessment area [24], one of the motivating aspects is to identify the types and degrees of image distortions that generally affect their local entropy.

Spatial entropy calculates the probability distribution of the mean pixel values, while spectral entropy calculates the probability distribution of the global DCT (Domain Cosine Transform) coefficient values. We hypothesize that the local Spatial and Spectral entropy applied in CG images may show statistical characteristics that correlate with perceptual data about CG faces. Indeed, this is the central hypothesis of the proposed *CCS* (Computed Comfort Score). To calculate the spatial entropy[3], we used the skimage.filters.rank library through function entropy(). To calculate the spectral entropy using FFT (Fast Fourier Transform) we use the scipy fftpack[4] library. To calculate the frequency map, the fft() function and then the dct() function were used to calculate the (DCT) domain cosine transform, both with default parameters.

(C) Features Pooling. At this stage, the entropy computation described in the previous step is used to calculate other characteristics for all pixel blocks of the face and its parts. The characteristics proposed in this work are mean, standard deviation, distortion, kurtosis, variance, Hu Moments [47] and Histogram of Oriented Gradients (HOG) [11]. Hu Moments were used with its default parameters [47], implemented using OpenCV[5] [16], generating a vector of 7 positions. For HOG, the detection window with gradient voting into five orientation bins and 3×3 pixels blocks of 4×4 pixel cells was used in the spectral entropy features and 16×16 pixel cells in the spatial entropy features, generating a vector of 11 positions. It implemented hOG using scikit-learn [43]. So, we have 23 features for spectral entropy and 23 for spatial entropy, proposing a total of 46 features.

The next section presents how the prediction of the face, and parts of the face, comfort score are computed. This step generates *CCS* for each CG face in the data set (5730 images) plus six parts of each 5730 faces.

4.3   Computing *CCS* Using Support Vector Regression

First, all 5730 19-character images are used for training, testing, and validating, varying in these three groups until all characters participate in all groups (cross validation). To run SVR (Support Vector Regression), we proposed nine models to test the impact of each group of Entropy features: *i)* Hu (7 features) and HOG (11 features), and *ii)* mean, standard deviation, distortion, kurtosis and variance. In addition, we want to assess the impact of spatial and spectral entropy, separately and together, and the face and its parts (7 ROIs tested, the whole face and six parts). Thus, we proposed nine combinations of the extracted data to use in the SVR model according to Table 2, in order to find the best accuracy of the cross validation mean perceptual score:

---

[3] https://scikit-image.org/docs/0.8.0/api/skimage.filter.rank.html.

[4] https://docs.scipy.org/doc/scipy/reference/fftpack.html.

[5] https://opencv.org/.

Table 2. Combination of nine models proposed to test the impact of each group of Entropy features. The column F.S. (Features Statistics) correspond to mean, standard deviation, distortion, kurtosis, variance. The column Total characteristics (T.C.) refers to the number of characteristics evaluating the entire face and the six face parts according to the features selected in the previous columns through the letter x.

Model	# Spatial Entropy	Spectral Entropy	F.S	HOG	Hu Moments	T. C
1	x	x	x	x	x	322
2	x	x	x	x		224
3	x	x	x		x	168
4	x		x	x	x	161
5	x		x	x		112
6	x		x		x	84
7		x	x	x	x	161
8		x	x	x		112
9		x	x		x	84

We computed the nine models to evaluate which features better correlate with the perceived comfort regarding CG characters, i.e., the ground truth with perceptual data (GT). The models generate individual values of comfort for each image from the short movie of each character, i.e., our proposed metric CCS_i for each character i in each frame f. Thus, to compute the CCS for each i character, in each video, we simply calculate the average CCS obtained at each f frame, from the movie that i participates in: $CCS_i = Avg(\sum_{i=0}^{N_i} CCS_{i,f})$, where i is the index of character, N_i is the number of frames of the short movie and f is the frame index.

It is important to mention that although we can compute $CCS_{i,f}$ for character i at frame f, we do not have such information in the ground truth, once we have one comfort value for each character, as informed by the participants. We chose to consider the average value, because when the participant saw the video, we do not know when (at which frame or frames) the participant perceives strangeness.

4.4   Preliminary Results

This section presents the preliminary results achieved with the two models presented in this work. We investigated the accuracy obtained with the nine implemented models to calculate CCS and compare with the binary model [10], where each character was classified. In addition, we evaluated the error obtained when we confronted the CCS_i obtained value and the perceived comfort for each character i. Then, we provide an analysis to find out the part of the faces that generates more discomfort with our method. We investigate the hypothesis, transforming all CG characters into cartoons and calculating the CCS again.

First, we want to investigate the accuracy obtained with the nine implemented models to calculate CCS and compare with the binary model [10], where the binary classification (Comfort/Discomfort) is generated for each character. In addition, we evaluated the error obtained when we confronted the CCS_i obtained value and the perceived comfort for each character i. Then, we provide an analysis to find out the part of the faces that generates more discomfort with our method. We investigate a hypothesis, transforming all CG characters into cartoons and calculating the CCS again.

Evaluating *CCS* Values as a Binary Classification of Comfort. First, we present the binary classification result regarding the CG characters, using the nine models and the whole face. We consider that characters in which perceptual comfort <60%, in the ground truth, can generate discomfort in the human perception. While remaining characters generate comfort, i.e., perceptual comfort ≥60%. Table 3 shows the five characters that generate discomfort in human perception and the result of binary classification using CCS values with the same threshold as in the ground truth, i.e., discomfort if $CCS < 60\%$ and comfort if $CCS \geq 60\%$. It presented a similar analysis in Table 5 with characters that generate comfort in human perception. In Table 6, "*" shows that classification was correct, while "–"was not correct.

Table 3. Percentage of class 0 and class 1 for each character after prediction by the implementation model.

Characters	% Class 0	% Class 1
character (a)	20.00	**80.00**
character (l)	2.36	**97.64**
character (c)	20.03	**79.97**
character (f)	44.65	**55.35**
character (i)	13.07	**86.93**

Table 4. Number of frames extracted from the videos of the 16 characters that not cause strangeness in subjective evaluation.

Characters	Number of Frames	Characters	Number of Frames
character (c)	610	character (n)	80
character (b)	552	character (k)	72
character (v)	427	character (p)	63
character (t)	402	character (s)	34
character (m)	207	character (d)	21
character (h)	175	character (r)	15
character (o)	145	character (q)	1

Table 5. Percentage of class 0 and class 1 for each character after prediction by the implementation model.

Characters	% Class 0	% Class 1	Characters	% Class 0	% Class 1
character (c)	**97.44**	2.56	character (n)	**76.61**	23.39
character (b)	**99.80**	0.20	character (k)	**99.03**	0.97
character (v)	**98.75**	1.25	character (p)	20.00	**80.00**
character (t)	**67.58**	32.42	character (s)	**99.72**	0.28
character (m)	**75.59**	24.41	character (d)	0.06	**99.94**
character (h)	**99.57**	0.43	character (r)	**99.83**	0.17
character (o)	20.36	**79.64**	character (q)	20.00	**80.00**

As we can see in Table 6, Models 1 and 6 seem to be more adequate than others to provide a correct classification of the last five characters that generate strangeness or discomfort in the individuals. Models 7 and 8, in Table 3, present 100% of correct classification with characters that are comfortable, according to human perception. When evaluating all the characters together that present discomfort and comfort in people's perception on Table 6, we noticed that the best model, in this case, is Model 1 with approximately 80% of average accuracy, considering both groups of characters. One can say that Models 7 and 8 also seem accurate, but in fact, such models classified incorrectly more than half of characters that generate strangeness/discomfort, maybe showing a tendency in generating high values of computed comfort (CCS). In addition, the Mean Absolute Error (MAE) between CCS obtained values and the comfort value in the ground truth, for the 19 evaluated characters is 23.59. Table 7 presents results of perceived and estimated comfort (CCS) in the second and third columns, for all 19 characters.

Figure 6 shows the CCS and perceived comfort values in the UV chart (Comfort X Human likeness). The yellow line refers to cartoons analyzed, and it is going to be discussed in Sect. 4.4. It is important to notice that Model 1 accuracy (80%) is very similar to results obtained in the previous work (also 80%) [10].

Perception of Comfort Through Entropy Analysis in CG Face Parts. Considering that a specific part of the face can cause discomfort, we investigated the parts of the face that cause more discomfort/strangeness. Analyzing the perceptual data, subjects comment that first part of the face that causes strangeness is the eyes followed by the mouth and nose. Taking the five characters that generate discomfort in the perceptual study, we observed that the nose and eyes are the parts of the face with smaller values of CCS. In the perceptual study, 11 from 14 characters that do not generate strangeness present the mouth as the region is less comfortable, being eyes and nose the less comfortable for the three remaining characters.

Table 6. Number of frames extracted from the videos of the 19 characters and result of binary classification with computed comfort using the 9 studied models. The symbol "–" shows the incorrect classification while "*" shows the opposite. The last 5 characters (a, c, f, i, l) correspond to the highlighted characters in bold in Fig. 1.

Character	Number of Frames	1	2	3	4	5	6	7	8	9
(b)	553	*	*	*	*	–	–	*	*	*
(d)	17	*	*	–	*	*	*	*	*	*
(e)	610	–	–	*	–	–	–	*	*	*
(g)	2	*	*	*	*	*	*	*	*	*
(h)	164	*	*	*	*	*	*	*	*	*
(k)	72	*	*	–	–	*	–	*	*	*
(m)	209	*	*	*	*	*	–	*	*	*
(n)	74	*	*	*	*	*	*	*	*	*
(o)	145	*	*	*	*	*	–	*	*	–
(p)	60	*	*	*	*	*	*	*	*	–
(r)	18	*	*	*	*	*	*	*	*	*
(s)	21	*	*	–	*	*	*	*	*	*
(t)	403	–	–	*	*	*	*	*	*	*
(v)	428	–	–	*	*	–	*	*	*	*
(a)	1786	–	–	*	*	*	*	–	–	–
(c)	745	*	*	–	*	–	*	*	*	–
(f)	148	*	*	–	*	–	*	*	*	–
(i)	250	*	*	–	–	–	*	–	–	–
(l)	33	*	–	–	–	–	–	–	–	–

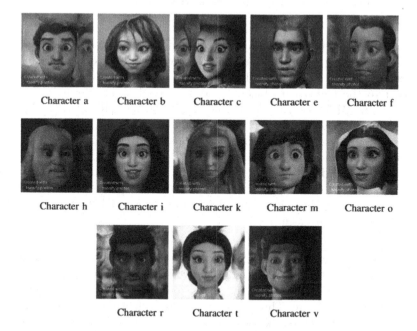

Fig. 5. The 13 characters shown in Fig. 1 that have been turned into cartoons.

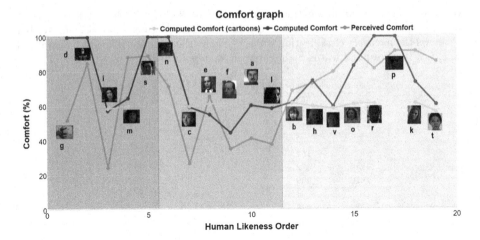

Fig. 6. Comfort chart with perceived comfort values shown on the green line (our ground truth, people assessment of the characters), CCS for each character shown on the blue line, and comfort values computed for each cartoon character presented on the yellow line. The X-axis represents the ordering of the characters according to the values of realism got by question Q1 (referring to realism) in the perceptual experiment. In addition, the colored backgrounds represent the groups of realism of each character, with the blue representing the Unrealistic characters, red representing Moderately Realistic, and yellow representing Very Realistic. (Color figure online)

It is interesting to remark, that there are few variations concerning the CCS computed for face parts and compared with perceived comfort. Values of MAE for each face part, compared with perceived comfort (ordered from the lowest error to the higher) are following presented: 21.15 for the nose, 22.40 for left_eyebrow, 22.52 for right_eyebrow, 22.93 for the left_eye, 23.89 for the right_eye, and 24.63 for the mouth. Although the average error of the parts of the face (22.92) is slightly less than CCS for the full face (23.59), these values are not got with the same model.

For example, Model 6 is used to get the best CCS for the left eye, left eyebrow, and right eyebrow; and Model 4 is the most suitable for the right eye. In fact, when analyzing model by model, none achieved better accuracy than Model 1 for the entire face.

The More Like a Cartoon, the More Comfortable the Character Is?
According to the UV theory [28] and other work presented in literature [9,12,17, 19,20,27], unrealistic characters (mostly cartoons) tend to be more comfortable to the human perception. Thus, to assess whether the comfort value could be if the character were cartoon-like, we decided to transform them into cartoons. We used Toonify[6] to cartoonize the characters, even the characters that are already be classified as cartoons. Only 13 characters had faces detected by Toonify.

---

[6] https://github.com/justinpinkney/toonify.

Figure 5 shows the 13 characters that have been transformed. We use Toonify because it is a free program developed in python language.

After transforming the characters into cartoons, the face detection was applied again, as well as the entire rest of the proposed method, as described in Sect. 4.2, thus generating CCS for each character. Table 7 presents some information regarding the transformed and original characters. First, for each character, we present (in the second column) the ground truth value of perceived comfort regarding the original character. Then, in the third column, we present the result of our method CCS calculated for the original character, and in the fourth column, the CCS for transformed characters. The fifth and sixth columns present data regarding the level of realism of the characters, as perceived by the subjects (explained in Sect. 4.1).

Table 7. Evaluation of 19 Characters from Fig. 1, according to following attributes: the subject evaluation, calculated CCS, transformed in cartoons and having CCS again, and finally the level of realism and classified group of realism. Characters in bold represent the ones that cause strangeness in the human perception.

Character	Comfort (%)	CCS (%)	CCS (Cartoons) (%)	Realism	Group Realism
a	**41.176**	**60.25**	**69.53**	**2.084**	**Moderately**
b	68.908	61.97	61.61	2.504	Very
c	**26.891**	**59.34**	**59.70**	**1.655**	**Moderately**
d	84,87	86.91	–	1.235	Unrealistic
e	**65.546**	**55.04**	**61.26**	**1.756**	**Moderately**
f	**35.294**	**44.52**	**61.35**	**1.915**	**Moderately**
g	52.1	100	–	1.109	Unrealistic
h	73.109	74.56	59.88	2.546	Very
i	24.37	57.3	58.56	1.386	Unrealistic
k	91.597	73.62	61.68	2.781	Very
l	**37.81**	**61.38**	–	**2.100**	**Moderately**
m	88.235	64.53	59.98	1.436	Unrealistic
n	71.43	100	–	1.563	Moderately
o	92.437	83.13	61.09	2.672	Very
p	92.437	73.98	–	2.731	Very
r	81.513	100	61.47	2.722	Very
s	89.08	93.51	–	1.436	Unrealistic
t	85.714	60.77	56.28	2.798	Very
v	79.832	59.71	58.40	2.605	Very

It is interesting to notice that only characters classified as moderately realistic, according to human perception, show an increase in the computed comfort score when transformed into a cartoon. The exception is the character (i), which is considered unrealistic, and the comfort score lightly increases. Very realistic characters have a reduced computed comfort score because there is a reduction in realism. This fact is in line with the literature [27] which shows a reduction in the comfort of cartoon characters compared to realistic characters. Characters a, c, e, and f are classified as moderately realistic. When transformed into cartoons, the comfort scores of characters a, c and f had comfort scores increased and above our threshold of 60%, so they became more comfortable in human perception. Characters b, h, k, o, r, t, and v, considered very realistic, had a reduction in CCS when transformed into cartoons. Indeed, it agrees with MacDorman [27] studies.

Figure 6 shows the perceived comfort and calculated CCS for original and transformed characters. It is interesting to note that when our method is applied to cartoon characters, the values got from computed comfort are more similar to each other than the original characters, which makes sense since they now have the same realism level. If we look at comfort averages, the group of moderately realistic characters was the only one that increased average comfort (42.226% before and 62.96% after), while the unrealistic (60.91% before and 59,27% after) and very realistic (with 81.872% before and 60.058% after) groups decreased their comfort scores.

5   Discussion and Final Considerations

Based on the few examples presented in the last sections, that discuss applications and studies on the referred domain, our goal in this section is to present some challenges, in our opinion, in the area.

The assessment of human perceptual data is always a challenge. Opinions and feelings, as perceptual data, can respond to cultural, personality and even emotional state of subjects. So, propose ways to capture and validate such information is very important and certainly a challenge. Secondly, to create experiments where CG characters are controllable is relevant, as mentioned in literature [46], e.g., to change the shape, the movement, the light. However, on the other hand, such experiments do not approach the CG characters as normally presented in digital entertainment, e.g., in a game context, in a virtual environment, interacting with others and etc. It means that maybe the controlled researches present characters very different from how they are presented in real life. It is also a relevant challenge, i.e., how to test hypothesis using games and movies characters, where we can not control them?

A very important challenge concerns with the area of computational aesthetics. The study of aesthetics from a computational angle began with Birkhoff, in work published in 1929 [5] [6] and formalized in his book in 1933 [7]. His work aimed to propose a way to measure the aesthetic value of certain shapes and objects mathematically. According to Birkhoff, aesthetic quality is related to the amount of attention required when observing an object, defined by the complexity and the notion of order of the object, in this case represented by elements mainly related to symmetry and repetition. In 2005, Hoenig [15] created the definition of the discipline of computational aesthetics intending to motivate the continued development of the area. According to Hoenig (2005, p. 16): "Computational Aesthetics is the research of computational methods that can make applicable aesthetic decisions in a similar fashion as humans can". This definition is intended to emphasize two aspects: one is the use of computational methods and the other is the enhancement of applicability. One example of methodology recently proposed in this area is the work of Pinho et al. [10]. In this work, she investigates the relationship between images features and the discomfort that human beings can perceive (UV). The authors extract image features based on Hu Moments (Hum), Histogram Oriented Gradient (Hog), saliency detection, and finally, a model using Support Vector Machine (SVM) to provide binary classification is suggested. The results indicate accuracy of around 80% in the image estimation process comparing with the subjective classification. As a contribution, some areas may benefit from this study for avoiding the creation of characters that may cause strangeness, such as the games, conversational agents and cinema industry, avoiding to develop perceptual studies with subjects.

Regarding our first case study, looking for realism and comparing the ordering of characters in levels of human likeness between individual perception and global perception, all ordering comparisons were similar. However, the ordering of images that had characters with equal skin colors in relation to global perception had the greatest similarity with the ordering of individual perception. So, it could be that there is a bias in people's perception when there are groups of characters with different skin colors. In this case, there was a limitation in our work, in which most participants responded that they considered themselves white people . So, if we could control this aspect, maybe the results would be different. Therefore, observing this factor, most participants were part of the group of characters with white skin color (in-group). According to the work by Saneyoshi et al. [36], the results showed that there may be a race bias in the Uncanny Valley context when white participants observe virtual human faces in an out-group, that is, following the same line as our results. Regarding perceived comfort, in all cases, the comfort perceived individually was always greater than the comfort perceived globally. So, in this case, we can say that the perceived discomfort increases when the characters are presented in groups. Regarding charisma, individual and global perceptions were similar, that is, perceived charisma is not influenced if groups of characters are presented instead of individual characters. Therefore, if the industry wants to include groups of characters with different realism and different skin colors, the ideal is to think of charismatic characters, as we are sure that perception will not be influenced.

In the second case study presented and discussed the preliminary results achieved so far refer to investigate whether we can estimate the strangeness caused by animated characters in humans using visual features; to propose a model for estimating the comfort a specific CG face should cause in humans' perception. Regarding these questions, we consider our model is promising in the sense that it seems to show that human perception can be represented using image features of CG characters. As an academic contribution, the main objective is to create a computational model that extracts different features from the image to try to capture the strangeness that human beings perceive in some CG characters. When there is a point of discomfort, we can make suggestions for changes. These skills can be used to improve the creation of new characters in

CG that can be used in a variety of areas, such as games, movies, health, legal, education, because the visualization or interaction with this virtual agent will be smoother and natural for people, making them more comfortable, including in a possible interaction.

Acknowledgements. The authors would like to thank CNPq and CAPES for partially funding this work.

References

1. Araujo, V., Dalmoro, B., Musse, S.R.: Analysis of charisma, comfort and realism in cg characters from a gender perspective. Vis. Comput. **37**, 1–14 (2021)
2. Araujo, V., Melgare, J., Dalmoro, B., Musse, S.R.: Is the perceived comfort with cg characters increasing with their novelty. IEEE Comput. Graph. Appl. 1 (2021). https://doi.org/10.1109/MCG.2021.3090198
3. Araujo, V., Melgare, J., Dalmoro, B., Musse, S.R.: Is the perceived comfort with CG characters increasing with their novelty. IEEE Comput. Graph. Appl. **42**, 32–46 (2021)
4. Awamleh, R., Gardner, W.L.: Perceptions of leader charisma and effectiveness: the effects of vision content, delivery, and organizational performance. Leadersh. Q. **10**(3), 345–373 (1999)
5. Birkhoff, G.D.: Quelques éléments mathématiques de l'art. In: Atti del Congresso Internazionale dei Matematici, pp. 315–333. Bologna, September 1929
6. Birkhoff, G.D.: Une théorie quantitative de l'esthétique. Bulletin de la Société française de Philosophia (1931)
7. Birkhoff, G.D.: Aesthetic measure. Bull. Am. Math. Soc. **40**, 7–10 (1933)
8. Bornemann, B., Winkielman, P., Van der Meer, E.: Can you feel what you do not see? using internal feedback to detect briefly presented emotional stimuli. Int. J. Psychophysiol. **85**(1), 116–124 (2012)
9. Chaminade, T., Hodgins, J., Kawato, M.: Anthropomorphism influences perception of computer-animated characters' actions. Soc. Cogn. Affect. Neurosci. **2**(3), 206–216 (2007)
10. Dal Molin, G.P., Nomura, F.M., Dalmoro, B.M., de A. Araújo, V.F., Musse, S.R.: Can we estimate the perceived comfort of virtual human faces using visual cues? In: 2021 IEEE 15th International Conference on Semantic Computing (ICSC), pp. 366–369 (2021). https://doi.org/10.1109/ICSC50631.2021.00085
11. Dalal, N., Triggs, B.: Histograms of oriented gradients for human detection. In: 2005 IEEE Computer Society Conference on Computer Vision and Pattern Recognition (CVPR 2005), vol. 1, pp. 886–893. IEEE (2005)
12. Flach, L.M., de Moura, R.H., Musse, S.R., Dill, V., Pinho, M.S., Lykawka, C.: Evaluation of the uncanny valley in cg characters. In: Proceedings of the Brazilian Symposium on Computer Games and Digital Entertainmen (SBGames)(Brasiília), pp. 108–116 (2012)
13. Goethals, G.R., Allison, S.T.: Kings and charisma, Lincoln and leadership: an evolutionary perspective. In: Goethals, G.R., Allison, S.T., Kramer, R.M., Messick, D.M. (eds.) Conceptions of Leadership, pp. 111–124. Jepson Studies in Leadership. Palgrave Macmillan, New York (2014). https://doi.org/10.1057/9781137472038_7
14. Goldenberg, A., Weisz, E., Sweeny, T.D., Cikara, M., Gross, J.J.: The crowd-emotion-amplification effect. Psychol. Sci. **32**(3), 437–450 (2021)

15. Hoenig, F.: Defining computational aesthetics. In: Neumann, L., Sbert, M., Gooch, B., Purgathofer, W. (eds.) 1st Eurographics Workshop on Computational Aesthetics in Graphics, Visualization, and Imaging, CAe 2005, Girona, Spain, 18–20 May 2005, Proceedings, pp. 13–18. Eurographics Association (2005). https://doi.org/10.2312/COMPAESTH/COMPAESTH05/013-018

16. Howse, J.: OpenCV Computer Vision with Python. Packt Publishing Ltd., Birmingham (2013)

17. Hyde, J., Carter, E.J., Kiesler, S., Hodgins, J.K.: Evaluating animated characters: facial motion magnitude influences personality perceptions. ACM Trans. Appl. Percept. (TAP) **13**(2), 8 (2016)

18. Jimenez, J., et al.: Separable subsurface scattering. In: Computer Graphics Forum, vol. 34, pp. 188–197. Wiley Online Library (2015)

19. Kätsyri, J., Förger, K., Mäkäräinen, M., Takala, T.: A review of empirical evidence on different uncanny valley hypotheses: support for perceptual mismatch as one road to the valley of eeriness. Front. Psychol. **6**, 390 (2015)

20. Kätsyri, J., Mäkäräinen, M., Takala, T.: Testing the uncanny valley hypothesis in semirealistic computer-animated film characters: an empirical evaluation of natural film stimuli. Int. J. Hum. Comput. Stud. **97**, 149–161 (2017)

21. Kim, T., et al.: Countering racial bias in computer graphics research. arXiv preprint arXiv:2103.15163 (2021)

22. Lamer, S.A., Sweeny, T.D., Dyer, M.L., Weisbuch, M.: Rapid visual perception of interracial crowds: racial category learning from emotional segregation. J. Exp. Psychol. Gen. **147**(5), 683 (2018)

23. Li, W., Zinbarg, R.E., Boehm, S.G., Paller, K.A.: Neural and behavioral evidence for affective priming from unconsciously perceived emotional facial expressions and the influence of trait anxiety. J. Cogn. Neurosci. **20**(1), 95–107 (2008)

24. Liu, L., Liu, B., Huang, H., Bovik, A.C.: No-reference image quality assessment based on spatial and spectral entropies. Signal Process. Image Commun. **29**(8), 856–863 (2014)

25. Ma, L., Deng, Z.: Real-time facial expression transformation for monocular RGB video. In: Computer Graphics Forum. vol. 38, pp. 470–481. Wiley Online Library (2019)

26. MacDorman, K.F.: Mortality salience and the uncanny valley. In: 5th IEEE-RAS International Conference on Humanoid Robots, 2005, pp. 399–405. IEEE (2005)

27. MacDorman, K.F., Chattopadhyay, D.: Reducing consistency in human realism increases the uncanny valley effect; increasing category uncertainty does not. Cognition **146**, 190–205 (2016)

28. Mori, M.: Bukimi no tani [the uncanny valley]. Energy **7**, 33–35 (1970)

29. Mustafa, M., Magnor, M.: EEG based analysis of the perception of computer-generated faces. In: Proceedings of the 13th European Conference on Visual Media Production (CVMP 2016), p. 4. ACM (2016)

30. Paleari, M., Lisetti, C.: Psychologically grounded avatars expressions. In: First Workshop on Emotion and Computing at KI (2006)

31. Rosenthal-von der Pütten, A.M., Krämer, N.C.: Individuals' evaluations of and attitudes towards potentially uncanny robots. Int. J. Soc. Robot. **7**(5), 799–824 (2015)

32. Queiroz, R.B., Musse, S.R., Badler, N.I.: Investigating macroexpressions and microexpressions in computer graphics animated faces. PRESENCE Teleoperators Virtual Environ. **23**(2), 191–208 (2014)

33. Riggio, R.E.: Charisma. Encycl. Ment. Health **1**, 387–396 (1998)

34. Rosebrock, A.: Facial landmarks with dlib opencv and python-pyimagesearch. PyImageSearch (2017)
35. Ruhland, K., Prasad, M., McDonnell, R.: Data-driven approach to synthesizing facial animation using motion capture. IEEE Comput. Graph. Appl. **37**(4), 30–41 (2017)
36. Saneyoshi, A., Okubo, M., Suzuki, H., Oyama, T., Laeng, B.: The other-race effect in the uncanny valley. Int. J. Hum. Comput. Stud. **166**, 102871 (2022)
37. Schwind, V.: Implications of the uncanny valley of avatars and virtual characters for human-computer interaction. (dissertation - university of stuttgart) (2018). http://dx.doi.org/10/gd6b7h
38. Schwind, V., Wolf, K., Henze, N.: Avoiding the uncanny valley in virtual character design. Interactions **25**(5), 45–49 (2018)
39. Shen, X.B., Wu, Q., Fu, X.l.: Effects of the duration of expressions on the recognition of microexpressions. J. Zhejiang Univ. Sci. B **13**(3), 221–230 (2012)
40. Sponring, J.: The entropy of scale-space. In: Proceedings of 13th International Conference on Pattern Recognition, vol. 1, pp. 900–904. IEEE (1996)
41. Tinwell, A., Grimshaw, M., Williams, A.: The uncanny wall. Int. J. Arts Technol. **4**(3), 326–341 (2011)
42. Viola, P., Jones, M., et al.: Rapid object detection using a boosted cascade of simple features. CVPR (1) **1**(511–518), 3 (2001)
43. Van der Walt, S., et al.: scikit-image: image processing in python. PeerJ **2**, e453 (2014)
44. West, P.T., Armstrong, J.: Charisma-studying its elusive nature. NASSP Bull. **64**(438), 70–77 (1980)
45. Zell, E., et al.: To stylize or not to stylize?: The effect of shape and material stylization on the perception of computer-generated faces. ACM Trans. Graph. (TOG) **34**(6), 184 (2015)
46. Zell, E., Zibrek, K., McDonnell, R.: Perception of virtual characters. In: ACM SIGGRAPH 2019 Courses, pp. 1–17. SIGGRAPH (2019)
47. Žunić, J., Hirota, K., Rosin, P.L.: A hu moment invariant as a shape circularity measure. Pattern Recogn. **43**(1), 47–57 (2010)

Nine Challenges for Immersive Entertainment

Wallace Santos Lages$^{(\boxtimes)}$ (iD)

Northeastern University, Boston, MA, USA
w.lages@northeastern.edu

Abstract. Immersive entertainment is an important driver of mixed reality platforms. As technology becomes better and cheaper, this will spark the next major shift in digital entertainment. We identify nine research topics on immersive entertainment across theoretical-scientific, creative, systems, and social dimensions. For each topic, we discuss possible research directions that can lead to advances in the field. This chapter is an extended version of a paper originally published in the proceedings of the XX Brazilian Symposium on Computer Games and Digital Entertainment. Each of the topics is discussed in more depth and a separate challenge for input devices and body tracking was added.

Keywords: Mixed reality · Virtual reality · Storytelling · Games

1 Introduction

The digital entertainment industry saw its latest great shift around mid-2000s with the growth of mobile gaming. Smartphones enabled a new ecosystem in which novel designs appeared and new technical solutions were developed. Mobile gaming broke many previous assumptions of the field, including the typical profile of players and how gaming hardware should look like. In less than 10 years, the mobile games sector revenue surpassed PC and consoles [56].

Although smartphones were not designed as primary gaming devices, their wide availability, new interaction methods, and ubiquitous connectivity also untapped new areas for research. We are now witnessing a similar shift, with the second generation of affordable and high-quality Virtual Reality (VR) headsets reaching the market. The consumer hardware evolved quickly from simple smartphone-based VR to standalone headsets with six degree of freedom tracking. Content also followed, moving from pure cinematic experiences to highly interactive and fast-paced games. New applications pushed the boundaries of storytelling and theatrical performance. Due to its more complex requirements, Augmented Reality (AR) devices have not yet reached the same stage, although they are likely to follow suit in the next few years.

How will immersive entertainment look like 10–15 years from now? If the trajectory of mobile gaming serves as indication, it is safe to assume that systems will become cheaper, better, and ubiquitous. Display, optics and processing

R. P. d. Santos and M. d. S. Hounsell (Eds.): GranDGamesBR 2020/2021, CCIS 1702, pp. 233–254, 2023.
https://doi.org/10.1007/978-3-031-27639-2_11

power will continue to improve, along with sensors and networking. We will also likely encounter true mixed reality devices, which will be able to operate in VR, AR, or blended modes. Improved quality and form factor will enable people to use these devices for many hours at a time. Social experiences will be common-place, either physically co-located or along with other users around the world.

In this chapter, we try to identify what these changes mean for immersive entertainment and discuss nine challenges and opportunities for designers work-ing towards the next level of immersive experiences. The chapter is structured in the following way: first we give a brief definition of what we consider immersive entertainment; next, each of the nine challenges is presented and discussed by presenting recent developments and their relevance to immersive entertainment. Finally, we conclude the chapter with brief summary.

This chapter is an extended version of a paper originally published in the proceedings of the XX Brazilian Symposium on Computer Games and Digital Entertainment [40]. Each challenge is now discussed in more depth and a separate challenge for Input Devices and Body Tracking was added.

1.1 Immersive Entertainment

Following Oriti et al., we will use the term 'immersive entertainment' to include any entertainment application designed for immersive systems [58]. As immersive systems, we consider any system that allows the creation of realistic experiences by matching human sensorimotor capabilities. Today, these systems are charac-terized by egocentric, head-tracked, stereoscopic rendering. These systems also provide some type of spatial input by means of six degree-of-freedom tracked controllers or hand-tracking. They typically also provide a 360°C field of regard, allowing the user to be completely surrounded by visual imagery (in contrast to a single screen display). Common displays include head-worn virtual reality displays, CAVE projection systems, or augmented-reality glasses.

In this chapter we focus primarily on entertainment applications such as games, narrative experiences, and performance work for VR, and AR systems [8]. However, there is a considerable overlap with productivity applications, ther-apeutic, training, or educational applications and the issues discussed here may be applicable to them as well.

2 Challenges

Advances in immersive entertainment have come from multiple adjacent fields, in particular from the interdisciplinary fields of play, games, and human-computer interaction. These are themselves supported by efforts in many other disci-plines including artificial intelligence, computer graphics, communication, the-ater, computer engineering, sociology, storytelling, and psychology. For the present discussion, we have selected nine topics which are likely to continue open in the next decade and in which advances could significantly transform immersive entertainment. They are:

1. Understanding user experience and presence
2. Creating believable characters and engaging storytelling
3. Design of novel interaction techniques
4. Improving rendering
5. Input devices and body tracking
6. Exploring uses for physiological sensing and biofeedback
7. Creating better social experiences
8. Safeguarding users and promoting responsible design
9. Improving and democratizing content generation

The topics are presented in no particular order, and we make no claim of completeness. They were chosen to provide a cross-cutting perspective of the field, including fundamental theoretical-scientific, creative, systems, and social dimensions.

2.1   Understanding User Experience and Presence

The ability to evaluate experiences is critical to understand how they affect users, how they can be improved, and to elucidate the underlying mechanisms. Questionnaires are a popular evaluation method for both immersive and non-immersive applications. Frequently used ones are the Game User Experience Satisfaction Scale (GUESS) [62], the Flow State Scale-2 and Dispositional Flow Scale-2 (FSS-2, DFS-2) [38], the User Experience Scale (UEQ and UEQ-S) [43, 65], the Game Experience Questionnaire (GEQ) [36], and the Game Engagement Questionnaire (GEQ) [15].

Questionnaires have the vantage of being convenient, generalizable, and easy to administer [24]. However, the most used questionnaires vary in the range of aspects they propose to measure and also on the level of reliability and validity [31]. There have been calls for more transparency on the use and also reporting of psychometric properties of these questionnaires, along with more systematical definition and operationalization of these constructs [1]. More important, although they can and have been applied to immersive entertainment, they were not specifically designed for them.

One of the qualities that distinguish immersive systems from other technologies is the enhanced sense of presence. The term is used to describe the feeling of realness that induce users to display behavioral, emotional, and physiological responses as they would in real life [46]. Presence is often framed as a result of an illusion of non-mediation, where human perception fails to accurately acknowledge the role of the technology in the experience [70]. Presence is, thus, a psychological response created by the delivery of sensory stimuli which approaches the fidelity of the real world [71].

Post-experiment questionnaires are the preferred method to measure presence. A recent survey by Souza et al. identified 29 different questionnaires used for quantifying presence, indicating that there is not a standard measurement method for it [74]. According to Grassini and Laumann [31], the three more frequently used questionnaires are the Witmer and Singer Presence Questionnaire (PQ) [89], the Slater-Usoh-Steed Questionnaire (SUS) [83], and the MEC

Spatial Presence Questionnaire [85]. Many studies have also tailored existing questionnaires to fit different situations.

The role of presence in immersive entertainment can only be elucidated if there is a reliable, consistent, quick, and non-intrusive way of measuring it. In this way, it could be included more often during playtesting and evaluation. However, current metrics for assessing presence do not satisfy those requirements. While questionnaires are practical, they are subjective and rely on participant's understanding of the concepts presented in the questions [70]. There are also concerns that asking questions may induce bias by making participants aware of it, thus capturing aspects unrelated to the phenomenon of interest [72,78].

Behavioral measures have the potential for being a better way to evaluate presence within experiences. Instead of relying on self-disclosure, behavior measures work by observing the response of the participants to a scenario, for example, dodging a ball or avoiding a cliff. The underlying idea is that as the virtual environment approaches reality, participants will respond to it in the same way they would do in reality. Freeman et al., proposed using postural responses, since they are unconscious and easy to monitor [29]. The main problem is that the experience needs to be modified to introduce behaviors that can be measured. It is also unlikely that a single standard could be used across the community. Other metrics have also been proposed, such as heart rate, electroencephalography, and skin conductance. However, published techniques often have conflicting results and are not considered reliable to be used alone [31].

> The ability to evaluate the user experience in immersive entertainment is critical to understanding the impact of design choices. Advancing this aspect will require establishing and validating new instruments that look into aspects of interest, such as engagement, flow, comfort, and presence. New studies with updated technology should provide a path forward regarding physiological and behavioral metrics.

2.2   Creating Believable Characters and Engaging Storytelling

Storytelling is a central part of games and other narrative experiences. An immersive story can range from a fixed narrative (e.g., a journalistic piece) to an open-ended, AI-managed, experience. To create engaging story worlds and make the most of the user's agency inside the virtual environment, it will be necessary to combine computational approaches with the creativity of human writers. Interactive storytelling and computational narratives are, thus, an integral part of the future of immersive entertainment [3].

The Holodeck, from the Star Trek series, is frequently used as vision of what immersive storytelling can be [54]. This imaginary facility can create high-fidelity simulations that allows users to step into vast and detailed experiences indistinguishable from reality. Story characters can touch, feel, eat and interact with simulated objects and people. Although it can be used for scientific and engineering simulations, they are more frequently used for *holonovels*. These are interactive stories with life-like characters in highly realistic settings. Holodeck users often experience the stories as one of the protagonists, while other characters are controlled by the computer and display very sophisticated reasoning and personality.

Several challenges exist on the way towards a Holodeck. The ones within reach are related to embodied Artificial Intelligence (AI) and story generation. Embodied AI alludes to fact that intelligence appears to the user in body (human, animal, or some sort of virtual agent) which occupies a location in space, has the ability to navigate, and can interact with the user in multiple ways (gestures, facial expressions, movement) [88]. Narrative control has been studied in the field of interactive storytelling. However, narratives in immersive environments may introduce new elements. For example, in AR narratives may need to adapt to the specific physical environment where it unfolds.

The concept of embodied AI in immersive entertainment is connected to the concepts of Plausibility Illusion, the illusion that what is apparently happening is really happening [20]. Compelling intelligent characters are necessary not only for story purposes, but also for increasing social presence and plausibility. There is also some evidence that narrative can improve the experience in other ways. Prior work investigated the association between cybersickness and presence in two conditions: 'enriched' and 'minimal' verbal narrative context. Enriched narrative was associated with increased presence and a reduction of cybersickness, mediated by gaming experience [87].

Virtual character believability depends on many aspects including 1) social understanding such as the ability to recognize the user, other agents, and learn and memorize the relationship between them. 2) maintaining causal representations (physical laws, psychological effects, and narrative impacts), 3) ability to plan and react consistently and according to their goals and beliefs [17]. While these are higher cognitive functions that would be necessary even in a text-based adventure, lower functions like walking, gaze, facial expressions, and gestures are more important on immersive experiences. Because of embodiment and presence, users connect to characters on a deeper level than on non-immersive entertainment. The narrative events are experienced through character actions and their existence in the environment [33].

Mobile AR will allow users to engage with entertainment content in different places, both indoors and outdoors. One of the challenges is, thus, creating narratives that will work on different physical environments. Narratives in AR should integrate coherently with the environment. For example, a character should walk through a door and sit on the couch rather than go through the walls. Tackling this challenge involves both advances in space understanding and story adaptation. However, the exact contribution of the physical space is still uncertain. A study of Fragments, a space-adaptive, indoor AR crime-solving game created for the Microsoft HoloLens, compared the player experience in four types of spatial conditions: (1) Large Room - Fully Furnished; (2) Large Room - Scarcely Furnished; (3) Small Room-Fully Furnished; and (4) Small Room - Scarcely Furnished. The authors found that the presence were rated significantly higher for participants who played Fragments in the two large room conditions. However, they found no significant effect of the amount of furniture on the room on presence or narrative engagement. In addition, more furniture had a negative impact on narrative engagement [68].

Storytelling is the foundation of many entertainment applications. In immersive environments it brings new challenges: 1-Developing believable agents that can reason and express themselves through real and virtual spaces, 2-Developing storytelling systems that can drive the characters in narratives considering the role of space in social contexts.

2.3   Design of Novel Interaction Techniques

Interaction techniques are at the core of every interactive application, connecting input and output hardware so that users can accomplish tasks. Early research on 3D interaction techniques have focused on fundamental problems, also called universal tasks: selection, manipulation, travel, and system control [13]. Selection refers to the task of identifying one object of interest from a set. A simple example is pointing or touching an object. Manipulation refers to operations that will change the position, orientation, scale of an object in 3D space. Travel refers to the task of moving from location to another. System control refers to the task of controlling the system. Inputting symbols, such as letters and numbers, is a form of system control [44]. The techniques are ultimately defined by the hardware available and will be discussed in its own section.

From the universal tasks, travel is required by a large number of entertaining applications. At the same time, it brings many challenges. Although natural walking has been recognized as the gold standard for travel techniques, a 1:1 mapping restricts the virtual space to the size of the physical space. For this reason, the techniques used in most consumer experiences avoid natural walking as a primary technique and use controller-based techniques derived from either teleportation or smooth locomotion (steering). Teleportation is a discrete movement from one point to another point [12]. It can be very simple and efficient, however, the discontinuous jump between the origin and destination leads to disorientation in unknown environments. While smooth locomotion does not have this problem, it induces simulator sickness in a segment of the population. This seems to be caused by conflicting sensory information between visual system (moving) and vestibular systems (still) [39].

If the space is large enough, it is possible to use an approach known as redirected walking. The idea is to slightly rotate the user's view while the user walks on a straight path in the virtual environment. As the user unconsciously compensates for the added virtual rotation, the real path bends in the opposite direction, resulting in a circular path in the real world [63]. This class of techniques, however, require a 40 m × 40 m space for imperceptible redirection, which is larger than the area available to most consumers.

While numerous techniques have been proposed and evaluated in the last 20 years, new techniques are continuously being developed to address specific applications needs. In entertainment applications, techniques are fundamental features that define the application experience. Because of this importance, rather than reusing generic techniques, designers often seek new techniques inspired by the application theme and that, although nonrealistic, can deliver a unique experience [76].

One example of such technique is JumpVR, which allows users to jump with superhuman strength to reach unnatural jump heights. While the player is standing or moving through the tracking space, a baseline is calculated based on the headset's height. When the player bends their knees the system is set into a monitoring state. If the headset's subsequent upwards acceleration surpasses the baseline plus an empirically defined threshold, the system recognises a jump and applies a vertical scaling factor to the actual movement vector. Forward movement is applied linearly by scaling the player's initial forward vector in each frame during the jump phase [90]. Bookshelf is a technique that combines natural walking with a secret passageway, disguised as rotating bookshelf. It allows players to traverse between two adjacent virtual rooms while walking on the same physical space. When the user steps onto the bookshelf, the virtual scene slowly rotates 180°C, placing the origin virtual room on the outside of the tracked space. As a result, the user is still physically still standing in the same room, but the destination virtual room is reoriented to lie on the same side as the physical room. The user can then simply turn around and walk to traverse towards the destination virtual room, which is now perfectly mapped to the physical room [92]. These narrative-led and hypernatural interaction techniques show great promise in 3D interaction [14].

> Interaction design research will continue to be one of the pillars supporting good user experience. Advancing on this topic will require research along three directions: 1-Design of techniques that consider the specific needs of entertainment applications, 2- Design of techniques that make use of new and improved hardware, 3-Understand how these techniques affect parameters of importance for entertainment applications, such as comfort and presence.

2.4   Improving Rendering

Immersive applications already have to balance several synthesis challenges: they must render stereoscopic views at low latency, provide enough visual quality to achieve creator's aesthetic goals, and run on standard consumer hardware. In addition, most future systems will also need to compute visual models of the physical surroundings (geometry of surfaces, materials, light sources) for composing augmentations and enable better interaction with the physical space.

Immersive systems share most of the traditional real-time rendering challenges: how to achieve fast and realistic rendering of illumination, shadows, surfaces, etc. In addition, they have stronger constraints on latency, since it is one of the major causes of cybersickness [18,75]. As experiences become more detailed, visual assets such as geometry and textures files become larger. This requires efficient ways to manage and render those datasets. Recent approaches to mitigate this problem include remote rendering/streaming and image-based techniques. Image-based rendering is an approach to rendering that reconstructs a given view directly from image data representing discrete samples of scene, instead of geometric primitives. The benefit is that the rendering cost becomes proportional to the number of pixels, instead of the number of polygons. On the other hand, a large number of image samples of the scene is required to achieve accurate renders of novel views. Neural radiance fields (NeRF) are a recent approach to view synthesis where a neural network is trained to estimate a volumetric representation of the scene radiance. This allows a strong reduction on the storage costs of creating volumetric representation of complex scenes at high-resolution.

The main disadvantage of NeRFs is that rendering requires many neural network evaluations per ray to approximate a volume accurately. Thus, rendering from a NeRF is usually slow. However, it is also possible to use a neural network to directly learn the light field. In this way, instead of multiples lookups per pixel to determine the final color of the ray from the volume, only one lookup is needed to directly retrieve the color of the ray. Attal et al. proposed a ray space embedding network that re-maps the input ray space into an embedded latent space [7]. This facilitates both the registration of rays observing same 3D points and the interpolation of unobserved rays, leading to better view synthesis. The technique has comparable storage costs to NeRF but has only been demonstrated against two-planes parametrizations. Neural rendering techniques are being recognized as promising technique for photo-realistic rendering needs of immersive applications [80], including human poses [45] and facial reconstruction [30].

A second approach to reducing rendering costs is to use remote computing power. However, VR streaming requires far more data than 2D content and latencies should be under 20–50 ms to prevent cybersickness [75]. Mehrabi et al. proposed an architecture to render virtual reality content on network edges with low latency and restricted bandwidth, supported by a cloud server with unlimited rendering resources and higher latency. To reduce the overall latency, the authors suggest rendering a locally navigable viewport that is larger than the field-of-view (FOV) of the user's HMD. This prevents the user from getting exposed to unrendered content before an updated frame is received from the server. The goal is then to minimize the computational overhead and network traffic considering the amount of rendered content required to compensate for the resulting end-to-end latency. Given a certain number of nodes, the allocation of clients to edge vs. cloud nodes can be framed as a mixed integer nonlinear programming problem. The authors' algorithm was able to balance quality and latency and achieve improvements of 22% and 12% in latency and 8% in quality compared to alternative solutions [51].

Augmented reality presents some unique challenges for rendering, which is the integration of virtual objects with real scenes. That requires using computer vision to develop inverse models that capture light sources and materials present in a scene. This allows a virtual character to be included and lighted appropriately to match the scene. Fast methods of acquisition and relighting [59] will be of increasingly importance in AR. Advanced scene mapping and understanding will allow more realistic integration between physical and virtual objects in mixed reality [94].

> Rendering will continue to be a major area of research in immersive entertainment. Advancing the topic involves finding more efficient ways to tackle the additional challenges of low latency stereoscopic rendering, and the acquisition of appearance models of the world. Some promising avenues include remote rendering architectures and image-based techniques that allow acquisition, religthing, and high-quality rendering of 3D models.

2.5   Input Devices and Body Tracking

Input devices are the foundation of interaction techniques. Although regular input devices like a keyboard and a mouse can be used in immersive environments, spatial devices have the advantage of providing information about the device position and orientation in 3D space. The challenge is to design controllers that can reproduce the affordances required by different applications. Although in some cases bare-hand interactions may be appropriate, controllers have the advantage of providing haptics and precise input.

As new input devices are developed, new affordances and capabilities become available for designers. Even small changes such as adding palm straps or touch sensors can enable new techniques and improvements to existing ones. One important limitation of current consumer controllers is the ability to let the users feel and manipulate virtual objects with similar tactile and force stimulation that would happen in the real world. A step towards this direction is CLAW, a controller which provides force feedback and actuated movement to the index finger. The controller has a force sensor and a servo motor that applies forces to the finger during grasping and touching. In addition, a voice coil actuator can generate vibrations for various textures synchronized with finger movement. As a result, the device can enable new interactions such as grasping virtual object and touching virtual surfaces [19]. However, interaction only works with the index finger and the fixed configuration limits the uses of the controller. Wee et al. lists additional challenges for haptic handhelds, including conforming to various hand shapes and allowing double hand manipulation [86].

Another way to make controllers more useful is to allow some level of reconfiguration so that they can support different experiences. HapTwist is a toolkit that allows the creation of interactive haptic proxies for VR objects. It consists of a set of software scaffoldings and hardware modules that can enable interactivity with different shapes [95]. The hardware module includes a set of twistable parts, Vive trackers with 3D-printed mounting structures, switches, triggers, and output components such as vibrators, fans, and thermo-electric elements. An algorithm is used to determine how to combine the twistable parts to build objects that approximate a desired 3D model. HapTwist significantly reduced the time spent to create new interactive haptic proxies, which indicates a direction for future exploration.

While many applications can benefit of the haptic sensation of a controller, buttons, thumbsticks, or triggers, some applications can feel more natural with bare-hand interaction. Recent consumer HMDs are capable of hand tracking using the embedded cameras and external cameras can be attached for tracking. Recent studies on bare-hand interaction have found mixed results. When using hand tracking, users switch from natural gestures towards exaggerated and power grasps [10,11]. Researchers also did not find significant differences in presence and realism [48,84]. Although hand tracking has been studied for a long time, it is still a hard problem because of the self-occlusions, the large variety of hand types, colors and dimensions, and the large space of hand configuration. More research is needed to understand if the unexpected results with bare-hand interaction come from tracking inaccuracies, interaction design, or the lack of other sensory information, such as haptic feedback.

An even harder challenge is tracking hand-object interactions [2]. Traditional techniques work on RGBD images and try to match the observations to a model of the hand [61]. More recently, researchers are exploring using only RGB images. Hampali et al. proposed a transformer neural network for processing appearance and spatial encodings of a set of potential 2D locations for the joints of both hands. Attention mechanisms were used to sort out the correct configuration of the joints and output the 3D poses of both hands [34].

In addition to hand tracking, facial and full body tracking will be very important to support interpersonal interaction on social mixed reality [47]. Oh Kruzic et al. studied the individual and joint contributions of face and upper body gesture in avatar mediated-virtual environments. The availability of facial expressions had a positive effect on interpersonal outcomes. More specifically, dyads that were able to see their partner's facial movements mapped onto their avatars liked each other more, formed more accurate impressions about their partners, and described their interaction experiences more positively compared to those unable to see facial movements. However, the latter was only true when their partner's bodily gestures were also available and not when only facial movements were available [57].

Input devices are the basis of new interaction techniques and gameplay. Advancing controllers involves finding efficient ways to provide the affordances needed for interaction. Some research directions includes haptics and controller reconfiguration. Body-tracking will continue to be relevant and advances will include tracking that works with the diversity of human beings and while interacting with objects.

2.6 Exploring Uses for Physiological Sensing and Biofeedback

Immersive systems will contain more physiological sensors than previous technologies. Physiological sensors can be used as input devices for games and other experiences, as indirect controls, or as a way to infer the emotional states of the users (affective computing) [67]. Current headsets already include sensors for tracking different facial features (e.g., pupil, eyebrow, mouth). Headsets under development are investigating how to incorporate other sensors, such as electroencephalogram (EEG), electrooculography (EOG), electromyography (EMG), electrodermal activity (EDA), and photoplethysmography (PPG) [9]. Information from these sensors can then be used to make immersive experiences more engaging.

An individual's emotional state and his body's physiological responses are often connected to each other. While we can control facial expressions or body position, some responses from the skin, the brain, or the heart are involuntary and cannot be controlled. They, thus, present a way to infer emotional and mental states that when integrated with gameplay can be used to close a biofeedback loop [35]. Emotional states can be used to detect the players' attitudes towards NPCs, adjust game difficulty based on frustration or excitement levels, or indicate player intention for an AI system. Physiological sensors will enable the creation of more immersive and dynamic game experiences.

Nacke et al. conducted a comprehensive study on different types of biometric sensors and their integration into a variety of game mechanics. The authors implemented five game mechanics in a side scrolling platform shooter game that was augmented to use physiological sensors. Directly controlled sensors included muscle flexion, breathing patterns, and temperature change. Indirectly controlled sensors included heart rate and galvanic skin response. Gaze location was also integrated to augment controller input. The sensors were used to control different aspects of the game: enemy target size, weapon flame length, speed and jump height, weather conditions and boss speed, and targeting. The relative appeal of direct and indirect physiological control was evaluated by participants playing three versions of the game: two augmented with physiological input and one control condition. Their study concluded that augmenting games with physiological input is challenging. Natural mappings may present more intuitive game interfaces, but also limit the flexibility and generality of the sensors for game control. Participants preferred physiological sensors that were directly controlled because of the visible responsiveness. Indirect control, on the other hand, was perceived as slow and inaccurate. However, participants recognized its potential to show passive reactions of the game world or as a dramatic device [55].

Dekker and Champion altered the commercial game Half-Life 2 to use heart rate variability and the skin response of the player to increase the game's 'horror' affordances. These included dynamic changes in the game shaders, screen shake, and the creation of new spawning points for the game's non-playing characters (zombies). The biometric information recorded by the prototype correlated well with the answers given in the evaluation interviews. While the visualizations were not related to the gameplay within the environment, engaged participants made connections between the gameplay and effects. The authors argue that the lack of connection for non-engaged participants may have been a factor in some participants preferring the standard game level. However, events that were triggered by biometric analysis but could not be related to the gameplay were considered confusing and lowered the participants' engagement [23].

Physiological measures are also an opportunity of measuring game experience [32]. An initial study by Meehan et al. reports on the use of heart rate, skin conductance, and skin temperature as measures of presence in virtual environments [50]. The study found evidence that heart rate could be used as reliable, valid, and objective measures of presence in stressful VEs. Burns et al., report on a study where facial expressions have been used to determine player affect and flow. It was very easy to distinguish between boring games and other game modes. However, was much more difficult to distinguish whether a player felt frustrated or achieved some type of flow [16]. Integrating multiple sensors seems a promising approach. Ishaque et al. used 3 types of physiological signals to analyze a VR fishing game: ECG, GSR, and Respiration. The authors evaluated five different binary classifiers to determine stress and relax conditions. The ensemble-based Gradient Boost classifier had the best performance, providing an accuracy of automated classification of 85% [37]. While this study performed binary classification, advances in learning algorithms and new sensors may allow a more fine-grained and robust classification.

Physiological signals have a strong potential to advance immersive entertainment. It will make possible to create experiences customized for each user, provide means for improving evaluation, and unlock new ways to interact. Advances will lead to better ways of inferring emotional and mental states to create new gaming and narrative experiences.

2.7   Creating Better Social Experiences

A significant part of future immersive entertainment will be social or have elements for sharing the experience with others. Some of these social experiences may be co-located, however, the large majority will likely be online. Unfortunately, online communities already suffer from hate speech [5,25], cyber bullying [6,21], and racism [49].

The increased sense of presence, body tracking, and voice communication allow users in immersive environments to engage in behaviors that are very similar to the ones in the physical world. However, that also opens space for potentially more harmful interactions than in other online platforms. In a study with social VR users, Freeman et al. identified several behaviors that caused users to feel anxious, uncomfortable, and even unsafe in these spaces. Half of the participants reported feeling harassed by others running around and shouting. They also felt that the predominance of audio communication forced them to experience involuntary unpleasant experiences. In addition, most of the users felt unsafe and uncomfortable when other users invaded their virtual personal space. The platforms most used by the participants in the study were Rec Room, VRChat, and AltspaceVR [28].

However, in another study about perceptions of non-verbal communication in social VR, Maloney et al. found that non-verbal communication in social VR can be both a benefit and a disadvantage for some users, such as the marginalized populations. Participants noted that they felt more comfortable employing non-verbal communication when approaching online strangers. For example, a handshake could be used to signal friendliness and avoid the awkwardness of the initial conversation. Non-verbal communication was also identified as an effective way for marginalized users in social VR to avoid unwanted interactions, attention, and behaviors. Members of these communities would turn off voice and communicate through gestures to avoid unwanted attention to their gender identity or accents. Another tactic was to employ specific gestures, such as extending one's arm with the palm of that hand facing towards the other person (talk to the hand), to reject potential harassment [47].

Understanding the behavior of these online communities is a starting point for both design and policy solutions, as it will vary with culture, maturity of the platform, and the features it provides. However, defining harassment is challenging. In fact, most social platforms lack specificity and consistency to what constitutes harassment and a coherent set of responses to violations of different severity [60].

Creating good platform policies help to protect users against unwanted behavior. However, as Pater et al. points out, equally important is to design platforms in a way that can encourage positive behavior [60]. Platform features developed for non-immersive experiences may also work well in VR, for example, using voice modulators to conceal gender and ethnicity, real-time reporting inside the experience (rather than a form), and attaching documentation for posterior analysis and dispute [28]. However, these solutions may also lead to their own problems. Meta's immersive platform, Horizon, implemented similar ideas: a rolling buffer that record the most recent interactions, ability to send the report upon blocking, and real-time evaluation (a trained safety specialist may invisibly observe the situation and recommend a response) [52]. Unfortunately, as others have argued, a solution where everyone is continuously recorded and observed by invisible moderators can also lead to privacy concerns and inhibit user expression [26,41].

In general, more studies are needed to understand the social dynamics in immersive environments. In particular, the interaction between groups (e.g., minors and adults) and communities outside North America and Europe [49]. The experience of marginalized groups also requires more attention, since the masculine, heteronormative culture prevalent at these spaces makes women and other communities (e.g., LGBTQ+ groups) vulnerable. Besides harassment, online users are exposed to other threats, among others, extorsion, false reporting, impersonation, stalking, and account takeover [81]. We will discuss privacy and protection of users in the next section.

> Supporting positive social experiences is challenging and foundational for many online immersive experiences. Advances will require a better understanding of users in online communities and the impact of design solutions in promoting a safe environment, while guaranteeing privacy and freedom of speech.

2.8   Safeguarding Users and Promoting Responsible Design

Immersive systems are a very intimate technology. Immersive applications can be extremely compelling and believable which may cause real psychological impacts [66]. The plethora of sensors provide multiple opportunities for capturing sensitive information about the user health, surroundings, and identity. Users may also be manipulated and misled to take actions against their best interests. Understanding how immersive entertainment can be misused and investigating ways to protect against these risks while delivering the best experience should be part of the research in the area.

Yee et al. found evidence that avatar characteristics may have a significant impact on how users behave online. Users who are deindividuated in online environments may unconsciously adhere to a new identity that is inferred from their avatars. To investigate this possibility, the authors designed a game in which two individuals take turns to decide how a pool of money should be split between the two of them. One individual makes the split, and the other must choose to either accept or reject the split. If the split is accepted, the money is shared accordingly. If the split is rejected, neither of them gets the money. The authors found that participants in the short condition were about twice as likely to accept the unfair offer (72%) than participants in the normal (31%) and tall condition (38%). The hypothesis is that participants with taller avatars were more confident and more willing to make unfair splits than participants in shorter avatars [91]. Prior studies have shown that avatar identification is positively correlated with Gaming Disorders [79], a condition characterized by impaired control over gaming. Researchers also speculate that repeated exposure to different bodies may also lead to after-affects. For example, people may prefer the virtual over the physical body, leading to a type of body dissatisfaction (dysmorphia) [73].

Unlike simply bad design, dark patterns are designs intentionally constructed to manipulate users to perform actions against their interests. Teseng et al. describe how perceptual manipulations can be used to provoke physical harm in VR. By hacking or tricking the user to run a malicious app, one can use redirection techniques to control the physical actions of the user (puppetry attacks) or to elicit a misinterpretation of the physical environment (mismatching attacks). A simple example of puppetry attack is to manipulate the trajectory of the hands, causing users to hit themselves. In one of the example scenario given by the authors, a VR user try on different baseball caps on their avatar. The application then increases the offset between the controller and the virtual hand, shifting the visual of the controller away from the real one. As a result, the user moves the controller even closer to the HMD, provoking collision. In a mismatching attack scenario, a VR user is playing a zombie game where they have to fight zombies using bare hands. A malicious actor then renders a virtual zombie over a bystander, leading the VR user to start a fight [82].

Tracking of the head and body parts are an integral part of the operation of mixed reality devices. In addition, many devices will include cameras, microphones, and sensors to scan and map the environment. In a study with 511 participants, Miller et al. demonstrated that 5 min of tracking data was sufficient to identify 85% of the users. The most important features were the headset Y, headset Z, and controller pitch and roll (placement of hand controllers when at rest). The content consisted of five 360-degree videos, 20 s long each, which caused participants to stand with little movement. It is worth noting that the interactions in the study were not designed for identification, which would not be the case in a malicious app [53]. Data from body motion can also be used to identify users and even diagnose certain medical conditions [4]. Some of these may be even unknown by the users, which brings additional concern to the way data is captured and processed [73].

Part of the solution could involve the removal of latent and sensitive information from the input stream at system level. While techniques for sanitizing video inputs have been studied (e.g., blurring faces, names or deleting sensitive footage), little research exist for real-time 3D. An alternative is to abstract the interfaces, reducing the need of untrusted applications to access raw data. One example is Prepose, an architecture that protects privacy, security, and reliability with untrusted applications by providing a high-level API to build gesture recognizers and only returning specific gesture events to applications [27]. Similar ideas could be applied to spatial data from AR and inside-out tracking system to limit the concern about capturing latent information about the environment. De Guzman et al. list and review different approaches and challenges in for the protection of input, data access, output, interaction, and device protection [22].

> From the existing and emerging platforms, immersive systems pose the highest risk to privacy of individuals due to its large number of sensors. Advancing this topic will require a better understanding of the risks and developing new architectures and algorithms to minimize them. Designers should also be careful with the content of the applications developed and about the choices offered to the user through interaction.

2.9   Improving and Democratizing Content Generation

One final important enabling aspect of immersive entertainment is the availability of content creation tools. Good tools can reduce the cost of production and allow non-specialists and minorities to have a voice in the space. For realistic experiences or ones depicting real places, tools for quickly capturing geometry and material information from real scenes will be essential. That will require a leap from complex and expensive multi-camera rigs to single-cameras or portable setups. Deep learning methods have recently allowed good quality 3D reconstruction of faces from single images [42]. Similar technology would need to be developed for full body reconstruction, including challenging parts like hair, eyes, and lips.

Computational narratives spaces and AI systems are becoming more sophisticated as well [69]. As a result, there is an increasing gap between the skills of writers and programmers. A promising area of research lies in the design of tools to facilitate prototyping, testing, and evaluation of characters behaviors and story outcomes. Sanghrajka et al. describe a tool for improving the ability of designers to visualize stories created by human authors or intelligent story generators. ShowRunner takes as inputs three elements: a specification of the actions in a story, a specification of the starting state for the story, and a data dictionary that maps descriptors in the start state and action descriptions to corresponding descriptors in the Unity game environment. The system first creates an internal database that maps the input story references to game engine-internal objects. Next, it modifies the starting state of the story world according to any customizations detailed in the input files. Finally, it executes the actions enumerated in the story script. During execution, the camera automatically films the unfolding action, creating a visualization for the user [64].

Developing immersive content adds an additional layer of complexity. One approach to make it more accessible is to allow authoring of content directly in VR. One example of such a tool is FlowMatic, an authoring tool that supports event-based programming of user actions, system timers, or collisions. Creating a VR scene basically involves creating virtual objects with their properties, arranging them in the scene, and specifying their behaviors in each frame. Scenes are composed of 3D models, data sources, and a diagram that represent the logic of the scene. FlowMatic uses a dataflow model that allows users to define relationships between objects in the scene and the state of the user [93]. The authors report that participants found immersive authoring intuitive, fun, and helpful for programming VR applications.

Testing AR stories can also be time consuming, since it often needs to be tested in different physical locations. Svensson applied the idea of mixed reality simulation to create a tool that makes it easier to construct and test interactive location-based storytelling by using simulated AR environments. This allows user testing to be done in a controlled environment with identical conditions between test groups/subjects. As an additional advantage, it also allows developers to emulate a range of existing or future AR devices [77].

As mentioned in the rendering section, advances in capture can also lead to simpler and better tools. Methods based on the training of statistical models of facial identity and expressions are a promising line of research. Gafni et al. describe a novel method that demonstrates that animated human faces can be learned from monocular camera recordings using neural rendering. A neural scene representation network stores a dynamic neural radiance field which is used during volumetric rendering. First, the facial expressions are captured with face tracking and the resulting low dimensional expression parameters are used to condition the neural scene representation network. Volumetric rendering is then used to render images from the implicit geometry and appearance representation [30]. This allows the use of a single view from a fixed camera, such as a webcam, instead of expensive calibrated multi-view rigs.

Good tools will be essential to the creation of more diverse and better entertainment experiences. Advancing this topic will require the development of new techniques and systems where the goal is to reduce the effort and increase accessibility to non-experts. In particular, immersive authoring tools and new interaction techniques may enable new processes that will give more power to authors of future experiences.

3   Conclusion

Immersive entertainment will grow to become a major category of digital entertainment in the next decade and will be the source of challenging problems in several computer science areas. Some of the open issues involve improving our understanding of the experience of individuals and groups in immersive systems, while others are related to design and technical solutions. In this chapter, we have identified nine topics of relevance: understanding presence and user experience; creating believable characters and engaging storytelling; designing novel interaction techniques; improving rendering; developing input devices; exploring uses for physiological sensing and biofeedback; creating better social experiences; safeguarding users and promoting responsible design; and improving and democratizing content generation. Although the penetration of mixed reality is still small when compared to the console and PC markets, this also provides 1) an opportunity for researchers to make contributions before it becomes widely adopted and 2) the ability to accelerate and define how these experiences will look like. Advances focusing immersive entertainment will also impact other immersive applications, such as education and training, which reinforce the benefits of working on these challenges.

References

1. Aeschbach, L.F., Perrig, S.A., Weder, L., Opwis, K., Brühlmann, F.: Transparency in measurement reporting: a systematic literature review of CHI PLAY. Proc. ACM Hum.-Comput. Interact. 5(CHI PLAY), 1–21 (2021)
2. Ahmad, A., Migniot, C., Dipanda, A.: Tracking hands in interaction with objects: a review. In: 2017 13th International Conference on Signal-Image Technology & Internet-Based Systems (SITIS), pp. 360–369. IEEE (2017)
3. Alabdulkarim, A., Li, S., Peng, X.: Automatic story generation: challenges and attempts. arXiv preprint arXiv:2102.12634 (2021)
4. Alcaniz Raya, M., Marín-Morales, J., Minissi, M.E., Teruel Garcia, G., Abad, L., Chicchi Giglioli, I.A.: Machine learning and virtual reality on body movements' behaviors to classify children with autism spectrum disorder. J. Clin. Med. 9(5), 1260 (2020)
5. Alkomah, F., Ma, X.: A literature review of textual hate speech detection methods and datasets. Information 13(6), 273 (2022)
6. Ashktorab, Z., Vitak, J.: Designing cyberbullying mitigation and prevention solutions through participatory design with teenagers. In: Proceedings of the 2016 CHI Conference on Human Factors in Computing Systems, pp. 3895–3905 (2016)
7. Attal, B., Huang, J.B., Zollhoefer, M., Kopf, J., Kim, C.: Learning neural light fields with ray-space embedding networks. arXiv preprint arXiv:2112.01523 (2021)
8. Azuma, R.: Fundamentals of wearable computers and augmented reality (2015)
9. Bernal, G., Hidalgo, N., Russomanno, C., Maes, P.: Galea: a physiological sensing system for behavioral research in virtual environments. In: 2022 IEEE Conference on Virtual Reality and 3D User Interfaces (VR), pp. 66–76. IEEE (2022)
10. Blaga, A.D., Frutos-Pascual, M., Creed, C., Williams, I.: Freehand grasping: an analysis of grasping for docking tasks in virtual reality. In: 2021 IEEE Virtual Reality and 3D User Interfaces (VR), pp. 749–758. IEEE (2021)

11. Blaga, A.D., Frutos-Pascual, M., Creed, C., Williams, I.: A grasp on reality: understanding grasping patterns for object interaction in real and virtual environments. In: 2021 IEEE International Symposium on Mixed and Augmented Reality Adjunct (ISMAR-Adjunct), pp. 391–396. IEEE (2021)

12. Bowman, D., Koller, D., Hodges, L.: Travel in immersive virtual environments: an evaluation of viewpoint motion control techniques. In: Proceedings of IEEE 1997 Annual International Symposium on Virtual Reality, pp. 45–52 (1997). https://doi.org/10.1109/VRAIS.1997.583043

13. Bowman, D.A., Kruijff, E., LaViola, J.J., Poupyrev, I.: An introduction to 3-D user interface design. Presence 10(1), 96–108 (2001)

14. Breyer, F., et al.: Narrative-led interaction techniques. In: Rouse, R., Koenitz, H., Haahr, M. (eds.) ICIDS 2018. LNCS, vol. 11318, pp. 217–229. Springer, Cham (2018). https://doi.org/10.1007/978-3-030-04028-4_22

15. Brockmyer, J.H., Fox, C.M., Curtiss, K.A., McBroom, E., Burkhart, K.M., Pidruzny, J.N.: The development of the game engagement questionnaire: a measure of engagement in video game-playing. J. Exp. Soc. Psychol. 45(4), 624–634 (2009)

16. Burns, A., Tulip, J.: Detecting flow in games using facial expressions. In: 2017 IEEE Conference on Computational Intelligence and Games (CIG), pp. 45–52. IEEE (2017)

17. Cavazza, M., Aylett, R., Dautenhahn, K., Fencott, C., Charles, F.: Interactive storytelling in virtual environments: building the "holodeck". In: Proceedings of VSMM, pp. 678–687. Citeseer (2000)

18. Chang, E., Kim, H.T., Yoo, B.: Virtual reality sickness: a review of causes and measurements. Int. J. Hum.-Comput. Interact. 36(17), 1658–1682 (2020)

19. Choi, I., Ofek, E., Benko, H., Sinclair, M., Holz, C.: Claw: a multifunctional handheld haptic controller for grasping, touching, and triggering in virtual reality. In: Proceedings of the 2018 CHI Conference on Human Factors in Computing Systems, pp. 1–13 (2018)

20. Cukor, J., Spitalnick, J., Difede, J., Rizzo, A., Rothbaum, B.O.: Emerging treatments for PTSD. Clin. Psychol. Rev. 29(8), 715–26 (2009). https://doi.org/10.1016/j.cpr.2009.09.001

21. Dadvar, M., De Jong, F.: Cyberbullying detection: a step toward a safer internet yard. In: Proceedings of the 21st International Conference on World Wide Web, pp. 121–126 (2012)

22. De Guzman, J.A., Thilakarathna, K., Seneviratne, A.: Security and privacy approaches in mixed reality: a literature survey. ACM Comput. Surv. 52(6), 1–37 (2019)

23. Dekker, A., Champion, E.: Please biofeed the zombies: enhancing the gameplay and display of a horror game using biofeedback. In: DiGRA 2007-Proceedings of the 2007 DiGRA International Conference: Situated Play, pp. 550–558 (2007)

24. Denisova, A., Nordin, A.I., Cairns, P.: The convergence of player experience questionnaires. In: Proceedings of the 2016 Annual Symposium on Computer-Human Interaction in Play, pp. 33–37. ACM (2016)

25. Djuric, N., Zhou, J., Morris, R., Grbovic, M., Radosavljevic, V., Bhamidipati, N.: Hate speech detection with comment embeddings. In: Proceedings of the 24th International Conference on World Wide Web, pp. 29–30 (2015)

26. Egliston, B., Carter, M.: Oculus imaginaries: the promises and perils of Facebook's virtual reality. New Media & Society, p. 1461444820960411 (2020)

27. Figueiredo, L.S., Livshits, B., Molnar, D., Veanes, M.: Prepose: privacy, security, and reliability for gesture-based programming. In: 2016 IEEE Symposium on Security and Privacy (SP), pp. 122–137. IEEE (2016)

28. Freeman, G., Zamanifard, S., Maloney, D., Acena, D.: Disturbing the peace: experiencing and mitigating emerging harassment in social virtual reality. Proc. ACM Hum.-Comput. Interact. **6**(CSCW1), 1–30 (2022)

29. Freeman, J., Avons, S.E., Meddis, R., Pearson, D.E., IJsselsteijn, W.: Using behavioral realism to estimate presence: a study of the utility of postural responses to motion stimuli. Presence: Teleoperators Virtual Environ. **9**(2), 149–164 (2000)

30. Gafni, G., Thies, J., Zollhofer, M., Nießner, M.: Dynamic neural radiance fields for monocular 4D facial avatar reconstruction. In: Proceedings of the IEEE/CVF Conference on Computer Vision and Pattern Recognition, pp. 8649–8658 (2021)

31. Grassini, S., Laumann, K.: Questionnaire measures and physiological correlates of presence: a systematic review. Front. Psychol. **11**, 349 (2020)

32. Halbig, A., Latoschik, M.E.: A systematic review of physiological measurements, factors, methods, and applications in virtual reality. Front. Virtual Real. **2**, 694557 (2021)

33. Hameed, A., Perkis, A.: Spatial storytelling: finding interdisciplinary immersion. In: Rouse, R., Koenitz, H., Haahr, M. (eds.) ICIDS 2018. LNCS, vol. 11318, pp. 323–332. Springer, Cham (2018). https://doi.org/10.1007/978-3-030-04028-4_35

34. Hampali, S., Sarkar, S.D., Rad, M., Lepetit, V.: Handsformer: keypoint transformer for monocular 3D pose estimation of hands and object in interaction. arXiv preprint arXiv:2104.14639 (2021)

35. Houzangbe, S., Christmann, O., Gorisse, G., Richir, S.: Fear as a biofeedback game mechanic in virtual reality: effects on engagement and perceived usability. In: Proceedings of the 13th International Conference on the Foundations of Digital Games, pp. 1–6 (2018)

36. IJsselsteijn, W.A., De Kort, Y.A., Poels, K.: The game experience questionnaire. Tech. rep., Technische Universiteit Eindhoven (2013)

37. Ishaque, S., Rueda, A., Nguyen, B., Khan, N., Krishnan, S.: Physiological signal analysis and classification of stress from virtual reality video game. In: 2020 42nd Annual International Conference of the IEEE Engineering in Medicine & Biology Society (EMBC), pp. 867–870. IEEE (2020)

38. Jackson, S.A., Eklund, R.C.: Assessing flow in physical activity: the flow state scale-2 and dispositional flow scale-2. J. Sport Exerc. Psychol. **24**(2), 133–150 (2002)

39. Kennedy, R.S., Lane, N.E., Berbaum, K.S., Lilienthal, M.G.: Simulator sickness questionnaire: an enhanced method for quantifying simulator sickness. Int. J. Aviat. Psychol. **3**(3), 203–220 (1993)

40. Lages, W.S.: Opportunities and challenges in immersive entertainment. Anais Estendidos do XX Simpósio Brasileiro de Jogos e Entretenimento Digital, pp. 943–946 (2021)

41. Lang, B.: In 'horizon' Facebook can invisibly observe users in real-time to spot rule violations. https://www.roadtovr.com/facebook-horizon-privacy-monitoring-moderation/

42. Lattas, A., et al.: Avatarme: realistically renderable 3D facial reconstruction "in-the-wild". In: CVF Conference on Computer Vision and Pattern Recognition (CVPR), IEEE (2020)

43. Laugwitz, B., Held, T., Schrepp, M.: Construction and evaluation of a user experience questionnaire. In: Holzinger, A. (ed.) USAB 2008. LNCS, vol. 5298, pp. 63–76. Springer, Heidelberg (2008). https://doi.org/10.1007/978-3-540-89350-9_6

44. LaViola, Jr, J.J., Kruijff, E., McMahan, R.P., Bowman, D., Poupyrev, I.P.: 3D user interfaces: theory and practice, 2nd edn. Addison-Wesley Professional (2017)

45. Liu, L., Habermann, M., Rudnev, V., Sarkar, K., Gu, J., Theobalt, C.: Neural actor: neural free-view synthesis of human actors with pose control. ACM Trans. Graph. **40**(6), 1–16 (2021)

46. Lombard, M., Ditton, T.: At the heart of it all: the concept of presence. J. Comput.-Mediat. Commun. **3**(2), JCMC321 (1997)

47. Maloney, D., Freeman, G., Wohn, D.Y.: "Talking without a voice" understanding non-verbal communication in social virtual reality. Proc. ACM Hum.-Comput. Interact. **4**(CSCW2), 1–25 (2020)

48. Masurovsky, A., Chojecki, P., Runde, D., Lafci, M., Przewozny, D., Gaebler, M.: Controller-free hand tracking for grab-and-place tasks in immersive virtual reality: design elements and their empirical study. Multimodal Technol. Interact. **4**(4), 91 (2020)

49. Matamoros-Fernández, A., Farkas, J.: Racism, hate speech, and social media: a systematic review and critique. Telev. New Media **22**(2), 205–224 (2021)

50. Meehan, M., Insko, B., Whitton, M., Brooks, F.P., Jr.: Physiological measures of presence in stressful virtual environments. ACM Trans. Graph. **21**(3), 645–652 (2002)

51. Mehrabi, A., Siekkinen, M., Kämäräinen, T., ylï Jski, A.: Multi-tier cloudvr: leveraging edge computing in remote rendered virtual reality. ACM Trans. Multimed. Comput. Commun. Appl. **17**(2), 1–24 (2021)

52. Meta: Notice of monitoring and recording to improve safety in horizon worlds. https://store.facebook.com/legal/quest/monitoring-recording-safety-horizon/

53. Miller, M.R., Herrera, F., Jun, H., Landay, J.A., Bailenson, J.N.: Personal identifiability of user tracking data during observation of 360-degree VR video. Sci. Rep. **10**(1), 1–10 (2020)

54. Murray, J.H.: Hamlet on the Holodeck, Updated Edition: The Future of Narrative in Cyberspace. MIT Press, Cambridge (2017)

55. Nacke, L.E., Kalyn, M., Lough, C., Mandryk, R.L.: Biofeedback game design: using direct and indirect physiological control to enhance game interaction. In: Proceedings of the SIGCHI Conference on Human Factors in Computing Systems, pp. 103–112 (2011)

56. NewZoo: The global games market reaches $99.6 billion in 2016, mobile generating 37%. https://newzoo.com/insights/articles/global-games-market-reaches-99-6-billion-2016-mobile-generating-37. Accessed 01 Sep 2021

57. Oh Kruzic, C., Kruzic, D., Herrera, F., Bailenson, J.: Facial expressions contribute more than body movements to conversational outcomes in avatar-mediated virtual environments. Sci. Rep. **10**(1), 1–23 (2020)

58. Oriti, D., Manuri, F., Pace, F.D., Sanna, A.: Harmonize: a shared environment for extended immersive entertainment. Virtual Real. **2021**, 1–14 (2021). https://doi.org/10.1007/s10055-021-00585-4

59. Park, J., Park, H., Yoon, S.E., Woo, W.: Physically-inspired deep light estimation from a homogeneous-material object for mixed reality lighting. IEEE Trans. Visual Comput. Graphics **26**(5), 2002–2011 (2020)

60. Pater, J.A., Kim, M.K., Mynatt, E.D., Fiesler, C.: Characterizations of online harassment: comparing policies across social media platforms. In: Proceedings of the 19th International Conference on Supporting Group Work, pp. 369–374 (2016)

61. Patten, T., Park, K., Leitner, M., Wolfram, K., Vincze, M.: Object learning for 6D pose estimation and grasping from RGB-D videos of in-hand manipulation. In: 2021 IEEE/RSJ International Conference on Intelligent Robots and Systems (IROS), pp. 4831–4838. IEEE (2021)

62. Phan, M.H., Keebler, J.R., Chaparro, B.S.: The development and validation of the game user experience satisfaction scale (GUESS). Hum. Factors **58**(8), 1217–1247 (2016)

63. Razzaque, S., Kohn, Z., Whitton, M.C.: Redirected walking. In: ACM (ed.) Proceedings of Eurographics, pp. 289–294. Citeseer (2001)

64. Sanghrajka, R., Young, R.M., Salisbury, B., Lang, E.W.: SHOWRUNNER: a tool for storyline execution/visualization in 3D game environments. In: Cardona-Rivera, R.E., Sullivan, A., Young, R.M. (eds.) ICIDS 2019. LNCS, vol. 11869, pp. 323–327. Springer, Cham (2019). https://doi.org/10.1007/978-3-030-33894-7_32

65. Schrepp, M., Hinderks, A., Thomaschewski, J.: Design and evaluation of a short version of the user experience questionnaire (UEQ-S). Int. J. Interact. Multim. Artifi. Intell. **4**(6), 103–108 (2017)

66. Segovia, K.Y., Bailenson, J.N.: Virtually true: children's acquisition of false memories in virtual reality. Media Psychol. **12**(4), 371–393 (2009)

67. Sekhavat, Y.A., Sisi, M.J., Roohi, S.: Affective interaction: using emotions as a user interface in games. Multimed. Tools Appl. **80**(4), 5225–5253 (2021)

68. Shin, J.E., Kim, H., Parker, C., Kim, H.I., Oh, S., Woo, W.: Is any room really ok? The effect of room size and furniture on presence, narrative engagement, and usability during a space-adaptive augmented reality game. In: 2019 IEEE International Symposium on Mixed and Augmented Reality (ISMAR), pp. 135–144. IEEE (2019)

69. Siler, C., Ware, S.: A good story is one in a million: solution density in narrative generation problems. In: Proceedings of the AAAI Conference on Artificial Intelligence and Interactive Digital Entertainment, vol. 16, pp. 123–129 (2020)

70. Skarbez, R., Brooks, F.P., Jr., Whitton, M.C.: A survey of presence and related concepts. ACM Comput. Surv. **50**(6), 1–39 (2017)

71. Slater, M.: A note on presence terminology. Presence Connect **3**(3), 1–5 (2003)

72. Slater, M.: How colorful was your day? Why questionnaires cannot assess presence in virtual environments. Presence **13**(4), 484–493 (2004)

73. Slater, M., et al.: The ethics of realism in virtual and augmented reality. Front. Virtual Real. **1**, 1 (2020)

74. Souza, V., Maciel, A., Nedel, L., Kopper, R.: Measuring presence in virtual environments: a survey. ACM Comput. Surv. **54**(8), 1–37 (2021)

75. Stauffert, J.P., Niebling, F., Latoschik, M.E.: Latency and cybersickness: impact, causes, and measures: a review. Front. Virtual Real. **1**, 582204 (2020)

76. Steed, A., Takala, T.M., Archer, D., Lages, W., Lindeman, R.W.: Directions for 3D user interface research from consumer VR games. IEEE Trans. Visual Comput. Graphics **27**(11), 4171–4182 (2021). https://doi.org/10.1109/TVCG.2021.3106431

77. Svensson, T.: Using VR to simulate interactable AR storytelling. In: Cardona-Rivera, R.E., Sullivan, A., Young, R.M. (eds.) ICIDS 2019. LNCS, vol. 11869, pp. 328–332. Springer, Cham (2019). https://doi.org/10.1007/978-3-030-33894-7_33

78. Szczurowski, K., Smith, M.: Measuring presence: hypothetical quantitative framework. In: 2017 23rd International Conference on Virtual System & Multimedia (VSMM), pp. 1–8. IEEE (2017)

79. Szolin, K., Kuss, D., Nuyens, F., Griffiths, M.: Gaming disorder: a systematic review exploring the user-avatar relationship in videogames. Comput. Hum. Behav. **128**, 107124 (2022)

80. Tewari, A., et al.: Advances in neural rendering. In: Computer Graphics Forum, vol. 41, pp. 703–735. Wiley Online Library (2022)

81. Thomas, K., et al.: Sok: hate, harassment, and the changing landscape of online abuse. In: 2021 IEEE Symposium on Security and Privacy (SP), pp. 247–267. IEEE (2021)
82. Tseng, W.J., et al.: The dark side of perceptual manipulations in virtual reality. In: CHI Conference on Human Factors in Computing Systems, pp. 1–15 (2022)
83. Usoh, M., Catena, E., Arman, S., Slater, M.: Using presence questionnaires in reality. Presence: Teleoperators Virtual Environ. 9(5), 497–503 (2000)
84. Voigt-Antons, J.N., Kojic, T., Ali, D., Möller, S.: Influence of hand tracking as a way of interaction in virtual reality on user experience. In: 2020 Twelfth International Conference on Quality of Multimedia Experience, pp. 1–4. IEEE (2020)
85. Vorderer, P., et al.: MEC spatial presence questionnaire. Retrieved Sept 18, 2015 (2004)
86. Wee, C., Yap, K.M., Lim, W.N.: Haptic interfaces for virtual reality: challenges and research directions. IEEE Access 9, 112145–112162 (2021)
87. Weech, S., Kenny, S., Lenizky, M., Barnett-Cowan, M.: Narrative and gaming experience interact to affect presence and cybersickness in virtual reality. Int. J. Hum. Comput. Stud. 138, 102398 (2020)
88. Wienrich, C., Latoschik, M.E.: Extended artificial intelligence: new prospects of human-AI interaction research. arXiv preprint arXiv:2103.15004 (2021)
89. Witmer, B.G., Singer, M.J.: Measuring presence in virtual environments: a presence questionnaire. Presence: Teleoperators Virtual Environ. 7(3), 225–240 (1998)
90. Wolf, D., Rogers, K., Kunder, C., Rukzio, E.: JumpVR: jump-based locomotion augmentation for virtual reality. In: Proceedings of the 2020 CHI Conference on Human Factors in Computing Systems, pp. 1–12 (2020)
91. Yee, N., Bailenson, J.N.: The Proteus effect: the effect of transformed self-representation on behavior. Hum. Commun. Res. 33(3), 271–290 (2007). https://doi.org/10.1111/j.1468-2958.2007.00299.x
92. Yu, R., et al.: Bookshelf and bird: enabling real walking in large VR spaces through cell-based redirection. In: 2017 IEEE Symposium on 3D User Interfaces (3DUI), pp. 116–119. IEEE (2017)
93. Zhang, L., Oney, S.: Flowmatic: an immersive authoring tool for creating interactive scenes in virtual reality. In: Proceedings of the 33rd Annual ACM Symposium on User Interface Software and Technology, pp. 342–353 (2020)
94. Zhao, X., Pang, Y., Yang, J., Zhang, L., Lu, H.: Multi-source fusion and automatic predictor selection for zero-shot video object segmentation. arXiv preprint arXiv:2108.05076 (2021)
95. Zhu, K., Chen, T., Han, F., Wu, Y.S.: Haptwist: creating interactive haptic proxies in virtual reality using low-cost twistable artefacts. In: Proceedings of the 2019 CHI Conference on Human Factors in Computing Systems, p. 693. ACM (2019)

Strategies to Promote Stakeholders' Autonomy While Creating Educational Digital Games

João Gabriel de Matos Dairel[1] , Isabela Gasparini[2] ,
and Rafael Dias Araújo[1(✉)]

[1] Universidade Federal de Uberlândia, Uberlândia, MG, Brazil
rafael.araujo@ufu.br
[2] Universidade do Estado de Santa Catarina, Joinville, SC, Brazil
isabela.gasparini@udesc.br

Abstract. The process of developing educational digital games presents several challenges. Authorship is one of them, intensified by the infinity of application domains and the time consumption for coding and making available each new game. Thus, there is a gap between the creative process of educational digital games and their development, causing a rupture of scale between the need to create these artifacts for specific purposes and their effective use. In this way, this work discusses the challenge of creating software architectures and ecosystems to provide greater autonomy in the construction of educational digital games by different actors, maintain characteristics of educational software, and, also, to allow proper monitoring of the learning process. With that aim, this chapter discusses the challenge from the point of view of digital games' authoring, stakeholders' autonomy, and the Brazilian context diversity.

Keywords: Educational digital games · Authoring · Creative process · Autonomy

1 Introduction and Contextualization

Teaching strategies beyond traditional teaching methodologies, especially those related to Digital Information and Communication Technologies (DICT), contribute positively to the teaching and learning process and also bring challenges [32]. The COVID-19 pandemic highlighted the need for computational solutions in many faces for the area of Social and Educational Technologies. There are also advances in discussions on digital transformation and the insertion of technologies in different sectors around the globe. In Brazil, there is a recently created Innovation Policy on Connected Education, instituted by Law No. 14.180 [7], which includes, among other actions, the "availability of free digital teaching materials, preferably open and in the public domain and free license, which counts on the effective participation of education professionals in their elaboration" and the "fostering the development and dissemination of digital teaching resources, preferably in an open format".

R. P. d. Santos and M. d. S. Hounsell (Eds.): GranDGamesBR 2020/2021, CCIS 1702, pp. 255–273, 2023.
https://doi.org/10.1007/978-3-031-27639-2_12

One of the possible alternatives in this scenario is the use of educational digital games as technological artifacts that facilitate the teaching and learning process of different areas of knowledge and ages [13,34,35] and stimulate concentration, perception, reasoning, and abstraction [8,21,39]. However, digital games that only focus on practicing repetitive tasks, like those created in the first generation of this type of game, or that are poorly designed, become obsolete quickly or may not be as effective in education [20,36]. Thus, it is important to create more dynamic mechanisms, as well as to involve the actors (whether teachers, students, or managers) in the process of creating the technological proposal, and not only the specialized professionals, in order to make this process more empathetic and improve its adoption [4].

However, the process of developing educational digital games presents several challenges, ranging from the survey of user needs to the design, implementation and evaluation [24,41]. In particular, it is important to highlight the challenge of authoring these artifacts, since there is a multitude of domains that can be applied, and it is necessary to have domain experts involved in the development process to define the learning objectives for specific content, and also to assess whether they are being effective as a learning support [39].

In this way, there is a gap between the creative process of educational digital games and their development, which causes a rupture of scale between the need to create these artifacts for specific purposes and their effective use. Usually, domain experts do not have the skills needed to implement the game, and programmers often lack domain knowledge fundamental to the context. In addition, the wide variety of game engines used for development and computing devices with different platforms used to run games are mitigating factors in this context. Although it can be a positive factor for the democratization and use of these artifacts in different platforms and scenarios, it amplifies the negative factor from the point of view of the complexity of creating and maintaining quality educational digital games.

Research in this area has sought to create processes, methodologies, and frameworks that involve multidisciplinary teams for creating educational digital games often focused on the issue of creativity. Nadolski et al. [31] state that serious game development requires using specific methodologies and makes the product more expensive. They proposed a methodology and a toolkit for serious game development in higher education called EMERGO that involves different actors in the process, such as teachers, educational technicians, and other specialists, such as graphic designers and game designers.

The AIMED method (*Agile, Integrative and open Method for open Educational resources Development*) [40] integrates instructional design practices, game design, simulation modeling, software engineering, and project management during the process of developing open educational resources, including serious digital games. The methodology proposed in [2] consists of creating the main game with missions and a set of related learning mechanisms (questionnaires, puzzles, or minigames), but independent and played in parallel with the main game. The idea of creating separate learning mechanisms potentially promotes the autonomy of authors, however, the methodology presented does not make it clear how and when actors are involved in the process.

The ABCDE [37] methodology presents an apparatus used to design serious game mechanics based on models and theories that foster creativity. Its proposal consists of running a workshop that uses the tools of brainstorming and game sketching in cycles that involve the generation, permutation, and visualization of ideas between the participants until they reach a point of convergence.

However, these proposals are still focused on creating each game one-by-one, without providing subsidies for non-technical adaptations. For example, teachers who are domain specialists, managers, and students, could eventually create new versions without the need to repeat the whole process to create a new game. That is, despite helping in the stages of the game development process, they do not effectively promote the autonomy of educational actors in the creation process, as they are still dependent on technical teams of programmers. Besides, autonomy is necessary for the learning context, since people's involvement in decision-making can lead to more effective learning.

Therefore, it is necessary to think about computing platforms and software ecosystems that allow domain experts (in this case, teachers) – or even end-users (in this case, students) – to be able to co-create and adapt the game design in a specific way to their educational context. For example, changing game elements, mechanics, and game phases to their needs and learning goals in an easier way and without the constant involvement of programmers for the implementation. This approach is similar to the so-called End-user Development (EUD) and End-User Programming (EUP) and refers to fields of research that study methods and techniques to enable end-users to modify and create digital artifacts [3]. EUD or EUP refers to tasks and tools that allow people who are not professional software developers - to program computers, i.e. they can use EUD tools to create or modify software artifacts without great knowledge of a programming language. Similar to that concept, we think teachers can be in charge of digital game adaptations, without having to learn how to code (as programming) or design a new game (as a game designer).

In this context, the technical team (e.g. programmers and developers) is still necessary, but with a different focus, to contribute to the development of artifacts and software ecosystems that facilitate the authoring process by teachers, managers, and/or students. Thus, this chapter aims to present a challenge in the context of the creation of educational digital games related to the promotion of the autonomy of non-technical stakeholders.

For this, Sect. 2 deals with concepts related to educational digital games, as well as issues related to authorship, autonomy, and the diversity of the Brazilian context; Sect. 3 addresses concepts related to software architecture and ecosystems and their importance in this context; Sect. 4 presents the proposed challenge and possibilities for evaluating progress; and, finally, Sect. 5 presents the final considerations of the chapter.

2   Educational Digital Games

Currently, there is a multitude of digital games available, whether commercial or not, with numerous design features. Many of them are similar while many are not. Thus, a taxonomy would facilitate the identification of both games with similar game design principles and those that have different characteristics.

There are different taxonomies for digital games in the literature. Novak [33] classifies by objective (entertainment, educational, social, recruitment and training, health, consciousness & change, aesthetics & creativity, marketing & advertising) and by genre (action, adventure, action-adventure, casino, puzzle, Role-playing games, simulation, strategy, Massively Multiplayer Online Games), with several subcategories. Crawford [14] focuses on perceptual and motor skills, called skill-and-action games (combat, maze, sports, paddle, race, and miscellaneous), and cognitive effort, called strategy games (adventures, Dungeons and Dragons, wargames, games of chance, educational and children's games, and interpersonal ones).

The rise of digital games in the industry and the educational environment today has attracted a variety of criticisms due to several limitations [10, 30, 36]. As learning is the result of several activities that stimulate cognition, the usual teaching environments through digital games use passive teaching means by distributing and consuming previously-stored content instead of learning. The use of traditional teaching mechanisms directly affects how the implementation of digital games is applied in education. Pedagogy is limited in short to the use of traditional teaching methods characterized mainly by the teacher, considered active, and students considered passive.

The technology evolution has provided appropriate support for methods that use games in education with devices capable of running the most diverse software, which is accessible to a large part of the population at a relatively low cost. This evolution has brought improvements in teaching support systems such as student monitoring, online assessments, and user feedback, among others. Such steps have gained greater attention from the pedagogical community, as they are easy to manage data commonly manually manipulated, such as an electronic diary [30].

Integrating these games into e-learning systems in a standards-compliant manner and allowing for two-way communication (system-game, game-system) opens new ways for the educational use of games while lowering costs and lowering requirements. The technological advances of educational games are also a desired objective as the use of specifically designed engines for the educational field with built-in features can increase their pedagogical value and can be used freely by instructors or organizations to develop educational games [30].

From the identification of the pedagogical requirements, game requirements can be gathered, and then we can choose a model that covers these requirements. Games may be included as learning objects in collaborative/community-oriented learning strategies and can interact with the environment during runtime. By definition, any initiative that mixes video games and education can be considered game-based learning [30]. To begin with, looking at current trends in online education, these educational games must be able to coexist in environments that follow the learning object model, which stands up for small games focused on very specific topics.

The motivational and immersive traits of game-based learning have been deeply studied in the literature, but the design and the systematic implementation of educational games remain an undefined topic. These approaches are categorized into three groups:

- multimedia approaches, strongly linked to content presentation;
- those who leverage pre-existing games for education;
- an intermediate category of specially designed games that seek a balance between fun and educational content.

On the other hand, putting a game into a specific state only requires setting the game's internal registers to certain values. When the entertainment aspects do not shine through the design, most of the game-based learning advantages in terms of motivation and engagement are lost, and the learning experience suffers.

Serious games (SGs) are games designed not only for entertainment but also aim to assist in a broad spectrum of application areas, e.g. military, government, education, healthcare, etc., through playful activities. They have gained space in the educational context due to the exploration of new technologies, which proposes daily challenges to the player to represent activities in a similar way to reality, offering the opportunity to explore the environment and generate interest when encountering different situations.

Mildner and 'Floyd' Mueller [27] point out that different roles such as game designers, artists, programmers, domain experts, and the users themselves, as shown in Fig. 1, must work together in the development process to create more attractive games. In addition, they also state that the inclusion of domain experts and the objective and message that a game conveys, in addition to the fun part, are the main differences between a serious game and a pure entertainment game.

From the point of view of elements that games must contain, there are several models in the literature. For example, Prensky [38] believes that games are a combination of twelve elements, namely: fun (for enjoyment and pleasure), play (for involvement), rules (for structure), goals (for motivation), interactivity, adaptivity, outcome, and feedback (for learning), win states (for gratification), conflict/competition/challenge/opposition (for adrenaline), problem-solving (for creativity), interaction (for socialization), and representation and story (for emotion).

Adams [1] points out ten elements: gameplay, aesthetics, harmony, storytelling, risks and rewards, novelty, learning, creative and expressive play, immersion, and socializing. Fundamentally, game elements focus on four basic elements heavily interconnected, with some of the more visible to end-users while others are less visible, as defined by Schell [42] and shown in Fig. 2:

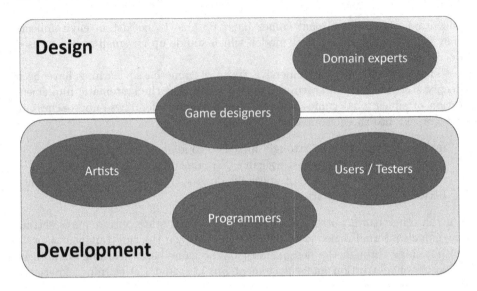

Fig. 1. Stakeholders involved in the serious game development process [27].

- Aesthetics: it refers to the general characteristics of the game environment;
- Mechanics: it is related to the set of rules and procedures that regulate how players achieve their objectives of the game;
- Story: it refers to the set of events (linear or not) by which the game's narrative is constructed;
- Technology: it is related to the set of tools and technology resources necessary for the game to be built according to the previous elements.

Specifically from the point of view of stories and narratives, it can be defined as broadly as the game: everything is a narrative/story [33]. We can define a narrative as an experience that is structured in time. Different structures represent different forms of narrative. In many games, the narrative manifests itself recursively with repetition of the structure at different levels of the time scale [14]. However, other elements such as aesthetics and mechanics with different levels of interactivity may vary in the meantime. Within the range of effort required for immersion and engagement, if gameplay consumes most of the player's available cognitive resources, there will be little room for perceiving complex narrative patterns. More than that, the narrative adds little to player immersion and engagement. On the other hand, focusing on developing a sense of storytelling only reduces the player's need and ability [14]. A good game design achieves better integration of gameplay and game narrative structures.

As can be observed, game development, especially serious ones, involves a complex process that is difficult to scale, as it is heavily dependent on technical teams. In addition, in the context of serious games for learning, domain experts are teachers of different levels of education who are usually already overloaded with the didactic workload that already requires a lot of effort [9,16,25].

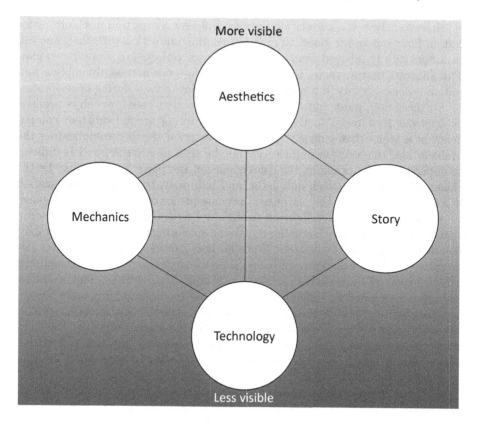

Fig. 2. Elemental Tetrad of game elements [42].

Thus, it becomes interesting to create educational materials that, in addition to promoting more effective learning, also facilitate teaching work. As a result, more and more new requirements are elicited, which leads to a longer development time and, consequently, a longer time to make the resource available for use.

The challenge proposed in this chapter is related to the authoring process of educational digital games, the stakeholders' autonomy while developing such digital artifacts, and also with the enormous diversity of teaching contexts in Brazil. Such subjects will be addressed in Subsects. 2.1, 2.2, and 2.3, respectively.

2.1 Authoring

The authoring process is based on tools created for programmers, and defining how game elements are used takes precedence over defining what they are used for. However, this is not the most suitable structure for education professionals whose objective is to teach through the game instead of programming it. As an element often depends on multiple interactions, it often becomes difficult for non-experts to understand.

However, there is a correlation between different interaction mechanisms for certain functions in the game. In many cases, the interaction with the game can be automatically inferred from the role that your objects are supposed to play. This suggests that a greater focus on function does not necessarily imply a limitation on interactivity, but implies a shift in point of view during development.

Furthermore, most authoring tools use content-based or object-centric descriptions that result in the game logic scattering around different components in a story that emerges from the interaction, further complicating the problem. So, the story is implicit, cannot be seen as a whole, and is difficult to understand. For example, the consequence of the player's action may be the change of a variable, which only later, and indirectly, triggers the modification of a feature that makes the player see the consequence of the action in the game.

Approaching game development to the story-writing process using a description based on a narrative metaphor makes the authoring process more natural for non-developers such as educators. Some authors consider video games as a new narrative medium. Educators, although generally unfamiliar with programming, can be expected to use other narrative materials (e.g., stories). This narrative metaphor is inspired by different heuristics, case studies, and proposals regarding story writing, and video game development. The explicit representation of the story creates a comprehensive description of the game, "weaving" the story using visual components and making the game easier to edit and understand. A description based on a narrative metaphor can also be considered in other approaches to creating educational video games.

There are interesting authoring platforms, such as Unity, Scratch, and Buildbox. Unity[1] is excellent for creating 2D and 3D games and educational experiences. It is well-suited for Virtual Reality (VR) and Augmented reality (AR) development. It is also a great platform for mobile games. It is less suited for non-game purposes (although it can certainly be used for those as well). It is also less suited for AR experiences that are highly complex, where you will probably want to write the native code in Android Studio or Xcode, as the case may be.

Scratch[2] is a visual programming language that allows students to create their own interactive stories, games, and animations. The platform helps students learn to think creatively, reason systematically, and work collaboratively [44]. It has a massive community for resources and support, easily integrated with different subjects. Although, it doesn't offer the next step into text-based coding languages and draws students of all types into coding, and lays a foundation for future learning.

Buildbox[3] is ideal for newcomers to the world of game-making. There aren't a lot of coding skills required. All you have to do is drag and drop to get the job done. There are a lot of options and tools to pick from. It aids in the creation of basic but enjoyable super casual games. It also aids in the development of cross-platform games. You may play them on Android, iOS, Windows, Mac OS

---

[1] https://unity.com/.

[2] https://scratch.mit.edu/.

[3] https://www.buildbox.com/.

X, and other platforms. A computer with a low specification can easily handle this software. It has a user interface that is straightforward to use, as well as tools that are simple to use.

Games authorship in the educational context directly involves developers due to the lack of platforms that allow the games' creation without the technical understanding of programming. This need, therefore, influences the motivation of educators who, in turn, choose not to use Serious Games. In this way, software applications that support the authoring process and that work synergistically and integrated as software ecosystems become an important requirement in this context.

2.2 Autonomy

First, it is important to point out that the term "autonomy" used in this chapter is based on Miller's definition [28], who says that "an autonomous person is someone who determines his/her own maxims or rules for action and acts in accordance with them".

Concerning the autonomy of learning, we expect that learners will take an active, independent attitude to learn and independently undertake a learning task. This autonomy is important to learning, students personal involvement in decision-making can lead to more effective learning. Autonomy can also be important to other stakeholders in other learning contexts. In this chapter, we think teachers can benefit from more powerful tools, by having part of the control and by personalizing their digital games to their students.

Currently, teachers who want to create a specific digital game for a particular subject in their discipline need to involve a technical team of programmers to make it viable. In practice, what we notice is that researchers in the field of educational technologies make this connection. However, this strategy is not scalable from the point of view of creating these artifacts. It is necessary to encourage and provide more autonomy to domain specialists, who are professors from different areas of knowledge who have specific needs in the context in which they are inserted.

According to Moran (2018) [29], neuroscience research shows that "each person learns what is most relevant and what makes sense to them, which generates cognitive and emotional connections". In addition to creation, it is also important to provide mechanisms for monitoring and evaluating the learning of its students, in order to facilitate and streamline the identification of difficulties through Learning Analytics techniques [15] and assist in the most appropriate intervention for each student. In the context of digital games, this area is also called Game Learning Analytics, given its potential and practical applicability of using data-based approaches to student interactions [18], as a way to find evidence of how learning occurs in this context.

Thereby, autonomy is still linked to developers, there is a need for a developer whenever there is a desire to create something new or to integrate existing games. However, several already structured games can, and are already used for learning, their main limitation is how much we can change their states and how players can achieve their goals, the vast majority of games do not provide the free creation of stages for users and dependence on creating new initiatives.

The game Calangos [26] is a 3D simulation game in first and third person which aims at presenting the process of ecological evolution by impersonating a lizard ("calango" in Portuguese). It has extremely relevant content for the discipline of biology, being important not only for the understanding of the field but also for the formation of individuals capable of making and critically evaluating decisions in the face of environmental problems.

"September 12th" [17] inspired the creation of the term "newsgame", which is related to electronic games based on journalistic news. In virtual reality, bombs not only kill, but cause collateral damage, and when civilians cry, the innocent dead turn into terrorists, while the player realizes that it is not possible to win by shooting. By conveying the timeless message that violence causes violence, the game has already been exhibited in museums in several countries and has been used by teachers as a tool to discuss terrorism.

The game "Myth of the Cave" [23] is inspired by the famous parable of the philosopher Plato, which shows how human beings can free themselves from the darkness that imprisons them through the light of truth. Aimed at students from the 1st to the 5th year of Elementary School, the pedagogical content of Myth of the Cave was built based on the National Curriculum Parameters. A Teacher's Guide is available, which guides how the game can be used as an educational practice and a system for evaluating and monitoring the student.

In the "Climate Challenge" game [22], the player assumes the role of president of Europe and must promote adequate public policies to meet the goal of reducing carbon emissions by 2100. At the same time, he must verify if there is enough water, energy, and food for the population, controlling their expenses.

As can be seen, in general, games are developed as standalone software and are used according to the elements defined in their design stage. This also reinforces the difficulty of scalability to adapt/fit them to very specific educational contexts.

2.3 Brazilian Context Diversity

Diversity, defined as the historical, social, cultural, and political creation of distinctions, occurs in the context of power relations, growing inequalities, and the economic crisis, which is expanding in the national and international environment. In this argument, it is impossible to ignore the effects of socioeconomic inequality on the whole of society, particularly on social groups considered different.

As a result, a study on inequality and diversity should be carried out. Considering its interaction with other elements, such as the problems of articulating equality and identity policies to the recognition of difference in the national and international context, the essential reinvention of the national and international environment. The State's approach to social emancipation, the worsening of poverty, and the unequal distribution of wealth are on the rise.

If the school can reinforce the inequality of capitalist society through official programming, it can also provide a space of struggle and conquest for socially marginalized groups. We all know that education is still heavily influenced by the hegemonic values of the ruling elites, but that doesn't mean it has to be that way. Only by getting to know the silenced cultures better (such as those of the indigenous peoples of the Amazon and Afro-descendants) will it be possible to include them in school curricula respectfully and purposefully, and not just as a reenactment of colonizing, putting their feet on our territory. In short, education still has a long way to go in terms of affirming identities and overcoming disparities, while respecting cultural diversity.

Cultural differences have been studied by many anthropologists (e.g. Hofstede, Trompenaars, and Hall) over the years and they categorized culture according to their findings presenting different cultural dimensions [19]. Cultural aspects are preferences and ways of behavior determined by the person's culture and it is the cumulative deposit of knowledge, beliefs, values, and attitudes, the rules of people's behavior in a society [19].

Considering Brazil's continental proportions and even different realities for different regions and groups, it is to be expected that there is great diversity so that authoring tools can be appropriated by different groups. In this way, a deeper analysis of structural, social, and value differences must be studied in depth.

3   Software Architecture and Ecosystems

As already contextualized, in general, digital games are developed individually as self-contained applications that perform a specific function. However, for this type of software to perform other functions desired in the educational context, such as analyzing student behavior and identifying learning difficulties, in addition to simply being created to support a specific theme, many hours of technical work are spent on the different stages of its development repeatedly for each game created. Thus, changing the mindset toward creating software ecosystems for this context can bring numerous benefits.

According to Bosch [5], a software ecosystem is a set of other software that allows and supports the activities and transactions made between stakeholders in an automated way. Among the benefits that the author mentions for the adoption of software ecosystems, we mention the possibility of collaboration with partners involved in the ecosystem to share the costs of innovation, the attractiveness for new users, and a greater perception of value to existing users. In addition, as games can also be understood as Information Systems [46], it is possible to design them aiming to create mechanisms to assist teachers and managers in decision-making processes.

Regarding game infrastructure, there are several software and frameworks for game development and analytics, some are specific to a computing platform such as a smartphone or desktop, and others are multiplatform, that is, they allow different platforms and operating systems to access the game. One way to guarantee cross-platform access is to use the browser to run the game. The choice of framework is essential to facilitate the development process and abstract platform-specific issues.

Several issues must be taken into account regarding infrastructure, the main ones are scalability, persistence, availability, and throughput. Regarding persistence, it must be taken into account in the development process where the data will be stored, and how it will be used so that developers can define data models that meet demand more efficiently, the most common means of storage and sharing are relational and non-relational databases for storage and JSON for exchanging data between the database and the server.

Relational databases are databases that mainly value referential integrity and transactions according to ACID (Atomicity, Consistency, Isolation, and Durability), databases store data in tables in sets of rows and columns with pre-defined relationships. During its creation, any action between two distinct tables, including relationships, take place through primary and foreign keys.

Otherwise, non-relational databases are databases that are not concerned with such characteristics mentioned above, they are used to be flexible, scalable, and able to respond quickly to data demand, they do not need so many modifications for their growth in scalability as relational databases, and the main difference between relational databases and non-relational databases is the non-use of the SQL language in queries, the queries are usually performed by specific drivers between the chosen programming language and the desired non-relational database.

For the process of intermediating data between systems, the JSON format is ideal because it is used by most programming languages for this purpose, and its model in the key value schema provides certain ease of accessing data in non-relational databases, as there are types of non-relational databases that use JSON as a file storage format. In terms of throughput, we are dealing with the speed at which data will flow from end to end, such as from server to database, and displayed to the client. In a system with a relevant number of users, this is necessary so that the experience is not impaired, and ensures greater availability of data access.

The game development life cycle is something fundamental, and it is made as an iteration in a cycle from the initial development to the reporting phase, following the DevOps standards, and can be divided into three main stages, being the first step by step, API management, consists of managing and maintaining applications, services, and microservices from initial implementation to updates, deployments, and support, controlling access to services, applications, and microservices. And it is involved in creating, managing, publishing, and sharing software artifacts.

One of the most important stages in the game's lifecycle is its development phase. The objective of this phase is the preparation of procedures, processes, tools, and mechanisms. This phase of development is based on service-oriented architecture and based on the microservices pattern. There are, of course, different engine game structures. They are classified into Monolithic Engines, Modular

Framework Engines, Modular Engines, and Compact Engines. The microservice idea is suitable for engines that support service-oriented architecture. Monolithic engines are not very advantageous in the use of microservices, however, it may be interesting to use them in smaller and independent systems.

It is important to reinforce the idea of the proposal of designing software ecosystems to allow not only the creation of learning games in a more autonomous way, but also the monitoring and follow-up of the learning process by school stakeholders (teachers, students, and supervisors), promoting transparency and a greater perception of self-knowledge. Thus, it is necessary to create specialized software around digital games so that, in an integrated and automated way, they provide a greater perception of value in the context in which they are inserted. Furthermore, it is also necessary to create structured and open repositories of educational digital games integrated into these ecosystems, as a fundamental part that also generates data to foster the analysis of the learning process through interactions.

Given the complexity and difficulties of the game development and maintenance processes, a review must be carried out in the support process and the possibility of automation and continuity of production, update, delivery, and test operations are provided in the shortest possible time and continuously. To achieve this approach, a shift in thinking is needed in game development and support. Through the DevOps culture, game development costs are greatly reduced. Version control systems such as Git[4], Perforce[5], and Subversion[6], continuous integration and delivery systems such as Jenkins[7], Bamboo[8], and TeamCity[9], and automation testing tools such as Selenium[10], Katalon Studio[11], UFT[12], and Watir[13] are part of this step.

4   Challenge

The challenge proposed in this chapter is to create architectural and design mechanisms that allow for educational context stakeholders to participate with more autonomy in the creative process and construction of educational digital games. Such digital games, published in repositories properly integrated into learning environments, should provide support for monitoring the learning process and be built in a scalable way so that there is no need for the constant involvement of a technical team of programmers to enable the creation of new games with the same Game Design.

---

[4] https://git-scm.com/.
[5] https://www.perforce.com/.
[6] https://subversion.apache.org/.
[7] https://www.jenkins.io/.
[8] https://www.atlassian.com/software/bamboo.
[9] https://www.jetbrains.com/teamcity/.
[10] https://www.selenium.dev/.
[11] https://katalon.com/.
[12] https://www.microfocus.com/products/uft-one/overview.
[13] http://watir.com/.

Currently, there is great variability in game engines, frameworks, and tools that can be used for the development of digital games. However, they require technical skills to create digital games and make them available to users, especially if there are specific context requirements. Thus, the central idea is to design software architectures and ecosystems that make it possible for non-technical people to be able to create game stories and mechanics with a certain autonomy, but that maintain characteristics of educational software to allow the monitoring of the learning process.

For example, imagine that a basic education science teacher - who is not a specialist in the area of computing - has access to a computing environment where he/she can create versions of digital games to explore specific content in his discipline. First, the teacher's concern should focus on creating different narratives and game mechanisms through intuitive authoring tools. Second, the environment must provide both data collection and initial analysis of behavior and use of games by students, to allow the identification of different factors related to the learning of students in a class. Finally, this kind of data and analysis should be useful as input for methods/tools/applications that support teachers, managers, and students themselves in decision-making processes.

In this way, both teachers and students can act as creators of contextualized digital games, promoting the scalability of solutions in specialized repositories (preferably open) and exercising the general competencies of Basic Education, particularly those defined by the Brazilian National Common Curricular Base (BNCC) [6]. In addition, supervisors and managers should also be included as facilitators and stimulators in this process, as well as providing them with evidence of the learning process in these environments.

In addition to the educational impact, the proposed challenge also has a potential social impact, since as it is explored, it will allow the insertion of innovative elements in the learning process, making the content taught to be increasingly contextualized with the reality in which people are included.

4.1   Progress Evaluation

We understand that this is a long-term challenge so it requires an incremental progress evaluation. Qualitative and quantitative means must be used in a participatory and formative way with all the stakeholders mentioned.

Findings from the meta-analysis conducted by Wang et al. [45] with works dealing with the use of digital games in STEM education showed that they have positive effects on student learning. Beyond that, the internal mechanism of digital games, such as gameplay design and game mechanisms, should be further explored in order to understand their effects on the learning process and, thereby, improve student motivation. Other studies in the literature have shown that gameplay, game mechanisms, competition strategies, and game platforms significantly improve student learning [11,12,43].

From a quantitative point of view, it is possible to evaluate points related to the repositories of digital games created/evolved regarding the number of artifacts and tools with the purpose of assisting the authoring, as well as the use of educational data mining and learning analytics techniques to evaluate students' learning process. In addition, investigations can look quantitatively at the domains of knowledge and contexts covered by digital games, and also at the number of hours played by students and spent on creation. It is also possible to observe the interaction of students both for co-creation and for the use of games, with measures concerning the interaction between the different actors and levels of collaboration, game-player interaction, individual performance, and team performance, among others.

From a qualitative point of view, it is possible to evaluate the evolution of the quality of digital games created in different contexts and scenarios, the pedagogical theories used for supporting their development, in addition to the perception of the user experience (UX) regarding the use of these artifacts and their contribution to the teaching and learning process. Among the possible analyzes and evaluations, one can think of engagement, motivation, satisfaction, impact on the level of knowledge, ease of learning the content addressed, accessibility, and others. The influence of learners' types and characteristics on their interest and motivation for digital games, as well as personalization and adaptation features that best meet their preferences and needs, should be further explored [45]. Campano Junior et al. [8] present a guide based on pedagogical theories to support the evaluation of Educational Games and can also be used in this context.

Finally, the study by [45] also points out the need to integrate digital games with other technologies and make full use of different information resources for the sustainable development of such artifacts in the context of practical teaching and learning applications. In this sense, it is also necessary to analyze not only functional requirements but also integration, security, and data privacy requirements, as well as evaluate the ecosystem as a whole. Thus, research in other areas such as software engineering and information systems can contribute with methodological and evaluative aspects at this point.

5 Final Considerations

This chapter presented a discussion about challenges for promoting stakeholders' autonomy in the process of creating educational digital games, which can be addressed from different points of view. We sought to present ways to increase the role of domain specialist teachers, students and supervisors, and managers in the process of authoring educational digital games, to encourage greater autonomous participation of education professionals in the creation of these artifacts as digital pedagogical materials.

In addition, we discuss issues related to the infrastructure for creating and maintaining such artifacts, as well as the breadth of the Brazilian context diversity, which reinforces the need to create mechanisms that depart from the well-known one-size-fits-all approach and allow stakeholders to get a deeper understanding of the learning process in each context. For this, it is necessary to change the mindset toward the creation of software ecosystems with specialized applications to support the decision-making processes of stakeholders in the educational context.

An important issue is that perspective does not exclude the dependency on the programmer or technical team but changes their role in the creation process, focusing on designing and developing computational solutions to foster the autonomy of other stakeholders in this context. It is known that this is a long-term process and that it requires the union of efforts and synergy of a multidisciplinary community to create solutions for the proposed challenge. In addition, it is important that the proposals are, in fact, viable and transferred to society.

Acknowledgements. The authors would like to thank the Federal University of Uberlândia and the State University of Santa Catarina for their support. This study was financed in part by the Coordenação de Aperfeiçoamento de Pessoal de Nível Superior - Brasil (CAPES) - Finance Code 001. We are also grateful for the support of the National Council for Scientific and Technological Development (CNPq) 308395/2020-4, and FAPESC/UDESC No 04/201 - Infrastructure Support for UDESC Research Groups, defined under the Technical and Financial Cooperation Agreement - T.O No2019TR585.

References

1. Adams, E.: Fundamentals of Game Design. Pearson Education, Berkeley, USA (2010)
2. Barbosa, A.F.S., Pereira, P.N.M., Dias, J.A.F.F., Silva, F.G.M.: A new methodology of design and development of serious games. Int. J. Comput. Games Technol. **2014**, 8 (2014). https://doi.org/10.1155/2014/817167
3. Barricelli, B.R., Cassano, F., Fogli, D., Piccinno, A.: End-user development, end-user programming and end-user software engineering: a systematic mapping study. J. Syst. Softw. **149**, 101–137 (2019). https://doi.org/10.1016/j.jss.2018.11.041
4. Battarbee, K., Suri, J.F., Howard, S.G.: Empathy on the edge: scaling and sustaining a human-centered approach in the evolving practice of design. IDEO, pp. 1–14 (2014). https://www.ideo.com/news/empathy-on-the-edge
5. Bosch, J.: From software product lines to software ecosystems SPLC 2009, pp. 111–119. Carnegie Mellon University, USA (2009)
6. Brasil: Base Nacional Comum Curricular (BNCC), Ministério da Educação. https://basenacionalcomum.mec.gov.br/abase
7. Brasil: Lei n° 14.180, de 1° de julho de 2021 (2021). https://www.in.gov.br/web/dou/-/lei-n-14.180-de-1-de-julho-de-2021-329472130. Diário Oficial da União, Edição 123, Seção 1, Página 1
8. Junior, M.M.C., de Souza, H.C.: Avaliação pedagógica com base na união dos componentes dos jogos educacionais e das teorias de aprendizagem. In: Proceedings of SBGames 2020, pp. 551–558 (2020)
9. Carlotto, M.S., da Dias, S.R.S., Batista, J.B.V., Diehl, L.: The mediational role of self-efficacy in the relation between workload and burnout' dimensions in teachers. Psico-USF **20**(1), 13–23 (2015). https://doi.org/10.1590/1413-82712015200102

10. Castro, D., Werner, C.M.L.: Unfolding for creation of educational games. In: Proceedings of SBGames 2020, pp. 822–825 (2020)
11. Chen, C.Y., Huang, H.J., Lien, C.J., Lu, Y.L.: Effects of multi-genre digital game-based instruction on students' conceptual understanding, argumentation skills, and learning experiences. IEEE Access **8**, 110643–110655 (2020). https://doi.org/10.1109/ACCESS.2020.3000659
12. Chen, C.-H., Shih, C.-C., Law, V.: The effects of competition in digital game-based learning (DGBL): a meta-analysis. Education Tech. Research Dev. **68**(4), 1855–1873 (2020). https://doi.org/10.1007/s11423-020-09794-1
13. Coelho, P.M.F., Valente, J.A.: O uso de games digitais como ferramenta pedagógica aplicada ao ensino de língua portuguesa e suas literaturas. Veredas Rev. Interdis. Humanidades **4**(7), 143–158 (2021)
14. Crawford, C.: The Art of Computer Game Design: Reflections of a Master Game Designer. McGraw-Hill/Osborne Media, California, USA (1984)
15. Ferguson, R.: Learning analytics: drivers, developments and challenges. Int. J. Technol. Enhanced Learn. **4**(5/6), 304–317 (2012). also translated into Italian. Learning analytics: fattori trainanti, sviluppi e sfide TD Tecnologie Didattiche **22**(3), 138–147
16. Ferreira, B.M.: A educação não pode salvar o mundo: reflexões acerca da sobrecarga de trabalho docente e da responsabilidade sobre a formação das crianças. Rev. Educ. Cultura Debate **7**(1), 220–225 (2021)
17. Frasca, G., Battegazzore, S., Olhaberry, N., Infantozzi, P., Rodriguez, F., Balbi, F.: September 12th, a toy world (2003). https://www.newsgaming.com/games/index12.htm
18. Freire, M., Serrano-Laguna, Á., Iglesias, B.M., Martínez-Ortiz, I., Moreno-Ger, P., Fernández-Manjón, B.: Game Learning Analytics: Learning Analytics for Serious Games. In: Spector, M., Lockee, B., Childress, M. (eds.) Learning, Design, and Technology, pp. 1–29. Springer, Cham (2016). https://doi.org/10.1007/978-3-319-17727-4_21-1
19. Gasparini, I., Pimenta, M.S., De Oliveira, J.P.M.: Vive la différence! a survey of cultural-aware issues in HCI. In: Proceedings of the 10th Brazilian Symposium on Human Factors in Computing Systems and the 5th Latin American Conference on Human-Computer Interaction, pp. 13–22 (2011)
20. Gros, B.: Digital games in education. J. Res. Technol. Educ. **40**(1), 23–38 (2007). https://doi.org/10.1080/15391523.2007.10782494
21. Hochsprung, J., Cruz, D.M.: Jogos digitais/eletrônicos em sala de aula: uma revisão sistemática. In: Proceedings of SBGames 2017, pp. 1132–1135. SBC (2017)
22. Intergovernmental Panel on Climate Change, Oxford University Centre for the Environment, Red Redemption Ltd: BBC Climate Challenge (nd). https://games4sustainability.org/gamepedia/bbc-climate-challenge/
23. Jungle Digital Games: O Mito da Caverna (nd). https://www.omitodacaverna.com.br/
24. Kaimara, P., Fokides, E., Oikonomou, A., Deliyannis, I.: Potential barriers to the implementation of digital game-based learning in the classroom: pre-service teachers' views. Technol. Knowl. Learn. **26**(4), 825–844 (2021). https://doi.org/10.1007/s10758-021-09512-7
25. Lelis, I.: Teaching in large classes: challenges and perspectives. Sociologias **14**(29), 152–174 (2012). https://doi.org/10.1590/S1517-45222012000100007
26. Loula, A.C., Calmon, J.H.S., de Castro, L.N., El-Hani, C.N.: Modelagem ecológica para um editor de criaturas de um jogo educativo. In: Proceedings of SBGames 2011, pp. 2–4 (2011)

27. Mildner, P., 'Floyd' Mueller, F.: Design of serious games. In: Dörner, R., Göbel, S., Effelsberg, W., Wiemeyer, J. (eds.) Serious Games, pp. 57–82. Springer, Cham (2016). https://doi.org/10.1007/978-3-319-40612-1_3

28. Miller, S.: Autonomy. In: Arrigo, B.A. (ed.) The SAGE encyclopedia of surveillance, security, and privacy, pp. 79–82. SAGE Publications, Inc. (2018). https://doi.org/10.4135/9781483359922.n38

29. Moran, J.: Metodologias ativas para uma aprendizagem mais profunda. In: Bacich, L., Moran, J. (eds.) Metodologias Ativas Para Uma Educação Inovadora: Uma Abordagem Teórico-prática. Desafios da Educação, Penso, Porto Alegre (2018)

30. Moreno-Ger, P., Burgos, D., Martínez-Ortiz, I., Sierra, J.L., Fernández-Manjón, B.: Educational game design for online education. Comput. Hum. Behav. 24(6), 2530–2540 (2008). https://doi.org/10.1016/j.chb.2008.03.012. Including the Special Issue: Electronic Games and Personalized eLearning Processes

31. Nadolski, R.J., et al.: Emergo: a methodology and toolkit for developing serious games in higher education. Simul. Gaming 39(3), 338–352 (2008). https://doi.org/10.1177/1046878108319278

32. Novaes, M.A.B.D., et al.: Active methodologies in the teaching and learning process: emerging didactic alternatives. Res. Soc. Dev. 10(4), e37710414091 (2021). https://doi.org/10.33448/rsd-v10i4.14091

33. Novak, J.: Game Development Essentials: An Introduction, 3rd edn. Delmar, Cengage Learning, New York, USA (2012)

34. Oliveira, F.M., Hildebrand, H.R.: Ludicidade, ensino e aprendizagem nos jogos digitais educacionais. Inf. Educ. Teoria Prática 21(1), 106–120 (2018)

35. Paiva, C.A., Tori, R.: Jogos digitais no ensino: processos cognitivos, benefícios e desafios. In: Proceedings of SBGames 2017, pp. 1052–1055 (2017)

36. Pimentel, C.A., Bergamo, M.L., de Freitas Melo, P.: Levantamento de requisitos para jogos educativos infantis. In: Proceedings of SBGames 2019, pp. 995–1004 (2019)

37. Possamai, D.S., Hounsell, M.d.S., Gasparini, I.: The ABCDE methodology: emphasizing creativity in the design of serious games. iSys - Brazilian J. Inf. Syst. 14(1), 24–55 (2021). https://doi.org/10.5753/isys.2021.993

38. Prensky, M.: Digital Game-Based learning. McGraw-Hill, New York, USA (2001)

39. Rocha, R., Bittencourt, I., Isotani, S.: Análise, projeto, desenvolvimento e avaliação de jogos sérios e afins: uma revisão de desafios e oportunidades. In: Anais do XXVI Simpósio Brasileiro de Informática na Educação (SBIE 2015), pp. 692–701 (2015). https://doi.org/10.5753/cbie.sbie.2015.692

40. Rocha, R.V., Valle, P.H.D., Maldonado, J.C., Bittencourt, I.I., Isotani, S.: AIMED: agile, integrative and open method for open educational resources development. In: 2017 IEEE 17th International Conference on Advanced Learning Technologies (ICALT), pp. 163–167 (2017). https://doi.org/10.1109/ICALT.2017.104

41. dos Santos, W.O., Isotani, S.: Desenvolvimento de jogos educativos? desafios, oportunidades e direcionamentos de pesquisa. RENOTE - Revi. Novas Tecnol. Educ. 16(2), 180–189 (2018)

42. Schell, J.: The Art of Game Design: A Book of Lenses. Morgan Kaufmann Publishers, Burlington, USA (2010)

43. Tsai, Y.L., Tsai, C.C.: A meta-analysis of research on digital game-based science learning. J. Comput. Assist. Learn. 36(3), 280–294 (2020). https://doi.org/10.1111/jcal.12430

44. UAB.EDU: Introduction to Scratch. https://www.uab.edu/icac/images/Scratch_Guides/Intro_to_Scratch.pdf

45. Wang, L.-H., Chen, B., Hwang, G.-J., Guan, J.-Q., Wang, Y.-Q.: Effects of digital game-based STEM education on students' learning achievement: a meta-analysis. Int. J. STEM Educ. **9**(1), 1–13 (2022). https://doi.org/10.1186/s40594-022-00344-0

46. Xexéo, G., Mangeli, E., Silva, F., Ouriques, L., Costa, L.F.C., Monclar, R.S.: Games as information systems. In: XVII Brazilian Symposium on Information Systems. SBSI 2021. Association for Computing Machinery, New York, NY, USA (2021). https://doi.org/10.1145/3466933.3466961

Author Index

R. P. d. Santos and M. d. S. Hounsell (Eds.): GranDGamesBR 2020/2021, CCIS 1702, p. 275, 2023.
https://doi.org/10.1007/978-3-031-27639-2

Printed in the United States
by Baker & Taylor Publisher Services